Get the eBook FREE!

(PDF, ePub, Kindle, and liveBook all included)

We believe that once you buy a book from us, you should be able to read it in any format we have available. To get electronic versions of this book at no additional cost to you, purchase and then register this book at the Manning website.

Go to https://www.manning.com/freebook and follow the instructions to complete your pBook registration.

That's it!
Thanks from Manning!

Infrastructure as Code,
Patterns and Practices

Infrastructure as Code, Patterns and Practices

WITH EXAMPLES IN PYTHON AND TERRAFORM

ROSEMARY WANG

MANNING
SHELTER ISLAND

For online information and ordering of this and other Manning books, please visit
www.manning.com. The publisher offers discounts on this book when ordered in quantity.
For more information, please contact

Special Sales Department
Manning Publications Co.
20 Baldwin Road
PO Box 761
Shelter Island, NY 11964
Email: orders@manning.com

Manning Publications Co.
20 Baldwin Road
PO Box 761
Shelter Island, NY 11964

Development editor:	Frances Lefkowitz
Technical development editors:	Garry Bargsley and Mike Shepard
Review editor:	Aleksandar Dragosavljević
Production editor:	Andy Marinkovich
Copy editor:	Sharon Wilkey
Proofreader:	Jason Everett
Technical proofreader:	Taylor Dolezal
Typesetter and cover designer:	Marija Tudor

ISBN 9781617298295
Printed in the United States of America

brief contents

contents

preface

The first time I toured a data center, I was fascinated by the entrance retinal scanner, flashing lights, cooling systems, and colorful wiring. Coming from an electrical engineering background, I could appreciate the complexity of managing hardware. I came upon the confusing concept of cloud computing when a company hired me to manage a private cloud platform. I no longer plugged in wires and crafted servers. Instead, I stared at progress bars in a user interface for thousands of servers and wrote terrible scripts to provision them.

At that point, I realized I needed to learn more. I wanted to automate more infrastructure and write more sustainable code that other team members could use. My learning journey reflected the growth of cloud computing and the DevOps philosophy. We needed to learn how to change and scale our infrastructure to keep up business innovation and avoid affecting critical systems! With the public cloud making it even easier to get infrastructure resources on demand, we could almost start treating our infrastructure as an extension of our software.

I traveled a rocky learning journey by becoming a generalist. I priced out public cloud migrations, paired with senior Java developers (the challenge that made me cry), applied design patterns and software development theory to code, tried out Agile methodology, and asked quality assurance and security professionals many questions. As I soaked up different perspectives and technical experiences, I tried to help other folks on their learning journeys as a consultant and, eventually, a developer advocate for open source infrastructure tools.

I decided to write this book because enough systems administrators, security professionals, and software developers expressed that they wanted to learn infrastructure as code (IaC) and needed a resource that organized patterns and practices for writing it. This book reflects everything I *wished* I learned earlier about IaC and the considerations and challenges of applying specific patterns and practices over others, agnostic of the tools and technologies.

I never expected the book to have so much detail. Whenever I released a chapter, I received a note from someone about something I forgot or a recommendation to expand one subject into a chapter. Many chapters cover topics that have entire books (or documentaries, even) dedicated to them but receive a general, high-level treatment in this book. I focus on the most important things you must know to apply the topic to IaC.

You might look at the examples in this book and ask, "Why not use this *other* tool?" I struggled to balance high-level theories with practical examples. The code listings generated spirited discussions from my reviewers and editors, many of whom suggested expansions or substitutions in a different language, tool, and platform! I tried my best to find a combination of languages, tools, and platforms to demonstrate the patterns. At the time of writing, you'll find the code listings written in Python, deployed by HashiCorp Terraform, and run on Google Cloud Platform (GCP). Each code listing comes with a high-level description of the pattern and practice, which you can apply irrespective of language, tool, or platform.

I hope you read this book and find one or two patterns that help you write cleaner IaC, collaborate on IaC in your team, and scale and secure your IaC across your company. Please don't expect to use every pattern and practice or apply all of them at once. You might feel overwhelmed! As you encounter challenges in your IaC, I hope you return to this book and reference a few more patterns.

acknowledgments

It takes a community to write a book, and the one that came together to help me is exceptional.

Thank you to my partner, Adam, who helped me make the time (and plenty of coffee) to focus and work on this book. Also thank you to my family, who encouraged me to pursue my interest in infrastructure. You provided words of encouragement and a listening ear, even if you didn't understand the technical concepts I was trying to untangle.

I am very grateful to my editors at Manning—Chris Philips, Mike Shepard, Tricia Louvar, and Frances Lefkowitz—for their patience, encouragement, guidance, and recommendations. Thank you for staying so consistent in your feedback and commitment through some very rough drafts. I want to also thank the team behind the production and promotion of this book.

A big thank you to the reviewers who read my manuscript and took the time and effort to provide me feedback: Cosimo Attanasi, David Krief, Deniz Vehbi, Domingo Salazar, Ernesto Cárdenas Cangahuala, George Haines, Gualtiero Testa, Jeffrey Chu, Jeremy Bryan, Joel Clermont, John Guthrie, Lucian Maly, Michael Bright, Ognyan Dimitrov, Peter Schott, Ravi Tamiri, Sean T. Booker, Stanford S. Guillory, Steffen Weitkamp, Steven Oxley, Sylvain Martel, and Zorodzayi Mukuya, your suggestions helped make this a better book.

To the community team at HashiCorp, thank you for lending your opinions, reviewing concepts, and encouraging me to write. You all inspired me to keep writing throughout technical challenges and the occasional bout of imposter syndrome. And a special thank you to my colleague and technical proofer, Taylor Dolezal, who bravely checked my code and read the book in various iterations.

To all the system administrators, testers, product managers, infrastructure engineers, business analysts, software developers, and security engineers I have ever worked with, you might recognize some of the patterns and practices we paired on, chatted about, or debated in this book. Thank you for teaching me something about infrastructure as code. You are part of the community that made this possible.

about this book

I wrote *Infrastructure as Code, Patterns and Practices* to help you write IaC that changes infrastructure resources without impacting critical business systems. The book focuses on the patterns and practices you can apply as an individual, team, or company across your infrastructure system. It focuses on high-level patterns and practices that you can apply to your IaC, while offering specific examples demonstrating implementation.

Who should read this book?

This book is for anyone (software developers, security engineers, quality assurance engineers, or infrastructure engineers) beginning to use cloud infrastructure and IaC and looking to scale it across their team or company. You will have written some IaC, run it manually, and created resources on a public cloud.

However, you now face the challenges of facilitating collaboration of IaC across your team or company. You must alleviate the friction of multiple team members and other teams making infrastructure changes and requesting updates for security, compliance, or functionality. While many resources introduce IaC in the context of a specific tool, this book generalizes the patterns and practices you can apply to a variety of infrastructure use cases, tools, and systems that will evolve over time.

How this book is organized: A roadmap

I organized this book into three sections with 13 chapters.

Part 1 introduces IaC and how you, as an individual, write it.

- Chapter 1 defines IaC and its benefits and principles. The chapter explains that the book has examples in Python, run by HashiCorp Terraform, and deployed to Google Cloud Platform (GCP). I also discuss the tools and use cases you'll encounter in your IaC journey.

- Chapter 2 dives into the principle of immutability and how you can migrate existing infrastructure resources to IaC. It also covers the practices of writing clean IaC.
- Chapter 3 offers a few patterns for dividing and grouping infrastructure resources into modules. Each pattern includes an example and a list of use cases.
- Chapter 4 covers how to manage dependencies among infrastructure resources and modules and decouple them with dependency injection and some common patterns.

Part 2 describes how to write and collaborate on IaC as a team.

- Chapter 5 organizes the practices and considerations for expressing IaC in different repository structures and sharing it across your team.
- Chapter 6 provides an infrastructure testing strategy. It describes each type of test and how to write them for IaC.
- Chapter 7 applies continuous delivery to IaC. It covers a high-level view of branching models and how your team can use them to change infrastructure.
- Chapter 8 provides techniques to build secure and compliant IaC, including testing and tagging.

Part 3 covers how to manage IaC across your company.

- Chapter 9 applies immutability to infrastructure changes, including an example for blue-green deployments.
- Chapter 10 refactors a large body of IaC to improve its maintainability and mitigate the blast radius of failed changes to one codebase.
- Chapter 11 describes reverting IaC and rolling forward changes to the system.
- Chapter 12 addresses the use of IaC to manage cloud computing costs. It includes an example for cost estimation of IaC.
- Chapter 13 completes the book with practices to manage and update IaC tools.

You will find that many concepts build on each other throughout the book, and it may help to read the chapters in order if you have not previously practiced IaC. Otherwise, you can choose the sections that best apply to the challenges you face in your IaC practice.

Before you read individual chapters for specific concepts, you may want to read chapter 1 or appendix A first to understand how to read and run the examples. Appendix A offers additional detail on the libraries, tools, and platforms related to the examples, while appendix B provides answers to the exercises.

About the code

Because of the verbosity of infrastructure configuration, some code listings in the book do not include the entire infrastructure definitions for clarity. Chapters 2 to 12 include code listings as examples of their concepts.

The existing code listings use a combination of Python 3.9, HashiCorp Terraform 1.0, and Google Cloud Platform. The appendix includes more information on how to run the examples and their tools and libraries. I update the source code on GitHub for minor versions of the tools.

This book contains many examples of source code both in numbered listings and in line with normal text. In both cases, source code is formatted in a `fixed-width font like this` to separate it from ordinary text. Sometimes code is also **in bold** to highlight code that has changed from previous steps in the chapter, such as when a new feature adds to an existing line of code.

In many cases, the original source code has been reformatted; we've added line breaks and reworked indentation to accommodate the available page space in the book. In rare cases, even this was not enough, and listings include line-continuation markers (➡). Additionally, comments in the source code have often been removed from the listings when the code is described in the text. Code annotations accompany many of the listings, highlighting important concepts. You can get executable snippets of code from the liveBook (online) version of this book at https://livebook.manning .com/book/essential-infrastructure-as-code. The complete source code is available for download from the Manning website at https://www.manning.com/books/ infrastructure-as-code-patterns-and-practices, and from GitHub at https://github .com/joatmon08/manning-book.

liveBook discussion forum

Purchase of *Infrastructure as Code, Patterns and Practices* includes free access to liveBook, Manning's online reading platform. Using liveBook's exclusive discussion features, you can attach comments to the book globally or to specific sections or paragraphs. It's a snap to make notes for yourself, ask and answer technical questions, and receive help from the author and other users. To access the forum, go to https://livebook .manning.com/book/infrastructure-as-code-patterns-and-practices/discussion. You can also learn more about Manning's forums and the rules of conduct at https:// livebook.manning.com/discussion.

Manning's commitment to our readers is to provide a venue where a meaningful dialogue between individual readers and between readers and the author can take place. It is not a commitment to any specific amount of participation on the part of the author, whose contribution to the forum remains voluntary (and unpaid). We suggest you try asking the author some challenging questions lest her interest stray! The forum and the archives of previous discussions will be accessible from the publisher's website for as long as the book is in print.

About the cloud provider

I had a challenge deciding which cloud provider to use for examples. While Amazon Web Services (AWS) or Microsoft Azure (Azure) may be more popular choices at publication, they require many resources to be created. For example, their networking requires a network, subnets, routing tables, gateways, and security groups before you can use it. Instead, I decided to use Google Cloud Platform (GCP) as the primary cloud provider to streamline the number of resources you need to create.

Though I use GCP for the examples, the concepts, processes, and guidelines are intended to be agnostic, and you should be able to adapt them to other cloud providers. For readers who prefer to use AWS or Azure, each example includes information on the equivalent service offerings in these two platforms. In addition, some examples include equivalents in the code repo.

In chapter 1, you can read more about my reasons for using GCP, and how to adapt the examples for Azure and AWS. And in appendix A, you'll find instructions for setting up and running the examples on GCP, along with tips for Azure and AWS users.

Other online resources

Refer to online resources for your specific IaC tool or infrastructure provider. Many of them provide examples of practices and patterns implemented in their tool.

about the author

 **ROSEMARY WANG** works to bridge the technical and cultural barriers between infrastructure, security, and application development. She is fascinated with solving intractable problems as a contributor, public speaker, writer, and advocate of open source infrastructure tools. When she is not drawing on whiteboards, Rosemary debugs stacks of various infrastructure systems on her laptop while watering her houseplants.

about the cover illustration

The figure on the cover of *Infrastructure as Code, Patterns and Practices* is captioned "Bayadere," a term meaning "a female Hindu dancer in India," taken from a collection by Jacques Grasset de Saint-Sauveur, published in 1797. Each illustration is finely drawn and colored by hand.

In those days, it was easy to identify where people lived and what their trade or station in life was just by their dress. Manning celebrates the inventiveness and initiative of the computer business with book covers based on the rich diversity of regional culture centuries ago, brought back to life by pictures from collections such as this one.

Part 1

First steps

What *is* infrastructure as code (IaC), and how do you go about writing it? Part 1 addresses these questions and introduces practices and patterns you can apply to writing IaC. In chapter 1, you'll learn how IaC works, the problems it solves, and how this book will help you to start using it. Chapter 2 discusses how to write clean code and guidelines for defining IaC in existing systems.

Chapters 3 and 4 dive into patterns for declaring groups of infrastructure, called *modules*, and their dependencies. You'll learn patterns for infrastructure modules and how to decouple module dependencies to support changes and minimize blast radius. The chapters also offer guidelines for choosing the most appropriate patterns for your scope and situation.

Introducing infrastructure as code

1

This chapter covers

- Defining *infrastructure*
- Defining *infrastructure as code*
- Understanding why infrastructure as code is important

If you just started working with public cloud providers or data center infrastructure, you might feel overwhelmed with all that you have to learn. You don't know *what* you need to know to do your job! Between data center infrastructure concepts, new public cloud offerings, container orchestrators, programming languages, and software development, you have a lot to research.

Besides learning everything you can, you also have to keep up with your company's requirements to innovate and grow. Building systems to support it all gets challenging. You need a way to support more complex systems, minimize your maintenance effort, and avoid disruption to customers using your application.

What do you need to know to work with cloud computing or data center infrastructure? How can you scale your systems across a team and your organization?

The answer to both questions involves *infrastructure as code* (*IaC*), the process of automating infrastructure changes in a codified manner to achieve scalability, reliability, and security.

Everyone can use IaC, from system administrators, site reliability engineers, DevOps engineers, security engineers, and software developers, to quality assurance engineers. Whether you've just run your first tutorial for IaC or passed a public cloud certification (congratulations!), you can apply IaC to larger systems and teams to simplify, sustain, and scale your infrastructure.

This book offers a practical approach to IaC by applying software development practices and patterns to infrastructure management. The book presents practices like testing, continuous delivery, refactoring, and design patterns with an infrastructure twist. You'll find practices and patterns to help you manage your infrastructure no matter the automation, tool, platform, or technology.

I divided this book into three parts (figure 1.1). Part 1 covers the practices you can apply to write IaC, while part 2 describes your team's patterns and practices to collaborate on it. Part 3 covers some approaches to scaling IaC across your organization.

This book covers the intersections of patterns and practices between you, your team, and your organization for infrastructure as code to scale your resources and systems and support mission-critical applications.

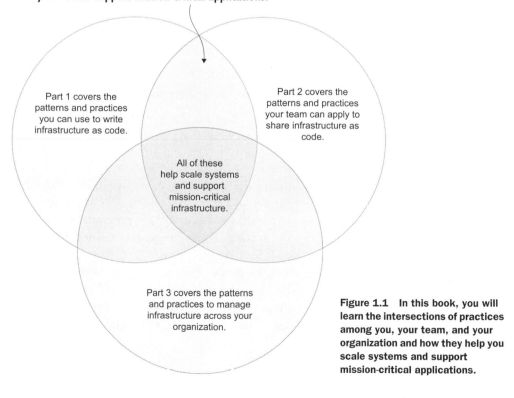

Part 1 covers the patterns and practices you can use to write infrastructure as code.

Part 2 covers the patterns and practices your team can apply to share infrastructure as code.

All of these help scale systems and support mission-critical infrastructure.

Part 3 covers the patterns and practices to manage infrastructure across your organization.

Figure 1.1   In this book, you will learn the intersections of practices among you, your team, and your organization and how they help you scale systems and support mission-critical applications.

Many of the patterns and practices in this book intersect these three interests. Writing good IaC individually helps you better share and scale it across your team and organization. Well-written IaC helps solve problems with *collaborating* on IaC, especially as more people adopt it.

Part 1 starts by defining *infrastructure* and explaining common IaC design patterns. These topics involve foundational concepts that help you scale IaC across your team. You may already be familiar with some of the material in this part, so review these chapters to establish foundations for more advanced concepts.

In parts 2 and 3, you'll learn the patterns and practices you need to scale systems and support infrastructure for mission-critical applications. These practices extend from you to your team and organization, from creating one application metrics alert for an application to implementing a network change across a 50,000-person organization. Many terms and concepts build on each other in these parts, so you might find it helpful to read the chapters in order.

1.1 What is infrastructure?

Before I dive into IaC, let's begin with the definition of *infrastructure*. When I began working in a data center, the literature often defined infrastructure as hardware or devices that provide network, storage, or compute capability. Figure 1.2 shows how applications run on servers (compute), connect through a switch (network), and maintain data on disks (storage).

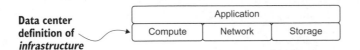

Figure 1.2 The data center definition of *infrastructure* includes networking, compute, and storage resources used to run an application.

These three categories matched the physical devices we managed in a data center. We made changes by scanning our IDs to get into a building, plugging into a device, typing commands, and hoping that everything still worked. With the advent of cloud computing, we continued to use these categories to discuss virtualization of specific devices.

However, the data center definition of infrastructure doesn't quite apply to today's services and offerings. Imagine that another team requests that you help them deliver their application to production for users. You run through a checklist that includes setting up the following:

- Enough servers
- Network connectivity for users
- A database for storing application data

Does completing this checklist mean the team can run this application in production? Not necessarily. You do not know if you set up enough servers or the proper access to log into the application. You also need to know if network latency affects the application's database connection.

In this narrow definition of infrastructure, you omit some critical tasks necessary for production readiness, including the following:

- Monitoring application metrics
- Exporting metrics for business reporting
- Setting up alerts for teams operating the application
- Adding health checks for servers and databases
- Supporting user authentication
- Logging and aggregating application events
- Storing and rotating database passwords in a secrets manager

You need these to-do items to deliver an application to production that will work reliably and securely. You might think of them as *operational* requirements, but they still require infrastructure resources.

Besides infrastructure related to operations, public cloud providers abstract the management of base networking, compute, and storage and offer platform as a service (PaaS) offerings instead, from object stores like storage buckets to event-streaming platforms like managed Apache Kafka. Providers even offer function as a service (FaaS) or containers as a service, additional abstractions for computing resources. The increasing marketplace of software as a service (SaaS), such as hosted application performance-monitoring software, might also be required to support an application in production and could also be infrastructure.

With so many services, we cannot describe infrastructure with just compute, network, and storage categories. We need to include operational infrastructure, PaaS, or SaaS offerings in our application delivery. Figure 1.3 adjusts the model of infrastructure to include additional service offerings like SaaS and PaaS that help us deliver applications.

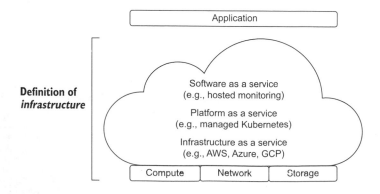

Figure 1.3   The infrastructure for an application might include queues on a public cloud, containers running applications, serverless functions for additional processing, or even monitoring services to check the system's health.

Because of the growing complexity, varying operating models, and user abstraction of data center management, you can't limit the definition of *infrastructure* to hardware or physical devices related to compute, network, or storage.

> **DEFINITION** *Infrastructure* refers to the software, platform, or hardware that delivers or deploys applications to production.

Here is a non-exhaustive list of infrastructure you might encounter:

- Servers
- Workload orchestration platforms (e.g., Kubernetes, HashiCorp Nomad)
- Network switches
- Load balancers
- Databases
- Object stores
- Caches
- Queues
- Event-streaming platforms
- Monitoring platforms
- Data pipeline systems
- Payment platforms

Expanding the *infrastructure* definition provides a common language across teams managing resources for various purposes. For example, a team managing an organization's continuous integration (CI) framework utilizes infrastructure from either a continuous integration SaaS or compute resources from a public cloud. Another team builds upon the framework, thus making it critical infrastructure.

1.2 What is infrastructure as code?

Before explaining infrastructure as code, we must understand the manual infrastructure configuration. In this section, I outline the problem with infrastructure and manual configuration. Then I define *infrastructure as code.*

1.2.1 Manual configuration of infrastructure

As part of a network team, I learned to change a network switch by copying and pasting commands from a text document. I once pasted `shutdown` instead of `no shutdown`, turning off a network interface! I quickly turned it back on, hoping that no one noticed and it didn't affect anything. A week later, however, I discovered that it shut off connectivity to a critical application and affected a few customer requests.

In retrospect, I ran into a few problems with my manual copying and pasting of commands and infrastructure configuration. First, I had no idea which resources my change would affect (also known as the *blast radius*). I did not know which networks or applications used the interface.

DEFINITION   The *blast radius* refers to the impact a failed change has on a system. A larger blast radius often affects more components or the most critical components.

Second, the network switch accepted my command without testing its effects or checking its intent. Finally, no one else knew what affected the application's processing of customer requests, and it took a week for them to identify the root cause as my miscopied command.

How does writing infrastructure in a codified manner help catch my miscopied network switch command? I could store my configuration and automation under source control to record the commands. To catch my mistake going forward, I create a virtual switch and a test that runs my script and checks the health of the interface.

After the tests pass, I promote the change to production because the tests check for the correct command. If I apply the wrong command, I can search infrastructure configuration to determine which applications run on the affected network. You can refer to chapter 6 for testing practices and chapter 11 for reverting changes.

Besides the risk of misconfiguration, my development momentum sometimes slows because of manual infrastructure configuration. Once, it took nearly two months for me to test my application against a database. Throughout those two months, my team submitted over 10 tickets related to creating the database, configuring new routing to connect the application to the database, and opening firewall rules to allow my application. The platform team manually configured everything in a public cloud. Development teams did not have direct access because of security concerns.

In other words, manual configuration of infrastructure often does not scale as systems and teams grow. Manual changes *increase the change failure rate of systems, slow development, and expose the system's attack surface to a potential security exploit.* You will always have the temptation to update some values into a console. However, these changes accumulate.

The next person who makes a change to the system may introduce a failure into the system that will be difficult to troubleshoot because changes haven't been audited or organized. Changes like updating a firewall to allow some traffic during the development process can inadvertently leave the system vulnerable to attack.

1.2.2 *Infrastructure as code*

What should you do to change infrastructure, if not manual changes? You can apply a software development life cycle for infrastructure resources and configuration in the form of IaC. However, an infrastructure development life cycle goes beyond configuration files and scripts.

Infrastructure needs to scale, manage failure, support rapid software development, and secure applications. A development life cycle for infrastructure involves more specific patterns and practices to support collaboration, deployment, and testing. In figure 1.4, a simplified workflow changes infrastructure by using configuration or scripts and committing them to version control. A commit automatically starts a workflow to deploy and test the changes to your infrastructure.

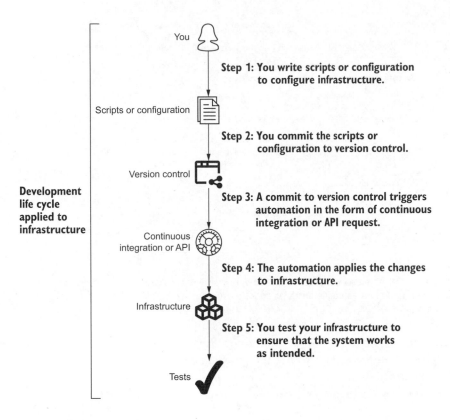

Figure 1.4   A development life cycle for infrastructure includes writing the code as documentation, committing it to version control, applying it to infrastructure in an automated way, and testing it.

Why should you remember the development life cycle? You can use it as a general pattern for managing changes and verifying that they don't affect your system. The life cycle captures *infrastructure as code*, which automates infrastructure changes in a codified manner and applies DevOps practices such as version control and continuous delivery.

> **DEFINITION**   *Infrastructure as code (IaC)* applies DevOps practices to automating infrastructure changes in a codified manner to achieve scalability, resiliency, and security.

I often find IaC cited as a necessary practice of DevOps. It certainly addresses the automation piece of the CAMS model (culture, automation, measurement, and sharing). Figure 1.5 positions IaC as part of automation practices and philosophy in the DevOps model. The practices of code as documentation, version control, software development patterns, and continuous delivery align with the development life cycle workflow we discussed previously.

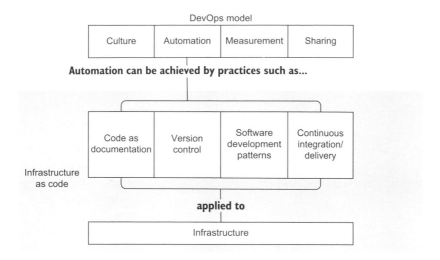

Figure 1.5   IaC applies version control, software development patterns, continuous integration, and code as documentation to infrastructure.

Why focus on IaC as part of automation in the DevOps model? Your organization does not have to adopt DevOps to use IaC. Its benefits improve DevOps adoption and metrics but still apply to any infrastructure configuration. You can still use IaC practices to improve the process of making infrastructure changes without affecting production.

> **NOTE**   You will see some DevOps practices included in this book, but I do not focus on its theory or principles. I recommend *Accelerate* by Nicole Forsgren et al. (IT Revolution Press, 2018) for a higher-level understanding of DevOps. You can also peruse *The Phoenix Project* by Gene Kim et al. (IT Revolution Press, 2013), which describes the fictional transformation of an organization adopting DevOps.

This book covers some approaches for codifying infrastructure to eliminate the friction of scale while maintaining the reliability and security of infrastructure for application users, whether you use the data center or cloud. Software development practices such as version control of configuration files, CI pipelines, and testing can help scale and evolve changes to infrastructure while mitigating downtime and building secure configuration.

1.2.3   *What is not infrastructure as code?*

Could you be doing IaC if you type out some configuration in a document? You might consider IaC to include adding configuration instructions in a change ticket. You can argue that a tutorial for building a queue or a shell script for configuring a server counts as IaC. Each of these examples *can* be forms of IaC if you can use them to do the following:

- Reliably and accurately reproduce the infrastructure it expresses
- Revert configuration to a specific version or point in time
- Communicate and assess the blast radius of a change to the resources

The configurations or scripts, however, are usually outdated, unversioned, or ambiguous in intent. You may even find yourself struggling to understand and change the configuration written in an IaC tool. The tool facilitates IaC workflows but not necessarily the practices and approaches that allow systems to grow while reducing operational responsibility and change failure. You need a set of principles to identify IaC.

1.3 Principles of infrastructure as code

As I mentioned, not every piece of code or configuration related to infrastructure will scale or mitigate downtime. Throughout the book, I highlight how IaC principles apply to certain code listings or practices. You can even use these principles to assess your IaC.

While others may add or subtract to this list of principles, I remember four of the most important principles with the mnemonic *RICE*. This stands for *reproducibility, idempotency, composability, and evolvability*. I define and apply each principle in the following sections.

1.3.1 Reproducibility

Imagine someone asks you to create a development environment with a queue and a server. You share a set of configuration files with your teammate. They use them to recreate a new environment for themselves in less than an hour. Figure 1.6 shows how you shared your configuration and enabled your teammate to reproduce a new environment. You discovered the power of *reproducibility*, the first principle of IaC!

Why should IaC conform to this principle of reproducibility? The ability to copy and reuse infrastructure configuration saves you and your team's initial engineering time. You don't have to reinvent the wheel to create new environments or infrastructure resources.

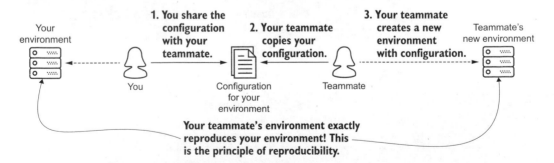

Figure 1.6   Manual changes introduce drift between version control and actual state and affect reproducibility, so you instead update changes in version control.

DEFINITION   The *principle of reproducibility* means that you can use the same configuration to reproduce an environment or infrastructure resources.

However, you'll find adhering to the principle of reproducibility more complicated than copying and pasting a configuration. To demonstrate this nuance, imagine you need to reduce a network address space from /16 to /24. You do have IaC written that expresses the network. However, you decide to choose the easy route of logging into the cloud provider and typing /24 into the text box.

Before you log into the cloud provider, you reflect on whether your change workflow adheres to reproducibility. You ask yourself the following questions:

- Will a teammate know that you've updated the network?
- If you run your configuration, will the network address space return to the /16?
- If you create a new environment with the configuration in version control, will it have an address space of /24?

You answer no to each of those questions. You cannot guarantee that you will reproduce the manual change successfully.

If you go ahead and type /24 in the cloud provider's console, your network has *drifted* from its desired state expressed in IaC (figure 1.7). To conform to reproducibility, you decide to update the version control configuration to /24 and apply the automation.

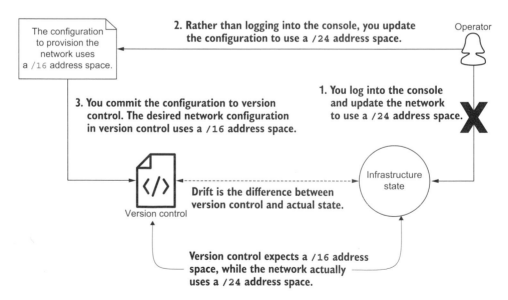

Figure 1.7   Manual changes introduce drift between version control and actual state and affects reproducibility, so you instead update changes in version control.

This scenario demonstrates the challenge of conforming to reproducibility. You need to minimize the inconsistency between the expected and actual infrastructure configuration, also known as *configuration drift*.

> **DEFINITION** *Configuration drift* is the deviation of infrastructure configuration from the desired configuration to the actual configuration.

As a practice, you can ensure the principle of reproducibility by placing your configuration files in version control and keeping version control as updated as possible. Maintaining the principle of reproducibility helps you collaborate better *and* manage testing environments similar to production.

In chapter 6, you'll learn more about infrastructure testing environments, which benefit from reproducibility. You'll also apply reproducibility to practices and patterns in testing and upgrading infrastructure, from creating test infrastructure mirroring production to deploying new infrastructure to replace older systems (blue-green deployments).

1.3.2 *Idempotency*

Some IaC includes *repeatability* as a principle, which means running the same automation and yielding consistent results. I pose that IaC needs a stricter requirement. Running automation should result in the same *end state* for an infrastructure resource. After all, I have one main objective when I write automation: the ability to run the automation multiple times and get the same result.

Let's consider why IaC needs a stricter requirement. Imagine you write a network script that first configures an interface and then reboots. The first time you run the script, the switch configures the interface and reboots. You save this script as version 1.

A few months later, your teammate asks you to run the script again on the switch. You run the script, and the switch reboots. However, the reboot disconnects some critical applications! You already configured the network interface. Why do you need to reboot the switch?

You figure out a way to prevent the switch reboot if you've already configured the network interface. In figure 1.8, you create version 2 of the script and add a conditional if statement. The statement checks whether you have configured the interface already before rebooting the switch. When you run the version 2 script again, you do not disconnect the applications.

The conditional statement conforms to the principle of idempotency. *Idempotency* ensures that you can repeat the automation without affecting the infrastructure unless you change the configuration or drift occurs. If an infrastructure configuration or script is idempotent, you can rerun the automation multiple times without affecting the state or operability of a resource.

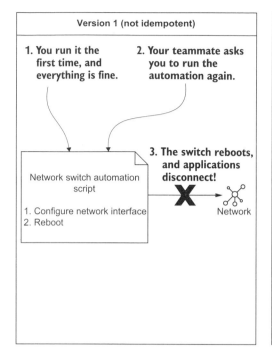
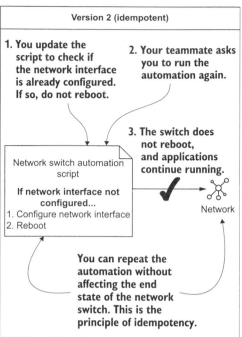

Figure 1.8   In version 1 of the script, you reboot the switch each time you run the script. In version 2, you check whether the network interface is configured before rebooting the switch. This preserves the working state of the network.

> **DEFINITION**   The *principle of idempotency* ensures that you can repeatedly run the automation on infrastructure without affecting its end state or having any side effects. You should affect infrastructure only when you update its attributes in automation.

Why should you adhere to idempotency in your IaC, such as in the case of your network script? In the example, you want to avoid rebooting the network switch to keep the network running correctly. You already configured the network interface; why configure it again? You should need to configure the interface only if it doesn't exist or change.

Without idempotency, your automation might break accidentally. For example, you may repeat a script and create a new set of servers, doubling their numbers. More catastrophically, you might automate a database update only to remove a critical database!

You can ensure the principle of idempotency by checking the repeatability of scripts and configuration. As a general practice, include a number of *conditional statements* checking whether a configuration matches the expected one before running your automation. Conditional statements help apply changes when required and avoid side effects that may affect the operability of infrastructure.

Designing automation with idempotency reduces risk, as it encourages the inclusion of logic to preserve the final expected state of the system. If the automation fails once and causes an outage in the system, organizations no longer want to automate again because of its perceived risk. Idempotency will become a guiding principle as you learn how to safely roll forward changes and preview automation changes before deployment in chapter 11.

1.3.3 Composability

You want to mix and match any set of infrastructure components, no matter the tool or configuration. You also need to update the individual configurations without affecting the entire system. Both of these requirements promote modularity and decoupling infrastructure dependencies, something you'll learn more about in chapters 3 and 4.

For example, imagine you create infrastructure for an application that someone accesses at hello-world.com. These are the minimum resources you need for a secure and production-ready configuration:

- A server
- A load balancer
- A private network for a server
- A public network for a load balancer
- A routing rule to allow traffic out of the private network
- A routing rule to allow public traffic to the load balancer
- A routing rule to allow traffic from the load balancer to the server
- A domain name for hello-world.com

You could write this configuration from scratch. However, what if you found preconstructed *modules* that group infrastructure components you can use to assemble the system? You now have multiple modules that create the following:

- Networks (private and public networks, gateways to route traffic from the private network, routing rules to allow traffic out of the private network)
- Servers
- Load balancers (domain name, routing rules to allow traffic from the load balancer to the server)

In figure 1.9, you pick the network, server, and load balancer modules to build your production environment. Later, you realize you need a premium load balancer. You swap out the standard load balancer with a premium one so you can serve more traffic. The server and network continue running without affecting users.

Your teammate can even add a database into the environment without affecting the load balancer, servers, or network. You group and select infrastructure resources in various combinations, which adheres to the principle of *composability*.

DEFINITION *Composability* ensures that you can assemble any combination of infrastructure resources and update each one without affecting the others.

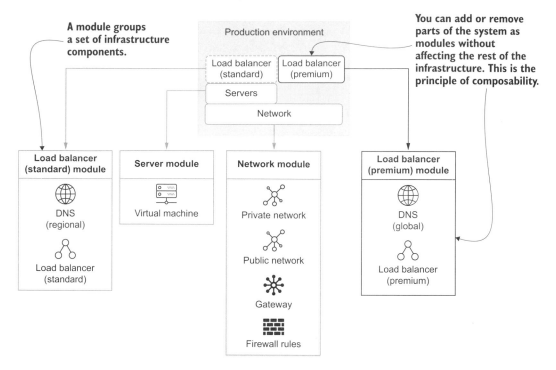

Figure 1.9   You build your production environment with building blocks of infrastructure so you can add new resources, like the premium load balancer, easily.

The more composable your configuration, the easier it is to create new systems with less effort. Think of constructing your IaC with building blocks. You want to be able to update or evolve subsets of resources without toppling the entire system! If you do not consider the composability of your IaC, you run the risk of change failures due to unknown dependencies in complex infrastructure systems.

The self-service benefit of composability can help your organization scale and empower teams to interact safely with infrastructure systems. Chapters 3 and 4 examine some patterns that can help you approach more modular infrastructure construction and improve composability.

1.3.4   *Evolvability*

You want to account for the scale and growth of your system but not optimize the configuration too early and unnecessarily. Much of infrastructure configuration will change over time, including its architecture.

As a practical example, you might initially name an infrastructure resource `example`. Later, you need to change the resource name to `production`. You start the change by finding and replacing hundreds of tags, names, dependent resources, and more. The procedure of find-and-replace requires a high rate of effort.

You notice that you forgot to change some fields as you apply the changes, and your new infrastructure changes fail. To ensure the future evolution of names, tags, and other metadata, you instead create a variable for the name, and the configuration references the variable. In figure 1.10, you update the global NAME variable, and the change propagates across the entire system.

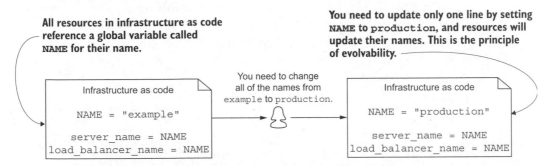

Figure 1.10 Rather than finding and replacing all instances of the name, you can set a top-level variable with the name for all resources.

The example seems almost too simple. Why does changing a name matter? IaC built with *evolvability* as a principle minimizes the effort (time and cost) to change a system and the risk of failure for the change.

> **DEFINITION** The *principle of evolvability* ensures that you can change your infrastructure resources to accommodate system scale or growth while minimizing effort and risk of failure.

System evolution includes changes beyond minor ones, such as name changes. A more disruptive change in infrastructure architecture might involve a replacement of Google Cloud Bigtable with Amazon Elastic Map Reduce (EMR). The application requiring the replacement has been future-proofed using Apache HBase, an open source distributed database that supports both offerings and simply requires the database endpoint.

We account for this evolution in the IaC by outputting the database endpoint to retrieve the application and completing the update behind the scenes by creating configurations for both offerings. After testing the Amazon Web Services (AWS) database, we output its endpoint for consumption by the application.

> **NOTE** I do not fully cover the theory behind evolving your architecture in this book. I highly recommend *Building Evolutionary Architectures* by Neal Ford et al. (O'Reilly, 2017) if you want to learn more. The book discusses how to build your infrastructure architecture to account for changes.

You might find yourself struggling to evolve your system because you have not used patterns and practices that allow it to change. Useful IaC focuses on techniques to facilitate future evolution. Many of the chapters in this book demonstrate patterns that help maintain evolvability and minimize the impact of changes to critical systems.

1.3.5   *Applying the principles*

Reproducibility, idempotency, composability, and evolvability seem specific in their definitions. However, they all help constrain your infrastructure architecture and define the behavior of many IaC tools. Your IaC must align with all four principles to scale, collaborate, and change your company. Figure 1.11 summarizes these four important principles and their definitions.

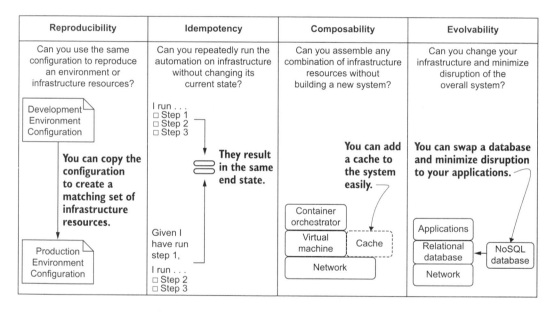

Figure 1.11   IaC should be reproducible, idempotent, composable, and evolvable. You can ask yourself a series of questions to determine whether your IaC conforms to all four principles.

As you write IaC, ask whether you conform to all four principles. These principles help you write and share your IaC with less effort and ideally minimize the impact of changes to your system. A missing principle can hinder updates to infrastructure resources or increase the blast radius of potential failure.

As you practice IaC, ask whether your configuration or tools align with the practices. For example, ask the following questions about your tool:

- Does the tool allow you to re-create entire environments?
- What happens when you rerun the tool to enforce configuration?

- Can you mix and match various configuration snippets to make a new set of infrastructure components?
- Does the tool offer capabilities to help you evolve an infrastructure resource without impacting other systems?

This book uses the principles to answer these questions and provide you with the skills to test, upgrade, and deploy infrastructure with resiliency and scalability in mind.

Exercise 1.1

Choose an infrastructure script or configuration in your organization. Assess whether it adheres to the principles of IaC. Does it promote reproducibility, use idempotency, help with composability, and ease evolvability?

See appendix B for answers to exercises.

1.4 Why use infrastructure as code?

IaC is typically considered a DevOps practice. However, you don't have to be applying DevOps across your entire organization to use it. You still want to manage your infrastructure in a way that reduces the change failure rate and mean time to resolution (MTTR), so you can sleep in on the weekends as an operator or spend more time writing code as a developer. There are a few reasons to use IaC, even if you think you don't need it.

1.4.1 Change management

You might experience a sinking feeling when you've applied a change to certain infrastructure, only to realize that someone reported it broke something. Organizations try to prevent this with *change management*, a set of steps and reviews to ensure that your changes do not affect production. The process often includes a change review board to review the changes, or change windows to block off time to execute the change.

> **DEFINITION** *Change management* outlines a set of steps and reviews that you take in your company to implement changes in production and prevent their failure.

However, no change is risk-free. Applying IaC practices can mitigate the risk of a change by modularizing your infrastructure (chapter 3) and rolling forward changes (chapter 11) to limit the blast radius.

In one regretful instance, I ignored my intuition to use IaC to mitigate the risk of a change. I had to roll out a new binary to servers, which required them to restart a set of dependent services. I wrote a script, asked my teammate to check it, and had the change review board sign off to run it. After applying and verifying the change over the weekend, I came in on Monday to several messages telling me servers supporting a reconciliation application went down overnight. My teammate traced it to an older operating system incompatibility with the dependencies in my script.

In retrospect, IaC could have mitigated the risk of the change. When I applied the RICE principles to the change, I realized that I forgot the following:

- *Reproducibility*—I did not reproduce my script on various test instances mimicking the various servers.
- *Idempotency*—I did not include logic to check the operating system before running the command.
- *Composability*—I did not limit the blast radius of the change to a small set of less critical servers.
- *Evolvability*—I did not update the servers with a newer operating system and reduce variation across the infrastructure.

Reducing variation allows for infrastructure evolution and risk mitigation because the actual configuration matches the one you expect during your automation, making changes more straightforward and reliable to apply. We'll discuss how to fit IaC into your change management process in chapter 7.

1.4.2   *Return on time investment*

IaC and time investment can be challenging to justify, especially if your devices or hardware do not have suitable automation interfaces. In addition to a lack of easy automation, it can be difficult to justify spending time automating a task that you do only once a year or even a decade. While IaC might take extra time to implement, it lowers the time to execute changes in the long term. How exactly does that work?

Imagine you need to update the same package on 10 servers. You used to do this without IaC. You'd manually log in, update the package, verify that everything works, fix errors, and move to the next one. On average, you'd spend 10 hours updating the servers.

Figure 1.12 shows that changes made without IaC have a constant level of effort over time. If you have additional changes, you may spend a few more hours fixing or updating the system. A failed change might mean you spend more effort over several days to fix the system.

You decide to invest time into building IaC for these servers (the solid line in figure 1.12). You reduce the servers' configuration drift, which takes about 40 hours. After your initial time investment, you spend less than 5 minutes updating all of the servers each time you make the change.

Why bother understanding the relationship between time and effort for IaC? Prevention helps reduce the effort of remediation. Without IaC, you might find yourself spending weeks trying to remediate a major system outage. You typically spend those weeks trying to reverse engineer the manual changes, revert specific changes, or at worst, building a new system from scratch.

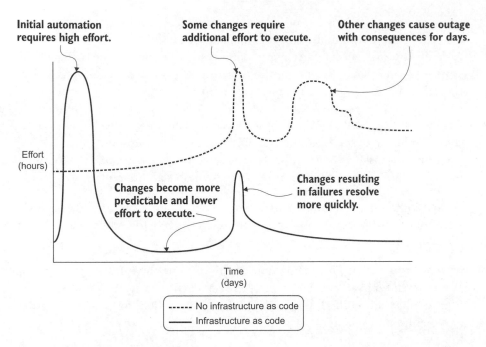

Figure 1.12   IaC requires less effort over time after the high initial automation effort. Without IaC, time to execute changes can be highly variable.

You *must* make an initial investment in writing IaC, even if it seems steep. This investment helps you over time as you spend less time debugging failed configurations or recovering broken systems in the long term. If your system completely fails one day, you can reproduce it easily by running your IaC.

The automation and tests encourage predictability and limit the blast radius of a failure change. They lower the change failure rate and MTTR of failed systems. As your infrastructure system evolves and scales, you can use the detailed testing practices covered in this book to improve the change failure rate in your system and alleviate the burden of future changes.

1.4.3   Knowledge sharing

IaC communicates infrastructure architecture and configuration, which helps reduce human error and improve reliability. An engineer once told me, "We don't need to do IaC for a network switch for a tertiary passive data center (used for backup). It's just me configuring stuff anyway, and we'd only need to make this change once and never touch it again."

The engineer left the organization shortly after configuring the switch. Later, my team needed to convert the tertiary passive data center to an active data center for compliance requirements. In a panic, we scrambled to reverse engineer the configuration on the switch. It took us a good part of two months to figure out the network connection, rework its configuration, and manage it with IaC.

Even if a task seems particularly obscure or the team configuring infrastructure consists of one person, investing the time and effort to approach infrastructure configuration in an "as code" manner can help accommodate evolution, especially as infrastructure systems and teams scale. You'll find that you spend more time remembering how you configured the obscure switch when someone reports an outage or when teaching the server configuration to a new team member.

Writing a task "as code," also known as *code as documentation*, communicates the expected state of the infrastructure and the system's architecture.

> **DEFINITION**   *Code as documentation* ensures that the code communicates the intent of the software or system without the need for additional reference documentation.

Someone unfamiliar with the system should examine the infrastructure configuration and understand its intent. You cannot expect all code to serve as documentation from a practical standpoint. However, the code should reflect most of your infrastructure architecture and system expectations.

1.4.4   *Security*

Auditing and checking for insecure configurations in IaC can highlight security concerns earlier in the development process. You hear this as *shifting security left*. If you incorporate security checks earlier in the process, you find fewer vulnerabilities when the system configuration runs in production. You'll learn more about security patterns and practices in chapter 8.

For example, you might temporarily increase access to an object store such that anyone can write and read from it in development. You push it to production. However, some of the objects in the store allow everyone to write to and read from them. While this seems like a simple mistake, the configuration has grave implications if the store contains customer data.

> **NOTE**   For more examples of insecure infrastructure configuration, you can search the news for a misconfigured object store that exposed driver's license information or even a database with a default password that revealed millions of consumer credit cards. Some security breaches involve legitimate vulnerabilities, but many involve insecure configuration. Organizations that prevent these misconfigurations in the first place can usually quickly examine configuration, audit access control, assess the blast radius, and remediate the breach.

IaC simplifies access control by expressing it in a single configuration. With IaC, you can test the configuration to ensure that the object store does not allow public access. Furthermore, you can include a production check to verify that your policy allows only read access to specific objects. Even security policies in a data center, such as firewall rules, can be expressed in IaC and audited to ensure that its rules allow only inbound connections from known sources.

If you experience a security breach, IaC allows you to examine configuration, audit access control quickly, assess the blast radius, and remediate the breach. You can use the same IaC practices to make all sorts of changes. You'll discover some practices in this book to help audit and secure your infrastructure in adherence to IaC principles.

1.5 Tools

IaC tooling varies quite widely because it applies to various resources. Most tools fall into one of three use cases, all of which address very different functions and vary widely in behavior, including the following:

- Provisioning
- Configuration management
- Image building

In this book, I primarily focus on tools used for provisioning, which deploy and manage sets of infrastructure resources. I include some sidebars and examples in configuration management and image building to highlight differences in approach.

1.5.1 Examples in this book

In this book, I faced a challenge to build concrete examples agnostic of tools or platforms. As a patterns and practices book, I needed to find a way to express the concepts in a general programming language without rewriting the logic of a tool.

PYTHON AND TERRAFORM

Figure 1.13 outlines the workflow of the code listings and examples. For more information, appendix A details the technical implementation. I wrote the code listings in Python to create a JavaScript Object Notation (JSON) file consumed by HashiCorp Terraform, a provisioning tool with various integrations across public clouds and other infrastructure providers.

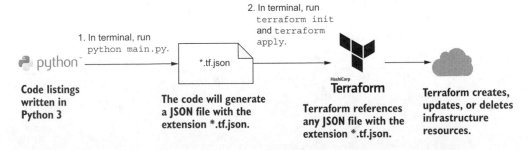

Figure 1.13 This book's examples use Python to create a JSON file that Terraform can consume.

When you run the Python script by using `python run.py`, the code creates a JSON file with the file extension *.tf.json. The JSON file uses syntax specific to Terraform. Then you can go into the directory with the *.tf.json file and run `terraform init` and `terraform apply` to create the resources. While the Python code seems to add unnecessary abstraction, it ensures that I can offer concrete examples agnostic of platform and tool.

I recognize that the complexity of this workflow seems nonsensical. However, it serves two purposes. The Python files provide a generalized implementation of patterns and practices with a programming language. The JSON configuration allows you to run and create the resources with a tool instead of me writing in abstractions.

> **NOTE** You can find the complete code examples at this book's code repository: https://github.com/joatmon08/manning-book.

You do not have to know Python or Terraform in depth to understand the code examples. If you would like to run the examples and create the resources, I recommend reviewing an introductory tutorial to Terraform or Python for syntax and commands.

> **NOTE** You can find numerous resources on Terraform and Python. Check out *Terraform in Action* by Scott Winkler (Manning, 2021), *The Quick Python Book* by Naomi R. Cedar (Manning, 2018), or *Python Workout* by Reuven M. Lerner (Manning, 2020).

GOOGLE CLOUD PLATFORM

While AWS or Microsoft Azure may be more popular choices at publication, I decided to use Google Cloud Platform (GCP) as the primary cloud provider for three main reasons. First, GCP requires overall fewer resources to achieve a similar architecture. This reduces the verbosity of the examples and focuses on the pattern and approach instead of the configuration.

Second, GCP's offerings use more straightforward naming and generic infrastructure terminology. If you work in a data center, you'll still be able to recognize what the services create. For example, Google Cloud SQL creates SQL databases.

If you run the examples, you will use the following resources in GCP:

- Networking (networks, load balancers, and firewalls)
- Compute
- Managed queues (Pub/Sub)
- Storage (Cloud Storage)
- Identity and access management (IAM)
- Kubernetes offerings (Kubernetes Engine and Cloud Run)
- Database (Cloud SQL)

You *do not* have to know the details of each service. I use them to demonstrate dependency management between infrastructure resources. I avoided using specialized services that are different for each cloud platform, such as machine learning.

AWS and Azure equivalents

Each example includes sidebars on equivalent AWS and Azure service offerings to further solidify specific patterns and techniques. To update the examples for the cloud provider of your choice, you may need to do some language replacements and change some of your dependencies. For example, you can create GCP networks with built-in gateways, while you must explicitly build them in AWS networks.

Some examples have an AWS equivalent in the book's code repository (https://github.com/joatmon08/manning-book). You'll also find more information on setting up AWS or Azure to run with examples in appendix A.

The third reason I wrote the examples in GCP involves cost. GCP offers a free usage tier. If you create a new account with GCP, you will receive a free trial of up to $300 (at time of publication). You can use offerings in the free usage tier if you have an existing account. I note any required resources that do not qualify for the free usage tier at the time of publication.

Using Google Cloud Platform

For more information on GCP's free program, refer to its program web page at https://cloud.google.com/free.

I recommend creating a separate GCP project to run all of the examples. A separate project will isolate your resources. When you finish this book, you can delete the project and its resources. Review the tutorial for creating GCP projects at http://mng.bz/e7QG.

1.5.2 Provisioning

Provisioning tools create and manage sets of infrastructure resources for a given provider, whether it's a public cloud, data center, or hosted monitoring solution. A *provider* refers to a data center, IaaS, PaaS, or SaaS responsible for providing infrastructure resources.

> **DEFINITION** A *provisioning tool* creates and manages a set of infrastructure resources for a public cloud, data center, or hosted monitoring solution.

Some provisioning tools work with only a specific provider, while others integrate with multiple providers (table 1.1).

Table 1.1 Examples of provisioning tools and providers

Tool	Provider
AWS CloudFormation	Amazon Web Services
Google Cloud Deployment Manager	Google Cloud Platform

Table 1.1 Examples of provisioning tools and providers *(continued)*

Tool	Provider
Azure Resource Manager	Microsoft Azure
Bicep	Microsoft Azure
HashiCorp Terraform	Various (for a complete list, see www.terraform.io/docs/providers/index.html)
Pulumi	Various (for a complete list, see www.pulumi.com/docs/intro/cloud-providers/)
AWS Cloud Development Kit	Amazon Web Services
Kubernetes manifests	Kubernetes (container orchestrator)

Most provisioning tools can preview changes to a system and express dependencies between infrastructure resources, also known as a *dry run.*

> **DEFINITION** A *dry run* analyzes and outputs expected changes to infrastructure before you apply the changes to resources.

For example, you can express a dependency between a network and a server. If you change the network, the provisioning tool will show that the server may also change.

1.5.3 *Configuration management*

Configuration management tools ensure that servers and computer systems run in the desired state. Most configuration management tools excel at device configuration, such as server installation and maintenance.

> **DEFINITION** A *configuration management tool* configures a set of servers or resources for the packages and attributes hosted on them.

For example, if you have 10,000 servers in your data center, how do you ensure that all of them run a specific version of the packages your security team approved? It does not scale for you to log into 10,000 servers and manually type commands to review. If you configure the servers with a configuration management tool, you can run a single command to review all 10,000 servers and execute the packages' updates.

A non-exhaustive list of configuration management tools that address this problem space includes the following:

- Chef
- Puppet
- Red Hat Ansible
- Salt
- CFEngine

While this book focuses on provisioning tools and managing multiprovider systems, I will address some configuration management practices related to infrastructure testing, updating infrastructure, and security. Configuration management can help tune your server and network infrastructure.

> **NOTE** I recommend books and tutorials for a configuration management tool of your choice for additional information. They will provide a more detailed guide specific to their design approach.

To add to the confusion, you might notice that some configuration management tools offer integrations with the data center and cloud providers. As a result, you might think of using your configuration tool as your provisioning tool. While possible, this approach may not be ideal because provisioning tools often have a different design approach for specifically addressing dependencies among infrastructure resources. I explore this nuance in the next chapter.

1.5.4 Image building

When you create a server, you must specify a machine image with an operating system. *Image-building* tools create images used for application runtime, whether a container or server.

> **DEFINITION** An *image-building tool* builds machine images for application runtimes, such as containers or servers.

Most image builders allow you to specify a runtime environment and build targets. Table 1.2 outlines a few tools, their supported runtime environments, and their build targets and platforms.

Table 1.2 Examples of image builders and providers

Tool	Runtime environment	Build target
HashiCorp Packer	Containers and servers	Various (for a complete list, see www.packer.io/docs/builders)
Docker	Containers	Container registries
EC2 Image Builder	Servers	Amazon Web Services
Azure VM Image Builder	Servers	Microsoft Azure

I do not include detailed discussions on image building in this book. However, the patterns for testing, delivery, and compliance do have sidebars for image building in chapters 6–8. In the next chapter, you'll learn about immutability, a critical paradigm that informs the approach of image builders.

Figure 1.14 shows how image building, configuration management, and provisioning tools work together. The process of deploying a new server configuration often starts with a configuration management tool, as you start building the foundations and testing whether your server configuration is correct.

After establishing the server configuration you want, you use an image builder to preserve the server's image with its versioning and runtime. Finally, your provisioning tool references the image builder's snapshot to create new production servers with the configuration you want.

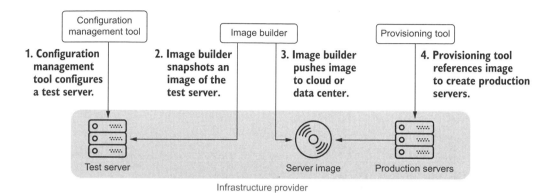

Figure 1.14   Each type of IaC tool contributes to the life cycle of a server infrastructure resource, from configuration to image capture and deployment.

This workflow represents the ideal end-to-end approach for managing and deploying servers with IaC tooling. However, as you will learn, infrastructure can be complex, and this workflow may not apply to every use case. Various infrastructure systems and their dependencies complicate provisioning, which I chose to be the primary focus of this book, and is why the examples use provisioning tools.

Summary

- Infrastructure can be software, a platform, or hardware that delivers or deploys applications to production.
- Infrastructure as code is a DevOps practice of automating infrastructure to achieve reliability, scalability, and security.
- The principles of IaC are reproducibility, idempotency, composability, and evolvability.
- By following the principles of IaC, you can improve change management processes, lower time spent on fixing failed systems in the long term, better share knowledge and context, and build security into your infrastructure.
- IaC tools include provisioning, configuration management, and image-building tools.

Writing
infrastructure as code

Imagine you've created a development environment for a hello-world application. You built it organically, adding new components as you needed them. Eventually, you need to reproduce the configuration for production use, which people can publicly access. You also need to scale production across three geographic regions for high availability.

To do this, you must create and update firewalls, load balancers, servers, and databases in new networks for the production environment. Figure 2.1 shows the complexity of the development environment with the firewall, load balancer, server, and database and the components you need to reproduce in production.

The figure also outlines the differences between development and production. The production configuration needs three servers for high availability, expanded firewall rules to allow all HTTP traffic, and stricter firewall rules for the servers to connect to the database. After reviewing all of the differences, you might have a lot of questions about the best and easiest way to make the changes.

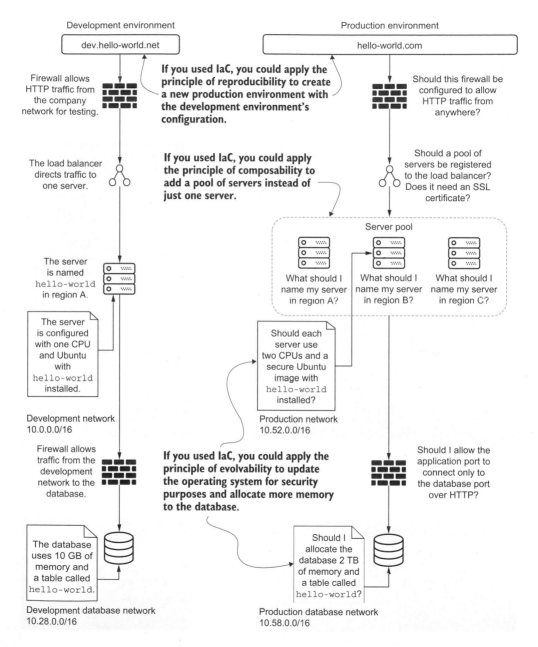

Figure 2.1   When you create a production environment based on the development, you must answer many questions about configurations for new infrastructure and reverse engineer the functionality of the development environment.

You might wonder, for example, why the lack of infrastructure as code for the *development* environment affects your ability to create the *production* one. The first reason is that you cannot easily *reproduce* the infrastructure resources. You have to reverse engineer a weeks' worth of manual configuration! With IaC, you can instead copy and paste some configuration and modify it for the production environment.

Second, you cannot easily *compose* the infrastructure resources with new ones. You need a pool of servers for production instead of a single server. If you built an infrastructure module, you could use that building block to create multiple servers without updating the configuration from scratch.

Finally, you cannot easily *evolve* the production environment with its specific requirements. The production environment requires some different infrastructure resources, like secure operating systems and a larger database. You'll have to manually tweak configuration that you've never run in the development environment.

You can solve these challenges and improve reproducibility, composability, and evolvability in two ways. First, you need a way to migrate manually configured infrastructure to IaC. Second, you need to write clean IaC to promote reproducibility and evolvability.

The first part of this chapter outlines fundamental concepts for writing IaC and migrating existing infrastructure to code. The second part of this chapter applies code hygiene practices to infrastructure. The combination of these practices will help you write reproducible IaC and set the stage for future composition and evolution of your system.

2.1 Expressing infrastructure change

I mentioned in chapter 1 that IaC automates changes. It turns out that reproducing and automating many changes over time takes effort. For example, if you want to provision and manage a server on GCP, you'll usually make the following changes over time:

1 Create the server in GCP by using the console, terminal, or code.
2 Read the server in GCP to check that you created the server with the correct specifications—for example, Ubuntu 18.04 as the operating system.
3 Update the server in GCP with a publicly accessible network address to log into it.
4 Delete the server in GCP because you no longer require it.

To make more complex updates or reproduce the server in another environment, you take the following steps:

1 Create the server.
2 Check if it exists by using a read command.
3 Update it if you need to log in.
4 Delete the server if you no longer need it.

No matter which resource you automate, you can always break down your changes to create, read, update, and delete (CRUD). You create an infrastructure resource, search for its metadata, update its properties, and delete it when you no longer need it.

> **NOTE**   You wouldn't usually have a change record that explicitly states "read the server." The record usually implies a read step to verify that a resource is created or updated.

CRUD allows you to automate your infrastructure step-by-step in a specific order. This approach, called the *imperative style*, describes how to configure infrastructure. You can think of it as an instruction manual.

> **DEFINITION**   The *imperative style* of IaC describes how to configure an infrastructure resource step-by-step.

While it seems intuitive, the imperative style does not scale as you make more changes to the system. I once had to create a new database environment based on a development environment. I started reconstructing the 200 change requests submitted to the development environment over two years. Each change request became a series of steps creating, updating, and deleting resources. It took me a month and a half to complete an environment that still didn't match the existing development one!

Rather than painstakingly re-create every step, I wished I could just describe the new database environment based on the running state of the development environment and let a tool figure out how to achieve the state. With most IaC, you will find it easier to reproduce environments and make changes in the declarative style. The *declarative style* describes the desired end state of an infrastructure resource. The tool decides the steps it needs to take to configure the infrastructure resource.

> **DEFINITION**   The *declarative style* of IaC describes the desired end state of an infrastructure resource. Automation and tooling decide how to achieve the end state without your knowledge.

This process with IaC takes a few steps. First, you need to search inventory sources for information on the database servers. Next, you get the database IP addresses. Finally, you write a configuration based on the information you've collected.

Your configuration in version control becomes the infrastructure *source of truth*. You declare the new database environment's desired state instead of describing a set of steps that may not end in the same result.

> **DEFINITION**   An infrastructure *source of truth* structures information about the state of your infrastructure system consistently and singularly.

You make all changes on the infrastructure source of truth. However, even in ideal circumstances (such as with GitOps in chapter 7), you probably have some configuration drift from manual changes over time. If you use the declarative style and create a source of truth, you can use immutability to change infrastructure and lower the risk of failure.

Exercise 2.1

Does the following use the imperative or declarative style of configuring infrastructure?

```
if __name__ == "__main__":
    update_packages()
    read_ssh_keys()
    update_users()
    if enable_secure_configuration:
        update_ip_tables()
```

See appendix B for answers to exercises.

2.2 Understanding immutability

How do you prevent configuration drift and quickly reproduce your infrastructure? It starts with changing the way you think about change. Imagine you create a server with Python version 2. You could update your scripts to log into the server and upgrade Python without restarting the server. You can treat the server as *mutable infrastructure* because you update the server in place without restarting it.

> **DEFINITION** *Mutable infrastructure* means that you can update the infrastructure resource in place without recreating or restarting it.

However, treating the server as mutable infrastructure raises an issue. Other packages on the server do not work with Python 3. Rather than update every other package and break the server, you can change your update scripts to create a *new* server with Python version 3 and compatible dependencies. Then you can delete the old server with Python 2. Figure 2.2 shows how to do this.

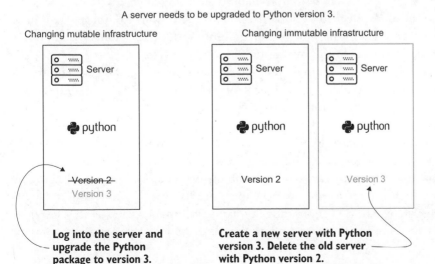

Figure 2.2 You treat the server mutably by logging in and updating the Python package version. By comparison, you treat the server immutably by replacing the old server with a new one upgraded to Python 3.

Your new scripts treat the server as *immutable infrastructure*, in which you can replace the existing infrastructure with changes. You do not update the infrastructure in place. *Immutability* means that after you create a resource, you do not change its configuration.

> **DEFINITION** *Immutable infrastructure* means you must create a new resource for any changes to infrastructure configuration. You do not modify the resource after creating it.

Why treat the server's update in two different ways? Some changes will break the resource if you do them mutably. To mitigate the risk of failure, you can create a whole new resource with the updates and remove the old one with immutability.

Immutability relies on a series of creation and deletion changes. Creating a new resource alleviates drift (difference in actual versus expected configuration) because the new resource aligns with the IaC you use to create it. You can expand this beyond server resources to even serverless functions or entire infrastructure clusters. You choose to create a new resource with changes instead of updating the existing one.

> **NOTE** Machine image builders work with the concept of immutable infrastructure. Any updates to a server require a new machine image, which the builder generates and provides. Modifications to the server, such as IP address registration, should be passed as parameters to a startup script defined by the image builder.

The enforcement of immutability affects the way you make changes. Creating a new resource requires the principle of reproducibility. As a result, IaC lends well to enforcing immutability as you make changes. For example, you might create a new firewall each time you need to update it. The new firewall overrides any manual rules someone added outside of IaC, facilitating security and reducing drift.

Immutability also promotes system availability and mitigates any failures to mission-critical applications. Instead of updating an existing resource in place, creating a new one isolates changes to the new resource, limiting the blast radius if something goes wrong. I discuss more on this in chapter 9.

However, immutability sometimes comes at the cost of time and effort. Figure 2.3 compares the effect of mutable versus immutable infrastructure. When you treat the server as a mutable resource, you localize the effect of the Python in-place update. Updating Python affects a small part of the server's overall state. When you treat a server immutably, you replace the *entire* server's state, affecting any resources dependent on that server.

Here, replacing the entire state for immutability can take *longer* than changing to mutable infrastructure! You cannot expect to treat all infrastructure immutably all the time. If you change tens of thousands of servers immutably, you spend a few days re-creating all of them. An in-place update may take only a day if you don't break anything.

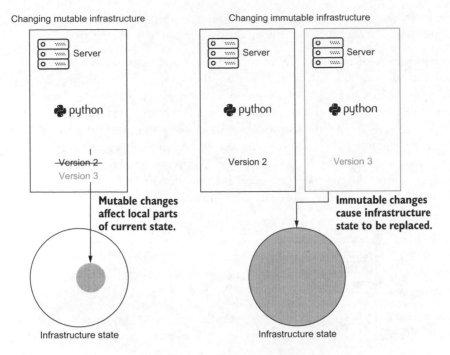

Figure 2.3 Changes to mutable resources affect a small portion of the infrastructure state, while immutable resources replace the entire resource state.

You'll find that you will switch between treating infrastructure as mutable *and* immutable, depending on the circumstance. Immutable infrastructure helps mitigate potential risk of failure across your system, while mutable infrastructure facilitates faster changes. You often treat infrastructure as mutable when you need to fix the system. How do you migrate between mutable and immutable infrastructure?

2.2.1 *Remediating out-of-band changes*

You cannot expect to deploy a new resource every time you make a change. Sometimes changes might seem minor in scope and impact. As a result, you decide to make the change mutably.

Imagine you and your friend meet at a coffee shop. Your friend orders a cappuccino with a nondairy alternative. However, the barista adds milk. The barista then needs to make a new cappuccino for your friend because the milk affects the whole cup. Your friend waits for another 5 to 10 minutes. You get a cup of coffee instead and add milk and sugar to taste. If you don't have enough sugar, you just add more.

You take less time to change your mutable coffee than your friend changing their immutable cappuccino. Similarly, it takes far less time, effort, and cost to execute changes to a mutable resource. When you temporarily treat infrastructure as a mutable resource, you make an *out-of-band* change.

DEFINITION   An *out-of-band change* is a quickly implemented change that temporarily treats immutable infrastructure as mutable infrastructure.

When you break immutability with an out-of-band change, you reduce the change time but increase the risk of affecting another change in the future. After you make the out-of-band change, you need to update your source of truth to return to immutable infrastructure. How do you start this remediation process?

You must reconcile the actual state and desired configuration when making an out-of-band change. Let's apply this to my server example in figure 2.4. First, you log into the server and upgrade Python to version 3. Then, you change the configuration in version control, so new servers install Python version 3. The configuration matches the server's state with the source of truth in version control.

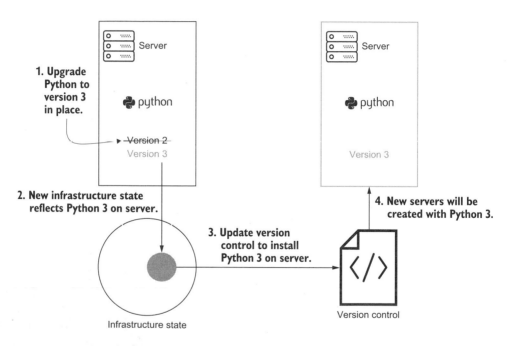

Figure 2.4   **After updating a mutable resource, you need to update version control to account for the out-of-band change.**

Why should you update IaC for the out-of-band change? Remember from chapter 1 that manual changes may affect reproducibility. Making sure that you transition a change made to mutable infrastructure to future immutable infrastructure preserves reproducibility. After remediating the out-of-band change and adding it to IaC, you can redeploy changes repeatedly to my server, and nothing should change. This behavior conforms to idempotency!

You will continuously reconcile state and source of truth if you make many mutable changes. You should *prioritize immutability* to promote reproducibility. A barista can always replace a drink in my coffee example, even if you spill the sugar container into your mutable coffee. I recommend using your organization's change procedures to limit out-of-band changes and ensure that the updates align with the configuration in IaC. You can always use the immutable infrastructure configuration to fix a failed mutable change.

> ### Exercise 2.2
>
> Which of the following changes benefit from the principle of immutability? (Choose all that apply.)
>
>   A   Reducing a network to have fewer IP addresses
>   B   Adding a column to a relational database
>   c   Adding a new IP address to an existing DNS entry
>   D   Updating a server's packages to backward-incompatible versions
>   E   Migrating infrastructure resources to another region
>
> See appendix B for answers to exercises.

2.2.2   *Migrating to infrastructure as code*

Immutability through IaC allows version control to manage infrastructure configuration as a source of truth and facilitate future reproduction. In fact, conforming to immutability means that you create new resources all the time. It works well for *greenfield* environments, which do not have active resources.

However, most organizations have *brownfield* environments, an existing environment with active servers, load balancers, and networks. Recall that the chapter example includes a brownfield development environment called hello-world. You went into your infrastructure provider and manually created a set of resources.

In general, a brownfield environment treats infrastructure as mutable. You need a way to change your practice of manually changing mutable infrastructure to automatically updating immutable IaC. How do you migrate the environment's infrastructure resources to immutability?

Let's migrate the hello-world development environment to immutable IaC. Before you begin, you make a list of infrastructure resources in the environment. It contains networks, servers, load balancers, firewalls, and Domain Name System (DNS) entries.

BASE INFRASTRUCTURE

To start, you find the base infrastructure resource that other resources need to use. For example, every infrastructure resource depends on the network in the development environment. You start writing IaC for the database and development networks because the server, load balancer, and database run on it. You cannot reconstruct any resources that run on the networks until the networks exist as code.

In figure 2.5, you use your terminal to access the infrastructure provider application programming interface (API). Your terminal command prints out the name and IP address range (classless inter-domain routing, or CIDR, block) of the development

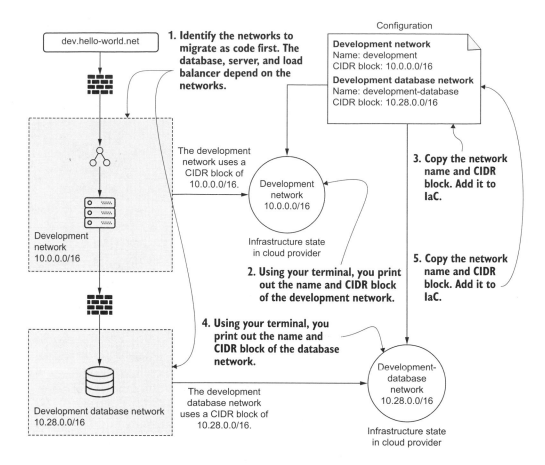

Figure 2.5   Reverse engineer the networks for the database and server first and write their configurations as code.

database and development networks. You reconstruct each network by copying the name and CIDR block of each network into IaC.

Why reverse engineer and reproduce the network in IaC? You must match the IaC with the network's actual resource state exactly. If you have a mismatch, called *drift*, you'll find that your IaC may break your network (and anything on it) by accident!

If possible, import the resource into an IaC state. The resource already exists, and you need your provisioning tool to recognize that. The import step migrates the existing resource to IaC management. To complete the network resource migration, run the IaC again and check that you don't have drift.

Many provisioning tools have a function for importing resources. For example, CloudFormation uses the `resource import` command. Similarly, Terraform offers `terraform import`.

If you write IaC without a provisioning tool, you do not need a direct import capability. Instead, you write code to create a new resource. Sometimes it's easier to use reproducibility to create a whole new resource. If you cannot easily create a new resource, write code with conditional statements that check whether the resources exist.

Figure 2.6 captures the entire decision workflow of reconstructing the network and whether you can use a provisioning tool to migrate your resource to immutability.

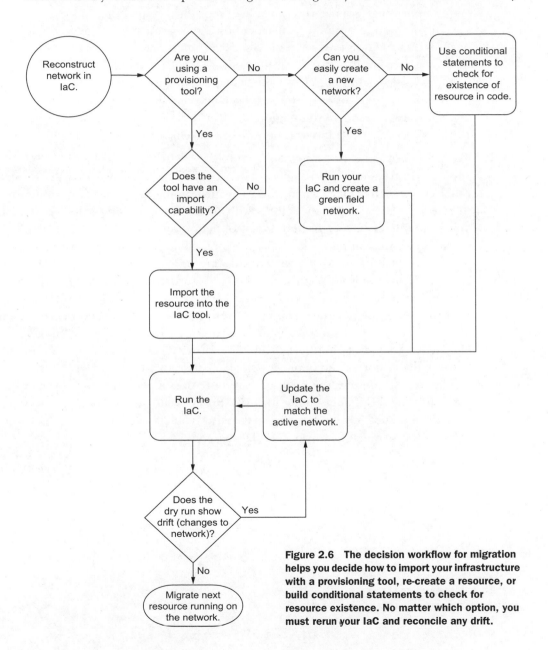

Figure 2.6   The decision workflow for migration helps you decide how to import your infrastructure with a provisioning tool, re-create a resource, or build conditional statements to check for resource existence. No matter which option, you must rerun your IaC and reconcile any drift.

The diagram includes the considerations for creating new resources or writing conditional statements for existing resources. As you migrate, you run your IaC multiple times to check for drift.

Why do you have so many decision workflows for migrating to immutability? All of these practices adhere to the principles of reproducibility, idempotency, and composability. You want to reproduce the resources in IaC as accurately as possible. If you can't import the resource, you can at least reproduce a new one.

Furthermore, rerunning the code uses the principle of idempotency, which ensures that you don't re-create the resource (unless necessary). If you reconcile drift, idempotency should not change the active network. Similarly, composability allows you to migrate each resource separately to avoid disrupting the system.

As you work on other resources, keep the decision workflow in mind. You can apply it to each resource you migrate to IaC until you complete the migration. You'll revisit parts of this decision workflow when you refactor IaC in chapter 10.

RESOURCES DEPENDENT ON BASE INFRASTRUCTURE

After reconstructing the base network infrastructure, you can work on the servers and other components. Once again, you use your terminal to print out attributes for the hello-world server. It runs in region A with an Ubuntu operating system and one CPU. You write the server specification in its configuration, making note of its dependency on the development network. Similarly, you use your terminal to learn that the database uses 10 GB of memory. You copy this into IaC and record its use of the development database network. Figure 2.7 shows the process of migrating the server and database to code.

You want to migrate the second set of resources that use the network. Use composability to isolate these infrastructure resources and make iterative updates. Small changes to next levels of infrastructure help prevent larger system failures. In chapter 7, you'll learn more about deploying small changes to infrastructure.

Before you move to the next set of resources, complete the cycle of migration by running your IaC and checking for drift. Ensure that the network, server, and database do not show changes in their IaC. After you reconcile any new drift, you can move onto the remaining resources (DNS, firewall rules, and load balancers).

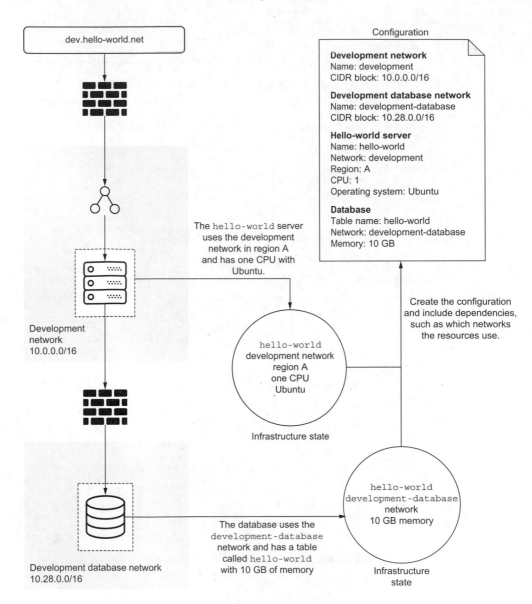

Figure 2.7 After migrating base infrastructure such as networks, migrate the server and database resources. They depend on base infrastructure but do not depend on each other.

Finally, figure 2.8 rebuilds the remaining configuration for DNS, firewall rules, and load balancers. They depend on the existing configuration of servers and databases. No other resources depend on them.

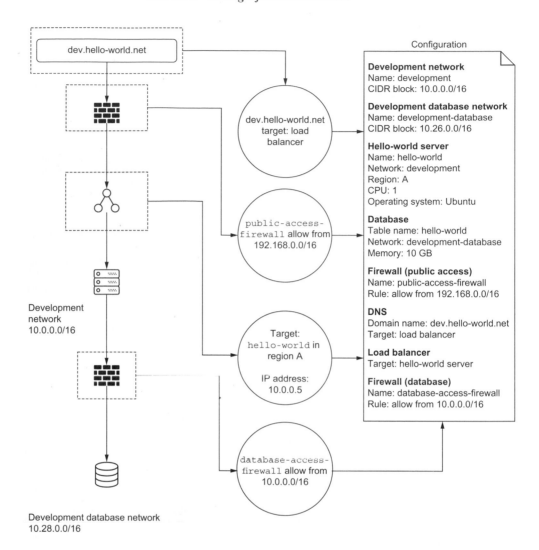

Figure 2.8   Finally, migrate resources with the fewest dependencies or require server and database configuration.

Why go through the painstaking process of reconstructing various levels of infrastructure? Your brownfield environment did not have a consistent *source of truth,* so you need to build one. When you finish adding the infrastructure resources to the configuration, you reconstruct a source of truth for the environment. A source of truth with IaC allows you to treat the brownfield environment as immutable infrastructure.

Outside of the example, you'll always migrate to immutability from base to top-level resources. Identify resources that others heavily depend upon when you start the migration. Write these low-level resources—such as networks, accounts or projects, and IAM—into IaC.

Next, choose resources such as servers, queues, or databases. Firewalls, load balancers, DNS, and alerts depend on the existence of servers, queues, and databases. You can migrate resources with the fewest dependencies at the end of the process. We'll discuss more about infrastructure dependencies in chapter 4.

> **NOTE** A *dependency graph* represents the dependencies among infrastructure resources. IaC tools, such as Terraform, use this concept to apply changes in a structured way. When you migrate resources, you reconstruct the dependency graph. You can investigate tooling that will map the live infrastructure state for you and highlight dependencies to make this easier.

MIGRATION STEPS

I usually follow general steps to assess dependencies and structure migrating existing resources to IaC:

1 Migrate *initial login, accounts, and provider resource isolation constructs.* For example, I write the configuration for a cloud provider's account or project and my initial service account for automation.

2 Migrate *networks, subnetworks, routing, and root DNS configuration,* if applicable. The root DNS configuration can include Secure Sockets Layer (SSL) certificates. For example, I created the root domain hello-world.net and its SSL certificate to prepare for subdomains such as dev.hello-world.net.

3 Migrate *computing resources* such as application servers or databases.

4 Migrate the *compute orchestration platform and its components* if you use a compute orchestration platform. For example, I migrate my Kubernetes cluster to schedule workloads across servers.

5 If you use a compute orchestration platform, migrate the *application deployments to the compute orchestration platform.* For example, I backport the configuration of the hello-world application deployed on Kubernetes.

6 Migrate *messaging queues, caches, or event-streaming platforms.* These services have application dependencies before you can reconstruct them. For example, I write the configuration for a messaging queue to communicate between hello-world and another application.

7 Migrate *DNS subdomains, load balancers, and firewalls.* For example, I re-create a configuration for a firewall rule between my hello-world application and its database.

8 Migrate *alerts or monitoring* related to resources. For example, I reconstruct my configuration to notify me if the hello-world application fails.

9 Finally, migrate *SaaS resources,* such as data processing or repositories, that do not depend on applications. For example, this could be a data transform job on GCP that has a singular dependency on a database.

Between each step, make sure you *test* that you've correctly migrated the initial resources by rerunning the configuration. You rarely get all the parameters and dependencies you need on the first try.

NOTE   Rerunning the migrated configuration should *not* change existing infrastructure because of idempotency. You should reapply the configuration and check the dry run. Changes in your dry run mean your configuration has not accurately captured the actual state of the resource.

If you run the configuration and it outputs changes, you must correct your configuration! The process requires trial and error. As a result, I recommend you test and verify each set of resources.

Migrating to immutability becomes an exercise in reducing drift. This process shows an extreme circumstance where the configuration has drifted far from the state. You work to reconcile the source of truth by updating its configuration in version control. The process of importing existing resources to a new source of truth applies to refactoring IaC, something we'll discuss in chapter 10.

2.3   *Writing clean infrastructure as code*

Besides using immutability, you can promote reproducibility by writing configuration cleanly. *Code hygiene* refers to a set of practices to enhance the readability and structure of code.

DEFINITION   *Code hygiene* is a set of practices and styles to enhance the readability and maintainability of code.

IaC hygiene helps save time when you need to reuse the configuration. I often find infrastructure configuration copied, pasted, and edited with hardcoded values. Hardcoded values reduce readability and reproducibility. While many of these practices come from software development, I suggest some practices specific to infrastructure.

2.3.1   *Version control communicates context*

How do you use version control effectively to enable reproducibility? Structured practices around version control help you quickly reproduce configuration and make informed changes. For example, you might update a firewall rule in development that allows traffic from `app-network` to `shared-services-network`. You add the following commit message to describe why you added the allowance:

```
$ git commit -m "Allow app to connect to queues
app-network needs to connect to shared-services-network
because the application uses queues.
All ports need to be open."
```

A few weeks later, you reproduce the network in production. However, you forgot why you added the allowance. When you examine the commit history, you remember your descriptive message. You now have information that the application needs to access queues.

When you write commit messages for IaC, you do not need to explain the configuration. The change already captures what the configuration will be. Instead, use the commit message to explain *why* you want to make the change and *how* it will affect other infrastructure.

> **NOTE** In this book, I address version control practices specific to IaC. To learn more about version control, check out the "Getting Started—About Version Control" Git tutorial at http://mng.bz/pOBR. For more on writing good commit messages, check out "Distributed Git—Contributing to a Project" at http://mng.bz/OoMj. Content for both is from *Pro Git* by Scott Chacon and Ben Straub (Apress, 2014).

You also might have an audit requirement to prefix an issue number or ticket number to the front of the commit message for traceability. For example, you might work on a ticket numbered TICKET-002. It contains a request to allow traffic between the application and shared services. To correlate the ticket to your commit, you add the ticket to the start of the commit message:

```
$ git commit -m "TICKET-002 Allow app to connect to queues
app-network needs to connect to shared-services-network
because the application uses queues.
All ports need to be open."
```

Adding the work item or ticket information to commit messages makes it easier to track changes. Configuration becomes change documentation because it is the source of truth for infrastructure resources. Version control also becomes a mechanism for documenting changes. You can reconstruct the history of changes and reproduce environments by examining version control and configuration.

2.3.2 Linting and formatting

Before you commit your code, you want to lint it and format it. IaC often will not execute because you missed a space (or two) or used the wrong field name. The wrong field name could lead to an error. Misaligned code can often cause you to misread or skip a configuration line.

Imagine you configure a server, and it needs a field called `ip_address`. Instead, you name the field `ip` and later realize you cannot create the server with your IaC. How can you make sure you've written the field as `ip_address`?

You can use *linting* to analyze your code and verify nonstandard or incorrect configurations. Most tools offer a way to lint the configuration or code. Linting for `ip_address` catches the wrong field name of `ip` early in development.

> **DEFINITION** *Linting* automatically checks the style of your code for nonstandard configuration.

Why check for nonstandard or incorrect configuration? You want to make sure you write the proper configuration and don't miss critical syntax. If the tool does not have a linting feature, you can always find a community extension or write your own linting rules with a programming language. You should include linting rules that address security standards, such as no secrets committed to version control (chapter 8).

Besides linting, you can use *formatting* to check for spacing and configuration formats. Formatting might seem obvious as a software development practice, but it becomes more critical in IaC.

> **DEFINITION**   *Formatting* automatically aligns your code for correct spacing and configuration formats.

Most tools use domain-specific languages (DSLs) that offer a higher level of abstraction for a programming language. A DSL provides a lower barrier to entry if you don't know a programming language. These languages use YAML or JSON data formats with particular format requirements. Having tools to check formatting, such as whether you missed a space in your YAML file, is helpful!

You can also add version control hooks to run formatting checks before committing your code. For example, you might create your infrastructure resources with CloudFormation in YAML data format. To validate the infrastructure resource fields and values, you use the AWS CloudFormation Linter (http://mng.bz/YGrj). You also format the YAML file with the AWS CloudFormation Template Formatter (http://mng.bz/GEVA).

Rather than remember to type these commands each time, you can add the commands as a pre-commit Git hook. Each time you run `git commit`, the command checks for a proper configuration and format before pushing them to a repository. You can also add them to a continuous delivery workflow, which I cover in chapter 7.

2.3.3   *Naming resources*

When your IaC becomes documentation, your resources, configuration, and variables need descriptive names. I once created a firewall rule to test something and called it `firewall-rule-1`. Two weeks later, when I wanted to reproduce it into production, I did not remember why I created the rule in development.

In retrospect, I should have named the firewall rule something more descriptive. I spent another 30 minutes tracking down the rule's IP addresses and allowances. Naming can affect the time you spend deciphering what the infrastructure does and how it differs in another environment.

Resource names should include the *environment*, the infrastructure *resource type*, and its *purpose*. Figure 2.9 names the firewall rule `dev-firewall-rule-allow-hello-world-to-database`, which includes the environment (`dev`), the resource type (`firewall-rule`), and the purpose (`allow-hello-world-to-database`).

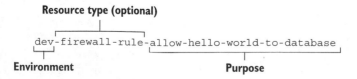

Figure 2.9   The resource name should include the environment, type, and purpose.

Why should names involve so much detail? You want to identify the resource quickly for troubleshooting, sharing, and auditing. Noticing the environment at a glance ensures that you configure the right one (and not production by accident). The purpose tells others and reminds yourself what the resource does.

Optionally, you can include the resource type. I usually omit resource type from the name because I identify it from resource metadata. Omitting the resource type allows you to conform to your cloud provider's character limit. If you want to include more information about the purpose or type of your resource, you can always include it in the resource's tags (chapter 8).

Describe the resource to someone else

When I name a resource, I try to describe it to someone else. If another person understands the resource based on the name, I know it is good. However, I know it needs more information if someone needs to ask additional questions about the environment or resource type.

This exercise can make the names a little long, but I err on the side of being more descriptive. Recognizing the resource's purpose based on its name saves valuable time reconstructing the environment.

Besides resource names, you also want to make variables and configurations as descriptive as possible. Most infrastructure providers have specific resource attribute naming. AWS refers to a network's IP address as the `CidrBlock`, while Azure refers to it as an `address_space`.

I lean toward using the provider's specific naming to facilitate looking up documentation for the provider for later changes and reproduction. If I rename the configuration for Azure to `cidr_block`, I have to remember to translate the parameter to `address_space` for Azure to consume it. You need to remember to translate a more generic field name for variables or configurations to another provider or environment.

2.3.4 Variables and constants

Besides naming variables, how do you know which values should be variables? Let's say the hello-world application always serves on port 8080. You don't plan on changing the port often, so you set it to `application_port = 8080` at the beginning of your configuration. However, you hardcode `hello-world` directly into the `name` attributes of your infrastructure resources.

One year later, you reproduce the environment for a new version of hello-world on port 3000. You want the new value of `name` as `hello-world-v2`. You update `application_port` at the beginning of your configuration to `3000`. Putting the port in a variable allows you to reference the `application_port` throughout your configuration and store the value in one place. You congratulate yourself on not needing to find and replace instances of 8080 in your configuration. However, you spend an hour searching for all instances of `hello-world` in your infrastructure configuration to change its name.

In this example, you have two types of inputs. A *variable* stores a value referenced by infrastructure configuration. Most infrastructure values are best stored in variables and referenced by the configuration.

> **DEFINITION**   A *variable* stores a value referenced by infrastructure configuration. You expect to change the value of a variable anytime you create a new resource or environment.

You should set the application's name, `hello-world`, as a variable because it will change depending on the environment, version, or purpose. However, the port does not change based on environment or purpose. A *constant* variable sets a common value across a set of resources and rarely changes with environment or purpose.

> **DEFINITION**   A *constant* variable establishes a common value across infrastructure configuration. You do not change constants often.

When deciding when to make a configuration value a variable or constant, consider the impact and security implications of changing the value. The frequency of change matters less. If changing the value affects infrastructure dependencies or compromises sensitive information, set it as a variable. You should always set names or environments as variables.

Unlike software development, which pushes for fewer constants, IaC *prioritizes constants over variables*. Avoid setting too many variables because they make the configuration challenging to maintain. Instead, you can set a constant by defining a local variable with a static configuration.

For example, Terraform uses local values (www.terraform.io/docs/language/valucs/locals.html) to store constants. Commonly defined constants include operating systems, tags, account identifiers, or domain names. Standardized values on infrastructure providers such as `internal` or `external` to describe a type of network can also be constant.

2.3.5   *Parametrize dependencies*

When you create a server, you need to specify the network it needs to use. You initially express this by hardcoding the name of the network you want, specifically `development`. When you read the configuration, you know precisely which network the server uses.

However, you realize that when you have to reproduce this for production, you need to search and replace any reference of `development` with `production`. Problematically, you have multiple references to `development`! Your search-and-replace mission becomes a few tedious hours.

CODE EXAMPLE

You decide to parametrize the GCP network as a variable so you can reproduce a server in another environment with a different network. When you pass the network name as a variable, you change the network for any server referencing it. Let's pass the name of the network as a variable in code as follows.

Listing 2.1   Parametrize the network as a variable

```
import json


                                              Passes the name and network as
def hello_server(name, network):      ◁──┘   parameters to the configuration
   return {
       'resource': [                          Uses Terraform's
           {                                   google_compute_instance
               'google_compute_instance': [ ◁──┘ resource to configure a server
                   {
                       name: [
                           {
                               'allow_stopping_for_update': True,
                               'zone': 'us-central1-a',
                               'boot_disk': [
                                   {
                                       'initialize_params': [
                                           {
                                               'image': 'ubuntu-1804-lts'
                                           }
                                       ]
                                   }
                               ],
                               'machine_type': 'f1-micro',
                               'name': name,
                               'network_interface': [
                                   {
          Sets the network     ─────▷  'network': network
            by using the           }
          "network" variable    ],
                               'labels': {
                                   'name': name,
                                   'purpose': 'manning-infrastructure-as-code'
                               }
                           }
                       ]
                   }
               ]
           }
       ]
   }
                                              Sets the network dependency
                                              as the default network when
                                              you run the script
if __name__ == "__main__":
    config = hello_server(name='hello-world', network='default')   ◁─────

    with open('main.tf.json', 'w') as outfile:                 Creates a JSON file with
        json.dump(config, outfile, sort_keys=True, indent=4)   the server object and
                                                               runs it with Terraform
```

> ### AWS and Azure equivalents
>
> In AWS, you would use the `aws_instance` Terraform resource with a reference to the network you want to use (http://mng.bz/z4j6). You can create this resource on the default virtual private cloud (VPC).
>
> In Azure, you would need to create a virtual network and subnets, then create the `azurerm_linux_virtual_machine` Terraform resource (http://mng.bz/064E) on the network.

Why pass the name and network as variables? You often change the name and network depending on the environment. Parametrizing these values helps with reproducibility and composability. You can create new resources on different networks *and* build multiple resources without worrying about conflicts.

RUNNING THE EXAMPLE

I'll run the example step-by-step to celebrate our first hello-world server. Refer to chapter 1 for more information on the tools required for the examples and appendix A for detailed usage instructions. Here are the steps:

1   Run the script in Python by entering the command in the terminal:

```
$ python main.py
```

The command creates a file with the extension *.tf.json. Terraform will automatically search for this file extension to create the resources.

2   Check whether the file exists by listing files in the terminal:

```
$ ls *.tf.json
```

The output should be as follows:

```
main.tf.json
```

3   Authenticate to GCP in the terminal:

```
$ gcloud auth login
```

4   Set the GCP project you want to use as the `CLOUDSDK_CORE_PROJECT` environment variable:

```
$ export CLOUDSDK_CORE_PROJECT=<your GCP project>
```

5   Initialize Terraform to retrieve the GCP plugin in the terminal:

```
$ terraform init
```

The output should include the following:

```
Initializing the backend...

Initializing provider plugins...
```

```
- Finding latest version of hashicorp/google...
- Installing hashicorp/google v3.58.0...
- Installed hashicorp/google v3.58.0 (signed by HashiCorp)

Terraform has created a lock file .terraform.lock.hcl to
⇒record the provider selections it made above.
⇒Include this file in your version control repository
⇒so that Terraform can guarantee to make the same
⇒selections by default when
⇒you run "terraform init" in the future.

Terraform has been successfully initialized!

You may now begin working with Terraform. Try running
⇒"terraform plan" to see any changes that are
⇒required for your infrastructure. All Terraform commands
⇒should now work.

If you ever set or change modules or backend configuration
⇒for Terraform, rerun this command to reinitialize
⇒your working directory. If you forget, other
⇒commands will detect it and remind you to do so if necessary.
```

6 Apply the Terraform configuration in the terminal. Ensure that you enter yes
to apply the changes and create the instance:

```
$ terraform apply
```

Your output should include the configuration and name of the server instance:

```
Do you want to perform these actions?
  Terraform will perform the actions described above.
  Only 'yes' will be accepted to approve.

  Enter a value: yes

google_compute_instance.hello-world: Creating...
google_compute_instance.hello-world: Still creating... [10s elapsed]
google_compute_instance.hello-world: Still creating... [20s elapsed]
google_compute_instance.hello-world: Creation complete after 24s
⇒[id=projects/infrastructure-as-code-book/zones
⇒/us-central1-a/instances/hello-world]

Apply complete! Resources: 1 added, 0 changed, 0 destroyed.
```

NOTE I do not go through all of the nuances of Terraform in this book. For
detailed information on getting started with Terraform, check out the
HashiCorp "Get Started" tutorial at https://learn.hashicorp.com/terraform.
You can find additional documentation on how Terraform works with GCP at
http://mng.bz/Kx2g.

7 You can examine the GCP console for the server's network and metadata. Otherwise, you can use the Cloud SDK command-line interface (CLI) to check the

network in the terminal. Enter the command to filter out the hello-world server:

```
$ gcloud compute instances list --filter="name=( 'hello-world' )" \
  --format="table(name,networkInterfaces.network)"
```

The output should include the GCP URL of the network:

```
NAME           NETWORK
hello-world    ['https://www.googleapis.com/compute/v1/projects/
➡<your GCP project>/global/networks/default']
```

The GCP server uses the `default` network, which you passed as a variable to the example. If you want to change the network, you update the new variable. Your IaC tooling will pick up the changes and create a new server.

To destroy the server, you can use Terraform in the terminal. Make sure you enter yes to remove the server altogether:

```
$ terraform destroy
```

When you define dependencies as variables, you loosely couple the two infrastructure resources. Chapter 4 covers specific patterns you can use to decouple infrastructure resources and dependencies further. If possible, you should avoid hardcoding dependencies and pass them in as parameters.

2.3.6   *Keeping it a secret*

IaC often needs to use *secrets* such as tokens, passwords, or keys to execute changes to a provider.

> **DEFINITION**   A *secret* is a piece of sensitive information such as a password, token, or key.

When you create servers in GCP, you need a service account key or token that accesses the project and server resources. To ensure that you can create resources, you maintain the secrets as part of the infrastructure configuration. Secrets in configuration can be problematic. If someone can read my secret, they can use it to access my GCP account to create resources and access restricted data!

You might also need to pass secrets as part of the configuration. For example, you use IaC to set the SSL certificate for a load balancer. The SSL certificate expires in two years. You re-create the environment two years later. However, you discover that the encrypted string of the certificate has expired. You cannot decrypt it and must now issue a new certificate.

Figure 2.10 shows how to best secure your certificate but improve its evolvability in the future. You pass the certificate as an input variable to have different certificates for each environment. Then you put the new certificates in a secrets manager, which stores and manages the certificate for you.

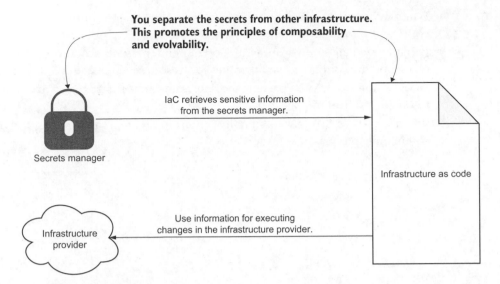

Figure 2.10 Retrieve sensitive information from a secrets manager to change resources with an infrastructure provider.

Anytime the certificate changes, you update it in the secrets manager. Your IaC updates its configuration when it reads the certificate from the secrets manager. Separating concerns for certificate management from configuration mitigates any problems you have later with certificate expiration.

Why store secrets outside of IaC? You just applied the principles of composability and evolvability to separating secrets from other infrastructure resources. This separation ensures that someone can't examine your IaC to get a password or username. You also minimize the impact of failure when you rotate a secret by rerunning the IaC.

Always pass secrets as variables into IaC and use it in memory. These include Secure Shell Protocol (SSH) keys, certificates, private keys, API tokens, passwords, and other login information. A separate entity should store and manage sensitive authentication data, such as a secrets manager. Separate secrets management facilitates reproduction, especially when you want different passwords and tokens for each environment. You should never hardcode or commit secrets to version control in plaintext.

Summary

- Prioritizing immutability reduces configuration drift, maintains a source of truth, and improves reproducibility.
- To conform to immutability, changes to a resource create an entirely new resource and replace its state.
- If you make mutable changes, you must reconcile the localized changes in the infrastructure state with your configuration.

- When writing IaC, use commits in version control to communicate changes and context and format the code for readability.
- Parametrize names, environments, and dependencies to other infrastructure. If you scope the configuration attributes to a resource, you can set it as a constant.
- Secrets should always be passed as variables and never hardcoded or committed to version control in plaintext.
- When writing scripts, always simplify actions to create, read, update, and delete commands to reproduce resources.

Patterns for infrastructure modules

This chapter covers

- Grouping infrastructure resources into composable modules based on function
- Building infrastructure modules with software development design patterns
- Applying module patterns to common infrastructure use cases

In the preceding chapter, I covered the fundamental practices for infrastructure as code. Even though I knew the fundamental practices, my first Python automation script grouped code into one file with messy functions. Years later, I learned software design patterns. They provided a standard set of patterns that made it easier for me to change the script and hand it over to another teammate for maintenance.

In the following two chapters, I show how to apply design patterns to IaC configuration and dependencies. Software *design patterns* help you identify common problems and build reusable, object-oriented solutions.

> **DEFINITION**   A *design pattern* is a repeatable solution to a common problem in software.

Applying software design patterns to IaC has its pitfalls. IaC has reusable objects (as infrastructure resources). However, its opinionated behaviors and DSLs do not map directly to software design patterns.

IaC offers an immutable layer of abstraction, which is why this chapter borrows both *creational* (used for creating objects) and *structural* (for structuring objects) design patterns to make approximations to infrastructure. Most IaC focuses on immutability, which automatically creates a new resource upon changes. As a result, the design patterns that rely on mutability do not apply.

> **NOTE**   I adapted many patterns from *Design Patterns: Elements of Reusable Object-Oriented Software* by Erich Gamma et al. (Addison-Wesley Professional, 1994) to IaC. If you would like to learn more about the original software design patterns, I recommend referencing that book.

I include Python code listings that create Terraform JSON files. They reference GCP resources. You can extend the patterns to DSLs, such as Terraform, CloudFormation, or Bicep. Depending on the DSL and tool you choose, it might use different mechanisms or features. When possible, I note limitations for DSLs and equivalents for AWS and Azure.

3.1   *Singleton*

Imagine you need to create a set of database servers in GCP from scratch. The database system needs a GCP project, custom database network, server template, and server group. The server template installs the packages on each server, while the server group describes the number of database servers you need.

Figure 3.1 shows how to add the project, database network, server template, and server group to one directory. You determine the attributes for the GCP project name and its organization. Next, you figure out the network should have the name `development-database-network` with an IP address range of 10.0.3.0/16. Finally, you express that the database should have three servers that use templates for MySQL. You write all these attributes as code into one configuration file.

The database system configuration uses the *singleton pattern*, which declares a set of resources as singular instances in a system.

> **DEFINITION**   The *singleton pattern* declares a set of resources as singular instances in a system. It deploys all the resources with a single command.

Why do we call it a *singleton* pattern? You create one file or directory with a static configuration. Furthermore, you define several parameters inline to create all infrastructure resources with a single command. That configuration expresses resources unique and specific to the environment created by the configuration.

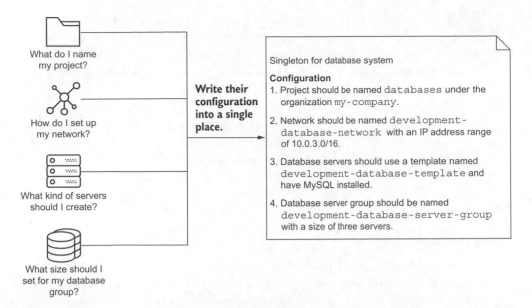

Figure 3.1   A singleton pattern expresses the configuration of an initial set of resources—such as a project, network, and database—in one file. This pattern captures the relationships among resources in one place.

The singleton pattern simplifies writing IaC because you put everything in one configuration. When you express every infrastructure resource in a single configuration, you get a single reference to debug and troubleshoot the provisioning order and required parameters.

However, starting with the singleton pattern often leads to challenges later. When I started using the singleton pattern, I treated infrastructure configuration like a junk drawer—storage for random items that don't have a place otherwise. The drawer becomes the first place you look if you cannot find something (figure 3.2).

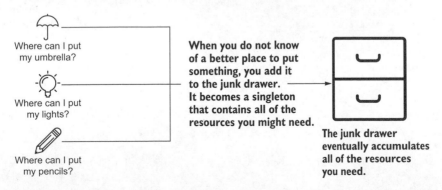

Figure 3.2   If you do not know where to put an object, add it to the junk drawer, which uses the singleton pattern to aggregate all resources.

Because I didn't know where else to configure infrastructure resources, I just added them to one file. Eventually, the singleton pattern became messy like a junk drawer! I had to search the singleton for an infrastructure resource. In addition, the number of infrastructure resources in the singleton means it takes time to identify, change, and create resources.

The singleton pattern challenges reproducibility as your system grows with more resources. Producing the configuration for production means copying and pasting it into a new file. Copying and pasting configuration does not scale when you have more resources to update! Singletons come at the cost of scalability and composability. It works for a few infrastructure resources but doesn't scale with complex systems.

When should you use a singleton? It works best when you have a resource that requires only a single instance and rarely changes, such as the GCP project. The network, database server template, and server group must go into another configuration.

All GCP projects must have a unique identifier, which makes it ideal for the singleton pattern. The project can have only a single instance. For example, you could create a project named *databases* and generate a unique identifier based on your current system username. The following listing shows the code to implement the singleton pattern for creating a GCP project with your system username.

Listing 3.1   Creating a project in GCP by using a singleton pattern

```
import json
import os

class DatabaseGoogleProject:              Creates an object
    def __init__(self):                   for the database
        self.name = 'databases'           Google project
        self.organization = os.environ.get('USER')     Gets the operating system
        self.project_id = f'{self.name}-{self.organization}'   user and sets it to the
        self.resource = self._build()                   organization variable

    def _build(self):
        return {
            'resource': [
                {
                    'google_project': [
                        {
                            'databases': [
                                {
                                    'name': self.name,
                                    'project_id': self.project_id
                                }
                            ]
                        }
                    ]
                }
            ]
        }
```

Creates an object for the database Google project

Gets the operating system user and sets it to the organization variable

Makes a unique project ID based on the project name and operating system user so GCP can create the project

Creates a DatabaseGoogle-Project to generate the JSON configuration for the project

Sets up the Google project using a Terraform resource with the name "databases"

```
if __name__ == "__main__":
    project = DatabaseGoogleProject()

    with open('main.tf.json', 'w') as outfile:
        json.dump(project.resource, outfile, sort_keys=True, indent=4)
```

Creates a DatabaseGoogleProject to generate the JSON configuration for the project

Writes the Python dictionary to a JSON file to be executed by Terraform later

---

AWS and Azure equivalents

You can equate a GCP project to an AWS account. To automate the creation of AWS accounts, you need to use AWS Organizations (https://aws.amazon.com/organizations/).

In Azure, you would create a subscription and a resource group. You can create a resource group by using the `azurerm_resource_group` Terraform resource (http://mng.bz/1orq).

Imagine you want to create a server in your database project. You can call the `DatabaseGoogleProject` singleton and extract the project identifier from the JSON configuration. A singleton contains unique resources that you can reference with a call to the module. For example, if you reference the `database` project, you will always get the correct project and not a different one.

You use a singleton for a GCP project because you create it *once* and change it *infrequently*. You can apply the singleton pattern to rarely changed *global* resources such as provider accounts, projects, domain name registrations, or root SSL certificates. It also works for static environments, such as low-use data center environments.

3.2 Composite

Instead of expressing the database system in one singleton, you can organize the components into modules. A *module* groups infrastructure resources that share a function or business domain. Modules allow you to change the automation of the parts without affecting the whole.

> **DEFINITION** A *module* organizes infrastructure resources by function or business domain. Other tools or resources may refer to them as *infrastructure stacks* or *sets*.

You can use modules as building blocks to construct your system. Other teams can use modules as building blocks for their unique infrastructure system.

Figure 3.3 shows how your company might organize itself into teams and create a reporting structure. Each team or manager reports to another manager, leading to the executive level. The company uses composition of teams to achieve a common objective.

**Your company uses composition to define teams and
put together the buildings blocks for a reporting structure.**

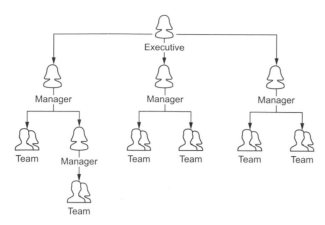

Figure 3.3 **Your company might
use the composite pattern to group
employees into a reporting
structure, thus allowing managers
to organize teams and their goals.**

Why would your company break reporting structures into modules? The pattern ensures that new initiatives or business opportunities have a team to support them. It promotes composability and evolvability as the company grows.

In a similar manner, most IaC depends on the *composite pattern* to group, rank, and structure a set of modules. You'll often find the composite pattern classified as a structural pattern because it structures objects in a hierarchy.

> **DEFINITION** The *composite pattern* treats an infrastructure module as a single instance and allows you to assemble, group, and rank modules in a system.

Tools usually have their own modularization feature. Terraform and Bicep use their own module frameworks to nest and organize modules. You can use nested stacks or StackSets in CloudFormation to reuse templates (modules) or create stacks across regions. A configuration management tool like Ansible lets you build top-level playbooks that import other tasks.

How do you implement a module? Imagine you need to set up a network for the database servers. However, the server needs a subnetwork (subnet). You composite the network and subnet into a module, as shown in figure 3.4. You determine how to set up the network first and write that into your module. Then you write down the configuration for the subnetwork and add it to the module.

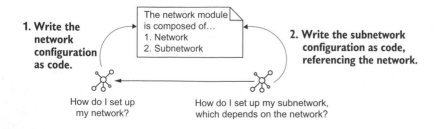

Figure 3.4 **A network
module can use the
composite pattern to
group the network and
subnetwork resources.**

The module contains the configuration for both the network and the subnetwork. If you need to reproduce the network system in your production environment, you can always copy and paste the entire module to create a new network and subnetwork. A composite pattern for the network ensures that you can always reproduce a group of resources that depend on one another.

You can implement the composite pattern for the network configuration in a module. As the following listing shows, the module creates a network and subnet. You pass the CIDR ranges for the network and subnet, and the module generates a standardized name for the network.

Listing 3.2 Creating a network and subnetwork

```python
import json

                          Creates a module for the network, which           Sets up the Google
                          uses the composition pattern to bundle             subnetwork using a
class Network:            the network and subnet together                    Terraform resource
    def __init__(self, region='us-central1'):                                with the name "my-
        self._network_name = 'my-network'                                    network-subnet"
        self._subnet_name = f'{self._network_name}-subnet'
        self._subnet_cidr = '10.0.0.0/28'         Sets the subnet's CIDR
        self._region = region                     block as 10.0.0.0/28
        self.resource = self._build()
                                          Uses the module to create the
    def _build(self):                     JSON configuration for the
        return {                          network and subnetwork
            'resource': [
                {
                    'google_compute_network': [
                        {
                            f'{self._network_name}': [
                                {
                                    'name': self._network_name
                                }
                            ]
                        }
                    ]
                },
                {
                    'google_compute_subnetwork': [
                        {
                            f'{self._subnet_name}': [
                                {
                                    'name': self._subnet_name,
                                    'ip_cidr_range': self._subnet_cidr,
                                    'region': self._region,
                                    'network': f'${{google_compute_network
                                    .{self._network_name}.name}}'
                                }
                            ]
                        }
                    ]
                }
            ]
        }
```

Sets the region to the default region, us-central1

Sets up the Google network using a Terraform resource with the name "my-network". GCP does not require a network CIDR block to be defined.

Sets up the Google subnetwork using a Terraform resource with the name "my-network-subnet"

Sets the subnet's CIDR block as 10.0.0.0/28

Creates the Google subnetwork on the network by using a Terraform variable. Terraform dynamically references the network ID and inserts it to the subnetwork's configuration for you.

```
        ]
      }
```

if __name__ == "__main__":   **Uses the module to create the**   **Writes the Python**
    network = Network()   ◁——⏐ **JSON configuration for the**   **dictionary to a JSON**
                                network and subnetwork   **file to be executed**
                                                                   by Terraform later

    with open('main.tf.json', 'w') as outfile:
        json.dump(network.resource, outfile, sort_keys=True, indent=4)

AWS and Azure equivalents

You can equate a GCP network and subnets to an AWS VPC and subnets, or to an Azure virtual network and subnets. However, in AWS and Azure, you need to define gateways and routing tables in each subnet. GCP automatically defines these for you when you create the network.

Why compose the module with the network and subnetwork? You can't use the GCP network unless you have a subnet! Composition allows you to create a set of resources together. Bundling the required resources together helps your teammate who might not know much about networking. The composite pattern improves the principle of composability because it groups and organizes common resources that you must deploy as one unit.

The composite pattern works well for infrastructure because infrastructure resources have a hierarchy. A module following this pattern reflects relationships among resources and facilitates their management. If you need to update routing, you update the network composite configuration. You can refer to the network configuration to determine subnet CIDR ranges and calculate network address space.

You apply the composite pattern by grouping resources based on function, business unit, or operational responsibility. As you draft the initial module, you may add variables to allow more flexible parameters or distribute the configuration to other teams. I discuss how to share modules in chapter 5. However, you can apply other patterns outside of a general composite pattern to further improve the reproducibility of IaC.

3.3 *Factory*

Previously, you used the singleton pattern to create a GCP project for the database system. Then you applied the composite pattern and built the network in a different module. However, now you realize you need a database network divided into three subnets. Rather than copying and pasting three subnets, you want to create a configuration that accepts inputs with the subnet name and IP address range.

A configuration to create three subnets and a network requires many parameters, which can be tedious to include and maintain. What if you had something like a factory to manufacture all of the resources with opinionated defaults? Figure 3.5 shows that you can create a network factory to stamp out similar networks. You can reduce the required parameters to two inputs and other configurations to default values.

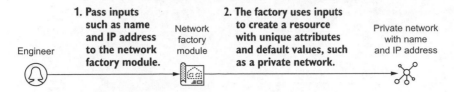

1. Pass inputs such as name and IP address to the network factory module.

Network factory module

2. The factory uses inputs to create a resource with unique attributes and default values, such as a private network.

Private network with name and IP address

Engineer

Figure 3.5 A factory pattern module includes a set of defaults for a minimal resource configuration and enables customization by accepting input variables.

When you know the network has specific default attributes, you can minimize the inputs and produce multiple resources with less effort. I call this approach the *factory pattern*. A module that uses the factory pattern takes a set of inputs, such as name and IP address range, and creates a set of infrastructure resources based on the inputs.

DEFINITION The *factory pattern* takes a set of input variables and creates a set of infrastructure resources based on input variables and default constants.

You want to offer just enough flexibility to make changes, such as the subnet's IP address and name. In general, you need to find a balance in your module between offering just enough customization and using opinionated default attributes. After all, you want to promote the principle of reproducibility but maintain the resource's evolvability. We'll discuss more about sharing resources such as modules in chapter 5, and standardizing secure practices for modules in chapter 8.

Let's return to our example. How do you create three subnets without passing a list of names? The module can automatically name the subnets so you avoid hardcoding them. Figure 3.6 shows how to add some logic into the network factory module to standardize the name of the subnet based on the network address.

Modules using factory patterns can transform input variables into standardized templates, a common practice to generate names or identifiers. When you implement the network module with the factory pattern in code, you add a `SubnetFactory` module. Listing 3.3 builds a factory module to generate names for the subnets.

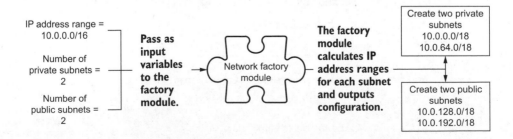

Figure 3.6 A network factory module can include transformations that calculate subnet addressing and create multiple subnet resources for a network.

Listing 3.3 Creating three subnets in GCP by using a factory pattern

```
import json
import ipaddress

def _generate_subnet_name(address):
    address_identifier = format(ipaddress.ip_network(
        address).network_address).replace('.', '-')
    return f'network-{address_identifier}'
```

For a given subnet, generates the subnet name by dash-delimiting the IP address range and appending it to the "network"

Creates a module for the subnet, which uses the factory pattern to generate any number of subnets

Passes the subnet's address to the factory

```
class SubnetFactory:
    def __init__(self, address, region):
        self.name = _generate_subnet_name(address)
        self.address = address
        self.region = region
        self.network = 'default'
        self.resource = self._build()
```

Creates the subnets on the "default" network in this example

Passes the subnet's region to the factory

Uses the module to create the JSON configuration for the network and subnetwork

```
    def _build(self):
        return {
            'resource': [
                {
                    'google_compute_subnetwork': [
                        {
                            f'{self.name}': [
                                {
                                    'name': self.name,
                                    'ip_cidr_range': self.address,
                                    'region': self.region,
                                    'network': self.network
                                }
                            ]
                        }
                    ]
                }
            ]
        }
```

Creates the Google subnetwork using a Terraform resource based on the name, address, region, and network

For each subnet defined with its IP address range and region, creates a subnet using the factory module

```
if __name__ == "__main__":
    subnets_and_regions = {
        '10.0.0.0/24': 'us-central1',
        '10.0.1.0/24': 'us-west1',
        '10.0.2.0/24': 'us-east1',
    }

    for address, region in subnets_and_regions.items():

        subnetwork = SubnetFactory(address, region)

        with open(f'{_generate_subnet_name(address)}.tf.json',
                  'w') as outfile:
            json.dump(subnetwork.resource, outfile,
                      sort_keys=True, indent=4)
```

Writes the Python dictionary to a JSON file to be executed by Terraform later

Why do I separate the subnets into their own factory module? Creating a separate module for subnets promotes the principle of evolvability. I can change the logic to generate names for any number of subnets. I can also update the name format without affecting the network.

Most factory modules include *transformation or dynamic generation* of attributes. For example, you can modify the network factory module to calculate the IP address ranges for subnets. The calculations automatically build the correct number of private or public subnets.

However, I recommend minimizing the transformations you add to factory modules when possible. They can add complexity to resource configuration. The more complex the logic for your transformation, the more you need tests to check for transformations. I'll cover how to test modules and infrastructure configuration in chapter 6.

The factory pattern balances reproducibility and evolvability of infrastructure resources. It manufactures similar infrastructure with minor differences for names, sizes, or other attributes. You'll want to build a factory module if the configuration applies to commonly built resources, such as networks or servers.

Anytime you run a factory module, you can expect to get the specific set of resources you request. The module does not contain much logic to determine *which* resources to build. Instead, a factory module focuses on setting attributes for resources.

I frequently write factory modules with *many default constants* and *few input variables*. This way, I reduce the overhead of maintaining and validating the inputs. Infrastructure that commonly uses factory modules includes networks and subnetworks, clusters of servers, managed databases, managed queues, or managed caches, and more.

3.4 Prototype

You can create the database servers now that you have created a module to build database networks. However, you must tag all resources in the database system with customer name, business unit, and cost center. The auditing team also asks you to include `automated=true` to identify the automated resources.

Ideally, tags (or labels in GCP) must be consistent across all your resources. Your automation should copy them to every resource if you update the tags. You'll learn more about the importance of tagging in chapter 8.

What if you could put all the tags in one place and update them at once? Figure 3.7 shows that you can put all of your tags into a module. The database server references the common module for tags and applies the static values to the server.

Rather than hardcoding every tag, you created a module implementing the *prototype pattern* to express a set of static defaults for consumption by other modules. Prototype modules produce a copy of the configuration to append to other resources.

> **DEFINITION** The *prototype pattern* takes a set of input variables to build a set of static defaults for consumption by other modules. They usually do not directly create infrastructure resources but export configuration values.

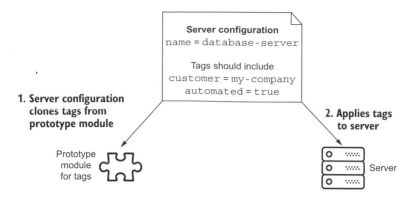

Figure 3.7   A module with the prototype pattern returns a copy of static values, such as tags, for consumption by other infrastructure resources.

You can think of a prototype as a dictionary that stores words and definitions (figure 3.8). The dictionary's creators change the words and definitions. You can reference it and update your text or vocabulary.

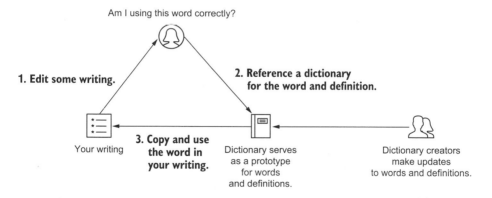

Figure 3.8   You use the dictionary as a prototype to reference words and definitions and update them in your writing.

Why use a prototype module to reference common metadata? The prototype pattern promotes the principle of evolvability and reproducibility. It ensures consistent configuration across resources and eases the evolution of common configuration. You don't have to find and replace strings in your files!

Let's implement the tag module with the prototype pattern. Listing 3.4 creates a module using the prototype pattern that returns a set of standard tags. In subsequent infrastructure resources, you reference the module for `StandardTags` for any tags that you need to include. The module does not create tag resources. Instead, it returns a copy of predefined tags.

Listing 3.4 Creating a tagging module using the prototype pattern

```
import json

class StandardTags():
    def __init__(self):
        self.resource = {
            'customer': 'my-company',
            'automated': True,
            'cost_center': 123456,
            'business_unit': 'ecommerce'
        }

class ServerFactory:
    def __init__(self, name, network, zone='us-central1-a', tags={}):
        self.name = name
        self.network = network
        self.zone = zone
        self.tags = tags
        self.resource = self._build()

    def _build(self):
        return {
            'resource': [
                {
                    'google_compute_instance': [
                        {
                            self.name: [
                                {
                                    'allow_stopping_for_update': True,
                                    'boot_disk': [
                                        {
                                            'initialize_params': [
                                                {
                                                    'image': 'ubuntu-1804-lts'
                                                }
                                            ]
                                        }
                                    ],
                                    'machine_type': 'f1-micro',
                                    'name': self.name,
                                    'network_interface': [
                                        {
                                            'network': self.network
                                        }
                                    ],
                                    'zone': self.zone,
                                    'labels': self.tags
                                }
                            ]
                        }
                    ]
                }
            ]
        }
```

Creates a module using the prototype pattern that returns a copy of standard tags, such as customer, cost center, and business unit

Creates a module using the factory pattern to create a Google computer instance (server) based on name, network, and tags

Passes tags as a variable to the server module

Uses the module to create the JSON configuration for a server on the "default" network

Creates the Google compute instance (server) using a Terraform resource

Adds the tags stored in the variable to the Google compute instance resource

```
    if __name__ == "__main__":
        config = ServerFactory(
            name='database-server', network='default',
            tags=StandardTags().resource)

    with open('main.tf.json', 'w') as outfile:
        json.dump(config.resource, outfile,
                    sort_keys=True, indent=4)
```

Uses the
standard tags
module to
add tags to
the server

Uses the module to create the
JSON configuration for a server
on the "default" network

Writes the Python dictionary
to a JSON file to be executed
by Terraform later

AWS and Azure equivalents

To convert listing 3.4 to another cloud provider, change the resource to an Amazon
EC2 instance or Azure Linux virtual machine. Then, pass `self.tags` to the `tags`
attribute for the AWS or Azure resource.

Let's run the Python script to create the server configuration, as shown in the listing 3.5.
When you examine the JSON output for the server, you'll notice that the server includes
a set of labels. Those labels match the standard tags from your prototype module!

Listing 3.5   Creating the server configuration with tags from the module

```
{
    "resource": [
        {
            "google_compute_instance": [
                {
                    "database-server": [
                        {
                            "allow_stopping_for_update": true,
                            "boot_disk": [
                                {
                                    "initialize_params": [
                                        {
                                            "image": "ubuntu-1804-lts"
                                        }
                                    ]
                                }
                            ],
                            "labels": {
                                "automated": true,
                                "business_unit": "ecommerce",
                                "cost_center": 123456,
                                "customer": "my-company"
                            },
                            "machine_type": "f1-micro",
                            "name": "database-server",
                            "network_interface": [
                                {
                                    "network": "default"
                                }
                            ],
                            "zone": "us-central1-a"
```

The JSON file defines a Google
compute instance using a
Terraform resource.

Terraform identifies the
resource as a database
server. The JSON
configuration matches
what you defined in the
server factory module
using Python.

Adds tags from the
standard tags
prototype module to
the labels field in the
server configuration

The JSON configuration
retrieves the zone variable and
populates it into the JSON file.

```
              }
            ]
          }
        ]
      }
    ]
  }
```

You'll notice that your server configuration contains a lot of hardcoded values, like operating system and machine type. The values behave as global defaults. Over time, you'll keep adding global defaults to your factory module and find that they overrun the module!

To detangle and organize the global defaults, you can define them in a prototype module. The module makes it easier to evolve the default over time and compose it with other values. The prototype becomes the static, well-defined default for a resource.

In one such situation, I started by writing a factory module to create a set of alerts on infrastructure. Initially, I passed the environment names and metrics thresholds to parametrize the alerts and their configuration. I discovered alerts did not need the environment names, and the metrics thresholds did not change across environments.

As a result, I converted this module into a prototype. Teams that needed to add metrics into their systems imported the module. The module added predefined alert resources to their configuration.

Domain-specific languages

DSLs for tools like Terraform, Kubernetes, CloudFormation, and Bicep do not have global constants as programming languages do. However, they do support module referencing and object structures. You can use the same pattern for DSLs and programming languages by creating the prototype as an object.

A prototype makes creating a standard set of resources or configurations easier. It eliminates the uncertainty in setting input values. However, you will have exceptions to standard values. As a solution, you can override or add configurations based on the resource. For example, I usually merge custom tags unique to a resource with the list of standard tags.

Besides tags, I commonly use prototype modules for regions, availability zones, or account identifiers. I create modules with the prototype pattern when I have *static configurations with many global defaults or complex transformations*. For example, you might have a server initialization script that runs when you use SSL. You can create a prototype module to template the script based on whether you use SSL.

3.5   *Builder*

You learned to apply the singleton pattern to create a project, the factory to create the networks, and the prototype to set the tags for the database server. Next, you'll build a load balancer that connects you to the database.

But first, you run into a challenging requirement. The module must allow you to create private or public load balancers! A private load balancer requires different server and network configuration. You must build a module that offers the flexibility to choose a private or public load balancer and configures the server and networks based on your choice.

Figure 3.9 demonstrates a module that chooses a firewall and server configuration based on your load balancer type. You can use the same module to create an external or internal load balancer. The module handles the correct configuration for the load balancer and its required firewall rules.

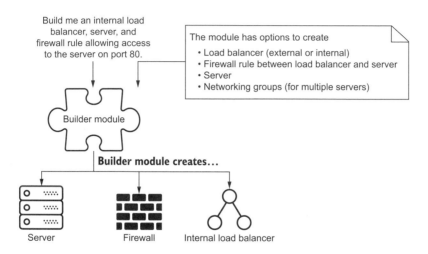

Figure 3.9   A builder module for the database would include parameters to select the type of load balancer and firewall rules that the module must create.

The module gives you the choice to build the system you want, helping with evolvability and composability. The module follows the *builder pattern*, which captures some default values but allows you to compose the system you need. The builder pattern organizes a set of related resources you enable or disable for your desired system.

> **DEFINITION**   The *builder pattern* assembles a set of infrastructure resources that you can enable or disable to achieve your desired configuration.

Implementing the builder pattern in your database module allows you to generate a combination of resources based on your selection. A builder pattern uses inputs to decide *which* resources it needs to build, while a factory module configures resource attributes based on input variables. The pattern works like building houses for a real estate development. You choose from preset blueprints and tell the builder which changes you want for the layout (figure 3.10). For example, some builders might add an extra room by removing the garage.

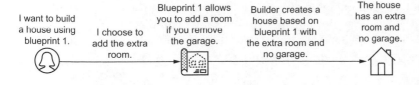

I want to build a house using blueprint 1.

I choose to add the extra room.

Blueprint 1 allows you to add a room if you remove the garage.

Builder creates a house based on blueprint 1 with the extra room and no garage.

The house has an extra room and no garage.

Figure 3.10 A builder module constructs a house with a preset blueprint that allows for layout changes, such as an extra room.

Let's start implementing the builder pattern, as in the following listing. First, you define a load balancer module by using the factory pattern. You use the factory pattern to customize the load balancer (also known as the *compute forwarding rule* in GCP). The module sets the scheme for the load balancer as external or internal.

Listing 3.6 Using the factory module for the load balancer

Creates a module for the load balancer, which uses the factory pattern to generate an internal or external load balancer

```
class LoadBalancerFactory:
    def __init__(self, name, region='us-central1', external=False):
        self.name = name
        self.region = region
        self.external = external
        self.resources = self._build()          ◁──  Uses the module to create the JSON
                                                       configuration for the load balancer
    def _build(self):
        scheme = 'EXTERNAL' if self.external else 'INTERNAL'          ◁──  Sets the scheme to internal
        resources = []                                                     or external load balancing.
        resources.append({                                                 The load balancer defaults to
          'google_compute_forwarding_rule': [{                             an internal configuration.
              'db': [
                  {
                      'name': self.name,
                      'target': r'${google_compute_target_pool.db.id}',   ◁──
                      'port_range': '3306',          ◁──
                      'region': self.region,
                      'load_balancing_scheme': scheme,
                      'network_tier': 'STANDARD'
                  }
              ]
          }
        ]
        })
        return resources
```

Creates the Google compute forwarding rule using a Terraform resource. This is GCP's equivalent of load balancing.

Allows traffic to port 3306, the MySQL database port

Sets the load balancer's target to the database server group. This uses Terraform's built-in variable interpolation feature to dynamically resolve the database server group's ID.

AWS and Azure equivalents

You can equate a GCP compute forwarding rule to AWS Elastic Load Balancing (ELB) or Azure Load Balancer. Similarly, an AWS security group or Azure network security group roughly equals a GCP firewall rule. For an example with AWS, refer to the code repository at https://github.com/joatmon08/manning-book.

However, an external load balancer requires additional configuration in the form of a firewall rule. You must allow traffic from external sources to the database ports. Let's define a module using the factory pattern for another firewall rule to allow traffic from external sources, as in the following listing.

Listing 3.7 Using the factory module for the firewall rule

```
class FirewallFactory:
    def __init__(self, name, network='default'):      ◁——  Creates a module for the firewall,
        self.name = name                                    which uses the factory pattern
        self.network = network                              to generate a firewall rule
        self.resources = self._build()        ◁——  Uses the module to create the JSON
                                                    configuration for the load balancer
    def _build(self):
        resources = []
        resources.append({
            'google_compute_firewall': [{
                'db': [
                    {
                        'allow': [
                            {
                                'protocol': 'tcp',
                                'ports': ['3306']
                            }
                        ],
                        'name': self.name,
                        'network': self.network
                    }
                ]
            }]
        })
        return resources
```

Creates the Google compute firewall using a Terraform resource. This is GCP's equivalent of a firewall rule.

The firewall rule should allow TCP traffic to port 3306 by default.

Thanks to the principle of composability, you put the load balancer and factory module into the database builder module. The module needs a variable that helps you choose the type of load balancer and whether you should include a firewall rule to allow traffic to the load balancer.

When you implement the database builder module in listing 3.8, you set it to create the database server group and networks by default. Then the builder accepts two options: an internal or external load balancer and the extra firewall rule.

Listing 3.8 Constructing a database with the builder pattern

```
import json
from server import DatabaseServerFactory
from loadbalancer import LoadBalancerFactory
from firewall import FirewallFactory


class DatabaseModule:
    def __init__(self, name):
```

Imports factory modules to create the database server group, load balancer, and firewall

Creates a module for the database, which uses the builder pattern to generate the required database server group, networks, load balancers, and firewalls

```
        self._resources - []
        self._name = name
        self._resources = DatabaseServerFactory(self._name).resources
```

Always create a database server group and networks by using the factory module. The builder module needs the database server group.

```
    def add_internal_load_balancer(self):
        self._resources.extend(
            LoadBalancerFactory(
                self._name, external=False).resources)
```

Adds a method so you can choose to build an internal load balancer

```
    def add_external_load_balancer(self):
        self._resources.extend(
            LoadBalancerFactory(
                self._name, external=True).resources)
```

Adds a method so you can choose to build an external load balancer

```
    def add_google_firewall_rule(self):
        self._resources.extend(
            FirewallFactory(
                self._name).resources)
```

Adds a method so you can choose to build a firewall rule to allow traffic to the databases

```
    def build(self):
        return {
            'resource': self._resources
        }
```

Uses the builder module to return the JSON configuration for your customized database resources

Uses the database builder module to create a database server group with external access (load balancer and firewall rule)

```
if __name__ == "__main__":
    database_module = DatabaseModule('development-database')
    database_module.add_external_load_balancer()
    database_module.add_google_firewall_rule()

    with open('main.tf.json', 'w') as outfile:
        json.dump(database_module.build(), outfile,
                  sort_keys=True, indent=4)
```

Writes the Python dictionary to a JSON file to be executed by Terraform later

After running the Python script, you will find a lengthy JSON configuration with the instance templates, server group, server group manager, external load balancer, and firewall rule. The builder generates all of the resources you need to build an externally accessible database. Note that the listing omits the other components for clarity.

Listing 3.9 Truncated database system configuration

```
[
  {
    "google_compute_forwarding_rule": [
      {
        "db": [
          {
            "load_balancing_scheme": "EXTERNAL",
            "name": "development-database",
            "network_tier": "STANDARD",
```

The JSON file defines a Google compute forwarding rule and firewall using a Terraform resource. The file omits the instance templates, server group, and server group for clarity.

Creates a load balancer with the EXTERNAL scheme, which makes it accessible from external source

Creates a firewall that allows TCP traffic on port 3306, the MySQL database ports

```json
          "port_range": "3306",
          "region": "us-central1",
          "target": "${google_compute_target_pool.db.id}"
        }
      ]
    }
  ]
},
{
  "google_compute_firewall": [
    {
      "db": [
        {
          "allow": [
            {
              "ports": [
                "3306"
              ],
              "protocol": "tcp"
            }
          ],
          "name": "development-database",
          "network": "default"
        }
      ]
    }
  ]
}
]
```

Sets the load balancer's target to the database server group. This uses Terraform's built-in variable interpolation feature to dynamically resolve the database server group's ID.

The JSON file defines a Google compute forwarding rule and firewall using a Terraform resource. The file omits the instance templates and server group for clarity.

The builder pattern helps you adhere to the principle of evolvability. You get to choose the set of resources you need. A module with this pattern takes away the challenge of configuring the right combination of attributes and resources.

Furthermore, you can use the builder pattern to wrap a generic interface around a cloud provider's resources. The Python example offers builder methods to `add_external_load_balancer`, which wraps around the GCP compute forwarding rule. When you use the module, the option describes the intent of creating a generic load balancer and not a GCP forwarding rule.

Domain-specific languages

Some DSLs offer an if-else (conditional) statement or loop (iteration) that you can use for the builder pattern. Terraform offers the `count` argument to create a set number of resources based on a conditional statement. CloudFormation supports conditionals for user inputs that can select stacks. Bicep uses deploy conditions. For Ansible, you can use conditional imports to select tasks or playbooks.

For example, you could set up a Boolean variable called `add_external_load_balancer`. If you pass `true` to the variable, the DSL adds a conditional statement to build an external load balancer resource. Otherwise, it creates an internal load balancer.

Some DSLs do not offer conditional statements. You will need some code similar to the code examples in this book that template the DSL. For example, you can use Helm to template and release Kubernetes YAML files.

The builder pattern best applies to modules that create multiple resources. These use cases include configuration for container orchestrators such as Kubernetes, platforms with cluster architectures, dashboards for application and system metrics, and more. A builder module for these use cases allows you to select the resource you want without passing specific input attributes.

However, builder modules can be complex because they reference other modules and multiple resources. The risk of module misconfiguration can be very high. Chapter 6 covers testing strategies to ensure a builder module's functionality and stability.

3.6 *Choosing a pattern*

Throughout this chapter, I've showed how to group some resources for a database system into various module patterns. How do you choose which module pattern to use? What about the other resources in the database system I did not mention?

You can create separate modules for new infrastructure resources with different business functions and purposes. The database example throughout this chapter separated the configuration of the Google project (singleton), network (factory), and database cluster (factory) into modules. Each evolves as different resources with different input variables and defaults.

The example uses the composite pattern to combine all of the module patterns in the system. It uses the factory pattern for network, load balancer, and database cluster modules to pass attributes and customize each resource. Tags often use the prototype pattern because they involve consistent metadata copied to other resources. You will use the factory and prototype patterns for most of the modules you write because they offer composability, reproducibility, and evolvability.

By contrast, you build the Google project as a singleton because no one else will change attributes for the single instance of my project. The project does not change much, so you use a less complex pattern. However, you solved the complex problem of creating a database system with the builder pattern. The builder module allows you to select the specific resources to create.

Figure 3.11 offers a decision tree for identifying which pattern to use. You ask yourself a series of questions on the purpose, reuse and update frequency, and composition of multiple resources. Based on these criteria, you create a module with a specific pattern.

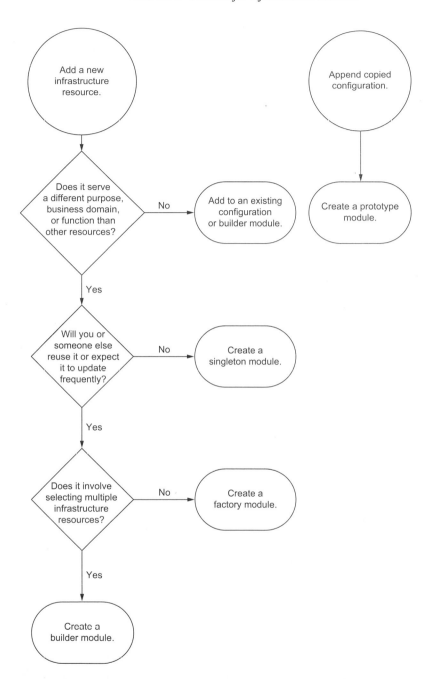

Figure 3.11   To decide which module pattern you want to use, you must assess how you use the resource and its behavior.

Following the decision tree helps build more composable and evolvable modules. You want to balance the predictability of standard attributes with the flexibility to override configuration for specific resources. However, keep an open mind. Modules can outgrow and change in function. Just because you build a module with one pattern doesn't mean you won't convert it to a different one in the future!

Exercise 3.1

To which module pattern(s) does the following IaC apply? (Choose all that apply.)

```python
if __name__ == "__main__":
  environment = 'development'
  name = f'{environment}-hello-world'
  cidr_block = '10.0.0.0/16'

  # NetworkModule returns a subnet and network
  network = NetworkModule(name, cidr_block)

  # Tags returns a default list of tags
  tags = TagsModule()

  # ServerModule returns a single server
  server = ServerModule(name, network, tags)
```

   A Factory
   B Singleton
   c Prototype
   D Builder
   E Composite

See appendix B for answers to exercises.

Note that many of the patterns in this chapter focus on building modules with IaC tooling. Sometimes you might write automation in a programming language because you cannot find IaC support. This situation happens most with legacy infrastructure. For example, imagine you need to create a database system in GCP. However, you do not have an IaC tool and can access the GCP API only directly.

To create the database system using the GCP API, you separate each infrastructure resource into a factory module with four functions: create, read, update, and delete. Changes to the resource use the composition of these functions. You can check for errors in each function depending on the action you want to execute for each resource.

Figure 3.12 implements factory modules for the server, network, and load balancer. You can create, read, update, and delete each module. A builder module for the database uses the composite pattern to create, read, update, and delete the network, server, and load balancer.

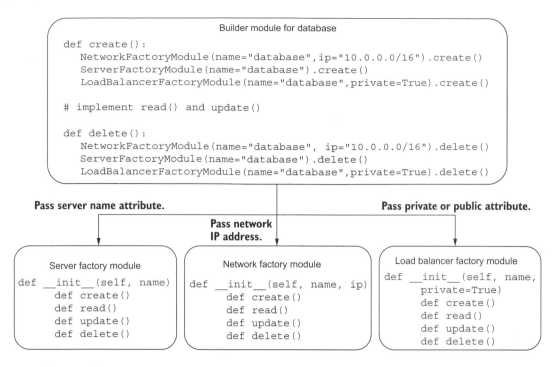

Figure 3.12   To write scripts for automation, create factory modules for individual resources, and then build functions to create, read, update, and delete resources.

Breaking down the updates you'll make to resources into four functions organizes the automation. Even the builder pattern uses the create, read, update, and delete functions. The functions define the automation behavior you want to use to configure resources. However, you should test each function for idempotency. Anytime you run the function, it should result in the same configuration.

You can apply the module patterns in this chapter to automating and implementing IaC on any infrastructure. As you develop IaC, identify where you can break your infrastructure system into modules. When deciding when and what to modularize, consider the following:

- Is the resource shared?
- What business domain does it serve?
- Which environment uses the resource?
- Which team manages the infrastructure?
- Does the resource use a different tool?
- How do you change a resource without affecting something else in the module?

By assessing which resources align with different business units, teams, or functions, you build smaller sets of infrastructure. As a general practice, write modules with as few resources as possible. Modules with fewer resources speed up the provisioning and minimize the blast radius of a failure. More important, you can deploy, test, and debug smaller modules before applying them to a more extensive system.

Grouping resources into modules offers a few benefits for you, your team, and your company. For you, modules improve the scalability and resiliency of infrastructure resources. You minimize the blast radius of changes to modules to improve the resiliency of the overall system.

For your team, a module provides the benefit of a self-service mechanism for other team members to reproduce your module and create infrastructure. Your teammate can use the module and pass the variables they want to customize instead of finding and replacing attributes. You'll learn more about sharing modules in chapter 5.

For your organization, a module helps you standardize better infrastructure and security practices across resources. You can use the same configurations to stamp out similar load balancers and restricted firewall rules. Modules also help your security team audit and enforce these practices across different teams, as covered in chapter 8.

Summary

- Apply module patterns such as singleton, factory, prototype, and builder so you can construct composable infrastructure configurations.
- Use the composite pattern to group infrastructure resources into a hierarchy and structure them for automation.
- You can use the singleton pattern to manage single instances of infrastructure, which applies to rarely changed infrastructure resources.
- Use the prototype pattern for copying and applying global configuration parameters, such as tags or common configuration.
- Factory modules take inputs to construct infrastructure resources with a specific configuration.
- Builder modules take inputs to decide which resources to create. Builder modules can be composed of factory modules.
- When deciding what and how to modularize, assess which functions or business domain the infrastructure configuration serves.
- If you write scripts to automate infrastructure, construct factory modules with capabilities to create, read, update, and delete. Reference them in builder modules.

Patterns for infrastructure dependencies

An infrastructure system involves a set of resources that depend on each other. For example, a server depends on the existence of a network. How do you know the network exists before creating a server? You can express this with an *infrastructure dependency*. An infrastructure dependency happens when a resource requires another one to exist before creating or modifying the first one.

> **DEFINITION** An *infrastructure dependency* expresses a relationship in which an infrastructure resource depends on the existence and attributes of another resource.

Usually, you identify the server's dependency on the network by hardcoding the network identifier. However, hardcoding more tightly binds the dependency

80

between server and network. Anytime you change the network, you must update the hardcoded dependency.

In chapter 2, you learned how to avoid hardcoding values with variables to promote reproducibility and evolvability. Passing the network identifier as a variable better decouples the server and network. However, a variable works between resources only in the same module. How can you express dependencies *between* modules?

The preceding chapter grouped resources into modules to enhance composability. This chapter covers patterns for managing infrastructure dependencies to enhance evolvability (change). You can more easily replace one module with another when they have a loose dependency.

In reality, infrastructure systems can be pretty complex, and you can't swap modules without some disruption. Loosely coupled dependencies offer mitigation for change failure but don't guarantee 100% availability!

4.1 Unidirectional relationships

Different dependency relationships affect infrastructure change. Imagine you add a firewall rule each time you create a new application. The firewall rule has a *unidirectional dependency* on the application IP address to allow traffic. Any change to the application gets reflected in the firewall rule.

> **DEFINITION** A *unidirectional dependency* expresses a one-way relationship in which only one resource refers to another.

You can express unidirectional dependencies between any set of resources or modules. Figure 4.1 describes the unidirectional relationship between the firewall rule and the application. The rule *depends on* the application, which makes it higher up the infrastructure stack than the lower-level application.

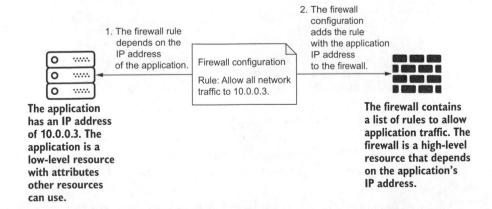

Figure 4.1 The firewall rule unidirectionally depends on the application's IP address.

When you express a dependency, you have a *high-level resource* like the firewall that depends on the existence of a *low-level resource* like the application.

> DEFINITION   A *high-level resource* depends on another resource or module. A *low-level resource* has high-level resources depending on it.

Let's say a reporting application needs a list of rules for the firewall. It sends the rules to an audit application. However, the firewall needs to know the IP address of the reporting application. Should you update the IP address of the reporting application or the firewall rule first? Figure 4.2 shows the conundrum of deciding which application you should update first.

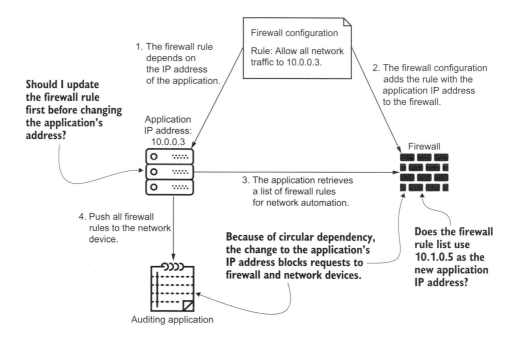

Figure 4.2   The reporting application and the firewall have a circular dependency on each other. Changes block connectivity to the application.

This example encounters a circular dependency, which introduces a chicken-or-egg problem. You cannot change one resource without affecting the other. If you first change the address of the reporting application, the firewall rule must change. However, the reporting application fails because it can't connect. You might have blocked its request!

Circular dependencies cause unexpected behaviors during changes, which ultimately affect composability and evolvability. You don't know which resource to update first. By contrast, you can identify how a low-level module's change might affect the high-level one. Unidirectional dependency relationships make changes more predictable. After all, a successful infrastructure change depends on two factors: predictability and isolation.

4.2 Dependency injection

Unidirectional dependencies help you engineer ways to minimize the impact of low-level module changes to high-level modules. For example, network changes should not disrupt high-level resources like queues, applications, or databases. This section applies the software development concept of dependency injection to infrastructure and further decouples unidirectional dependencies. Dependency injection involves two principles: inversion of control and dependency inversion.

4.2.1 Inversion of control

When you enforce unidirectional relationships in your infrastructure dependencies, your high-level resource gets information about the low-level resource. Then it can run its changes. For example, a server gets information about the network's ID and IP address range before it claims an IP address (figure 4.3).

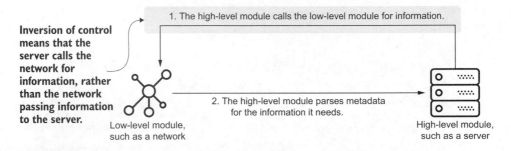

Figure 4.3 With inversion of control, the high-level resource or module calls the low-level module for information and parses its metadata for any dependencies.

The server calls the network, naturally applying a software development principle called *inversion of control*. The high-level resource calls for information about the low-level resource before updating.

> **DEFINITION** *Inversion of control* is the principle by which the high-level resource calls the low-level one for attributes or references.

As a nontechnical example, you use inversion of control when you call to schedule a doctor's appointment instead of the doctor's office automatically scheduling your appointment.

Let's apply inversion of control to implement the server's dependency on the network. You create the network by using a network module. In the following listing, the network module outputs a network name and saves it in a file called terraform.tfstate. High-level resources, like the server, can parse the network name from this JSON file.

Listing 4.1   Network module outputs in JSON file

```
{
  "outputs": {
    "name": {
      "value": "hello-world-subnet",
      "type": "string"
    }
  }
}
```

Creating the network with Terraform generates a JSON file with a list of outputs. Terraform uses this file to track the resources it creates.

The network module outputs the subnet name as a string.

The remainder of the JSON file has been omitted for clarity.

Using inversion of control, the server *calls* the network's terraform.tfstate file in listing 4.2 and reads the subnet name. Since the module expresses outputs in the JSON file, your server module needs to parse for the value of the subnet name (`hello-world-subnet`).

Listing 4.2   Applying inversion of control to create a server on a network

```python
import json

class NetworkModuleOutput:
    def __init__(self):
        with open('network/terraform.tfstate', 'r') as network_state:
            network_attributes = json.load(network_state)
        self.name = network_attributes['outputs']['name']['value']

class ServerFactoryModule:
    def __init__(self, name, zone='us-central1-a'):
        self._name = name
        self._network = NetworkModuleOutput()
        self._zone = zone
        self.resources = self._build()

    def _build(self):
        return {
            'resource': [{
                'google_compute_instance': [{
                    self._name: [{
                        'allow_stopping_for_update': True,
                        'boot_disk': [{
                            'initialize_params': [{
                                'image': 'ubuntu-1804-lts'
                            }]
                        }],
                        'machine_type': 'f1-micro',
                        'name': self._name,
                        'zone': self._zone,
                        'network_interface': [{
                            'subnetwork': self._network.name
                        }]
                    }]
                }]
            }]
        }
```

Creates an object that captures the schema of the network module's output. This makes it easier for the server to retrieve the subnet name.

The object for the network output parses the value of the subnet name from the JSON object.

Creates a module for the server, which uses the factory pattern

The server module calls the network output object, which contains the subnet name parsed from the network module's JSON file.

Uses the module to create the JSON configuration for the server using the subnetwork name

Creates the Google compute instance using a Terraform resource with a name and zone

The server module references the network output's name and passes it to the "subnetwork" field.

```
        }]
    }

if __name__ == "__main__":
    server = ServerFactoryModule(name='hello-world')
    with open('main.tf.json', 'w') as outfile:
        json.dump(server.resources, outfile, sort_keys=True, indent=4)
```

> **Writes the Python dictionary to a JSON file to be executed by Terraform later**

AWS and Azure equivalents

In AWS, you would use the `aws_instance` Terraform resource with a reference to the network you want to use (http://mng.bz/PnPR). In Azure, use the `azurerm_linux_virtual_machine` Terraform resource (http://mng.bz/J2DZ) on the network.

Implementing inversion of control eliminates a direct reference to the subnet in your server module. You can also control and limit the information the network returns for high-level resources to use. More important, you improve my composability because you can create other servers and high-level resources on the subnet name offered by the network module.

What if other high-level resources need other low-level attributes? For example, you might create a queue that needs the subnet IP address range. To solve this problem, you evolve the network module to output the subnet IP address range. The queue can reference the outputs for the address it needs.

Inversion of control improves evolvability as high-level resources require different attributes. You can evolve low-level resources without rewriting the infrastructure as code for high-level resources. However, you need a way to protect the high-level resources from any attribute updates or renaming on the low-level resources.

4.2.2 Dependency inversion

While inversion of control enables the evolution of high-level modules, it does not protect them from changes to low-level modules. Let's imagine you change the network name to its ID. The next time you deploy changes to your server module, it breaks! The server module does not recognize the network ID.

To protect your server module from changes to the network outputs, you add a layer of abstraction between the network output and server. In figure 4.4, the server accesses the network's attributes through an API or a stored configuration instead of the network output. All of these interfaces serve as abstractions to retrieve network metadata.

You can use dependency inversion to isolate changes to low-level modules and mitigate disruption to their dependencies. *Dependency inversion* dictates that high-level and low-level resources should have dependencies expressed through abstractions.

DEFINITION *Dependency inversion* is the principle of expressing dependencies between high-level and low-level modules or resources through abstractions.

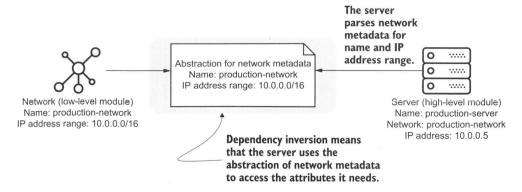

Figure 4.4   Dependency inversion returns an abstraction of the low-level resource metadata to the resource that depends on it.

The abstraction layer behaves as a translator that communicates the required attributes. It serves as a buffer for changes to the low-level module away from the high-level one. In general, you can choose from three types of abstraction:

- Interpolation of resource attributes (within modules)
- Module outputs (between modules)
- Infrastructure state (between modules)

Some abstractions, such as attribute interpolation or module outputs, depend on your tool. Abstraction by infrastructure state will depend on your tool or infrastructure API. Figure 4.5 shows the abstractions by attribute interpolation, module output, or infrastructure state to pass network metadata to the server.

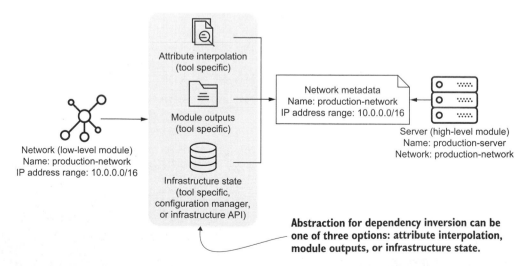

Figure 4.5   Depending on the tool and dependencies, abstractions for dependency inversion can use attribute interpolation, module outputs, or infrastructure state.

Let's examine how to implement the three types of abstraction by building modules for the network and server in listing 4.3. I'll start with attribute interpolation. Attribute interpolation handles attribute passing between resources or tasks within a module or configuration. Using Python, a subnet interpolates the name of the network by accessing the `name` attribute assigned to the network object.

Listing 4.3   Using attribute interpolation to get the network name

```python
import json


class Network:
    def __init__(self, name="hello-network"):
        self.name = name
        self.resource = self._build()

    def _build(self):
        return {
            'google_compute_network': [
                {
                    f'{self.name}': [
                        {
                            'name': self.name
                        }
                    ]
                }
            ]
        }


class Subnet:
    def __init__(self, network, region='us-central1'):
        self.network = network
        self.name = region
        self.subnet_cidr = '10.0.0.0/28'
        self.region = region
        self.resource = self._build()

    def _build(self):
        return {
            'google_compute_subnetwork': [
                {
                    f'{self.name}': [
                        {
                            'name': self.name,
                            'ip_cidr_range': self.subnet_cidr,
                            'region': self.region,
                            'network': self.network.name
                        }
                    ]
                }
            ]
        }
```

Uses the module to create the JSON configuration for the network

Creates the Google network using a Terraform resource named "hello-network"

Creates the Google subnetwork using a Terraform resource named after the region, us-central1

Passes the entire network object to the subnet. The subnet calls the network object for the attributes it needs.

Interpolates the network name by retrieving it from the object

```
if __name__ == "__main__":
    network = Network()
    subnet = Subnet(network)

    resources = {
        "resource": [
            network.resource,
            subnet.resource
        ]
    }

    with open(f'main.tf.json', 'w') as outfile:
        json.dump(resources, outfile, sort_keys=True, indent=4)
```

Uses the module to create the JSON configuration for the network

Uses the module to create the JSON configuration for the subnet and passes the network object to the subnet

Merges the network and subnet JSON objects into a Terraform-compatible JSON structure

Writes the Python dictionary to a JSON file to be executed by Terraform later

Domain-specific languages

IaC tools that use DSLs offer their own variable interpolation format. The example in Terraform would use `google_compute_network.hello-world-network.name` to dynamically pass the name of the network to the subnet. CloudFormation allows you to reference parameters with `Ref`. You can reference `properties` of a resource in Bicep.

Attribute interpolation works between modules or resources in a configuration. However, interpolation works for only specific tools and not necessarily across tools. When you have more resources and modules in composition, you cannot use interpolation.

One alternative to attribute interpolation uses explicit module outputs to pass resource attributes between modules. You can customize outputs to any schema or parameters you need. For example, you can group the subnet and network into one module and export its attributes for the server to use. Let's refactor the subnet and network and add the server, as in the following listing.

Listing 4.4   Setting the subnet name as the output for a module

```
import json

class NetworkModule:
    def __init__(self, region='us-central1'):
        self._region = region
        self._network = Network()
        self._subnet = Subnet(self._network)
        self.resource = self._build()

    def _build(self):
        return [
            self._network.resource,
            self._subnet.resource
        ]
```

Network and subnet objects omitted for clarity

Refactors network and subnet creation into a module. This follows the composite pattern. The module creates the Google network and subnet using Terraform resources.

Uses the module to create the JSON configuration for the network and subnet

```
class Output:
    def __init__(self, subnet_name):
        self.subnet_name = subnet_name
```

Creates a nested class for the network module output. The nested class exports the name of the subnet for high-level attributes to use.

```
    def output(self):
        return self.Output(self._subnet.name)
```

Creates an output function for the network module to retrieve and export all network outputs

```
class ServerModule:
    def __init__(self, name, network,
                 zone='us-central1-a'):
        self._name = name
        self._subnet_name = network.subnet_name
        self._zone = zone
        self.resource = self._build()
```

Using the network output object, gets the subnet name and sets it to the server's subnet name attribute

Uses the module to create the JSON configuration for the server

```
    def _build(self):
        return [{
            'google_compute_instance': [{
                self._name: [{
                    'allow_stopping_for_update': True,
                    'boot_disk': [{
                        'initialize_params': [{
                            'image': 'ubuntu-1804-lts'
                        }]
                    }],
                    'machine_type': 'e2-micro',
                    'name': self._name,
                    'zone': self._zone,
                    'network_interface': [{
                        'subnetwork': self._subnet_name
                    }]
                }]
            }]
        }]
```

This module creates the Google compute instance (server) using a Terraform resource.

Passes the network outputs as an input variable for the server module. The server will choose the attributes it needs.

```
if __name__ == "__main__":
    network = NetworkModule()
    server = ServerModule("hello-world",
                          network.output())
    resources = {
        "resource": network.resource + server.resource
    }

    with open(f'main.tf.json', 'w') as outfile:
        json.dump(resources, outfile, sort_keys=True, indent=4)
```

Refactors network and subnet creation into a module. This follows the composite pattern. The module creates the Google network and subnet using Terraform resources.

Merges the network and server JSON objects into a Terraform-compatible JSON structure

Writes the Python dictionary to a JSON file to be executed by Terraform later

> **Domain-specific languages**
>
> For a provisioning tool like CloudFormation, Bicep, or Terraform, you generate outputs for modules or stacks that higher-level ones can consume. A configuration management tool such as Ansible passes variables by standard output between automation tasks.

Module outputs help expose specific parameters for high-level resources. The approach copies and repeats the values. However, module outputs can get complicated! You'll often forget which outputs you exposed and their names. Contract testing in chapter 6 might help you enforce required module outputs.

Rather than use outputs, you can use infrastructure state as a state file or infrastructure provider's API metadata. Many tools keep a copy of the infrastructure state, which I call *tool state*, to detect drift between actual resource state and configuration and track which resources it manages.

> **DEFINITION** *Tool state* is a representation of infrastructure state stored by an IaC tool. It tracks the configuration of resources managed by the tool.

Tools often store their state in a file. You already encountered an example of using tool state in listing 4.2. You parsed the name of the network from a file called terraform.tfstate, which is the tool state for Terraform. However, not all tools offer a state file. As a result, you may have difficulty parsing low-level resource attributes across tools.

If you have multiple tools and providers in your system, you have two main options. First, consider using a configuration manager as a standard interface to pass metadata. A *configuration manager*, like a key-value store, manages a set of fields and their values.

The configuration manager helps you create your own abstraction layer for tool state. For example, some network automation scripts might read IP address values stored in a key-value store. However, you have to maintain the configuration manager and make sure your IaC can access it.

As a second option, consider using an infrastructure provider's API. Infrastructure APIs do not often change; they provide detailed information and account for out-of-band changes that a state file may not include. You can use client libraries to access information from infrastructure APIs.

> **Domain-specific languages**
>
> Many provisioning tools offer a capability to make API calls to an infrastructure API. For example, AWS-specific parameter types and `Fn::ImportValue` in CloudFormation retrieve values from the AWS API or other stacks. Bicep offers a keyword called `existing` to import resource properties outside of the current file.
>
> Terraform offers data sources to read metadata on an infrastructure resource from the API. Similarly, a module can reference Ansible facts, which gather metadata about a resource or your environment.

You will encounter a few downsides to using the infrastructure API. Unfortunately, your IaC needs network access. You won't know the *value* of the attribute until you run the IaC because the code must make a request to the API. If the infrastructure API experiences an outage, your IaC may not resolve attributes for low-level resources.

When you add an abstraction with dependency inversion, you protect high-level resources from changing attributes on lower-level resources. While you can't prevent all failures or disruptions, you minimize the blast radius of potential failures due to updated low-level resources. Think of it as a contract: if both high- and low-level resources agree on the attributes they need, they can evolve independently of one another.

4.2.3   Applying dependency injection

What happens when you combine inversion of control and dependency inversion? Figure 4.6 shows how you can combine both principles to decouple the server and network example. The server calls the network for attributes and parses the metadata using the infrastructure API or state. If you make changes to the network name, it updates the metadata. The server retrieves the updated metadata and adjusts its configuration separately.

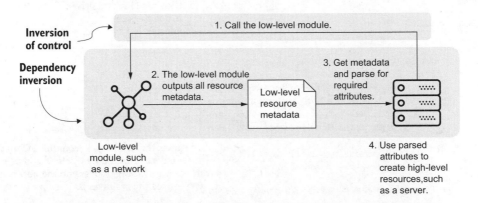

Figure 4.6   Dependency injection combines inversion of control and dependency inversion to loosen infrastructure dependencies and isolate low-level and high-level resources.

Harnessing the power of both principles helps promote evolution and composability because the abstraction layer behaves as a buffer between each building block of your system. You use *dependency injection* to combine inversion of control and dependency inversion. Inversion of control isolates changes to the high-level modules or resources, while dependency inversion isolates changes to the low-level resources.

> **DEFINITION**   *Dependency injection* combines the principles of inversion of control and dependency inversion. High-level modules or resources call for attributes from low-level ones through an abstraction.

Let's implement dependency injection for the server and network example with Apache Libcloud, a library for the GCP API, as shown in listing 4.5. You use Libcloud to search for the network. The server calls the GCP API for the subnet name, parses the GCP API metadata, and assigns itself the fifth IP address in the network's range.

Listing 4.5   Using dependency injection to create a server on a network

```python
import credentials
import ipaddress
import json
from libcloud.compute.types import Provider
from libcloud.compute.providers import get_driver


def get_network(name):
    ComputeEngine = get_driver(Provider.GCE)
    driver = ComputeEngine(
        credentials.GOOGLE_SERVICE_ACCOUNT,
        credentials.GOOGLE_SERVICE_ACCOUNT_FILE,
        project=credentials.GOOGLE_PROJECT,
        datacenter=credentials.GOOGLE_REGION)
    return driver.ex_get_subnetwork(
        name, credentials.GOOGLE_REGION)


class ServerFactoryModule:
    def __init__(self, name, network, zone='us-central1-a'):
        self._name = name
        gcp_network_object = get_network(network)
        self._network = gcp_network_object.name
        self._network_ip = self._allocate_fifth_ip_address_in_range(
            gcp_network_object.cidr)
        self._zone = zone
        self.resources = self._build()



    def _allocate_fifth_ip_address_in_range(self, ip_range):
        ip = ipaddress.IPv4Network(ip_range)
        return format(ip[-2])


    def _build(self):
        return {
            'resource': [{
                'google_compute_instance': [{
                    self._name: [{
                        'allow_stopping_for_update': True,
                        'boot_disk': [{
                            'initialize_params': [{
                                'image': 'ubuntu-1804-lts'
                            }]
```

Imports the Libcloud library, which allows you to access the GCP API. You must import the provider object and Google driver.

Imports the Google Compute Engine driver for Libcloud

This function retrieves the network information using the Libcloud library. The network and subnet were created separately. Their code has been omitted for clarity.

Passes the GCP service account credentials you want Libcloud to use for accessing the GCP API

Uses the Libcloud driver to get the subnet information by its name

This module creates the Google compute instance (server) using a Terraform resource

Parses the CIDR block from the GCP network object returned by Libcloud and uses it to calculate the fifth IP address on the network. The server uses the result as its network IP address.

Uses the module to create the JSON configuration for the server

Parses the subnet name from the GCP network object returned by Libcloud and uses it to create the server

```
                                          }],
                                          'machine_type': 'f1-micro',
                                          'name': self._name,
                                          'zone': self._zone,
                                          'network_interface': [{
                                              'subnetwork': self._network,
                                              'network_ip': self._network_ip
                                          }]
                                      }]
                                  }]
                              }]
                          }

        if __name__ == "__main__":
            server = ServerFactoryModule(name='hello-world', network='default')
            with open('main.tf.json', 'w') as outfile:
                json.dump(server.resources, outfile, sort_keys=True, indent=4)
```

Parses the CIDR block from the GCP network object returned by Libcloud and uses it to calculate the fifth IP address on the network. The server uses the result as its network IP address.

Parses the subnet name from the GCP network object returned by Libcloud and uses it to create the server

This module creates the Google compute instance (server) using a Terraform resource.

Writes the Python dictionary to a JSON file to be executed by Terraform later

---

AWS and Azure equivalents

To convert listing 4.5, you need to update the IaC to create an Amazon Elastic Compute Cloud (EC2) instance or Azure Linux virtual machine. You need to update the Libcloud driver to use Amazon EC2 Driver (http://mng.bz/wo95) or Azure ARM Compute Driver (http://mng.bz/qY9x).

Using the infrastructure API as an abstraction layer, you account for the evolution of the network independent of the server. For example, what happens when you change the IP address range for the network? You deploy the update to the network before you run the IaC for the server. The server calls the infrastructure API for network attributes and recognizes a new IP address range. Then it recalculates the fifth IP address.

Figure 4.7 shows the responsiveness of the server to the change because of dependency injection. When you change the IP address range for the network, your server gets the updated address range and reallocates the IP address if needed.

Thanks to dependency inversion, you can evolve low-level resources separately from dependencies. Inversion of control helps high-level resources respond to changes in low-level resources. Combining the two as dependency injection ensures the composability of the system, as you can add more high-level resources on the low-level ones. Decoupling due to dependency injection helps you minimize the blast radius of failed changes across modules in your system.

In general, you should apply dependency injection as an essential principle for infrastructure dependency management. If you apply dependency injection when you write your infrastructure configuration, you sufficiently decouple dependencies so

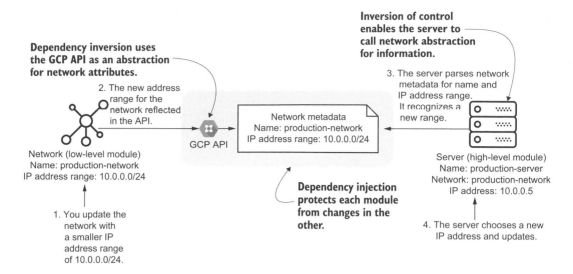

Figure 4.7   Dependency injection allows me to change the low-level module (the network) and automatically propagate the change to the high-level module (the server).

that you can change them independently without affecting other infrastructure. As your module grows, you can continue to refactor to more specific patterns and further decouple infrastructure based on the type of resources and modules.

4.3   *Facade*

Applying the principle of dependency injection generates similar patterns for expressing dependencies. The patterns align with structural design patterns in software development. In the pursuit of decoupling dependencies, I often find myself repeating the same three patterns in my IaC.

Imagine you want to create a storage bucket to store static files. You can control who accesses the files with an access control API in GCP. Figure 4.8 creates the bucket and sets the outputs to include the bucket's name. The access control rules for the bucket can use the outputs to get the bucket's name.

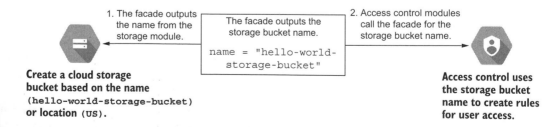

Figure 4.8   The facade simplifies attributes to the name of the storage bucket for use by the access control module.

The pattern of using outputs and an abstraction layer seems *very* familiar. In fact, you encountered it in the chapter's first half. You've been unknowingly using the facade pattern to pass multiple attributes between modules!

The *facade pattern* uses module outputs as the abstraction for dependency injection. It behaves like a mirror, reflecting the attributes to other modules and resources.

> **DEFINITION** The *facade pattern* outputs attributes from resources in a module for dependency injection.

A facade reflects the attributes and nothing more. The pattern does decouple dependencies between high- and low-level resources and conforms to the principle of dependency injection. The high-level resource still calls the low-level resource for information, and outputs serve as the abstraction.

The following listing implements the facade pattern in code by building an output method. Your bucket module returns the bucket object and name in its output method. Your access module uses the output method to retrieve the bucket object and access its name.

Listing 4.6 Outputting the bucket name as a facade for access control rules

```python
import json
import re


class StorageBucketFacade:
    def __init__(self, name):
        self.name = name
```
Using the facade pattern, outputs the bucket name as part of the storage output object. This implements dependency inversion to abstract away unnecessary bucket attributes.

Creates a low-level module for the GCP storage bucket, which uses the factory pattern to generate a bucket

```python
class StorageBucketModule:
    def __init__(self, name, location='US'):
        self.name = f'{name}-storage-bucket'
        self.location = location
        self.resources = self._build()

    def _build(self):
        return {
            'resource': [
                {
                    'google_storage_bucket': [{
                        self.name: [{
                            'name': self.name,
                            'location': self.location,
                            'force_destroy': True
                        }]
                    }]
                }
            ]
        }

    def outputs(self):
```

Creates the Google storage bucket using a Terraform resource based on the name and location

Sets an attribute on the Google storage bucket to destroy it when you delete Terraform resources

Creates an output method for the module that returns a list of attributes for the storage bucket

```
        return StorageBucketFacade(self.name)
```

Creates a high-level module to add access control rules to the storage bucket

```
    class StorageBucketAccessModule:
        def __init__(self, bucket, user, role):
            if not self._validate_user(user):
                print("Please enter valid user or group ID")
                exit()
            if not self._validate_role(role):
                print("Please enter valid role")
                exit()
            self.bucket = bucket
            self.user = user
            self.role = role
            self.resources = self._build()

        def _validate_role(self, role):
            valid_roles = ['READER', 'OWNER', 'WRITER']
            if role in valid_roles:
                return True
            return False

        def _validate_user(self, user):
            valid_users_group = ['allUsers', 'allAuthenticatedUsers']
            if user in valid_users_group:
                return True
            regex = r'^[a-z0-9]+[\._]?[a-z0-9]+[@]\w+[.]\w{2,3}$'
            if(re.search(regex, user)):
                return True
            return False

        def _change_case(self):
            return re.sub('[^0-9a-zA-Z]+', '_', self.user)

        def _build(self):
            return {
                'resource': [{
                    'google_storage_bucket_access_control': [{
                        self._change_case(): [{
                            'bucket': self.bucket.name,
                            'role': self.role,
                            'entity': self.user
                        }]
                    }]
                }]
            }


    if __name__ == "__main__":
        bucket = StorageBucketModule('hello-world')
        with open('bucket.tf.json', 'w') as outfile:
            json.dump(bucket.resources, outfile, sort_keys=True, indent=4)

        server = StorageBucketAccessModule(
            bucket.outputs(), 'allAuthenticatedUsers', 'READER')
        with open('bucket_access.tf.json', 'w') as outfile:
            json.dump(server.resources, outfile, sort_keys=True, indent=4)
```

Passes the bucket's output facade to the high-level module

Validates that the roles passed to the module match valid roles in GCP

Validates that the users passed to the module match valid user group types for all users or all authenticated users

Creates Google storage bucket access control rules using a Terraform resource

AWS and Azure equivalents

A GCP storage bucket is similar to an Amazon Simple Storage Service (S3) bucket or Azure Blob Storage.

Why output the entire bucket object and not just the name? Remember that you want to build an abstraction layer to conform to the principle of dependency inversion. If you create a new module that depends on the bucket location, you can update the bucket object's facade to output the name and location. The update does not affect the access module.

You can implement a facade with low effort and still get the benefits from decoupling of dependencies. One such benefit includes the flexibility to make isolated, self-contained updates in one module without affecting others. Adding new high-level dependencies does not require much effort.

The facade pattern also makes it easier to debug problems. It mirrors the outputs without adding logic for parsing, making it simple to trace problems to the source and fix the system. You'll learn more about reverting failed changes in chapter 11.

Domain-specific languages

Using a DSL, you can mimic a facade by using an output variable with a customized name. The high-level resource references the customized output names.

As a general practice, you'll start a facade with one or two fields. Always keep this to the minimum number of fields you'll need for high-level resources. Review and prune the fields when you don't need them every few weeks.

The facade pattern works for simpler dependencies, such as a few high-level modules to one low-level one. However, when you add many high-level modules and the depth of your dependencies increases, you will have difficulty maintaining the facade pattern for the low-level modules. When you need to change a field name in the output, you must change every module that references it. Changing every module reference does not scale when you have hundreds of resources that depend on one low-level module.

4.4 Adapter

The facade mirrors the values as outputs for one infrastructure module to high-level modules in the previous section. It works well for simple dependency relationships but falls apart with more complex modules. More complex modules usually involve one-to-many dependencies or span multiple infrastructure providers.

Let's say you have an identity module that passes a list of users and roles for configuring infrastructure. The identity module needs to work across multiple platforms. In figure 4.9, you set up the module to output a JSON-formatted object that maps permissions such as `read`, `write`, or `admin` with the corresponding usernames. Teams must map these usernames and their generic permissions to GCP-specific terms. GCP's access management uses `viewer`, `editor`, and `owner`, which transform to `read`, `write`, and `admin`.

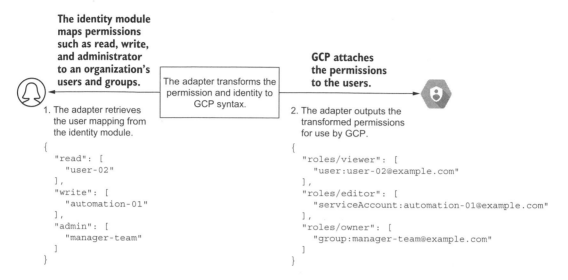

The identity module maps permissions such as read, write, and administrator to an organization's users and groups.

The adapter transforms the permission and identity to GCP syntax.

GCP attaches the permissions to the users.

1. The adapter retrieves the user mapping from the identity module.

```
{
  "read": [
    "user-02"
  ],
  "write": [
    "automation-01"
  ],
  "admin": [
    "manager-team"
  ]
}
```

2. The adapter outputs the transformed permissions for use by GCP.

```
{
  "roles/viewer": [
    "user:user-02@example.com"
  ],
  "roles/editor": [
    "serviceAccount:automation-01@example.com"
  ],
  "roles/owner": [
    "group:manager-team@example.com"
  ]
}
```

Figure 4.9   The adapter pattern transforms attributes to a different interface that high-level modules can consume.

How do you map a generic set of roles to the specific infrastructure provider roles? The mapping needs to ensure that you can reproduce and evolve the module over multiple infrastructure providers. You want to extend the module in the future to add users to equivalent roles across platforms.

As a solution, the *adapter pattern* transforms metadata from the low-level resource so that any high-level resource can use it. An adapter behaves like a travel plug. You can change the plug depending on the country's outlet and still use your electronic devices.

DEFINITION   The *adapter pattern* transforms and outputs metadata from the low-level resource or module so any high-level resource or module can use it.

To start, you create a dictionary that maps generic role names to users. In listing 4.7, you want to assign a read-only role to the audit team and two users. These generic roles and usernames do not match any of the GCP permissions and roles.

Listing 4.7   Creating a static object that maps generic roles to usernames

```
class Infrastructure:
    def __init__(self):
        self.resources = {
```

```
        'read': [
            'audit-team',
            'user-01',
            'user-02'
        ],
```
Assigns the audit-team, user-01, and user-02 to a read-only role. The mapping describes that the user can only read information on any infrastructure provider.

```
        'write': [
            'infrastructure-team',
            'user-03',
            'automation-01'
        ],
```
Assigns the infrastructure-team, user-02, and automation-01 to a write role. The mapping describes that the user can update information on any infrastructure provider.

```
        'admin': [
            'manager-team'
        ]
    }
```
Assigns the manager team to the administrator role. The mapping describes that the user can manage any infrastructure provider.

AWS and Azure equivalents

For those more familiar with AWS, the equivalent policies for each permission set would be `AdministratorAccess` for `admin`, `PowerUserAccess` for `write`, and `ViewOnlyAccess` for `read`. Azure role-based access control uses `Owner` for `admin`, `Contributor` for `write`, and `Reader` for `read`.

However, you cannot do anything with the static object in role mappings. GCP does not understand the usernames or roles! Implement the adapter pattern to map generic permissions to the infrastructure-specific permissions.

The following listing builds an identity adapter specific to GCP, which maps generic permissions like read to GCP-specific terms like `roles/viewer`. GCP can use the map to add users, service accounts, and groups to the correct roles.

Listing 4.8 Using the adapter pattern to transform generic permissions

```
import json
import access


class GCPIdentityAdapter:
    EMAIL_DOMAIN = 'example.com'

    def __init__(self, metadata):
        gcp_roles = {
            'read': 'roles/viewer',
            'write': 'roles/editor',
            'admin': 'roles/owner'
        }
        self.gcp_users = []
        for permission, users in metadata.items():
            for user in users:
                self.gcp_users.append(
                    (user, self._get_gcp_identity(user),
                        gcp_roles.get(permission)))

    def _get_gcp_identity(self, user):
```

Creates an adapter to map generic role types to Google role types

Sets the email domain as a constant, which you'll append to each user

Creates a dictionary to map generic roles to GCP-specific permissions and roles

Transforms the usernames to GCP-specific member terminology, which uses user type and email address

For each permission and user, builds a tuple with the user, GCP identity, and role

If the username has "team," the GCP identity needs to be prefixed with "group" and suffixed with the email domain.

If the username has "automation," the GCP identity needs to be prefixed with "serviceAccount" and suffixed with the email domain.

```python
    if 'team' in user:
        return f'group:{user}@{self.EMAIL_DOMAIN}'
    elif 'automation' in user:
        return f'serviceAccount:{user}@{self.EMAIL_DOMAIN}'
    else:
        return f'user:{user}@{self.EMAIL_DOMAIN}'
```

For all other users, the GCP identity needs to be prefixed with "user" and suffixed with the email domain.

```python
def outputs(self):
    return self.gcp_users
```

Outputs the list of tuples containing the users, GCP identities, and roles

```python
class GCPProjectUsers:
    def __init__(self, project, users):
        self._project = project
        self._users = users
        self.resources = self._build()

    def _build(self):
        resources = []
        for (user, member, role) in self._users:
            resources.append({
                'google_project_iam_member': [{
                    user: [{
                        'role': role,
                        'member': member,
                        'project': self._project
                    }]
                }]
            })
        return {
            'resource': resources
        }
```

Creates a module for the GCP project users, which uses the factory pattern to attach users to GCP roles for a given project

Uses the module to create the JSON configuration for the project's users and roles

Creates a dictionary to map generic roles to GCP-specific permissions and roles

Creates a list of Google project IAM members using a Terraform resource. The list retrieves the GCP identity, role, and project to attach a username to read, write, or administrator permissions in GCP.

Creates an adapter to map generic role types to Google role types

```python
if __name__ == "__main__":
    users = GCPIdentityAdapter(access.Infrastructure().resources).outputs()

    with open('main.tf.json', 'w') as outfile:
        json.dump(
            GCPProjectUsers(
                'infrastructure-as-code-book',
                users).resources, outfile, sort_keys=True, indent=4)
```

Writes the Python dictionary to a JSON file to be executed by Terraform later

---

AWS and Azure equivalents

To convert the code listing to AWS, you would map references to the GCP project to an AWS account. GCP project users align with an AWS IAM user and their attached roles. Similarly, you would create an Azure subscription and add a user account and their API permissions in Azure Active Directory.

You could extend your identity adapter to map the generic dictionary of access requirements to another infrastructure provider, like AWS or Azure. In general, an adapter translates the provider-specific or prototype module-specific language into generic terms. This pattern works best for modules with different infrastructure providers or dependencies. I also use the adapter pattern to create a consistent interface for infrastructure providers with poorly defined resource parameters.

For a more complex example, imagine configuring a virtual private network (VPN) connection between two clouds. Instead of passing network information from each provider through a facade, you use an adapter, as in figure 4.10. Your network modules for each provider output a network object with more general fields, such as `name` and `IP address`. This use case benefits from an adapter because it reconciles the semantics of two different languages (e.g., a GCP Cloud VPN gateway and AWS customer gateway).

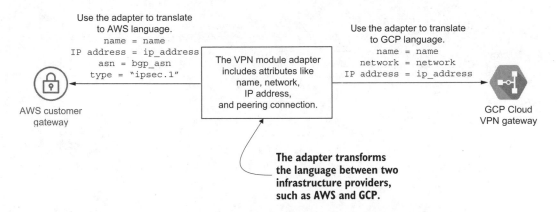

Figure 4.10 An adapter translates language and attributes between two cloud providers.

Azure equivalent

An Azure VPN gateway achieves similar functionality to an AWS customer gateway and GCP Cloud VPN gateway.

Why use an adapter to promote composability and evolvability? The pattern heavily relies on dependency inversion to abstract any transformation of attributes between resources. An adapter behaves as a contract between modules. As long as both modules agree on the contract outlined by the adapter, you can continue to change high-level and low-level modules somewhat independently of each other.

Domain-specific languages

A DSL translates the provider- or resource-specific language or resource. DSLs implement an adapter within their framework to represent infrastructure state. Infrastructure state often includes the same resource metadata as the infrastructure API. Some tools will allow you to interface with the state file and treat the schema as an adapter for high-level modules.

However, the adapter pattern works only if you *maintain the contract* between modules. Recall that you built an adapter to transform permissions and usernames to GCP. What happens if your teammate accidentally updates the mapping for read-only roles to `roles/reader`, which doesn't exist? Figure 4.11 demonstrates that if you don't use the right role specific to GCP, your IaC fails.

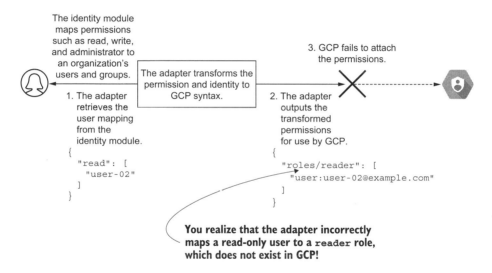

Figure 4.11   You need to troubleshoot and test the adapter to map the fields correctly.

In the example, you broke the contract between the generic and GCP roles! The broken contract causes your IaC to fail. Make sure you maintain and update the correct mappings in your adapter to minimize failure.

Furthermore, troubleshooting becomes more difficult with an adapter. The pattern obfuscates the resources depending on a specific adapter attribute. You need to investigate whether an error results from the wrong field output from the source module, an incorrect attribute in the adapter, or the wrong field consumed by the dependent module. Module versioning and testing in chapters 5 and 6, respectively, can alleviate the challenges and troubleshooting of an adapter.

4.5 Mediator

The adapter and facade patterns isolate changes and make it easy to manage one dependency. However, IaC often includes complex resource dependencies. To detangle the web of dependencies, you can build opinionated automation that structures when and how IaC should create resources.

Imagine you want to add a firewall rule to allow SSH to the server's IP address in our canonical server and network example. However, you can create the firewall rule only if the server exists. Similarly, you can create the server only if the network exists. You need automation to capture the complexity of the relationships among firewall, server, and network.

Let's try to capture the logic of creating the network, the server, and the firewall. Automation can help *mediate* which resources to create first. Figure 4.12 diagrams the workflow for the automation. If the resource is a server, IaC creates the network and then the server. If the resource is a firewall rule, IaC creates the network first, the server second, and the firewall rule third.

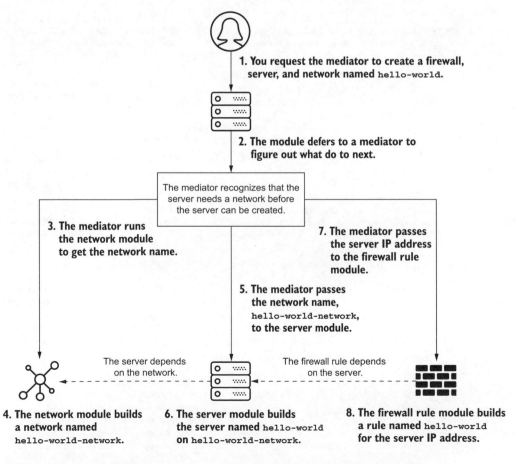

Figure 4.12 The mediator becomes the authority on which resource to configure first.

The IaC implements dependency injection to abstract and control network, server, and firewall dependencies. It relies on the principle of idempotency to run continuously and achieve the same end state (network, server, and firewall), no matter the existing resources. Composability also helps establish the building blocks of infrastructure resources and dependencies.

This *mediator pattern* works like air-traffic control at an airport. It controls and manages inbound and outbound flights. A mediator's sole purpose is to organize the dependencies among these resources and to create or delete objects as needed.

> **DEFINITION**   The *mediator pattern* organizes dependencies among infrastructure resources and includes logic to create or delete objects based on their dependencies.

Let's implement the mediator pattern for the network, server, and firewall. Implementing a mediator in Python requires a few if-else statements to check each resource type and build its low-level dependencies. In listing 4.9, the firewall depends on creating the server and the network first.

Listing 4.9   Using the mediator pattern to organize server and dependencies

```
import json
from server import ServerFactoryModule
from firewall import FirewallFactoryModule
from network import NetworkFactoryModule


class Mediator:
    def __init__(self, resource, **attributes):
        self.resources = self._create(resource, **attributes)

    def _create(self, resource, **attributes):
        if isinstance(resource, FirewallFactoryModule):
            server = ServerFactoryModule(resource._name)
            resources = self._create(server)
            firewall = FirewallFactoryModule(
                resource._name, depends_on=resources[1].outputs())
            resources.append(firewall)
        elif isinstance(resource, ServerFactoryModule):
            network = NetworkFactoryModule(resource._name)
            resources = self._create(network)
            server = ServerFactoryModule(
                resource._name, depends_on=network.outputs())
            resources.append(server)
        else:
            resources = [resource]
        return resources
```

Imports the factory modules for the network, server, and firewall

Creates a mediator to decide how and in which order to automate changes to resources

When you call the mediator to create a resource like a network, server, or firewall, you allow the mediator to decide all the resources to configure.

After the mediator creates the server configuration, it builds the firewall rule configuration.

If you want to create a firewall rule as a resource, the mediator will recursively call itself to create the server first.

After the mediator creates the network configuration, it builds the server configuration.

If you want to create a server as a resource, the mediator will recursively call itself to create the network first.

If you pass any other resource to the mediator, such as the network, it will build its default configuration.

```
def build(self):
    metadata = []
    for resource in self.resources:
        metadata += resource.build()
    return {'resource': metadata}
```

Uses the module to create a list of resources from the mediator and render the JSON configuration

```
if __name__ == "__main__":
    name = 'hello-world'
    resource = FirewallFactoryModule(name)
    mediator = Mediator(resource)
```

Passes the mediator a firewall resource. The mediator will create the network, server, and then the firewall configuration.

```
    with open('main.tf.json', 'w') as outfile:
        json.dump(mediator.build(), outfile, sort_keys=True, indent=4)
```

Writes the Python dictionary to a JSON file to be executed by Terraform later

---

AWS and Azure equivalents

Firewall rules for GCP are similar in behavior to rules for an AWS security group or Azure network security group. The rules control ingress and egress traffic to and from IP address ranges to tagged targets.

If you have a new resource, such as a load balancer, you can expand the mediator to build it after the server or firewall. The mediator pattern works best with modules that have many levels of dependencies and multiple system components.

However, you might find the mediator challenging to implement. The mediator pattern must follow idempotency. You need to run multiple times and achieve the same target state. You have to write and test all of the logic in a mediator. If you do not test your mediator, you may accidentally break a resource. Writing your own mediator takes lots of code!

Fortunately, you do not have to implement your own mediator often. Most IaC tools behave as mediators to resolve complex dependencies and decide how to create resources. The majority of provisioning tools have built-in mediators to identify dependencies and order of operations. For example, the container orchestration of Kubernetes uses a mediator to orchestrate changes to the resources in the cluster. Ansible uses a mediator to determine which automation steps to compose and run from various configuration modules.

NOTE Some IaC tools implement the mediator pattern by using graph theory to map dependencies between resources. The resources serve as nodes. Links pass attributes to dependent resources. If you want to create resources without a tool, you can manually diagram dependencies in your system. Diagrams can help organize your automation and code. They also identify which modules you can decouple. The exercise of graphing dependencies might help you implement a mediator.

I implement the mediator pattern only when I cannot find it in a tool or need something between tools. For example, I sometimes write a mediator to control creating a Kubernetes cluster in one tool before another tool deploys services on the Kubernetes cluster. A mediator reconciles automation between these two tools, such as checking cluster health before deploying services with the second tool.

4.6   *Choosing a pattern*

The facade, adapter, and mediator all use dependency injection to decouple changes between high-level and low-level modules. You can apply any of the patterns, and they will express dependencies between modules and isolate changes within them. As your system grows, you may need to change these patterns depending on the structure of your module.

Your choice of pattern depends on the number of dependencies you have on a low-level module or resource. The facade pattern works for one low-level module to a few high-level ones. Consider an adapter if you have a low-level module with many high-level module dependencies. When you have many dependencies among modules, you may need a mediator to control resource automation. Figure 4.13 outlines the decision tree for identifying which dependency pattern to use.

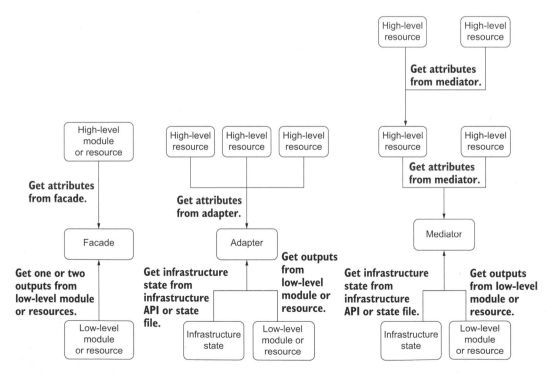

Figure 4.13   Choosing your abstraction depends on the relationship of the dependency, whether it is intra-module, one to one, or one to many.

All of the patterns promote idempotency, composability, and evolvability through dependency injection. However, why would you start with a facade and then consider the adapter or mediator? As your system grows, you will need to optimize your dependency management pattern to reduce the operational burden of changes.

Figure 4.14 shows the relationship between troubleshooting and implementation effort and scalability and isolation for facade, mediator, and adapter patterns. For example, a facade has the benefit of minimal effort for implementation and troubleshooting but does not scale or isolate changes with more resources. Adapters and mediators offer improved scalability and isolation at the cost of troubleshooting and implementation effort.

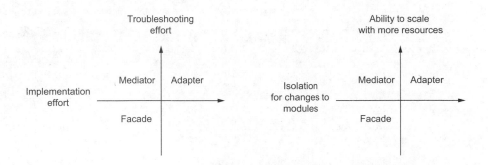

While the adapter pattern may have a high cost associated with troubleshooting and implementation efforts, it provides better scalability with more resources and isolation for changes to modules.

Figure 4.14   Some patterns may have a low cost of troubleshooting and implementation but cannot isolate changes to modules and scale.

Lower your initial effort by choosing a tool with a mediator implementation. Then use the tool's built-in facade implementation to manage dependencies between modules or resources. When you find it difficult to manage a facade because you have multiple systems depending on each other, you can start examining an adapter or mediator.

An adapter takes more effort to implement but provides the best foundation for expanding and growing your infrastructure system. You can always add new infrastructure providers and systems without worrying about changing low-level modules. However, you cannot expect to use the adapter for every module because it takes time to implement and troubleshoot.

A tool with a mediator chooses which components get updated and when. An existing tool lowers your overall implementation effort but introduces some concerns during troubleshooting. You need to know your tool's behavior to troubleshoot failed changes for dependencies. Depending on how you use the tool, a tool with a mediator allows you to scale but may not fully isolate changes to modules.

Exercise 4.1

How can we better decouple the database's dependency on the network via the following IaC?

```
class Database:
  def __init__(self, name):
    spec = {
      'name': name,
      'settings': {
        'ip_configuration': {
          'private_network': 'default'
        }
      }
    }
```

A The approach adequately decouples the database from the network.

B Pass the network ID as a variable instead of hardcoding it as `default`.

C Implement and pass a `NetworkOutput` object to the database module for all network attributes.

D Add a function to the network module to push its network ID to the database module.

E Add a function to the database module to call the infrastructure API for the `default` network ID.

See appendix B for answers to exercises.

Summary

- Apply infrastructure dependency patterns such as facade, adapter, and mediator to decouple modules and resources, and you can make changes to modules in isolation.
- Inversion of control states that the high-level resource calls the low-level one for attributes.
- The dependency inversion principle states that the high-level resource should use an abstraction of low-level resource metadata.
- Dependency injection combines the principles of inversion of control and dependency inversion.
- If you do not recognize an applicable pattern, you can use dependency injection for a high-level resource to call a low-level resource and parse its object structure for the values it needs.
- Use the facade pattern to reference a simplified interface for attributes.
- Use the adapter pattern to transform metadata from one resource for another to use. This pattern works best with resources across different infrastructure providers or prototype modules.
- The mediator pattern organizes the dependencies between these resources and creates or deletes objects as needed. Most tools serve as a mediator between resources.

Part 2

Scaling with your team

After you learn the practices and patterns for writing infrastructure as code, you often want to share it with your team. This part discusses considerations and guidelines for sharing and collaborating on IaC. Establishing patterns across multiple teams minimizes conflicts and potential failures.

Chapter 5 describes how to structure, version, and release modules so every team member can update them safely. In chapter 6, you'll learn about testing strategies for IaC. The tests will help you verify the stability of changes before you push them to production.

You'll add testing to delivery pipelines in chapter 7, which describes development and deployment models. The chapter offers guidance to branch (or not to branch!) and safely deploy changes to production. Finally, chapter 8 discusses practices you can add to IaC testing and delivery pipelines to ensure secure and compliant configurations.

Structuring and sharing modules

This chapter covers

- Constructing module versions and tags for infrastructure changes
- Choosing a single repository versus multiple repositories
- Organizing shared infrastructure modules across teams
- Releasing infrastructure modules without affecting critical dependencies

Up to this point in the book, you've learned practices and patterns for writing infrastructure as code and breaking them into groups of infrastructure components. However, you can write the most optimal configurations but still have trouble maintaining and mitigating the risk of failure to your systems. The difficulties happen because your team does not standardize collaboration practices when updating infrastructure modules.

Imagine a company, Datacenter for Veggies, starts by automating its growing operations for herbs. Applications in GCP monitor and adjust for optimal herb growth. Each team uses the singleton pattern and creates a unique infrastructure configuration.

Over time, Datacenter for Veggies becomes more popular and wants to expand to all vegetables. It hires a new application development team specializing in software for growing various vegetables, from herbs to leafy greens to root vegetables. Each team creates an infrastructure configuration independent of the others.

Datacenter for Veggies hires you to develop an application to grow fruit. You realize you cannot reuse any infrastructure configurations because they are unique to each vegetable team. The company needs a consistent, reusable way to build, secure, and manage infrastructure.

You realize that Datacenter for Veggies could use some module patterns from chapter 3 to organize infrastructure configuration into modules for composability. You sketch out a diagram, depicted in figure 5.1, to organize and coordinate groups of infrastructure for multiple teams. The teams for herbs, root vegetables, leafy green vegetables, and fruit can all use standardized configuration for networks, databases, and servers.

Sharing modules across teams promotes reproducibility, composability, and evolvability. The teams do not have to spend as much time building IaC because they reproduce established configurations. Team members can choose how they compose their systems and override the configurations for their specific needs.

To fully realize the benefit of standardized modules, you need to treat them with a development life cycle outside of regular infrastructure changes. This chapter covers practices for sharing and managing infrastructure modules. You'll learn techniques and practices to release stable modules without introducing critical failures to higher-level dependencies.

5.1 Repository structure

Imagine that each team in Datacenter for Veggies uses a singleton pattern for its infrastructure. The Herbs and Leafy Greens teams realize they use similarly configured servers, networks, and databases. Can they merge their infrastructure configuration into one module?

Rather than copy and paste each other's configuration, the Herbs and Leafy Greens teams want to update it in one place and reference it in their configuration. Should Datacenter for Veggies put all infrastructure in one repository? Or should it divide its modules across multiple repositories?

5.1.1 Single repository

At first, each Datacenter for Veggies team stores its infrastructure configuration in a single code repository. Each team organizes its configuration into a dedicated directory to avoid mixing up configurations. If a team wants to reference a module, the team imports the module by using a local file path.

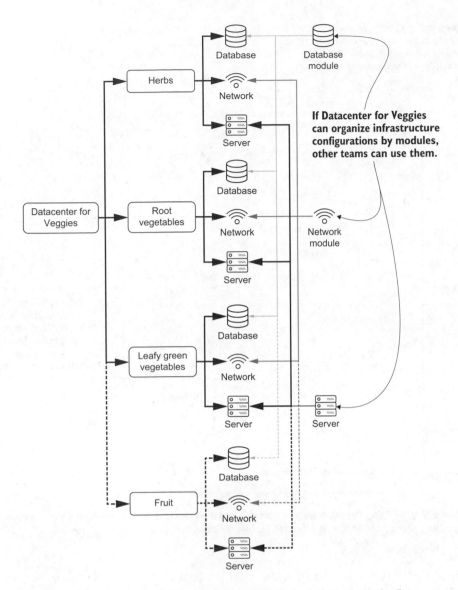

Figure 5.1   Datacenter for Veggies can use modules to organize and standardize infrastructure configuration across application teams.

Figure 5.2 shows how Datacenter for Veggies structures its single code repository. The repository contains two folders at the top level, separating modules and environments. The company subdivides the environments directory for each team, such as the Leafy Greens team. The Leafy Greens team separates configurations by development and production environments.

When using a single repository for infrastructure configuration, subdivide modules and configurations into different subdirectories.

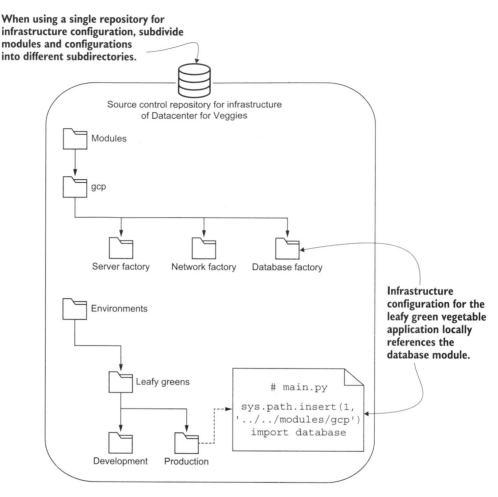

Figure 5.2   The Leafy Greens team's production and development environments use the directories containing server, network, and database factory modules in a single repository structure.

When the Leafy Greens team members want to create a database, they can use a module in the modules folder. In their IaC, they import the module by setting a local path. After importing, they can use the database factory and build the resource in production.

Datacenter for Veggies started defining infrastructure with a *single repository* (also known as a *mono repository,* or *monorepo*) to contain all configuration and modules for each team.

> **DEFINITION**   A *single repository* structure (also known as *mono repository,* or *monorepo*) contains all IaC (configuration and modules) for a team or function.

In general, the company likes the single repository structure. All teams can reproduce their configuration by copying and pasting, and can compose new resources by adding a new folder for a module. In listing 5.1, the Leafy Greens team members build a new database module. Using Python, they insert a local file path to modules by using the `sys.path` method. They use the database by importing its module into the codebase.

Listing 5.1 Referencing infrastructure modules in a different directory

```
import sys
sys.path.insert(1, '../../modules/gcp')           ⊲─  Imports the directory with
                                                      the modules because it exists
                                                      in the same repository

from database import DatabaseFactoryModule
from server import ServerFactoryModule
from network import NetworkFactoryModule

import json
                                                      Imports the server, database,
                                                      and network factory modules
if __name__ == "__main__":                            for the production environment
    environment = 'production'
    name = f'{environment}-hello-world'
    network = NetworkFactoryModule(name)
    server = ServerFactoryModule(name, environment, network)
    database = DatabaseFactoryModule(name, server, network, environment)
    resources = {
        'resource': network.build() + server.build() + database.build()
    }
                                                                    Uses the
    with open('main.tf.json', 'w') as outfile:                     modules to
        json.dump(resources, outfile, sort_keys=True, indent=4)  create the JSON
                                                                configuration for
Writes the Python dictionary                                     the network,
out to a JSON file to be                                         server, and
executed by Terraform later                                      database
```

Using local folders to store modules helps the teams reference the infrastructure they want. Everyone can look in the same repository for modules or examine other teams' configurations. If someone on the Herbs team wants to learn about the Fruits team's IaC, they can use the `tree` command to examine the directory structure:

```
$ tree .
.
├── environments
│   ├── fruits
│   │   ├── development
│   │   └── production
│   ├── herbs
│   │   ├── development
│   │   └── production
│   ├── leafy-greens
│   │   ├── development
│   │   └── production
│   └── roots
│       ├── development
│       └── production
```

```
└── modules
    └── gcp
        ├── database.py
        ├── network.py
        ├── server.py
        └── tags.py
```

To better organize configurations, each team puts development and production environment configurations into separate folders. These directories isolate configurations and changes for each environment. Ideally, all environments should be the same. Realistically, you will have differences between environments to address cost or resource constraints.

Other tools

A single repository structure applies to many other IaC tools. You can apply the single repository structure for reusing roles and playbooks to configuration management tools like Ansible. You can reference and build playbooks or configuration management modules based on each local directory in the single repository.

CloudFormation works a bit differently. You can host all of your stack definition files in a single repository. However, you must release the child template (which I consider a module) into an S3 bucket and reference it with the `TemplateURL` parameter in the `AWS::CloudFormation::Stack` resource. Later in this chapter, you'll learn how to deliver and release changes to modules.

Datacenter for Veggies uses one infrastructure provider, GCP. In the future, teams can add new directories for different infrastructure tools or providers. These tools can update servers or networks (ansible directory), build virtual machine images (packer directory), or deploy the database to AWS (aws directory):

```
$ tree .
.
├── environments
│   ├── development
│   └── production
└── modules
    └── ansible
    └── aws
    └── gcp
    └── packer
```

You may encounter the principle of *don't repeat yourself* (*DRY*) in other IaC materials. DRY promotes reuse and composability. Infrastructure modules reduce duplication and repetition in configuration, which conforms to DRY. If you can have identical development and production environments, you could omit the development and production directories and reference one module instead of separate environment files.

You cannot fully comply with DRY in infrastructure. Depending on the infrastructure or tool's language and syntax, you will always have repetitive configuration. As a result, you can have occasional repetition for clearer configuration or within the limitations of tools or platforms.

5.1.2 Multiple repositories

As Datacenter for Veggies grows, its infrastructure repository has hundreds of folders. Each folder contains many more nested ones. Every week, you spend time rebasing the configuration with all the updates from every repository. You also wait 20 minutes each time you push to production because your CI framework must recursively search for changes. The security team also expresses concern because contractors working with the Leafy Greens team have access to all of the Fruits team's infrastructure!

You divide network, tag, server, and database modules into individual repositories. Each repository has its workflow for building and delivering the module, which takes less time for the CI framework. You can control access to each repository, allowing contractors on the Leafy Greens team to access only the Leafy Greens configuration.

Different teams in Datacenter for Veggies can use the module's repository or packaged version. Each team stores its configuration and modules in a separate repository. Anyone in the company can download and use the modules in their configurations.

Figure 5.3 shows the code repositories Datacenter for Veggies uses to create IaC. Each team and module gets its own code repository. When the Leafy Greens team

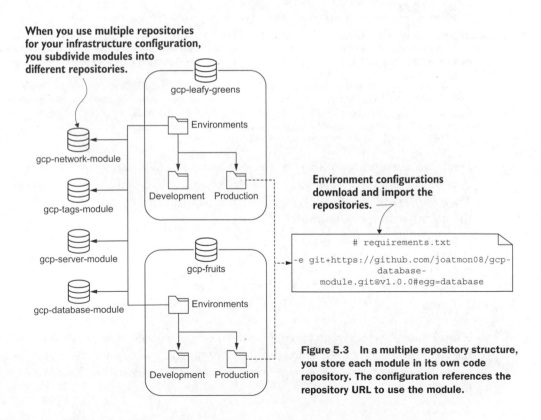

Figure 5.3 In a multiple repository structure, you store each module in its own code repository. The configuration references the repository URL to use the module.

wants to create a database, it downloads and imports the database module from a GitHub repository URL instead of the local folder. If teams have multiple environments, they subdivide their code repository into folders.

Datacenter for Veggies has migrated from a single repository structure to a *multiple repository*, or *multi repo*, structure. The company separated modules into various repositories based on the teams.

> **DEFINITION**   A *multiple repository* (also known as a *multi repo*) structure separates IaC (configuration or modules) into different repositories based on team or function.

Recall that a single repository pattern promotes reproducibility and composability. A multiple repository pattern helps improve the principle of evolvability. Separating the modules into their own repositories helps structure each module's life cycle and management.

To implement a multiple repository structure, you split the modules into their own version control repository. In the following listing, you configure Python's package manager to download each module by adding it as a library requirement in requirements.txt. Each library requirement must include a URL to the version control repository and a specific tag to download.

Listing 5.2   Python requirements.txt references module repositories

Downloads the prototype module for tags from a GitHub repository. Picks the module version based on the tag.

Downloads the factory module for the network, server, and database from a GitHub repository. Picks the module version based on the tag.

```
-e git+https://github.com/joatmon08/gcp-tags-module.git@1.0.0#egg=tags
-e git+https://github.com/joatmon08/gcp-network-module.git@1.0.0#egg=network
-e git+https://github.com/joatmon08/gcp-server-module.git@0.0.1#egg=server
-e git+https://github.com/joatmon08/gcp-database-
      module.git@1.0.0#egg=database
```

First, you create a repository for the production configuration of the fruit application's infrastructure. After you create the repository, you add requirements.txt to it. Then you run Python's package installation manager to download each module for the infrastructure configuration:

```
$ pip install -r requirements.txt
Obtaining tags from
git+https://github.com/joatmon08/
➥gcp-tags-module.git@1.0.0#egg=tags
...
Successfully installed database network server tags
```

Rather than set a local path and import the modules, you need to run Python's package installation manager to download from the remote repository first. After downloading the modules, teams can import them in environment configurations by using Python in listing 5.3.

Listing 5.3   Importing the modules for use in infrastructure configuration

```
from tags import StandardTags
from server import ServerFactoryModule                Imports the modules
from network import NetworkFactoryModule              downloaded by the
from database import DatabaseFactoryModule            package manager

import json

if __name__ == "__main__":
    environment = 'production'
    name = f'{environment}-hello-world'               Uses the modules to create the
                                                      JSON configuration for the
    tags = StandardTags(environment)                  network, server, and database
    network = NetworkFactoryModule(name)
    server = ServerFactoryModule(name, environment, network, tags.tags)
    database = DatabaseFactoryModule(
        name, server, network, environment, tags.tags)
    resources = {
        'resource': network.build() + server.build() + database.build()
    }

    with open('main.tf.json', 'w') as outfile:
        json.dump(resources, outfile, sort_keys=True, indent=4)
```

Writes the Python dictionary out to a JSON
file to be executed by Terraform later

Recall that Datacenter for Veggies separately configures the development and production environments. The teams would implement code to reference the same factory and prototype modules hosted in version control. Consistent modules for development and production environments prevent drift between environments and help you test module changes before production. You'll learn more about testing and environments in chapter 6.

The IaC implementation for a multiple repository does not differ too much from a single repository. Both structures support reproducibility and composability. However, they differ in that you independently evolve a module in an external repository.

Updating a configuration in a multiple repository structure involves re-downloading new modules with your package manager. Running the package manager to use a new module can introduce friction in your IaC workflow. Someone may update a module, and you won't know unless you review its repository. Later in this chapter, you'll learn about solving this problem with versioning.

Domain-specific languages

If a tool can reference modules or libraries with version control or artifact URLs, it can support a multiple repository structure.

When you adopt a multiple repository structure, you must establish a few standard practices to share and maintain modules. First, standardize a module file structure and format. It helps the teams across your organization identify and filter modules in version control. Consistent file structures and naming for module repositories also help with auditing and future automation.

For example, infrastructure modules in Datacenter for Veggies follow the same pattern and file structure. Their names include *infrastructure provider, resource,* and *tool* or *purpose.* In figure 5.4, the `gcp-server-module` describes GCP as the infrastructure provider, `server` as the resource type, and `module` as the purpose.

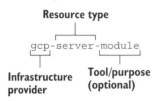

Figure 5.4   The repository name should include the infrastructure provider, resource type, and purpose.

If your modules use a specific tool or have a unique purpose, you can append it to the end of the repository name. It helps to add the tool to the name to identify the module type. Similar to the practices outlined in chapter 2, you want your module name descriptive enough for a teammate to identify.

You can apply the repository naming approach to naming folders in a single repository as well. However, subdirectories in a single repository make it easier to nest and identify infrastructure provider and resource type. Depending on your organization and team's preferences, you can always add more fields to a repository name.

5.1.3   *Choosing a repository structure*

The scalability of your system and CI framework determine whether you use a single repository or multiple repositories. Datacenter for Veggies started with a single repository, which worked well because it had tens of modules and a few environments. Each module has two environments, for development and production. Each environment needs a few servers, one database, a network, and a monitoring system.

Using a single repository provides a few benefits. Figure 5.5 outlines some of the advantages and limitations. First, anyone on your team can access modules and configurations in one repository. Second, you need to go to only one place to compare and identify differences between environments. For example, you can compare two files in the repository to check whether development uses three servers and production uses five servers.

Drawing on the IaC principles, a single repository structure still offers composability, evolvability, and reproducibility. Anyone can go into a folder and evolve a module. You can still build modules on one another because you have a singular view of all infrastructure and configuration.

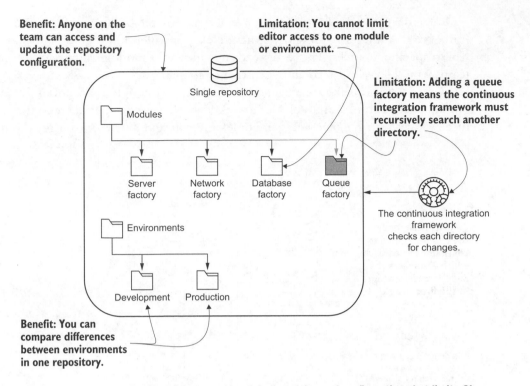

Benefit: Anyone on the team can access and update the repository configuration.

Limitation: You cannot limit editor access to one module or environment.

Limitation: Adding a queue factory means the continuous integration framework must recursively search another directory.

Single repository

Modules

Server factory

Network factory

Database factory

Queue factory

The continuous integration framework checks each directory for changes.

Environments

Development   Production

Benefit: You can compare differences between environments in one repository.

Figure 5.5   A single repository offers one view for all modules and configurations but limits CI frameworks or granular access control.

On the other hand, a single repository structure has some limitations. If anyone can go and change a module, it could break the IaC that depends on it! Furthermore, your CI system might break down as it recursively checks each directory for changes.

As a result, you need to adopt practices and tools to handle single repositories. These include opinionated versioning and specialized build systems. If your organization cannot build or adopt a tool that helps alleviate single repository management, you may choose a multiple repository structure.

> **NOTE**   You will find a few tools that help with building and managing single repositories. They have additional code to handle nested subdirectories and individual build workflows. Some of them include Bazel, Pants, and Yarn.

The migration from single to multiple repository structure happens more than you think. I had to do it twice! One organization started with three environments and four modules. Over a few years, the IaC grew to hundreds of modules and environments.

Unfortunately, the CI framework (Jenkins) took nearly three hours to run a standard change scaling up servers. The framework spent most of its time searching each directory and nested directory for changes! We eventually refactored the configurations and modules into multiple repositories.

Refactoring into multiple repositories alleviated some of the problems with the CI framework. A multiple repository structure also provided more granular access control to specific modules. The security team could grant module edit access to specific teams. You'll learn more about refactoring in chapter 10.

Figure 5.6 shows the benefits and limitations of multiple repositories, including granular access control and scalable CI workflows. However, a multiple repository structure reduces your singular view of modules and configurations for your organization.

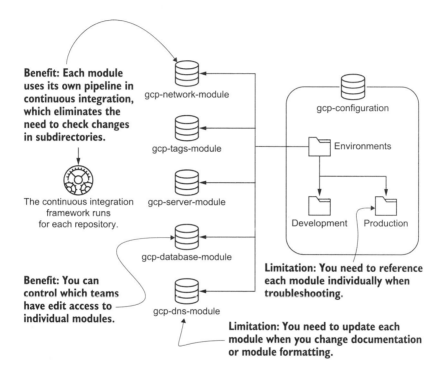

Figure 5.6   Multiple repositories help reduce the burden of running tests and configurations with CI frameworks but require constant verification of conformance to formatting and troubleshooting.

By refactoring the configuration into a multiple repository structure, you can isolate access to and evolve the infrastructure configuration for specific teams. You have greater control over the evolution and life cycle of modules. Most CI frameworks support multiple repositories and will run workflows in parallel when the framework detects changes to a given repository.

However, multiple repositories do have some downsides. Imagine Datacenter for Veggies has ten or more modules in different repositories. How do you know if they all conform to the same file standards and naming?

Figure 5.7 shows one solution to the problem of file and standard conformance. You can capture all of the tests for formatting and linting checks into a prototype module. Then, the CI framework downloads the tests and checks for README and Python files in the server, network, database, and DNS modules.

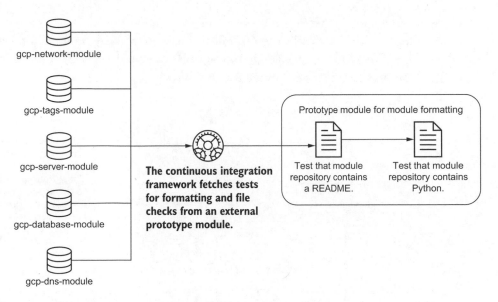

Figure 5.7 Creating a prototype module that contains all of the checks for module repository format will help fix older repositories that do not conform to new standards.

The prototype module with tests help enforce formatting for older modules that you don't use as often, like DNS. If you want to add a new standard, you update the prototype module with a new test. The next time someone updates a module or configuration, they need to update their module format to conform.

A standardized set of checks helps alleviate the operational burden of finding and replacing files in hundreds of repositories. It distributes the responsibility of updating the module repository to the module's maintainers. For more on module conformance testing and integrating modules in your workflow, you can apply the practices in chapters 6, 7, and 8.

A second disadvantage to a multiple repository structure involves the challenge of troubleshooting. When you reference a module in your configuration, you need to search for the module repository to identify which inputs and outputs it needs. The search adds extra effort and time when you debug failures in configuration.

If you have a build system that can handle single repository building requirements, you can use a single repository for everything. However, most build systems do not scale with recursive directory searching. To solve this problem, you can use a combination of single and multiple repositories.

Let's apply this solution to Datacenter for Veggies. They separate each configuration for different types of fruits and vegetables. Leafy Greens uses one repository, while Fruits uses another. Both of them reference shared modules for network, tags, database, and DNS.

Figure 5.8 shows that the Fruits team needs a queue but the Leafy Greens team does not. As a result, the Fruits repository includes a local module for creating queues. The Fruits team uses a single repository for its unique configurations but references multiple repositories for common modules.

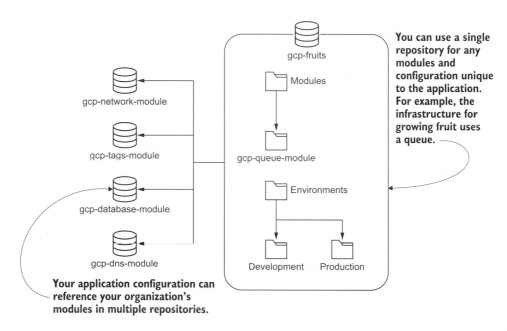

Figure 5.8   Your organization can combine multiple repositories with a single repository for application or system-specific configuration.

When you use this mix-and-match approach, recognize the kind of access control you want for individual repositories or shared configurations. If you want to improve composability and reproducibility for other teams, you might put a module in its own repository. However, if you want to maintain evolvability for a specialized configuration, you might manage the module locally with your configuration.

As you choose your repository structure, recognize the trade-off between approaches and refactor as the number of modules and configurations grows. When you add more configuration and resources into a single repository, you need to make sure the tools and processes scale with it!

5.2   *Versioning*

Throughout this chapter, you've used the practice of keeping infrastructure configuration or code in version control. For example, Datacenter for Veggies teams can always reference infrastructure based on the commit hash. One day, the security team for Datacenter for Veggies expressed concern about the age of usernames and passwords for soil-monitoring databases.

The team recommends using a secret manager to store and rotate the password every 30 days. Problematically, *all* teams use the soil-monitoring database module. Figure 5.9 shows that the application currently references the output of the database module. The module outputs the password for the database, which applications use to write and read data. The security team wants you to use a secrets manager instead.

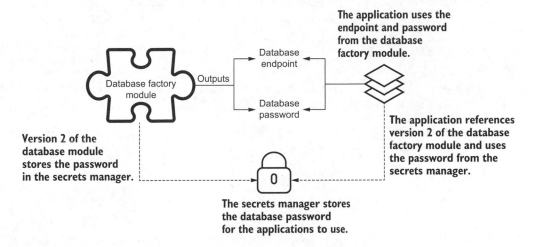

Figure 5.9   The applications reference the database endpoint and password from the soil-monitoring module but should use the password from the secrets manager.

The database module output affects the secret's evolvability and security. How can we update the database to use the secrets manager without disrupting soil data collection? The infrastructure team at Datacenter for Veggies decides to add *versioning* to the database module.

> **DEFINITION**   *Versioning* is the process of assigning unique versions to iterations of code.

Let's examine how the Datacenter for Veggies team implements module versions. The team uses version control to tag the current version of the database module as `v1.0.0`. Version v1.0.0 will output the database password for applications:

```
$ git tag v1.0.0
```

They push the tag for v1.0.0 to version control:

```
$ git push origin v1.0.0
Total 0 (delta 0), reused 0 (delta 0), pack-reused 0
 * [new tag]         v1.0.0 -> v1.0.0
```

You must refactor configurations for Fruit, Leafy Greens, Grain, and Herb growth to use the v1.0.0 version of the database module in a process called *version pinning*. Version pinning preserves idempotency. When you run the IaC, the configurations continue to use the database module outputs. You should not detect any drift between a pinned module and the existing infrastructure.

After all of the teams pin the versions to v1.0.0, you can rewrite the module to use a secrets manager. The database module stores the password in the secrets manager. The team tags the new database module as v2.0.0, which outputs the database endpoint and location of the password in the secrets manager:

```
$ git tag v2.0.0
```

They push the tag for v2.0.0 to version control:

```
$ git push origin v2.0.0
Total 0 (delta 0), reused 0 (delta 0), pack-reused 0
 * [new tag]         v2.0.0 -> v2.0.0
```

You can examine the difference between the two versions of the module based on the commit history:

```
$ git log --oneline
7157d3e (HEAD -> main, tag: v2.0.0, origin/main)
➡Change database module to store password in secrets manager
5c5fd65 (tag: v1.0.0) Add database factory module
```

Now that you've created a new version of the database factory module, you ask some of the teams to try it. The Fruits team bravely volunteers. The Fruits team currently uses version 1.0.0. That module version outputs the database endpoint and password.

When updating to module version 2.0.0, as shown in figure 5.10, the Fruits team needs to account for changes in the module's workflow. The team cannot use the database password in the module's output. The module outputs an API path to the database password stored in the secrets manager. As a result, the Fruits team refactors its IaC to get the database password from the secrets manager before creating the database.

You'll apply a few essential practices to module versioning. First, make sure you run your IaC and eliminate any drift before you update. Second, establish a versioning approach that *does not* reference the latest version of the module.

Datacenter for Veggies follows *semantic versioning*, assigning version numbers that convey essential information about the configuration. You can specify module versions in a few ways, including tagging the commit with a number in version control or packaging and labeling the module in an artifact repository.

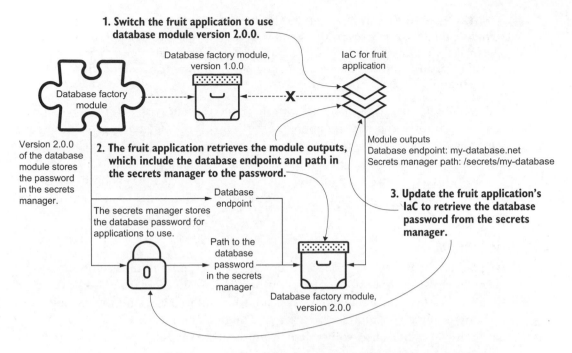

1. Switch the fruit application to use database module version 2.0.0.

Database factory module, version 1.0.0

IaC for fruit application

Database factory module

Version 2.0.0 of the database module stores the password in the secrets manager.

2. The fruit application retrieves the module outputs, which include the database endpoint and path in the secrets manager to the password.

Module outputs
Database endpoint: my-database.net
Secrets manager path: /secrets/my-database

The secrets manager stores the database password for applications to use.

Database endpoint

3. Update the fruit application's IaC to retrieve the database password from the secrets manager.

Path to the database password in the secrets manager

Database factory module, version 2.0.0

Figure 5.10   You can refactor the Fruit application to reference version 2.0.0 of the database module and retrieve the database password from the secrets manager.

NOTE I often update the major version for significant updates that remove inputs, outputs, and resources. I usually update the minor version if I update configuration values, inputs, or outputs to modules that do not affect dependencies using previous versions. Finally, I will change the patch version for minor configuration value changes scoped to the module and its resources. For additional details on semantic versioning and its approaches, you can reference https://semver.org/.

Using a consistent versioning approach, you can more effectively evolve downstream infrastructure resources without breaking upstream ones because you control their dependencies. Versioning also helps with the auditing of active versions. To save resources, reduce confusion, and promote the latest changes, versioning allows you to identify and deprecate older, inactive versions of the module.

However, you must continuously remember and enforce certain versioning practices. The longer you wait to update the application to use v2.0.0 of the database, the higher chance it will fail. You might consider putting a timeline on how long you can use the module version v1.0.0. You do not need to immediately delete v1.0.0 of the database module. Generally, I upgrade dependent modules within a few minor version changes. Trying to upgrade with a broader "jump" between versions increases the change's risk and possible failure rate.

> **NOTE**   If you use feature-based development or Git Flow, you can accommodate patches or hotfixes in the same workflow as software development. You can make a branch based on the version tag, update the changes, increase the patch version, and add a new tag for the hotfix branch. You will need to keep the branch for the commit history.

This versioning process works well for a multiple repository structure. What about a single repository? You can still apply the version control tagging approach. You may want to add a prefix to the tag with the module name (`module-name-v2.0.0`). Then you can package and release your module to an artifact repository. Your build system packages the contents of the module subdirectory and tags the version in the artifact store. Your configuration references the remote modules in the artifact repository instead of a local file.

5.3   *Releasing*

I explained the practice of module versioning to help with module evolution and minimize disruption to your system. However, you don't want every team to update its IaC to the newest module immediately. Instead, you want to make sure the module works and doesn't break your infrastructure *before* you use it in production.

Figure 5.11 shows how you evaluate your database module update before allowing all Datacenter for Veggies teams to use it. After you update the database module to store a password in the secrets manager, you push the changes to version control. You ask the Fruits team to *test* the module in a separate environment and confirm that the module works. They confirm it works correctly. You tag the release with a new version, 2.0.0, and update the documentation on the secrets manager.

In the previous section, the Datacenter for Veggies infrastructure team updated the module and tested it with the Fruits team's development environment first. Now that the module passed the test, other teams can use the new database module with a secret manager. The team followed a *release* process to certify that other teams can use the new module.

> **DEFINITION**   *Releasing* is the process of distributing software to a consumer.

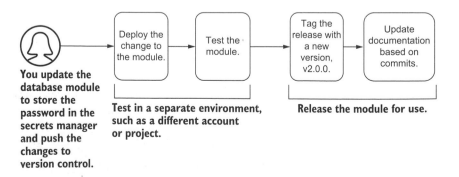

Figure 5.11   When you make module updates, ensure that you include a testing stage before releasing the module and updating its documentation.

A release process identifies and isolates any problems from module updates. You do not package a new module unless the tests certify that it works.

I recommend running module tests in a dedicated testing environment away from development and production workloads. A separate account or project for module testing helps you track the cost of running the tests and isolates failures away from active environments. You'll learn more about testing and testing environments in chapter 6.

> **NOTE** For a detailed code listing of a continuous delivery pipeline for releasing modules, check out http://mng.bz/PnaR. The GitHub Actions pipeline automatically builds a GitHub release when the tests succeed based on a commit message.

After testing the modules, you tag the release with a new version for your team to use. Datacenter for Veggies releases the database module as version v2.0.0 and uses the Python package manager to reference the tag. Alternatively, you can package the module and push it to an artifact repository or storage bucket.

For example, imagine Datacenter for Veggies has some teams that use CloudFormation. These teams prefer to reference modules (or CloudFormation stacks) stored in an Amazon S3 bucket. In figure 5.12, the teams add a step to their delivery pipeline to compress their modules and upload them to an S3 storage bucket. As a last step, they update documentation outlining the changes they made.

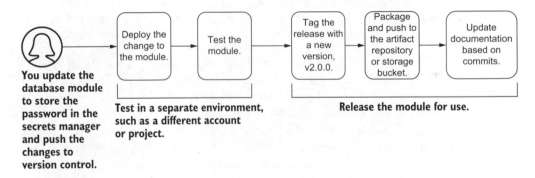

Figure 5.12   After testing, you optionally choose to package and push the module to an artifact repository or storage bucket.

Some organizations prefer packaging the artifact and storing it in a separate repository for additional security control. If you have a secure network that cannot access an external version control endpoint, you can reference the artifact repository instead. Just make sure to keep the tag in version control so someone can correlate the artifact to the correct code version.

After packaging and pushing the artifact, you should update documentation outlining your changes. That documentation, called *release notes*, outlines breaking changes to outputs and inputs. Release notes communicate a summary of changes to other teams.

> **DEFINITION**   *Release notes* list changes to code for a given release. You should store them in a document in the repository, often called a changelog.

You can manually update the release notes, but I prefer an automated semantic release tool (such as semantic-release) to examine the commit history and build release notes for me. Make sure that you use the correct commit message format for the tool to match and parse changes. Chapter 2 emphasized the importance of writing descriptive commit messages. You'll also find them helpful for an automated release tool.

For example, the database module stores the password in a secret manager. Datacenter for Veggies considers this a major feature, so you prefix the commit message with `feat`:

```
$ git log -n 1 --oneline
1b65555 (HEAD -> main, tag: v0.0.1, origin/main, origin/HEAD)
 feat(security): store password in secrets manager
```

A commit analyzer in an automated release tool automatically updates the major version of the tag to v2.0.0 based on this commit.

Image building

You might encounter the practice of using image-building tools to build immutable server or container images. By baking the packages you want into a server or container image, you can create new servers with updates without the problems of in-place updates. When you release immutable images, use a workflow to create a test server based on the image, check that it runs correctly, and update the version of the image tag. Chapter 7 covers some of these workflows.

Besides updating release notes, make sure you update commonly used files and documentation. Common files help your teammates use the module. For instance, Datacenter for Veggies agrees that teams must always include a README file. A README documents the purpose, inputs, and outputs of each module.

> **DEFINITION**   A *README* is a document in a repository that explains usage and contribution instructions for code. For IaC, use it to document a module's purpose, inputs, and outputs.

Use a linting rule to check for the existence of a README file. In chapter 2, I discussed some linting practices to ensure clean IaC. Applying the pattern to commonly used files and documentation helps you format and organize large amounts of IaC.

In the Python examples, the modules include common files like `__init__.py` for identifying the package and `setup.py` for module configuration. I often refer to

files with configuration or metadata that help specific tools or languages as *helper files.*
They change depending on the tool and platform you use. You will want to standardize them across your organization so you can change or search them in parallel by
using automation.

5.4 *Sharing modules*

As Datacenter for Veggies grows more produce, it adds *new teams* that automate the
growth of grains, tea, coffee, and beans. The company also creates a new team for
researching wild strains of produce. Each team needs to be able to expand the existing modules but also create new ones.

For example, the Beans team needs to change a database module to use PostgreSQL version 12. Should those team members be able to edit the module with the
version update? Or should they file a ticket with you, the infrastructure team, to
update it?

You need to empower different teams to create and update modules with IaC.
However, you want to make sure that teams do not change an attribute and compromise security or functionality. You'll find a few practices that can help you share modules across your organization.

Imagine that all teams in Datacenter for Veggies need a database. You create a new,
opinionated database module that establishes a default set of parameters to provide
security and functionality. The database module uses embedded defaults for module
inputs to cover many Datacenter for Veggies use cases. Even if the Coffee team doesn't
know how to create a database, that team can use the module to build a secure, working database.

As a general practice, set *opinionated defaults* in your module. You want to err on the
prescriptive side. If a team needs more flexibility, it can update the module or override the default attributes. Preset defaults help teach secure and standard practices for
deploying specific infrastructure resources.

In this scenario, the Beans team expresses a need for more flexibility. The module
does not use a new version of the database, PostgreSQL version 12. No other team
uses that version of PostgreSQL. The Beans team decides to update the database version and push the changes into the repository.

However, the changes do not get released immediately. The build system sends a
notification to module approvers in the infrastructure team. In figure 5.13, the infrastructure team pauses the build system and reviews the changes. If the changes pass
the team's approval, the build system releases the module. The Beans team can use
the new version of the database module with PostgreSQL version 12.

Why should you allow the Beans team to change the infrastructure module? *Self-
service* of module changes empowers all teams to update their systems and reduce the
burden on infrastructure and platform teams. You want to balance their development
progress with security and infrastructure availability. Adding an approval before module release identifies potential failures or nonstandard changes to infrastructure.

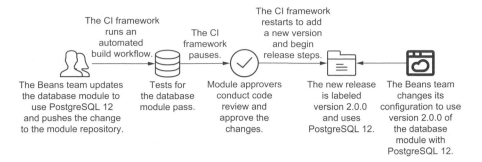

Figure 5.13   An application team can update the database module. However, the team must wait for approval from subject-matter experts before being able to use the new release.

The practice of allowing any team to use modules and edit them with approvers works best with established module development standards and processes. If you don't establish module standards, this approach falls apart and adds friction to delivering the infrastructure change to production.

Let's return to the example. The infrastructure team does not have much confidence in the change, so the team asks a database administrator for additional review. The database administrator points out that if the Beans team upgrades its module version, the resulting behavior deletes the previous database and creates an empty one with the new version! This would significantly disrupt the application supporting bean growth.

In figure 5.14, the Beans team submits a request for help from the database team. An administrator recommends some practices that will help update the database without deleting data. The Beans team implements these practices and asks module approvers for a second review. Once the module gets released, the team can use the module without worrying about disrupting its applications.

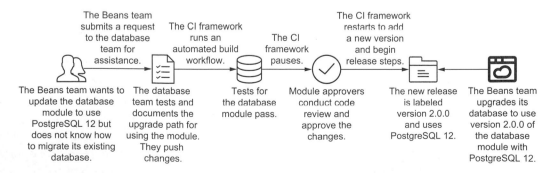

Figure 5.14   For disruptive module updates, the application team submits a ticket to the database team to verify database migration steps before releasing a new module version.

If you have concerns that a change might be particularly disruptive to a system's architecture, security, or availability, *ask for review from a subject-matter expert* before releasing a new version. A subject-matter expert can help identify any problems that will affect other teams using the module and advise on the best way to update it. The process of review helps you evolve your IaC and identify potential failures from infrastructure changes.

In general, you need a process that empowers your team to make infrastructure changes *and* provides the team the knowledge and support to complete those changes successfully without disrupting critical systems. Manual review may seem tedious but helps educate your team and prevent problems in production. Your team must find a balance between quickly deploying changes to production and waiting for manual review from a subject-matter expert, something I'll expand on in chapter 7.

By working collaboratively on modules, you share IaC knowledge across teams and collectively identify potential disruptions to critical infrastructure. You can treat modules as *artifacts* for use across an organization, similar to shared application libraries, container images, or virtual machine images. Anyone in the company can use and update modules (with additional help, if needed!) to evolve infrastructure architecture, security, or availability.

Summary

- Structure and share modules and configurations in a single repository or multiple repositories.
- A single repository structure organizes all configuration and modules in one place, making it easier to troubleshoot and identify usable resources.
- A multiple repository structure organizes all configuration and modules into their own code repositories, divided by business domain, function, team, or environment.
- A multiple repository structure allows better access control for individual infrastructure configuration or modules and streamlines pipeline execution for each repository.
- A single repository may not scale as more people collaborate on IaC and require additional resources for a build system to process changes quickly.
- Refactor a single repository into multiple repositories, one for each module.
- Choose a consistent versioning methodology for modules and update them using Git tags.
- Package and release a module to an artifact repository, which will allow anyone in the organization to retrieve a specific module version.
- When sharing modules across teams, establish opinionated default parameters in modules to maintain security and functionality.
- Allow anyone in the organization to suggest updates to modules, but add governance to identify potentially disruptive changes to modules that affect architecture, security, or infrastructure availability.

Testing

This chapter covers

- Identifying which type of tests to write for infrastructure systems
- Writing tests to verify infrastructure configuration or modules
- Understanding the cost of various types of tests

Recall from chapter 1 that infrastructure as code involves an entire process to push a change to a system. You update scripts or configurations with infrastructure changes, push them to a version control system, and apply the changes in an automated way. However, you can use every module and dependency pattern from chapters 3 and 4 and still have failed changes! How do you catch a failed change before you apply it to production?

You can solve this problem by implementing tests for IaC. *Testing* is a process that evaluates whether a system works as expected. This chapter reviews some considerations and concepts related to testing IaC to reduce the rate of change failure and build confidence in infrastructure changes.

> **DEFINITION** *Testing* IaC is a process that evaluates whether infrastructure works as expected.

Imagine you configure a network switch with a new network segment. You can manually test existing networks by pinging each server on each network and verifying their connectivity. To test that you set up the new network correctly, you create a new server and check whether it responds when you connect to it. This manual test takes a few hours for two or three networks.

As you create more networks, you can take days to verify your network connectivity. For every network segment update, you must manually verify the network connectivity and the servers, queues, databases, and other resources running on the network. You *cannot* test everything, so you check only a few resources. Unfortunately, this approach can leave hidden bugs or issues that appear only weeks, even months, later!

To reduce the burden of manual testing, you can instead *automate* your tests by scripting each command. Your script creates a server on the new network, checks its connectivity, and tests connections to existing networks. You invest some time and effort into writing the tests but save hours of manual verification by running an automated script for any subsequent changes to the network.

Figure 6.1 shows the amount of effort in hours compared to the number of infrastructure resources when you do manual and automated testing. When you run the

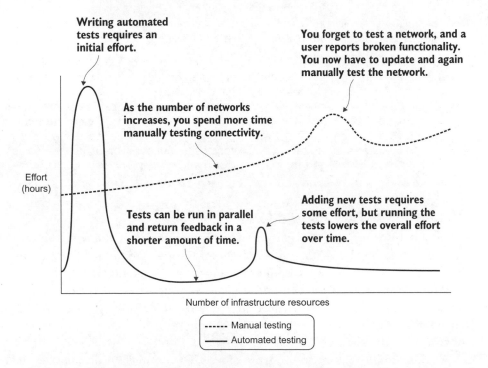

Figure 6.1 Manual testing may require lower effort initially, but as the number of infrastructure resources in your system increases, that effort increases. Automated testing takes a high initial effort that decreases as you grow your system.

network tests manually, you have to spend a lot of time on testing. The effort increases the more resources you add to your system. By comparison, writing automated tests takes an initial effort. However, the effort to maintain the test generally decreases as your system grows. You can even run automated tests in parallel to reduce the overall testing effort.

Of course, testing doesn't catch every problem or eliminate all failures from your system. However, automated testing serves as documentation for what you should test in your system every time you make a change. If a hidden bug chooses to appear, you spend some effort writing a new test to verify the bug doesn't happen again! Tests lower the overall operational effort over time.

You can use testing frameworks for your infrastructure provider or tool or native testing libraries in programming languages. The code listings use a Python testing framework called `pytest` and Apache Libcloud, a Python library to connect to GCP. I wrote the tests to focus on *what the test verifies* and not the syntax. You can apply the general approach to any tool or framework.

> **For more on pytest and Apache Libcloud**
>
> To run the tests, refer to the code repository at https://github.com/joatmon08/manning-book for instructions, examples, and dependencies. It includes links and references for getting started with pytest and Libcloud.
>
> *Do not* write tests for every single bit of IaC in your system. Tests can become difficult to maintain and, on occasion, redundant. Instead, I'll explain how to assess when to write a test and which type of test applies to the resource you're changing. Infrastructure testing is a heuristic; you're never going to be able to predict or simulate a change to production fully. A helpful test provides insight and practice into configuring infrastructure or how a change will impact a system. I'll also separate which tests apply to *modules* such as factories, prototypes, or builders versus general composite or singleton *configuration* for a live environment.

6.1   *The infrastructure testing cycle*

Testing helps you gain confidence and assess the impact of changes to infrastructure systems. However, how can you test a system without creating it first? Furthermore, how do you know that your system works after applying changes?

You can use the infrastructure testing cycle in figure 6.2 to structure your testing workflow. After you define an infrastructure configuration, you run initial tests to check your configuration. If they pass, you can apply the changes to active infrastructure and test the system.

In this workflow, you run two types of tests. One kind statically analyzes the configuration before you deploy the infrastructure changes, and the other dynamically analyzes the infrastructure resource to make sure it still works. Most of your tests follow this pattern by running before and after change deployment.

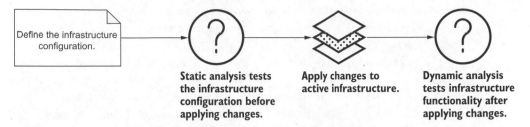

Figure 6.2   Infrastructure testing indicates whether you can apply changes to a system. After applying changes, you can use additional tests to confirm that the changes succeeded.

6.1.1   Static analysis

How would you apply the infrastructure testing cycle to our network example? Imagine you parse your network script to verify that the new network segment has the correct IP address range. You don't need to deploy the changes to the network. Instead, you analyze the script, a static file.

In figure 6.3, you define the network script and run static analysis. If you find the wrong IP address, the tests fail. You can revert or fix your network changes and rerun the tests. If they pass, you can apply the correct network IP address to the active network.

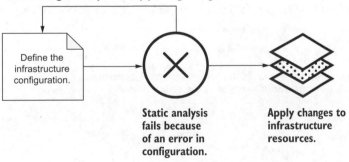

Figure 6.3   You can either fix the configuration to pass the tests or revert to a previously successful configuration when static analysis fails.

Tests that evaluate infrastructure configuration before deploying changes to infrastructure resources perform *static analysis.*

> **DEFINITION**   *Static analysis* for IaC verifies plaintext infrastructure configuration before deploying changes to live infrastructure resources.

Tests for static analysis do not require infrastructure resources since they usually parse the configuration. They do not run the risk of impacting any active systems. If static analysis tests pass, we have more confidence that we can apply the change.

I often use static analysis tests to check for infrastructure naming standards and dependencies. They run before applying changes, and in a matter of seconds, they identify any inconsistent naming or configuration concerns. I can correct the changes, rerun the tests to pass, and apply the changes to infrastructure resources. Refer to chapter 2 for clean IaC, linting, and formatting rules.

Tests for static analysis do not apply changes to active infrastructure, making rollback more straightforward. If tests for static analysis fail, you can return to the infrastructure configuration, correct the problems, and commit the changes again. If you cannot fix the configuration to pass static analysis, you can revert your commit to a previous one that succeeds! You'll learn more about reverting changes in chapter 11.

6.1.2   *Dynamic analysis*

If the static analysis passes, you can deploy changes to the network. However, you don't know whether the network segment actually works. After all, a server needs to connect to the network. To test connectivity, you create a server on the network and run a test script to check inbound and outbound connectivity.

Figure 6.4 shows the cycle of testing network functionality. Once you apply changes to the live infrastructure environment, you run tests to check the functionality of the system. If the test script fails and shows the server cannot connect, you return to the configuration and fix it for the system.

Note that your testing script needs a live network to create a server and test its connectivity. The tests that verify infrastructure functionality after applying changes to live infrastructure resources perform *dynamic analysis*.

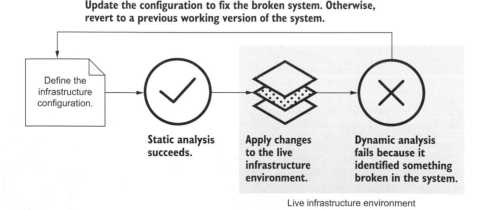

Figure 6.4   When dynamic analysis fails, you can fix the testing environment by updating the configuration or reverting to a previously working configuration.

DEFINITION   *Dynamic analysis* for IaC verifies system functionality after applying changes to live infrastructure resources.

When these tests pass, we have more confidence that the update succeeded. However, if they fail, they identify a problem in the system. If the tests fail, you know that you need to debug, fix the configuration or scripts, and rerun the tests. They provide an early warning system for changes that might break infrastructure resources and system functionality.

You can only dynamically analyze a live environment. What if you don't know whether the update will work? Can you isolate these tests from a production environment? Rather than apply all changes to a production environment and test it, you can use an intermediate testing environment to separate your updates and test them.

6.1.3   *Infrastructure testing environments*

Some organizations duplicate entire networks in a separate environment so they can test larger network changes. Applying changes to a testing environment makes it easier to identify and fix the broken system, update configuration, and commit the new changes without affecting business-critical systems.

When you run your tests in a separate environment before promoting to the active one, you add to the infrastructure testing cycle. In figure 6.5, you keep the static analysis step. However, you apply your network change in a testing environment and run dynamic analysis. If it passes the testing environment, you can apply the changes to production and run dynamic analysis in production.

A *testing environment* isolates changes and tests from the production environment.

DEFINITION   A *testing environment* is separate from production and used for testing infrastructure changes.

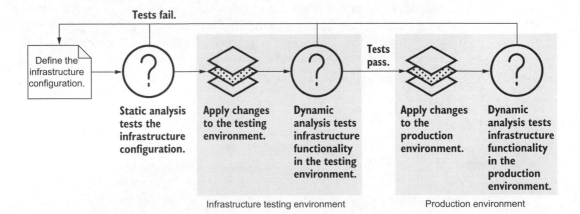

Figure 6.5   You can run a static and dynamic analysis of infrastructure in a testing environment before applying the changes to production.

A testing environment before production helps you *practice* and *check* changes before deploying to production. You better understand how they affect existing systems. If you cannot fix the updates, you can revert the testing environment to a working configuration version. You can use testing environments for the following:

- Examining the effect of an infrastructure change before applying it to a production system
- Isolating testing for infrastructure modules (refer to chapter 5 for module-sharing practices)

However, keep in mind that you have to maintain testing environments like production environments. When possible, an infrastructure testing environment should adhere to the following requirements:

- Its configuration must be as similar to production as possible.
- It must be a different environment from the application's development environment.
- It must be persistent (i.e., do not create and destroy it each time you test).

In previous chapters, I mentioned the importance of reducing drift across environments. If your infrastructure testing environment duplicates production, you will have more accurate testing behavior. You also want to test infrastructure changes in isolation, away from a development environment dedicated to applications. Once you've confirmed that your infrastructure changes have not broken anything, you can push them to the application's development environment.

It helps to have a persistent infrastructure testing environment. This way, you can test whether updates to running infrastructure will potentially affect business-critical systems. Unfortunately, maintaining an infrastructure testing environment may not be practical from a cost or resources standpoint. I outline some techniques for cost management of testing environments in chapter 12.

In the remainder of this chapter, I'll discuss the different types of tests that perform static and dynamic analysis and how they fit into your testing environment. Some tests will allow you to reduce your dependency on a testing environment. Others will be critical to assessing the functionality of a production system after changes. In chapter 11, I cover rollback techniques specific to production and incorporate testing into continuous infrastructure delivery.

6.2   *Unit tests*

I mentioned the importance of running static analysis on IaC. Static analysis evaluates the files for specific configurations. What kinds of tests can you write for static analysis?

Imagine you have a factory module to create a network named `hello-world-network` and three subnets with IP address ranges on 10.0.0.0/16. You want to verify their network names and IP ranges. You *expect* the subnets to divide the 10.0.0.0/16 range among themselves.

As a solution, you can write tests to check the network name and subnet IP address ranges in your IaC without creating the network and subnet. This static analysis verifies the configuration parameters for expected values in a matter of seconds.

Figure 6.6 shows that your static analysis consists of several tests run simultaneously. You check the network name, number of subnets, and IP ranges for subnets.

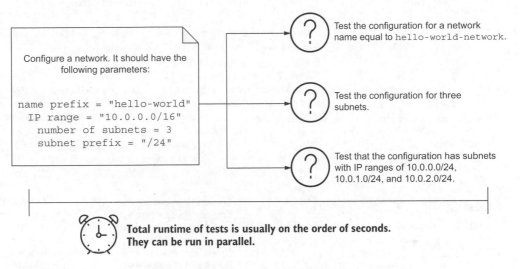

Figure 6.6   Unit tests verify that a configuration parameter, such as network name, equals an expected value.

We just ran unit tests on the network IaC. A *unit test* runs in isolation and statically analyzes infrastructure configuration or state. These tests do not rely on active infrastructure resources or dependencies and check for the smallest subset of configuration.

> **DEFINITION**   *Unit tests* statically analyze plaintext infrastructure configuration or state. They do not rely on live infrastructure resources or dependencies.

Note that unit tests can analyze metadata in infrastructure configuration *or* state files. Some tools offer information directly in configuration, while others expose values through state. The next few sections provide examples to test both types of files. Depending on your IaC tool, testing framework, and preference, you may test one, the other, or both.

6.2.1   Testing infrastructure configuration

We'll start by writing unit tests for modules that use templates to generate infrastructure configuration. Our network factory module uses a function to create an object with the network configuration. You need to know whether the function `_network_configuration` generates the correct configuration.

For the network factory module, you can write unit tests in pytest to check the functions that generate the JSON configuration for networks and subnets. The testing file includes three tests, one for the network name, the number of subnets, and IP ranges.

Pytest will identify tests by looking for files and tests prefixed by test_. In listing 6.1, we named the testing file test network.py so pytest can find it. The tests in the file each have the prefix test_ and descriptive information on what the test checks.

Listing 6.1   Using pytest to run unit tests in test_network.py

Imports pytest, a Python testing library. You need to name the file and tests prefixed with test_ for pytest to run them.

Imports the network factory module from main.py. You need to run the method for network configuration.

```
import pytest
from main import NetworkFactoryModule
```

Sets expected values as constants, such as network prefix and IP range

```
NETWORK_PREFIX = 'hello-world'
NETWORK_IP_RANGE = '10.0.0.0/16'
```

Creates the network from the module as a test fixture based on expected values. This fixture offers a consistent network object for all tests to reference.

Creates a separate fixture for the network configuration since you need to parse google_compute_network. One test uses this fixture to test the network name.

```
@pytest.fixture(scope="module")
def network():
    return NetworkFactoryModule(
        name=NETWORK_PREFIX,
        ip_range=NETWORK_IP_RANGE,
        number_of_subnets=3)
```

```
@pytest.fixture
def network_configuration(network):
    return network._network_configuration()['google_compute_network'][0]
```

Creates a separate fixture for the subnet configuration since you need to parse for google_compute_subnetwork. Two tests use this fixture for checking the number of subnets and their IP address ranges.

```
@pytest.fixture
def subnet_configuration(network):
    return network._subnet_configuration()[
        'google_compute_subnetwork']
```

```
def test_configuration_for_network_name(network, network_configuration):
    assert network_configuration[network._network_name][
        0]['name'] == f"{NETWORK_PREFIX}-network"
```

```
def test_configuration_for_three_subnets(subnet_configuration):
    assert len(subnet_configuration) == 3
```

Pytest will run this test to check the configuration for the number of subnets to equal 3. It references the subnet_configuration fixture.

Pytest will run this test to check the configuration for the network name to match hello-world-network. It references the network_configuration fixture.

```
def test_configuration_for_subnet_ip_ranges(subnet_configuration):
    for i, subnet in enumerate(subnet_configuration):
        assert subnet[next(iter(subnet))
                ][0]['ip_cidr_range'] == f"10.0.{i}.0/24"
```

**Pytest will check the correct subnet IP range
in the network example configuration. It
references the subnet_configuration fixture.**

AWS and Azure equivalents

To convert listing 6.1 to AWS, use the `aws_subnet` Terraform resource (http://
mng.bz/J2vZ) and retrieve the value for the `cidr_block` attribute.

For Azure, use the `azurerm_subnet` Terraform resource (http://mng.bz/wo05) and
retrieve the value for the `address_prefixes` attribute.

The testing file includes a static network object passed between tests. This *test fixture*
creates a consistent network object that each test can reference. It reduces repetitive
code used to build a test resource.

DEFINITION A *test fixture* is a known configuration used to run a test. It often
reflects known or expected values for a given infrastructure resource. Some of
the fixtures separately parse the network and subnet information. Anytime we
add new tests, we don't have to copy and paste the parsing. Instead, we reference the fixture for the configuration.

You can run pytest at your command line and pass an argument with a test file. Pytest
runs a set of three tests and outputs their success:

```
$ pytest test_network.py
==================== test session starts ====================
collected 3 items

test_network.py ...                                   [100%]

==================== 3 passed in 0.06s ====================
```

In this example, you import the network factory module, create a network object with
configuration, and test it. You don't need to write any configuration to a file. Instead,
you reference the function and test the object.

   This example uses the same approach I take to unit testing application code. It
often results in smaller, more modular functions that you can test more efficiently.
The function that generates the network configuration needs to output the configuration for the test. Otherwise, the tests cannot parse and compare the values.

6.2.2   *Testing domain-specific languages*

How do you test your network and subnet configuration if you use a DSL? You don't have functions that you can call in your test. Instead, your unit tests must parse values out of the configuration or dry-run file. Both types of files store some kind of plaintext metadata about infrastructure resources.

Imagine you use a DSL instead of Python to create your network. This example creates a JSON file with Terraform-compatible configuration. The JSON file contains all three subnetworks, their IP address ranges, and names. In figure 6.7, you decide to run the unit tests against the network's JSON configuration file. The tests run quickly because you do not deploy the networks.

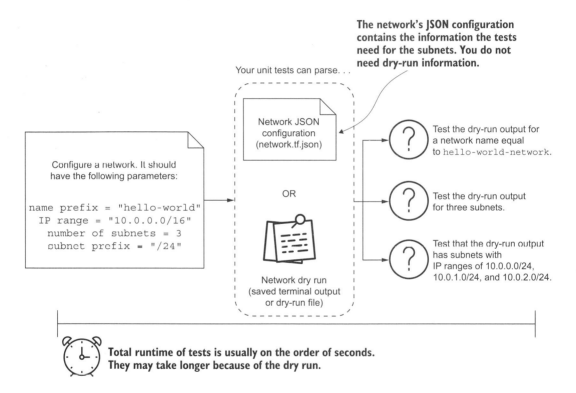

Figure 6.7   Unit tests against dry runs require generating a preview of changes to infrastructure resources and checking it for valid parameters.

In general, you can always unit-test the files you used to define IaC. If a tool uses a configuration file, like CloudFormation, Terraform, Bicep, Ansible, Puppet, Chef, and more, you can unit-test any lines in the configuration.

In listing 6.2, you can test the network name, number of subnets, and subnet IP address ranges for your network module *without* generating a dry run. I run similar tests with pytest to check the same parameters.

Listing 6.2   Using pytest to run unit tests in test_network_configuration.py

Imports Python's JSON library because you will need to load a JSON file

Sets a constant with the expected filename for the network configuration. The tests read the network configuration from network.tf.json.

```python
import json
import pytest

NETWORK_CONFIGURATION_FILE = 'network.tf.json'

expected_network_name = 'hello-world-network'
```

Sets the expected network name to hello-world-network

```python
@pytest.fixture(scope="module")
def configuration():
    with open(NETWORK_CONFIGURATION_FILE, 'r') as f:
        return json.load(f)
```

Opens the JSON file with the network configuration and loads it as a test fixture

```python
@pytest.fixture
def resource():
    def _get_resource(configuration, resource_type):
        for resource in configuration['resource']:
            if resource_type in resource.keys():
                return resource[resource_type]
    return _get_resource
```

Creates a new test fixture that references the loaded JSON configuration and parses for any resource type. It parses the JSON based on Terraform's JSON resource structure.

Gets the google_compute_network Terraform resource out of the JSON file

```python
@pytest.fixture
def network(configuration, resource):
    return resource(configuration, 'google_compute_network')[0]
```

Gets the google_compute_subnetwork Terraform resource out of the JSON file

```python
@pytest.fixture
def subnets(configuration, resource):
    return resource(configuration, 'google_compute_subnetwork')
```

```python
def test_configuration_for_network_name(network):
    assert network[expected_network_name][0]['name'] \
        == expected_network_name
```

Pytest will run this test to check the configuration for the network name to match hello-world-network. It references the network fixture.

```python
def test_configuration_for_three_subnets(subnets):
    assert len(subnets) == 3
```

```python
def test_configuration_for_subnet_ip_ranges(subnets):
    for i, subnet in enumerate(subnets):
        assert subnet[next(iter(subnet))
            ][0]['ip_cidr_range'] == f"10.0.{i}.0/24"
```

Pytest will check for the correct subnet IP range configuration. It references the subnet fixture.

Pytest will run this test to check the configuration for the number of subnets to equal 3. It references the subnet fixture.

> **AWS and Azure equivalents**
>
> To convert listing 6.2 to AWS, use the `aws_subnet` Terraform resource (http://mng.bz/J2vZ) and retrieve the value for the `cidr_block` attribute.
>
> For Azure, use the `azurerm_subnet` Terraform resource (http://mng.bz/wo05) and retrieve the value for the `address_prefixes` attribute.

You might notice that the unit tests for DSLs look similar to those of programming languages. They check the network name, number of subnets, and IP addresses. Some tools have specialized testing frameworks. They usually use the same workflow of generating a dry-run or state file and parsing it for values.

However, your configuration file may not contain everything. For example, you won't have certain configurations in Terraform or Ansible until *after* you do a dry run. A *dry run* previews IaC changes without deploying them and internally identifies and resolves potential problems.

> **DEFINITION** A *dry run* previews IaC changes without deploying them. It internally identifies and resolves potential problems.

Dry runs come in different formats and standards. Most dry runs output to a terminal, and you can save the output to a file. Some tools will automatically generate the dry run to a file.

> **Generating dry runs for unit tests**
>
> Some tools save their dry runs in a file, while others output the changes in a terminal. If you use Terraform, you write the Terraform plan to a JSON file by using the following command:
>
> ```
> $ terraform plan -out=dry_run && terraform show -json dry_run >
> dry_run.json
> ```
>
> AWS CloudFormation offers change sets, and you can parse the change set description after it completes. Similarly, you can get Kubernetes dry-run information with the `kubectl run`'s `--dry-run=client` option.

As a general practice, I prioritize tests that check configuration files. I write tests to parse dry runs when I cannot get the value from configuration files. A dry run typically needs network access to the infrastructure provider API and takes a bit of time to run. On occasion, the output or file contains sensitive information or identifiers that I do not want a test to explicitly parse.

While dry-run configuration may not adhere to the more traditional software development definition of unit tests, the parsing of dry runs does not require any changes to active infrastructure. It remains a form of static analysis. The dry run itself serves as a unit test to validate and output the expected change behavior before applying the change.

6.2.3   *When should you write unit tests?*

Unit tests help you verify that your logic generates the correct names, produces the correct number of infrastructure resources, and calculates the correct IP ranges or other attributes. Some unit tests may overlap with formatting and linting, concepts I mentioned in chapter 2. I classify linting and formatting as part of unit testing because they help you understand how to name and organize your configuration.

Figure 6.8 summarizes some use cases for unit tests. You should write additional unit tests to verify any logic you used to generate infrastructure configuration, especially with loops or conditional (if-else) statements. Unit tests can also capture wrong or problematic configurations, such as the wrong operating system.

Write unit tests to check. . .

Logic for generating configuration, such as conditionals (if-else) or loops (for, while)	**Wrong or problematic configuration**	**Conformance to expected or team standards**
Example: The configuration should have the right number of subnets.	Example: The configuration should have a specific IP address range. Any other range will conflict with another team.	Example: The network name in the configuration should match the team's standard.

Figure 6.8   Write unit tests to verify the resource logic, highlight potential problems, or identify team standards.

Since unit tests check the configuration in isolation, they do not precisely reflect the way a change will affect a system. As a result, you can't expect a unit test to prevent a major failure during production changes. However, you should still write unit tests! While they won't identify problems while running a change, unit tests can *prevent* problematic configurations before production.

For example, someone might accidentally type a configuration for 1,000 servers instead of 10 servers. A test to verify the maximum number of servers in a configuration can prevent someone from overwhelming the infrastructure and manage the cost. Unit tests can also prevent any insecure or noncompliant infrastructure configuration from a production environment. I cover how to apply unit tests to secure and audit infrastructure configuration in chapter 8.

In addition to early identification of wrong configuration values, unit tests help automate checking complex systems. When you have many infrastructure resources managed by different teams, you can no longer manually search through one resource list and check each configuration. Unit tests communicate the most critical or standard configurations to other teams. When you write unit tests for infrastructure modules, you verify that the internal logic of the module produces the expected resources.

Unit testing your automation

Good unit tests require an entire book to describe! I scoped my explanation in this section to testing infrastructure configuration. However, you might write a custom automation tool directly accessing an infrastructure API. Automation uses a more sequential approach to configure a resource step-by-step (also known as the *imperative style*).

You should use unit tests to check the individual steps and their idempotency. Unit tests should run the individual steps with various prerequisites and check that they have the same result. If you need to access an infrastructure API, you can mock the API responses in your unit tests.

Use cases for unit tests include checking that you've created the expected number of infrastructure resources, pinned specific versions of infrastructure, or used the correct naming standard. Unit tests run quickly and offer rapid feedback at virtually zero cost (after you've written them!). They run on the order of seconds because they do not post updates to infrastructure or require the creation of active infrastructure resources. If you write unit tests to check the output of a dry run, you add a bit of time because of the initial time spent generating the dry run.

6.3   *Contract tests*

Unit tests verify configuration or modules in isolation, but what about dependencies between modules? In chapter 4, I mentioned the idea of a contract between dependencies. The output from a module must agree with the expected input to another. You can use tests to enforce that agreement.

For example, let's create a server on a network. The server accesses the network name and IP address by using a facade, which mirrors the name and IP address range of the network. How do you know that the network module outputs the network name and IP CIDR range and not another identifier or configuration?

You use a contract test in figure 6.9 to test that the network module outputs the facade correctly. The facade must contain the network name and IP address range. If the test fails, it shows that the server cannot create itself on the network.

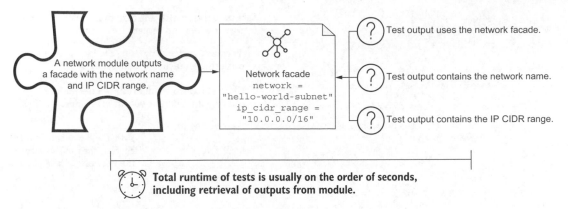

Figure 6.9   **Contract tests can quickly verify that a configuration parameter equals an expected value, such as a network facade with proper outputs.**

A *contract test* uses static analysis to check that module inputs and outputs match an expected value or format.

> **DEFINITION**   *Contract tests* statically analyze and compare module or resource inputs and outputs to match an expected value or format.

Contract tests help enable evolvability of individual modules while preserving the integration between the two. When you have many infrastructure dependencies, you cannot manually check all of their shared attributes. Instead, a contract test automates the verification of the type and value of attributes between modules.

You'll find contract tests most useful for checking inputs and outputs of heavily parameterized modules (such as factory, prototype, or builder patterns). Writing and running contract tests helps detect wrong inputs and outputs and documents the module's minimum resources. When you do not have contract tests for your modules, you won't find out if you broke something in the system until the next time you apply the configuration to a live environment.

Let's implement a contract test for the server and the network in listing 6.3. Using pytest, you set up the test by creating a network with a factory module. Then you verify that the network's output includes a facade object with the network name and IP address range. You add these tests to the server's unit tests.

> **Listing 6.3   Contract test to compare the module outputs with inputs**

```
from network import NetworkFactoryModule, NetworkFacade
import pytest
```
                   Pytest will run this test to check if the network
```
network_name = 'hello-world'        ◁┘ name matches the expected value, hello-world.
network_cidr_range = '10.0.0.0/16'  ◁┐ Pytest will run this test to check that the network
```
                                 output's IP CIDR range matches 10.0.0.0/16.

```
@pytest.fixture
def network_outputs():
    network = NetworkFactoryModule(
        name=network_name,
        ip_range=network_cidr_range)
    return network.outputs()
```

Sets up the test with a fixture that uses a network
factory module and returns its outputs

Creates a network by using the factory module
with the name and IP address range

The test fixture should return a network
facade with different output attributes.

```
def test_network_output_is_facade(network_outputs):
    assert isinstance(network_outputs, NetworkFacade)
```

Pytest will run this test to
check if the module outputs
the network facade object.

```
def test_network_output_has_network_name(network_outputs):
    assert network_outputs._network == f"{network_name}-subnet"

def test_network_output_has_ip_cidr_range(network_outputs):
    assert network_outputs._ip_cidr_range == network_cidr_range
```

Pytest will run this test to check if the network
name matches the expected value, hello-world.

Pytest will run this test to check
that the network output's IP CIDR
range matches 10.0.0.0/16.

Imagine you update the network module to output the network ID instead of the name. That breaks the functionality of the upstream server module because the server expects the network name! Contract testing ensures that you do not break the *contract* (or interface) between two modules when you update either one. Use a contract test to verify your facades and adapters when expressing dependencies between resources.

Why should you add the example contract test to the server, a higher-level resource? Your server *expects* specific outputs from the network. If the network module changes, you want to detect it from the high-level module first.

In general, a high-level module should defer to changes in the low-level module to preserve composability and evolvability. You want to avoid making significant changes to the interface of a low-level module because it may affect other modules that depend on it.

Domain-specific languages

Listing 6.3 uses Python to verify the module outputs. If you use a tool with a DSL, you might be able to use built-in functionality that allows you to validate that inputs adhere to certain types or regular expressions (such as checking for a valid ID or name formatting). If a tool does not have a validation function, you may need to use a separate testing framework to parse the output types from one module's configuration and compare them to the high-level module inputs.

Infrastructure contract tests require some way to extract the expected inputs and outputs, which may involve API calls to infrastructure providers and verifying the responses against expected values for modules. Sometimes this involves creating test resources to examine the parameters and understand how fields like ID should be structured. When you need to make API calls or create temporary resources, your contract tests can run longer than a unit test.

6.4   Integration tests

How do you know that you can apply your configuration or module changes to an infrastructure system? You need to apply the changes to a testing environment and *dynamically analyze* the running infrastructure. An *integration test* runs against test environments to verify successful changes to a module or configuration.

> **DEFINITION**   *Integration tests* run against testing environments and dynamically analyze infrastructure resources to verify that they are affected by module or configuration changes.

Integration tests require an isolated testing environment to verify the integration of modules and resources. In the next sections, you'll learn about the integration tests you can write for infrastructure modules and configurations.

6.4.1   Testing modules

Imagine a module that creates a GCP server. You want to make sure you can create and update the server successfully, so you write an integration test, as shown in figure 6.10.

First, you configure the server and apply the changes to a testing environment. Then, you run integration tests to check that your configuration update succeeds, create a server, and name it `hello-world-test`. The total runtime of the test takes a few minutes because you need to wait for a server to provision.

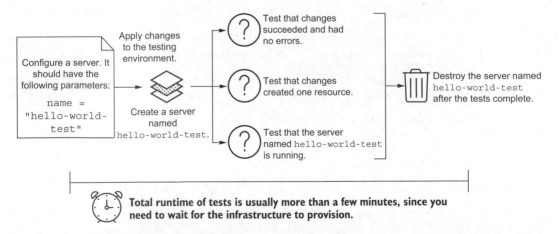

Figure 6.10   Integration tests usually create and update infrastructure resources in a testing environment, test their configuration and status for correctness or availability, and remove them after the tests.

When you implement an integration test, you need to compare the active resource to your IaC. The active resource tells you whether your module deployed successfully. If someone cannot deploy the module, they potentially break their infrastructure.

An integration test must retrieve information about the active resource with the infrastructure provider's API. For example, you can import a Python library to access the GCP API in your server module's integration test. The integration test imports Libcloud, a Python library, as a client SDK for the GCP API.

The test in listing 6.4 builds the server's configuration by using the module, waits for the server to deploy, and checks the server's state in the GCP API. If the server returns a `running` status, the test passes. Otherwise, the test fails and identifies a problem with the module. Finally, the test tears down the test server it created.

Listing 6.4   Integration tests for server creation in test_integration.py

```python
from libcloud.compute.types import NodeState
from main import generate_json, SERVER_CONFIGURATION_FILE
import os
import pytest
import subprocess
import test_utils


TEST_SERVER_NAME = 'hello-world-test'


@pytest.fixture(scope='session')
def apply_changes():
    generate_json(TEST_SERVER_NAME)
    assert os.path.exists(SERVER_CONFIGURATION_FILE)
    assert test_utils.initialize() == 0
    yield test_utils.apply()
    assert test_utils.destroy() == 0
    os.remove(SERVER_CONFIGURATION_FILE)


def test_changes_have_successful_return_code(apply_changes):
    return_code = apply_changes[0]
    assert return_code == 0


def test_changes_should_have_no_errors(apply_changes):
    errors = apply_changes[2]
    assert errors == b''


def test_changes_should_add_1_resource(apply_changes):
    output = apply_changes[1].decode(encoding='utf-8').split('\n')
    assert 'Apply complete! Resources: 1 added, 0 changed, ' + \
        '0 destroyed' in output[-2]
```

Pytest uses Libcloud to call the GCP API and get the server's current state. It checks that the server is running.

During the test session, uses a pytest test fixture to apply the configuration and creates a test server on GCP

Generates a Terraform JSON file that uses the server module

Using Terraform, initializes and deploys the server using the Terraform JSON file

Deletes the test server with Terraform and removes the JSON configuration file at the end of the test session

Pytest will run this test to verify that the output status of the changes has succeeded.

Pytest will run this test to verify that the changes do not return with an error.

Pytest will run this test and check that the configuration adds one resource, the server.

```
def test_server_is_in_running_state(apply_changes):
    gcp_server = test_utils.get_server(TEST_SERVER_NAME)
    assert gcp_server.state == NodeState.RUNNING
```

Pytest uses Libcloud to call the GCP API and get the server's current state. It checks that the server is running.

AWS and Azure equivalents

To convert listing 6.4, you need to update the IaC to create an Amazon EC2 instance or Azure Linux virtual machine. Then you need to update the Apache Libcloud driver to use Amazon EC2 Driver (http://mng.bz/qYex) or Azure ARM Compute Driver (http://mng.bz/7yjQ). The initialization of the driver and IaC will change, but the test does not.

When you run the tests in this file at your command line, you'll notice that it takes a few minutes because the test session creates the server and deletes it:

```
$ pytest test_integration.py
========================== test session starts ==========================
collected 4 items

test_integration.py ....                                         [100%]

==================== 4 passed in 171.31s (0:02:51) ====================
```

The integration tests for the server apply two main practices. First, the tests follow this sequence:

1 Render configuration, if applicable
2 Deploy changes to infrastructure resources
3 Run tests, accessing the infrastructure provider's API for comparison
4 Delete infrastructure resources, if applicable.

This example implements the sequence using a fixture. You can use it to apply any arbitrary infrastructure configuration and remove it after testing.

NOTE Integration tests work very similarly for configuration management tooling. For example, you can install packages and run processes on your server. After running the tests, you can expand the server integration tests by checking the server's packages and processes and destroying the server. Rather than writing the tests using a programming language, I recommend evaluating specialized server testing tooling that logs into the server and runs tests against the system.

Second, you run module integration tests in a separate *module-testing environment* (such as a test account or project) away from testing or production environments supporting applications. To prevent conflicts with other module tests in the environment, you label and name the resources based on the specific module type, version, or commit hash.

> **DEFINITION**   A *module-testing environment* is separate from production and used for testing module changes.

Testing modules in a different environment than a testing or production environment helps isolate failed modules from an active environment with applications. You can also measure and control your infrastructure cost from testing modules. Chapter 12 covers the cost of cloud computing in greater detail.

6.4.2 *Testing configuration for environments*

Integration tests for infrastructure modules can create and delete resources in a testing environment, but integration tests for environment configurations cannot. Imagine you need to add an A record to your current domain name configured by a composite or singleton configuration. How do you write integration tests to check that you added the record correctly?

You encounter two problems. First, you cannot simply create and then destroy DNS records as part of your integration tests because it may affect applications. Second, the A record depends on a server IP address to exist before you can configure the domain.

Instead of creating and destroying the server and A record in a testing environment, you run the integration tests against a *persistent* testing environment that matches production. In figure 6.11, you update the DNS record in IaC for the testing environment. Your integration tests check that the DNS in the testing environment matches the expected correct DNS record. After the test passes, you can update the DNS record for production.

Why run the DNS test in a *persistent* testing environment? First, it can take a long time to create a testing environment. As a high-level resource, DNS depends on many

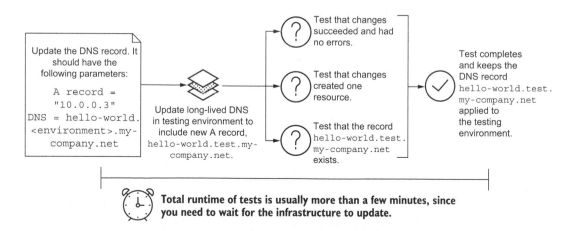

Figure 6.11   You can run integration tests against a testing environment with long-lived resources to isolate the changes from production and reduce the dependencies you need to create for the test.

low-level ones. Second, you want an accurate representation of how the change behaves before you update production.

The testing environment captures a subset of dependencies and complexities of the production system so you can check that your configuration works as expected. Keeping similar testing and production environments means that a change in testing provides an accurate perspective of its behavior in production. You want to aim for early detection of problems in the testing environment.

6.4.3 Testing challenges

Without the integration tests, you would not know whether a server module or DNS record updates successfully until you manually check it. They expedite the process of verifying that your IaC works. However, you will encounter a few challenges with integration testing.

You might have difficulty determining which configuration parameters to test. Should you write integration tests to verify that every configuration parameter you've configured in IaC matches the live resource? Not necessarily!

Most tools already have *acceptance tests* that create a resource, update its configuration, and destroy the resource. Acceptance tests certify that the tool can release new code changes. These tests must pass in order for the tool to support changes to infrastructure.

You don't want to spend additional time or effort writing tests that match the acceptance tests. As a result, your integration tests should cover whether *multiple* resources have the correct configuration and dependencies. If you write custom automation, you will need to write integration tests to create, update, and delete resources.

Another challenge involves deciding whether you should create or delete resources during each test or run a persistent testing environment. Figure 6.12 shows a decision tree for whether to create, delete, or use a persistent testing environment for an integration test.

In general, if a configuration or module does not have too many dependencies, you can create, test, and delete it. However, if your configuration or module takes time to create or requires the existence of many other resources, you will need to use a persistent testing environment.

Not all modules benefit from a create-and-delete approach in integration testing. I recommend running integration tests for low-level modules, such as networks or DNS, and avoid removing the resources. These modules usually require in-place updates in environments with a minimal financial cost. I often find it more realistic to test the update instead of creating and deleting the resource.

Resources created by integration tests for mid-level modules, such as workload orchestrators, may be persistent or temporary depending on the size of the module and resource. The larger the module, the more likely it will need to be long-lived. You can run integration tests for high-level modules, such as application deployments or SaaS, and create and delete the resources each time.

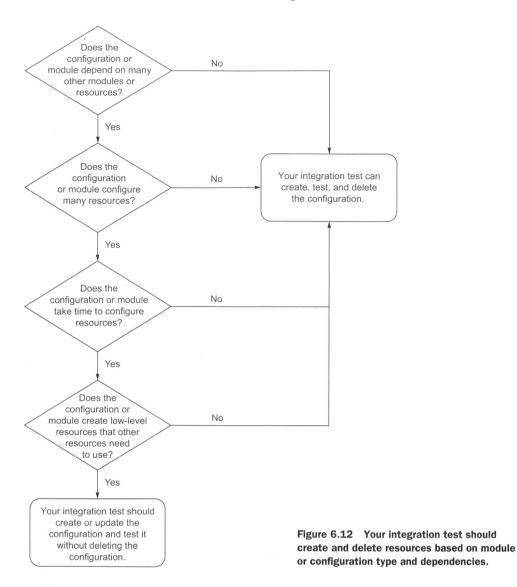

Figure 6.12   Your integration test should create and delete resources based on module or configuration type and dependencies.

A persistent testing environment does have its limits. Integration tests tend to take a long time to run because creating or updating resources takes time. As a rule, keep modules smaller with fewer resources. This practice reduces the amount of time you need for a module integration test.

Even if you keep configurations and modules small with few resources, integration tests often become the culprit of your infrastructure provider bill's increasing cost. A number of tests need long-lived resources like networks, gateways, and more. Weigh the cost of running an integration test and catching problems against the cost of misconfiguration or a broken infrastructure resource.

You may consider using infrastructure mocks to lower the cost of running an integration test (or any test). Some frameworks replicate an infrastructure provider's APIs for local testing. I do not recommend relying heavily on mocks. Infrastructure providers change APIs frequently and often have complex errors and behaviors, which mocks do not often capture. In chapter 12, I discuss techniques to manage the cost of testing environments and avoid mocks.

6.5   End-to-end tests

While integration tests dynamically analyze configuration and catch errors during resource creation or update, they do not indicate whether an infrastructure resource is *usable*. Usability requires that you or a team member use the resource as intended.

For example, you might use a module to create an application, called a *service*, on GCP Cloud Run. GCP Cloud Run deploys any service in a container and returns a URL endpoint. Your integration tests pass, indicating that your module correctly creates the service resource and permissions to access the service.

How do you know whether someone can access the application URL? Figure 6.13 shows how to check that the service endpoint works. First, you write a test to retrieve the application URL as an output from your infrastructure configuration. Then, you make an HTTP request to the URL. The total run time takes a few minutes, most of it from creating the service.

You've created a test for dynamic analysis that differs from an integration test called an *end-to-end test*. It verifies the end-user functionality of the infrastructure.

> **DEFINITION**   *End-to-end tests* dynamically analyze infrastructure resources and end-to-end system functionality to verify that they are affected by IaC changes.

The example end-to-end test verifies the end-to-end workflow of the end user accessing the page. It does *not* check for the successful configuration of infrastructure.

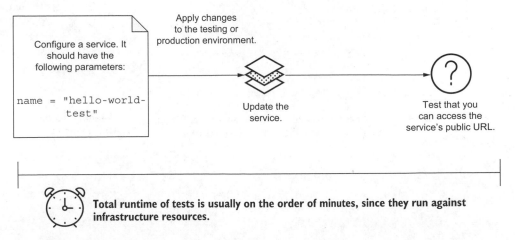

Figure 6.13   End-to-end tests verify the end user's workflow by accessing the web page at the application's URL.

End-to-end tests become vital for ensuring that your changes don't break upstream functionality. For example, you might accidentally update a configuration that allows authenticated users to access the GCP Cloud Run service URL. Your end-to-end test fails after applying the change, indicating that someone may no longer access the service.

Let's implement an end-to-end test for the application URL in Python in the following listing. The test for this example needs to make an API request to the service's public URL. It uses a pytest fixture to create the GCP Cloud Run service, test the URL for the running page, and delete the service from a testing environment.

Listing 6.5   End-to-end test for GCP Cloud Run service

```
from main import generate_json, SERVICE_CONFIGURATION_FILE
import os
import pytest
import requests
import test_utils

TEST_SERVICE_NAME = 'hello-world-test'


@pytest.fixture(scope='session')
def apply_changes():
    generate_json(TEST_SERVICE_NAME)
    assert os.path.exists(SERVICE_CONFIGURATION_FILE)
    assert test_utils.initialize() == 0
    yield test_utils.apply()
    assert test_utils.destroy() == 0
    os.remove(SERVICE_CONFIGURATION_FILE)


@pytest.fixture
def url():
    output, error = test_utils.output('url')
    assert error == b''
    service_url = output.decode(encoding='utf-8').split('\n')[0]
    return service_url


def test_url_for_service_returns_running_page(apply_changes, url):
    response = requests.get(url)
    assert "It's running!" in response.text
```

During the test session, uses a pytest test fixture to apply the configuration and create a test service on GCP

Using Terraform, initializes and deploys the service using the Terraform JSON file

Generates a Terraform JSON file that uses the GCP Cloud Run module

Destroys the GCP Cloud Run service in the testing environment, so you do not have a persistent service in your GCP project

Uses a pytest fixture to parse the output of the configuration for the service's URL

In the test, checks the service's URL response containing a specific string to indicate the service is running

In the test, makes an API request to the service's URL using Python's requests library

AWS and Azure equivalents

AWS Fargate with Amazon Elastic Kubernetes Service (EKS) or Azure Container Instances (ACI) roughly equates to GCP Cloud Run.

Note that if you want to run an end-to-end test in production, you do not want to delete the service. You usually run end-to-end tests against existing environments without creating new or test resources. You apply changes to the existing system and run the tests against the active infrastructure resources.

> **Smoke tests**
>
> As a type of end-to-end test, a *smoke test* provides rapid feedback on whether a change has broken critical business functionality. Running all end-to-end tests can take time, and you need to fix a change failure quickly.
>
> If you can run a smoke test first, you can verify that the change has not gone catastrophically and proceed with further testing. As a quality assurance analyst once told me, "If you power up some hardware and it smokes, you know something is wrong. It's not worth your time to test it further."

More complex infrastructure systems benefit from end-to-end tests because they become the primary indicator of whether a change has affected critical business functionality. As a result, they help test composite or singleton configurations. You do not usually run end-to-end tests on modules unless they have many resources and dependencies.

I write most of my end-to-end tests for network or compute resources. For example, you can write a few tests to check network peering. The tests provision a server on each network and check whether the servers can connect.

Another use case for end-to-end tests involves submitting a job to a workload orchestrator and completing it. This test determines whether the workload orchestrator functions properly for application deployment. I once included end-to-end tests that issued Hypertext Transfer Protocol (HTTP) requests with varying payloads to ensure that upstream services could call each other without disruption, no matter the payload size or protocol.

Outside of network or compute use cases, end-to-end tests can verify the expected behavior of any system. If you use configuration management with a provisioning tool, your end-to-end tests verify that you can connect to the server and run the expected functionality. For monitoring and alerts, you can run end-to-end tests to simulate the expected system behavior, verify that metrics have been collected, and test the triggering of the alert.

However, end-to-end tests are the most expensive tests to execute in terms of time and resources. Most end-to-end tests need every infrastructure resource available to fully evaluate the system. As a result, you may run end-to-end tests only against production infrastructure. You may not run them in a testing environment because it often costs too much money to procure enough resources for the test.

6.6 *Other tests*

You may encounter other types of tests outside of unit, contract, integration, and end-to-end tests. For example, say you want to roll out a configuration change to a production server that reduces memory. However, you don't know whether the memory reduction will affect the overall system.

Figure 6.14 shows that you can check whether your change affected the system by using system monitoring. Monitoring continuously aggregates metrics on the server's memory. If you receive an alert that the server's memory reaches a percentage of its capacity, you know that you may affect the overall system.

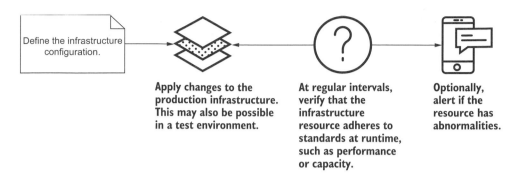

Define the infrastructure configuration.

Apply changes to the production infrastructure. This may also be possible in a test environment.

At regular intervals, verify that the infrastructure resource adheres to standards at runtime, such as performance or capacity.

Optionally, alert if the resource has abnormalities.

Figure 6.14   Continuous tests run at short intervals to verify that a set of metrics does not exceed a threshold.

Monitoring implements *continuous testing* with "tests" to check that metrics do not exceed thresholds run at regular, frequent intervals.

> **DEFINITION**   *Continuous tests* (such as monitoring) run at regular, frequent intervals to check that the current value matches an expected value.

Continuous testing includes monitoring system metrics and security events (when the root user logs into a server). They offer dynamic analysis on an active infrastructure environment. Most continuous tests take the form of alerts, which notify you of any problems.

You may encounter another type of test called a *regression test*. For example, you may run a test over a period of time to check whether your server configuration conforms to your organization's expectations. Regression tests run regularly but do not have the frequency of monitoring or other forms of continuous testing. You may choose to run them every few weeks or months to check for out-of-band, manual changes.

> **DEFINITION**   *Regression tests* run periodically over an extended period of time to check whether infrastructure configuration conforms to the expected state or functionality. They can help mitigate configuration drift.

Continuous and regression tests often require special software or systems to run. They ensure that running infrastructure behaves with expected functionality and performance. These tests also set a foundation for automating a system to respond to anomalies.

For example, systems configured with IaC and continuous tests can use autoscaling to adjust resources based on the metrics such as CPU or memory. These systems can also implement other self-healing mechanisms, such as diverting traffic to an older version of an application upon errors.

6.7 Choosing tests

I explained some of the most common tests in infrastructure, from unit tests to end-to-end tests. However, do you need to write all of them? Where should you spend your time and effort in writing them? Your *infrastructure testing strategy* will evolve, depending on the complexity and growth of your system. As a result, you will constantly be assessing which tests will help you catch configuration issues before production.

I use a pyramid shape as a *guideline* for infrastructure testing strategy. In figure 6.15, the widest part of the pyramid indicates you should have more of that type of test, while the narrowest part indicates that you should have fewer. At the top of the pyramid are end-to-end tests, which may cost more time and money because they require active infrastructure systems. At the bottom of the pyramid are unit tests, which run in seconds and do not require entire infrastructure systems.

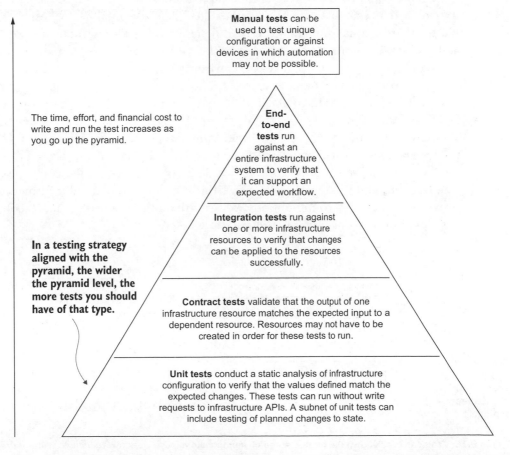

Figure 6.15 Based on the test pyramid, you should have more unit tests than end-to-end tests because it costs less time, money, and resources to run them.

This guideline, called the *test pyramid*, provides a framework for different types of tests, their scope, and frequency. I adapted the test pyramid from software testing to infrastructure, modifying it to infrastructure tools and constraints.

> **DEFINITION**   The *test pyramid* serves as a guideline for your overall testing strategy. As you go up the pyramid, the type of test will cost more time and money.

In reality, your test pyramid may be shaped more like a rectangle or pear, sometimes with missing levels. You *will not* and *should not* write every type of test for every infrastructure configuration. At some point, the tests become redundant and impractical to maintain.

Depending on the system you want to test, it may not be practical to adhere to the test pyramid in its ideal. However, avoid what I jokingly call the *test signpost*. A signpost favors many manual tests and not much of anything else.

6.7.1   *Module-testing strategy*

I alluded to the practice of testing modules before releasing them in chapter 5. Let's return to that example, where you updated a database module to PostgreSQL 12. Rather than manually creating the module and testing to see whether it works, you add a series of automated tests. They check for the module's formatting and create a database in an isolated module-testing environment.

Figure 6.16 updates the module release workflow with the unit, contract, and integration tests you can add to check that your module works. After the contract tests pass, you run an integration test that sets up the database module on a network and checks whether the database runs. After completing the integration test, you delete the test database created by the module and release the module.

A combination of unit, contract, and integration tests adequately represents whether a module will work correctly. Unit tests check for module formatting and your team's standard configurations. You run them first, so you get fast feedback on any violations in formatting or configurations.

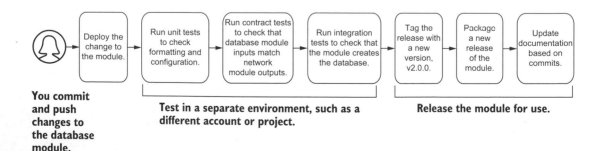

Figure 6.16   You can break down the testing stage of your module release workflow to include unit, contract, and integration tests.

Next, you run a few contract tests. In the case of the database module, you check whether the network ID input to the database module matches the output of the network ID from the network module. Catching these mistakes will identify problems between dependencies earlier in your deployment process.

Focus on unit or contract testing to enforce proper configuration, correct module logic, and specific inputs and outputs. The testing workflow outlined in figure 6.16 works best for modules that use the factory, builder, or prototype patterns. These patterns isolate the smallest subset of infrastructure components and provide a flexible set of variables for your teammates to customize.

Depending on the cost of your development environment, you can write a few integration tests to run against temporary infrastructure resources, which you delete at the end of the test. By investing some time and effort into writing tests for modules with many inputs and outputs, you ensure that changes do not affect upstream configuration and that the module can run successfully on its own.

Exercise 6.1

You notice that a new version of a load balancer module is breaking your DNS configuration. A teammate updated the module to output private IP addresses instead of public IP addresses. What can you do to help your team better remember that the module needs public IP addresses?

    A Create a separate load balancer module for private IP addresses.

    B Add module contract tests to verify that the module outputs both private and public IP addresses.

    C Update the module's documentation with a note that it needs public IP addresses.

    D Run integration tests on the module and check that the IP address is publicly accessible.

See appendix B for answers to exercises.

6.7.2 *Configuration testing strategy*

Infrastructure configurations for active environments use more complex patterns like singleton or composite. A singleton or composite configuration has many infrastructure dependencies and often references other modules. Adding end-to-end tests to your testing workflow can help identify issues between the infrastructure and modules.

Imagine you have a singleton configuration with an application server on a network. Figure 6.17 outlines each step after you update the size of the server. After pushing the change to version control, you deploy the change to a testing environment. Your testing workflow begins with unit tests to verify formatting and configuration quickly.

Next, you run integration tests to apply changes and verify that the server still runs and has a new size. You complete your verification by using an end-to-end test to test the entire system. The end-to-end test issues an HTTP GET to the application endpoint. Figure 6.17 repeats the process in production to ensure that the system did not break.

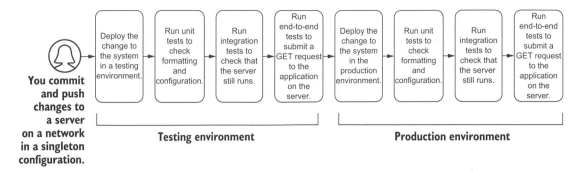

Figure 6.17   IaC using the singleton and composite patterns should run unit, integration, and end-to-end tests in a testing environment before deploying the changes to production.

Just because you created or updated a server successfully does not mean the application it hosts can serve requests! With a complex infrastructure system, you need additional tests to verify dependencies or communication between infrastructure. End-to-end tests can help preserve the functionality of the system.

Repeating the same tests between testing and production environments offers quality control. If you have any configuration drift between testing and production environments, your tests may reflect those differences. You can enable or disable specific tests depending on the environment.

Image building and configuration management

Tests for image building and configuration management tools follow a similar approach to testing the configuration for provisioning tools. Unit testing image building or configuration management metadata involves checking configuration. You do not need contract tests unless you modularize your configuration management, in which you follow the testing approach for modules. Integration tests should run in a testing environment, either to test that the server successfully starts with a new image or applies the correct configuration. End-to-end tests ensure that your new images and configurations do not impact the functionality of the system.

Exercise 6.2

You add firewall rules to allow an application to access a new queue. Which combination of tests would be most valuable to your team for the change?

- A Unit and integration tests
- B Contract and end-to-end tests
- C Contract and integration tests
- D Unit and end-to-end tests

See appendix B for answers to exercises.

6.7.3 Identifying useful tests

The testing strategies for modules and configurations can help guide your initial approach to writing valuable tests. Figure 6.18 summarizes the types of tests you might consider for modules and configurations. Modules rely on unit, contract, and integration tests, while configurations rely on unit, integration, and end-to-end tests.

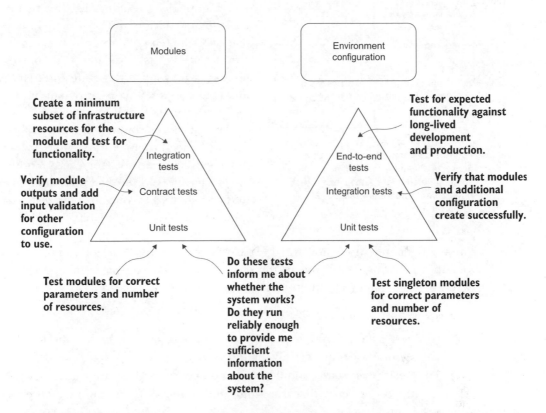

Figure 6.18 Your testing approach will differ depending on whether you write a module or environment configuration.

How do you know *when* to write a test? Imagine your teammate might know that a database password needs to have alphanumeric characters with a 16-character limit. However, you might not know this fact until you update a 24-character password, deploy the change, and wait five minutes for the change to fail.

I consider the practice of updating your tests a matter of turning unknown knowns into known knowns in your system. After all, you use observability to debug unknown unknowns and monitoring to track the known unknowns. In figure 6.19, you convert siloed knowledge (unknown knowns) that someone else knows into tests (known knowns) for team knowledge. New tests often reflect siloed knowledge that the team should know and acknowledge.

**Convert siloed knowledge
to valuable tests.**

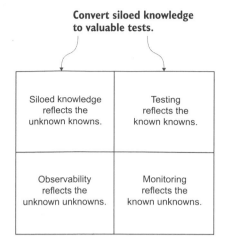

Figure 6.19 **Infrastructure testing
converts siloed knowledge, something
someone else might know, into a test to
reflect the team's knowledge.**

A good test shares knowledge to the rest of the team. You don't always need to build a new test. Instead, you might find an existing test that doesn't check for everything. Use a test to prevent your team from repeating problems.

Besides adding tests, you'll remove tests. You might write a test and discover that it fails half the time. It does not provide helpful information or increase your confidence in the system because of its unreliability. Removing the test cleans up your testing suite and helps eliminate flaky tests that constantly fail but do not indicate a true failure in the system.

Furthermore, you'll remove tests because you don't need them. For example, you might not need contract tests for every module, or integration tests for every environment configuration. Always ask yourself if the tests provide value and if they run reliably enough for you to get sufficient information about the system.

The next chapter shows how to add tests to a delivery pipeline for your IaC. Even if you do not choose to automate the testing workflow, you have an opportunity to examine how changes could potentially affect your infrastructure.

Summary

- The test pyramid outlines an approach to testing. The higher the test level in the pyramid, the more costly the test.
- Unit tests verify static parameters in modules or configurations.
- Contract tests verify that the inputs and outputs of a module match expected values and formats.
- Integration tests create test resources, verify their configuration and creation, and delete them.
- End-to-end tests verify that the end user of an infrastructure system can run the expected functionality.
- Modules using factory, builder, or prototype patterns benefit from unit, contract, and integration tests.
- Configurations using composite or singleton patterns applied to environments benefit from unit, integration, and end-to-end tests.
- Other tests include monitoring for continuously testing system metrics, regression tests for out-of-band manual changes, or security tests for misconfigurations.

Continuous delivery and branching models

This chapter covers

- Designing delivery pipelines to avoid pushing failures to production systems
- Choosing a branching model for infrastructure configuration for team collaboration
- Reviewing and managing changes to infrastructure resources within your team

In the previous chapters, you learned how to write patterns for modules and dependencies. You also applied some general practices for writing infrastructure as code and sharing modules. The patterns, practices, and workflows had a lot of steps.

Furthermore, many of the workflows require careful coordination of changes. One day, you might try to make a change only to find out that your teammate's updates might overwrite yours! How do you make sure you manage conflicts during the development process?

One solution involves submitting change requests to a ticketing system. For example, if you want to change a server, you'd need to fill out a change request in your ticketing system. This change request then gets reviewed by your peers (usually your team) and the change advisory board (on behalf of the company).

Most companies use this process, called *change management*, to figure out which changes conflict. Infrastructure change management involves submitting a change request detailing rollout and rollback steps for peer reviewers' approval.

> DEFINITION   *Change management* for infrastructure is a process that facilitates a change to a system. It often involves detailing and reviewing the change across a company before approving it for production.

Change management depends on peer review to prevent changes from overwriting each other. The peer review and change advisory board in the example serve as quality gates. *Quality gates* verify that the change request does not compromise a system's security or availability. Once your change passes the gates, you can schedule it and update the server accordingly.

> DEFINITION   *Quality gates* for IaC enforce a system's security, availability, and resiliency through review or tests.

How do change management and quality gates help solve conflicts between changes? Imagine you applied the change management process to your and your teammate's conflicting changes. In figure 7.1, you and your teammate submit change requests to the ticketing system. Peers across the organization manually review each change and determine that your teammate's change has a minimal impact on users. They reschedule your change for another day to avoid conflict with your teammate's change.

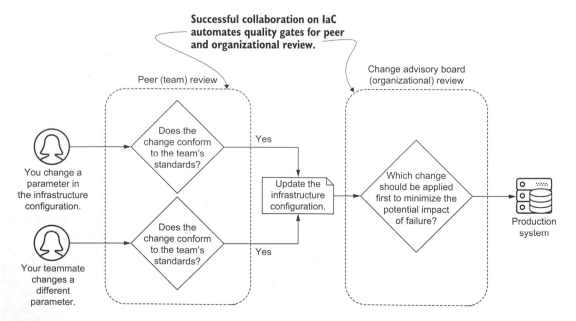

Figure 7.1   Collaboration on IaC involves streamlining the process of peer and organizational review of changes.

Change management can take weeks to complete. Manual review doesn't catch every problem or prevent every infrastructure change conflict. You still need to understand how to revert changes. You'll learn about fixing change failures in chapter 11.

Rather than rely on change management, you can use IaC to *communicate* changes through code and *automate* change management. This chapter focuses on streamlining change management by scaling and automating IaC development processes across your team and company. You'll face the challenge of people working on the same or dependent resources while trying not to break a production system.

Image building and configuration management

Throughout this book, I focus on the use case of provisioning infrastructure. Use cases for image building and configuration management should follow the general pattern for delivery pipelines in this chapter. The patterns and practices to assess infrastructure changes and incorporate automated testing remain consistent for all use cases.

7.1   Delivering changes to production

How do you control IaC changes to a production environment? You apply software development practices like continuous integration, delivery, or deployment (CI/CD) to organize code changes from various collaborators and prepare to release IaC to a production environment.

CI/CD requires automated testing to automate the release and management of changes. I'll explain how you can automate infrastructure changes and make the most of its benefits. It uses the testing practices you learned from the preceding chapter with the delivery pipeline patterns in this chapter.

7.1.1   Continuous integration

Recall the IaC conflict you ran into with your teammate. You did not know your teammate's change would affect yours, and vice versa. How do you automatically identify the conflicts before your peers review your change?

One solution in figure 7.2 involves asking your team to regularly merge its changes into the main IaC. If your team continuously *integrates* its changes into the main configuration, you and your teammate can identify the conflicts earlier, before they overwrite your updates.

You can apply the practice of *continuous integration* (*CI*) to merge your changes into the main configuration multiple times a day and check whether they conflict with collaborators.

> **DEFINITION**   *Continuous integration* (*CI*) for IaC is a practice of regularly and frequently merging changes into your repository after verifying the change in a testing environment.

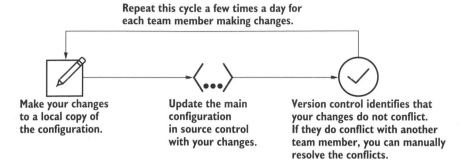

Figure 7.2   Continuous integration involves merging changes to the main configuration often, allowing earlier identification of conflicts in changes.

How often should you merge? Knowing when to merge requires a bit of experience and depends on the type of change you want to make. As a general rule, I merge when I accumulate a few lines of configuration change that (likely) will not break the system. Sometimes, this means I merge several times a day. Other times, for a difficult change, I might merge once or twice a day. The rest of the team also continues to work on and merge their changes a few times a day.

Each time a team member merges their changes, a build tool (such as a CI framework) should start a workflow to test the changes and deploy them. Figure 7.3 shows an example workflow that a build tool might run. The workflow checks IaC for merge conflicts, runs unit tests to verify formatting, and pauses for peer review. Once it passes peer review, the build tool deploys the changes to production.

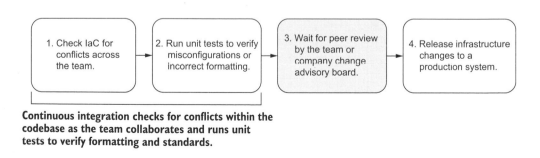

Figure 7.3   CI in a delivery pipeline includes automated unit tests before waiting for manual approval to production.

You can express this workflow as part of a *delivery pipeline*. A pipeline organizes and automates a set of stages to build, test, deploy, and release your IaC.

> **DEFINITION** A *delivery pipeline* for IaC expresses and automates a workflow to build, test, deploy, and release a change to infrastructure.

An infrastructure delivery pipeline starts by checking configuration conflicts or syntax problems. Unit testing in a CI pipeline offers you some confidence that you don't have change conflicts. You can then submit the change to your team or company for review. The pipeline automatically releases (or applies) it to production.

Why should you design a delivery pipeline and add it to your build tool? You might not remember all the steps you need to release a change to production. A delivery pipeline codifies the process so you don't have to remember it. Agreeing on a delivery pipeline for infrastructure helps you scale infrastructure changes consistently and reproducibly, no matter the infrastructure resource.

7.1.2   Continuous delivery

You used CI to merge changes and check for conflicts, but how do you know if the system functions as you expect? CI validates formatting and standards, but you don't know if the configuration works until release. You have some confidence in your unit test, but you need more tests to feel comfortable with the updates.

Figure 7.4 reimagines the CI workflow you started for IaC. You update your delivery pipeline with extra stages after unit tests. Before you submit the change for peer review, you deploy the configuration to a testing environment and test it with integration and end-to-end tests. After peer review, you *deliver* the changes to production and rerun the end-to-end tests to verify production functionality.

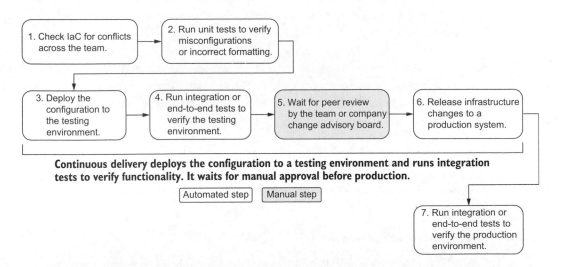

Figure 7.4   Continuous delivery automatically deploys and runs infrastructure changes in a testing environment and waits for manual approval for production.

You expanded your delivery pipeline with the practice of *continuous delivery* (*CD*). CD adds a step to your delivery pipeline that deploys your infrastructure configuration to a testing environment for integration or end-to-end testing after passing unit tests.

> **DEFINITION** *Continuous delivery* (*CD*) for IaC deploys your infrastructure change to a testing environment for integration or end-to-end testing after merging your changes to a repository. It can involve a manual quality gate before releasing the changes to production.

Whenever someone pushes a change to source control, it starts the pipeline's workflow to verify the changes in a testing environment. Once the integration and end-to-end tests pass, the pipeline can wait for manual approval before deploying the changes to production.

Why use CD over CI? CD incorporates all of the automated tests you worked hard to write in chapter 6. Furthermore, its delivery pipeline includes *tests as quality gates*. A teammate reviewing your change might feel more confident about whether the tests verify the change implementation.

> **NOTE** Continuous delivery requires an entire book! I've applied it directly to infrastructure and tried to cover it in one section. If you want to review a more practical example, I created an example pipeline at http://mng.bz/mOy8. The pipeline uses GitHub Actions to deploy the hello-world service to Google Cloud Run. Its stages include unit tests, testing environment deployment, and integration tests.

CD should involve small and frequent changes to code. You push these changes automatically to a testing environment and wait for manual approval before pushing them to production. However, changes waiting for manual approval accumulate like a traffic jam. A few cars that slow down can cascade to many cars, ultimately affecting your expected arrival time!

A manual approval step builds a batch of changes, which introduces some problems. When you push a large batch of changes into production in figure 7.5, you wait for the system to process and deploy the changes. Unfortunately, you also introduce an unintended failure because some changes conflict. Your team spends days tracking down which combination of changes caused the failure.

When you use CD, approve changes as quickly as possible. Implement a shorter feedback cycle for manual approval. You can also limit how many changes you approve at once. Both solutions mitigate some of the risk introduced by manual approval. I'll cover another solution in the next section that entirely omits the manual approval process.

7.1.3 *Continuous deployment*

Can you prevent large batches of changes by eliminating manual stages in your delivery pipeline? You can! However, you must practice CI/CD before removing manual approval.

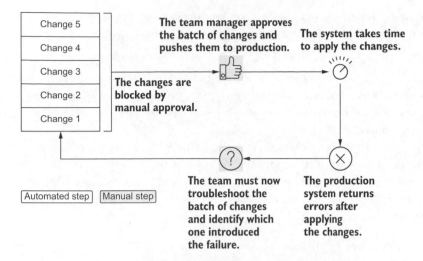

Figure 7.5   Avoid pushing large batches of changes to production whenever you introduce a manual approval to prevent complex troubleshooting.

Removing manual approval from your pipeline means you must have confidence in your *testing*. The pipeline in figure 7.6 adds more integration and end-to-end tests to verify the system and automatically pushes the changes to production. You feel confident that your tests sufficiently check system functionality *and* you can easily revert changes. You remove the manual approval and promote changes immediately to a production environment.

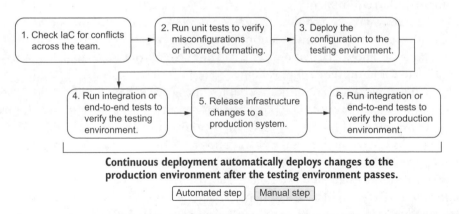

Figure 7.6   Continuous deployment fully automates the testing and applying of changes to production.

Continuous deployment removes the manual approval step and promotes changes directly from a testing environment into production.

> **DEFINITION**   *Continuous deployment* for IaC deploys and tests your infrastructure change to a testing environment and automatically promotes the change to production when the tests pass.

Automatic deployment prevents a traffic jam of changes. Pushing infrastructure changes often takes hours and affects unknown dependencies. You can use continuous deployment for infrastructure if you have a thorough testing strategy and familiarity in fixing failures.

Using the techniques in chapter 11 to fix failures can help you practice continuous deployment. However, most organizations do not fully embrace continuous deployment for their infrastructure because they do not feel confident in testing or reverting changes. Investing time and practice in these patterns can help you move closer to a continuous deployment model.

7.1.4   *Choosing a delivery approach*

Continuous delivery and deployment create a workflow to test and deliver IaC to a production environment. However, you cannot expect your organization to feel comfortable automating all changes directly to production! I recommend applying a combination of continuous delivery and deployment to infrastructure change management. First, you must categorize the type of changes you implement before choosing a delivery approach.

TYPES OF INFRASTRUCTURE CHANGE

The type of change affects how you deliver it to production. You need to work with your organization's change review board to classify the type of change and automate the testing and review for each one. Otherwise, you may find yourself noncompliant with an audit requirement.

Imagine you make a routine change every week to a server. You update the server's IaC with a new tag. The automation never changes and does not fail often. When it does fail, you know exactly how to fix it. The server's routine change becomes a good candidate for continuous deployment.

In figure 7.7, you continuously deploy the server change directly to production without manual approval. The pipeline replaces a manual approval step after the testing environment with a test to check for a prefix in the commit message. Your server change has the commit message of a `standard` change, so the pipeline bypasses manual approval.

You routinely make *standard changes* to your infrastructure. Examples of standard changes include upgrading container images in an orchestrator, deploying a new queue, or adding a new alert into your monitoring system. If the change fails, you can reference a runbook to roll back the change without impacting anything.

> **DEFINITION**   A *standard change* to infrastructure is a commonly implemented change with well-defined behavior and a rollback plan.

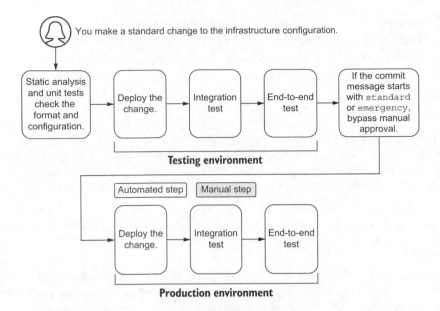

Figure 7.7   A standard or emergency change can have an initial peer review before your delivery pipeline automatically pushes it to production.

Why should you consider continuous deployment for standard changes? A standard change often involves a commonly automated, well-defined fix. You don't want your team members pausing to review and approve a repetitive change. The standard change distracts them from more important changes.

Other types of changes benefit from continuous deployment. Imagine you discover that an application on a server stopped running. You need the application up and running again quickly. Rather than run a standard change, you implement the fix in IaC and update its commit message with `emergency`. After pushing the change, your build system bypasses the manual approval stage because the commit message identifies the change as an emergency.

Besides continuously delivering standard changes, you can opt to continuously deliver *emergency changes* for emergency scenarios to fix production. When possible, push fixes by using IaC and the commit message to identify the emergency change.

> **DEFINITION**   An *emergency change* to infrastructure is a change that you must quickly implement in production to fix system functionality.

Emergency changes go directly to production without manual approval because you often need to fix the system quickly. A manual approval may hinder the resolution of a problem. As a result, adding a bypass for emergency changes helps you quickly resolve the problem and record your resolution history.

To continuously deploy standard and emergency changes, you *must* have automated testing in your pipeline before adding the ability to bypass the manual approval step. Furthermore, you need to standardize the bypass commit message structure. A bypass allows engineers to deploy fixes without a backlog of changes. It also allows compliance and security teams to audit the sequence of changes.

Can't I just run an emergency change manually?

I highly recommend you use IaC and your delivery pipeline to make emergency changes. The commits record a history of your resolution steps, and your pipeline tests your changes before you run automation that makes the system worse.

However, you might find the deployment pipeline can take too long to run when you're trying to push out a fix quickly. You may consider making a manual change, recognizing that you may not benefit from the automated tests and checks addressed by the pipeline.

After you make a manual change, reconcile the actual infrastructure state with the expected IaC. The practice of reconciliation involves manually updating the configuration to match the infrastructure resource (review this technique in chapter 2).

Other changes should not use continuous deployment. Imagine you've been assigned a new project. You need to enable IPv6 on all networks. By making this networking change, you could affect every application and system in the network!

For this new and major change, you *do not* want to skip manual approval. You want skilled network engineers reviewing your IaC. In figure 7.8, you update your networks' IaC with IPv6 and wait for manual approval before production. The manual approval

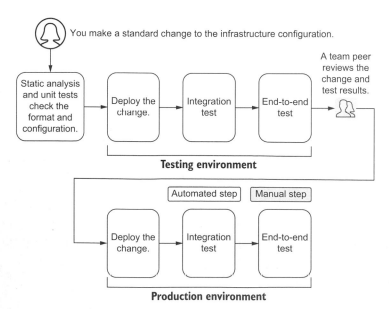

Figure 7.8 New or major changes should have manual peer approval before applying to production.

step communicates to the other application and engineering teams that your changes may have a large blast radius if they fail.

New or major changes can affect a system's architecture, security, or availability. These changes should require filing an issue or ticket with some justification and discussion. They also involve a manual change review from your peers in the team or company.

> **DEFINITION** A *new or major change* to infrastructure potentially affects a system's architecture, security, or availability. These changes do not have well-defined implementation or rollback plans.

Major changes have the potential for significant impact or a high risk of failure. Similarly, new or unknown changes can cause unpredictable results and complex rollback steps. Asking for manual approval signals that you may need some help if the changes fail. Other examples of new or major changes often include updates to network CIDR blocks (if they affect other allocations), DNS, certificate changes, upgrades to workload orchestrators, or platform refactoring (such as adding a secrets manager to applications).

DELIVERY APPROACH BASED ON CHANGE TYPE

After categorizing the changes you make and their types, you can decide on your delivery approach. For the most part, standard and emergency changes use continuous deployment, while new and major changes use CD.

Table 7.1 outlines some of the types of changes, their delivery approach, and an example. However, these general practices have exceptions. Some standard changes may require CD because they impact other resources. By contrast, changes related to greenfield (new) environments could implement a continuous deployment approach because it does not impact other systems.

Table 7.1 Types of changes and delivery approach

Type of change	Delivery approach	Manual approval before production?	Example
Standard	Continuous deployment	No	Adding servers to a scaling group
Emergency	Continuous deployment or manual change	No	Rolling back an operating system image to a previous version
Major	Continuous delivery	Yes	Enabling SSL for all services and infrastructure
New	Continuous delivery	Yes	Deploying a new type of infrastructure component

Continuous integration, delivery, and deployment also apply to the software development life cycle. However, applying the concepts to the infrastructure life cycle pushes the limits of your organization's change and review processes. Regularly categorizing your changes and evaluating your change and review process can help balance productivity and governance, something I mentioned as part of module-sharing practices.

> **Configuration management**
>
> Configuration management tools should follow a similar approach for assessing change types and applying continuous delivery or deployment.

As a general rule, make sure to quickly review and approve changes and *push them into production as soon as possible.* A larger batch of changes has a larger blast radius. If you push every change in one batch and affect a business-critical application, you must troubleshoot each change in the batch. The complexity of troubleshooting grows when you need to identify which change affected the system.

> **Exercise 7.1**
>
> Choose a standard infrastructure change in your organization. What do you need in order to confidently continuously deliver the change to production? What about continuous deployment? Outline or diagram stages in your delivery pipelines for both.
>
> See appendix B for answers to exercises.

7.1.5 *Modules*

What about delivery pipelines for modules? You learned about sharing, releasing, and managing versions of infrastructure modules in chapter 5 and testing their functionality in chapter 6. I alluded to the idea of automating the process of testing and releasing modules but did not fully explain their delivery pipelines.

Delivery pipelines for infrastructure modules differ slightly from the examples I outlined for production configuration. You alter the delivery pipeline in figure 7.9 to

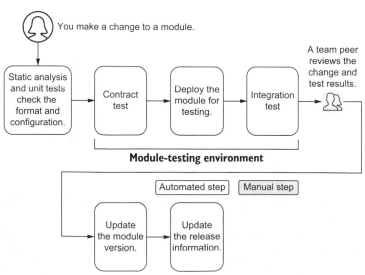

Figure 7.9 After testing the module, wait for the team to review the change and test results before updating and releasing the new module version.

release a module after testing instead of delivering to production. You keep a manual approval step for your team to review the module.

You can categorize module changes with the same types of changes as configurations, including standard, emergency, major, and new changes. Table 7.2 outlines the types of changes, their delivery approach, and an example. For the most part, they match the approach recommended for configurations.

Table 7.2 Types of module changes and delivery approach

Type of change	Delivery approach	Manual approval before production?	Example
Standard	Continuous deployment	No	Enabling an override for an existing default parameter
Emergency	Continuous deployment or branch	No	Rolling back an operating system image to a previous version
Major	Continuous delivery	Yes	Updating a database or infrastructure by using data
New	Continuous delivery	Yes	Deploying a new server module

Some module changes benefit from review or pair programming with a subject-matter expert, such as database configurations or other specialized infrastructure involving data. However, emergency changes on modules may have a different delivery approach.

Emergency changes on modules mean isolating a quick fix to a different version of the module. You can achieve isolation in one of two ways. You could implement the fix and continuously deploy and release a new version of the module with the changes. Alternatively, you could create a *branch* of a module repository and update your infrastructure configuration to reference the branch.

> **DEFINITION** A *branch* in version control is a pointer to a snapshot of code. It allows you to separately implement changes based on that snapshot.

After validating the branch, you can update the main branch of the module with a standard change. Branching the module helps you quickly implement the emergency module change and reconcile the module changes later.

If I know other teams pin their versions, I prefer to continuously deploy a new version of the module with the fix. While a branch can isolate the emergency change, I have to remember to merge it back into the main release of the module. In the next section, you'll learn about branching models and how to apply them to IaC changes.

Image building and configuration management

Delivery pipelines for image building and configuration management modules follow a similar approach to modules for provisioning tools. Make sure to version and test changes to images before deploying them to production.

7.2   Branching models

Besides implementing continuous delivery or deployment, you need to standardize the way changes merge to your main configuration. The main branch in version control serves as a source of truth for configuration. Updating the configuration requires additional coordination and collaboration within your team.

Imagine you want to reduce access for a firewall while your teammate refreshes its license. Your team has a CD pipeline to test and manually approve changes to the production firewall. However, you and your teammate's changes present two problems.

First, how can both of you work on and test your changes in isolation? Second, how do you control which change should go first? Figure 7.10 outlines your and your teammate's dilemma of who should deploy their changes first. You want to avoid pushing both changes at the same time. If the firewall causes network access failure, you won't know which change caused the problem.

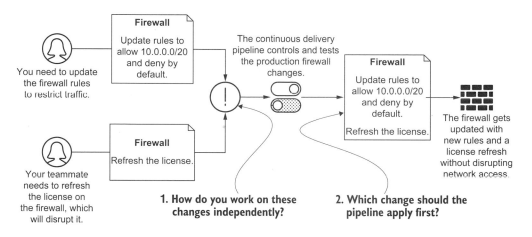

Figure 7.10   Even if you have a CD pipeline to deliver changes to the firewall, you need additional development coordination to identify which change must apply first.

A *branching model* coordinates how your team uses version control to enable parallel work while minimizing disruption and troubleshooting complexity. You can choose from two types of branching models: feature-based or trunk-based development.

> **DEFINITION**   A *branching model* defines how your team uses version control to enable parallel work and resolve conflicts in their efforts.

Each branching model comes with its complexities in implementation, especially in IaC. I'll describe how you can apply both development models to coordinate the firewall rule and license changes between you and your teammate. Then, I'll discuss some limitations to each approach and how your teams can choose.

7.2.1 *Feature-based development*

What if you and your teammate could work on your changes in isolation before combining them? If your teammate creates a *branch* with their license change and you create a branch with your firewall changes, you isolate your changes from each other. When you both finish, you merge your changes to the main branch and resolve conflicts with each other.

Figure 7.11 demonstrates how you and your teammate choreograph your changes on different branches. You name your branch TICKET-002 for the firewall rule, and your teammate names their branch TICKET-005 for the license update. Your firewall rule changes get approved first, so you put them into the main branch and deploy them to production. Your teammate continues working on the license update. They retrieve your firewall rule updates into their branch for further testing before merging their changes back to the main branch.

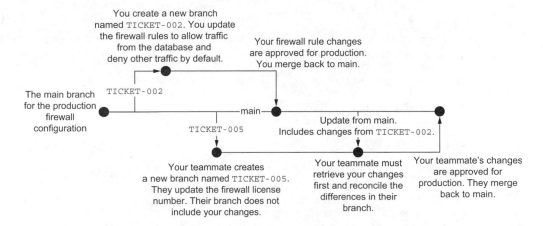

Figure 7.11 When you use feature-based development, you isolate your changes to your branch and reconcile conflicts with the main configuration.

Feature-based development allows you to evolve your changes independent of your teammates by isolating those changes to a branch.

> **DEFINITION** *Feature-based development* (also known as *feature branching*, or *Git Flow*) is a branching pattern that separates different changes into individual branches. You merge the changes on a specific branch to the main configuration after testing.

The flow of feature-based development helps you focus on the composability of your change independent of others. However, you need to constantly fetch changes from the main branch and reconcile them with your branch. Feature-based development works best when each team member diligently updates and tests their branches.

Let's examine feature-based development in action. Imagine you start your feature-based development workflow for the firewall by cloning a local copy of the configuration from version control:

```
$ git clone git@github.com:myorganization/firewall.git
```

You create a branch, which creates a pointer for your updates. I recommend naming the branch after the ticket number (such as TICKET-002) associated with the change, although you can also use a descriptive dash-delimited name:

```
$ git checkout -b TICKET-002
```

You make your changes to the firewall rules on the branch. Then you use your command line to commit your changes to your local branch:

```
$ git commit -m "TICKET-002 Only allow traffic from database"
[TICKET-002 cdc9056] TICKET-002 Only allow traffic from database
 1 file changed, 0 insertions(+), 0 deletions(-)
 create mode 100644 firewall.py
```

You have your changes locally, but you want others to review your change. You push the changes to a remote branch:

```
$ git push --set-upstream origin TICKET-002
Enumerating objects: 7, done.
Counting objects: 100% (7/7), done.
Delta compression using up to 8 threads
Compressing objects: 100% (3/3), done.
Writing objects: 100% (5/5), 1.06 KiB | 1.06 MiB/s, done.
Total 5 (delta 1), reused 0 (delta 0), pack-reused 0
remote: Resolving deltas: 100% (1/1), completed with 1 local object.
To github.com:myorganization/firewall.git
 * [new branch]        TICKET-002 -> TICKET-002
Branch 'TICKET-002' set up to track remote branch
➥'TICKET-002' from 'origin'.
```

Meanwhile, your teammate works on TICKET-005, which updates the license. They create a new branch called TICKET-005 with changes that *do not* include your firewall rule updates. Notice that your branch does not include their updated license, and their branch does not include your updated firewall rules. You can review the difference between the two branches:

```
$ git diff TICKET-002..TICKET-005
diff --git a/firewall.py b/firewall.py
index 74daecd..aaf6cf4 100644
--- firewall.py
+++ firewall.py
@@ -1,3 +1,3 @@
-print("License number is 1234")
+print("License number is 5678")

-print("Firewall rules should allow from database and deny by default.")
\ No newline at end of file
```

```
+print("Firewall rules allow all.")
\ No newline at end of file
```

You open a *pull request*, notifying your team that you finished your changes.

> **DEFINITION** A *pull request* notifies the maintainers of a repository that you
> have external changes you would like to merge into the main configuration.

You add members of the change advisory board to review your pull request. They
approve the changes, and you merge your changes back to the main branch.

Your teammate has not received approval to update the license yet. To ensure that
they don't affect the production configuration, they need to retrieve all changes from
the main branch, including yours in TICKET-002:

```
$ git checkout main
Switched to branch 'main'
Your branch is behind 'origin/main' by 1 commit, and can be fast-forwarded.
  (use "git pull" to update your local branch)

$ git pull --rebase
Updating 22280e7..084855a
Fast-forward
 firewall.py | 2 +-
 1 file changed, 1 insertion(+), 1 deletion(-)
```

Then they return to their branch named TICKET-005 and merge changes from the
main branch into the TICKET-005 branch:

```
$ git checkout TICKET-005
Switched to branch 'TICKET-005'
Your branch is up to date with 'origin/TICKET-005'.

$ git merge main
Auto-merging firewall.py
Merge made by the 'recursive' strategy.
 firewall.py | 2 +-
 1 file changed, 1 insertion(+), 1 deletion(-)
```

When your teammate reviews the firewall configuration, they'll find your changes
from TICKET-002. They can update their branch with the changes from the main
one:

```
$ git push --set-upstream origin TICKET-005
Enumerating objects: 7, done.
Counting objects: 100% (7/7), done.
Delta compression using up to 8 threads
Compressing objects: 100% (3/3), done.
Writing objects: 100% (5/5), 1.06 KiB | 1.06 MiB/s, done.
Total 5 (delta 1), reused 0 (delta 0), pack-reused 0
remote: Resolving deltas: 100% (1/1), completed with 1 local object.
To github.com:myorganization/firewall.git
 * [new branch]      TICKET-005 -> TICKET-005
Branch 'TICKET-005' set up to track remote branch 'TICKET-005' from 'origin'.
```

Once your teammate's changes receive approval, your teammate can merge the new firewall license to the main branch.

Feature-based development requires numerous steps for each team member. You can simplify the workflow by automating the testing and merging process. Use a delivery pipeline to organize the changes across branches.

Figure 7.12 organizes the feature-based development workflow of the delivery pipeline for you and your teammate. You and your teammate each get a branch pipeline with its own testing environment. For example, you have a branch named TICKET-002 and a new firewall environment that isolates your changes. You run unit tests, deploy the change, and run integration and end-to-end tests in the TICKET-002 firewall environment.

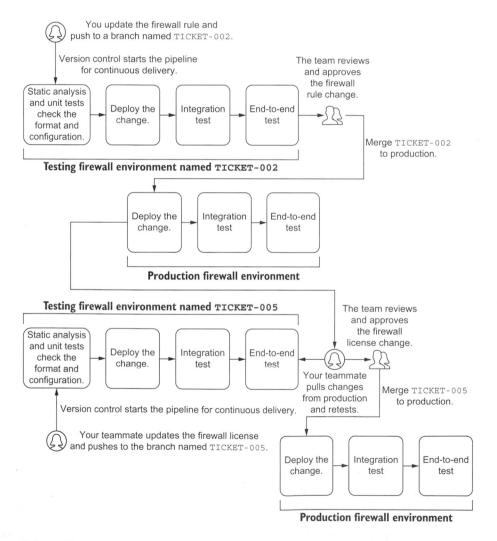

Figure 7.12   **You can use feature-based development to isolate testing of your changes on the branch.**

Once your branch tests pass, you merge the changes to the main branch. While you worked on your change, your teammate separately created their own branch and firewall environment named `TICKET-005`. Your teammate realizes that you recently made updates to the firewall configuration.

In figure 7.12, your teammate retrieves changes from the main branch and makes sure those changes still work with their branch and environment. Once your teammate runs the same unit, integration, and end-to-end tests on their branch, they merge `TICKET-005` changes to the main branch for production deployment.

Why create a testing environment for each branch? A testing environment per branch isolates your changes and tests them relative to the main branch. As a temporary environment, the branch's testing environment can minimize the need for a persistent testing environment and reduce the overall cost of infrastructure. However, a testing environment may take some time to create.

Your team gets a few benefits from feature-based development, including the following:

- Ability to isolate changes to a branch.
- Ability to test changes within the branch.
- Implicit step for peer review. You can merge your changes to production only if someone approves the change.
- Separation of emergency changes on a branch. After validating the emergency change, you can merge it to the main branch.

Fortunately, repository hosting services (e.g., GitHub or GitLab) have functionality that can help you automate a feature-based development model. Such functionality includes labels for tracking specific features, status checks with integration tests before merging your branch, and automated deletion of old branches. You can also define a list of reviewers and automatically add them to pull requests.

7.2.2   *Trunk-based development*

Imagine your organization does not want to create a testing environment per branch, and many of the engineers do not feel comfortable with a feature-based development workflow. Instead of creating a branch, you and your teammate work together on the main branch.

Figure 7.13 shows how you and your teammate can collaborate on the main branch. You update the firewall rule and push the changes first. Then your teammate updates their local repository to include your changes and pushes their changes to the main branch.

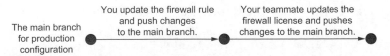

Figure 7.13   When you use trunk development, you maintain one main branch and update the production configuration directly.

The workflow seems more streamlined since you both push to one branch. *Trunk-based development* means that you push changes directly to the main branch without isolating your changes in version control.

> **DEFINITION**   *Trunk-based development* (also known as *pushing to main*) is a branching pattern that pushes all changes directly to the main branch. It favors making small changes and using testing environments to verify that changes succeed.

Trunk-based development does not allow you to evolve your changes independently of your teammates. However, this limitation becomes a benefit. Trunk-based development forces you to implement changes in a *specific order.* You can quickly identify which commit causes the change and resolve it. The pattern offers an opinionated way to orchestrate and apply IaC changes.

Let's apply trunk-based development to your firewall rule and your teammate's firewall license updates. You start by cloning a local copy of the firewall configuration from version control. When you clone the configuration, you can check the main branch:

```
$ git clone git@github.com:myorganization/firewall.git
$ git branch --show-current
main
```

You make the firewall rule changes to the main branch. Commit your changes:

```
$ git commit -m "TICKET-002 Only allow traffic from database"
[TICKET-002 cdc9056] TICKET-002 Only allow traffic from database
 1 file changed, 0 insertions(+), 0 deletions(-)
 create mode 100644 firewall.py
```

Update your local copy to make sure you retrieve new changes from main. Use `git pull --rebase` to fetch the changes from the remote repository, merge them into your local copy, and rebase the local history with the remote one:

```
$ git pull --rebase
Already up to date.
```

Now, you can push the changes to the main branch. Your push should start the delivery pipeline in figure 7.14. Your pipeline runs unit and integration tests against a testing environment. After all testing stages pass, the pipeline waits for manual approval from your team. Your teammate can review your changes and approve them. Once they approve your change, the pipeline deploys your firewall rule change to production.

If your firewall rule change fails, it stops the delivery pipeline before it goes to production. You'll notice the failure in the testing environment stage and revert the change. Everyone else can proceed with their changes to production while you implement a fix.

Trunk-based development heavily depends on delivery pipelines to test and deploy changes. The delivery pipeline should include a persistent testing environment to evaluate conflicts between changes. While a persistent testing environment incurs a cost, the environment more accurately reflects the change's behavior in production.

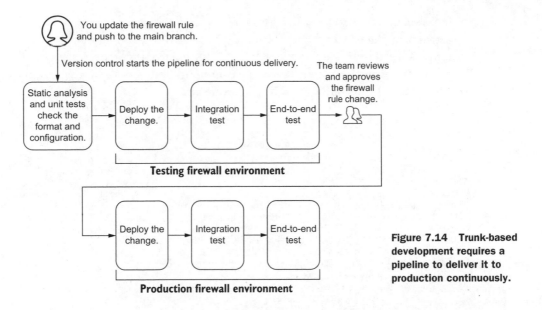

Figure 7.14   Trunk-based development requires a pipeline to deliver it to production continuously.

The workflow for trunk-based development has very few steps. Most infrastructure teams find this workflow helpful in making changes because it sequences the changes in a particular order. Trunk-based development creates a continuous feedback loop of how different changes affect each other. It also promotes a practice of making minor changes, resolving updates from the main configuration, and pushing the changes to production. When your team's changes conflict, you can quickly identify which dependencies affected the testing environment.

However, trunk-based development does require practice to resolve changes and discipline to reconcile changes. You do not isolate your changes, and working on one branch can make it challenging to collaborate. Once you work through the initial collaboration conflicts, you might find that trunk-based development provides better visibility into IaC changes across your team.

7.2.3   Choosing a branching model

I've spent hours with software and infrastructure teams debating the merits of feature-based or trunk-based development. At the conclusion of those meetings, I always came to the realization that the branching model choice depended on the team's comfort level, size, and environment setup. This section covers some limitations and concerns when applying both branching models to infrastructure.

CHALLENGES OF FEATURE-BASED DEVELOPMENT

Many open source projects for applications and infrastructure successfully use feature-based development. Feature-based development provides the framework to test and assess critical changes independent of one another. It separates changes across many collaborators and enforces a manual review stage before merging to the main branch. Source control or CI frameworks offer native integrations to support feature-based development.

IaC gets the same benefit from feature-based development. Teams enjoy isolating infrastructure changes to a branch before pushing it to production. Figure 7.15 tests your firewall rule changes in the `TICKET-002` environment from your teammate's license changes in the `TICKET-005` environment. You can apply changes on top of your branch without conflicting with someone else.

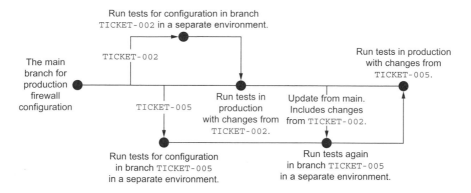

Figure 7.15   You can create a new testing environment for each feature branch to verify individual changes.

However, feature-based development has a few challenges. First, new environments can cost time and money to create (refer to chapter 12 for cost management). Your pipeline might struggle to spin up new environments when multiple team members work on the configuration with many branches.

To speed up the creation of testing environments, you could invest in runners for your pipeline framework to run tests in parallel. Alternatively, you could also create one persistent testing environment for all branches to use. However, feature-based development might cause conflicts in a persistent testing environment because each branch applies changes asynchronously.

Rather than create a persistent testing environment, you could also omit the integration and end-to-end tests from every branch except the main one to optimize costs. For example, your firewall change might require only static analysis, unit tests, and team review before merging to production, as shown in figure 7.16. You do not need to create a unique testing environment for the branch and merge the branch to production after manual review.

Another challenge you face with feature-based development involves the discipline and familiarity with version control. If you haven't used version control, you need to get used to the feature-branching workflow. The workflow adds the challenge of reverse engineering merged changes and troubleshooting conflicts.

For example, someone could make a branch to fix the firewall rule over the weekend. They forget to merge the hotfix, and you did not know they changed the firewall. You overwrite their configuration by accident when updating the firewall rules! Over time, you accumulate a lot of branches and must troubleshoot which ones you've applied.

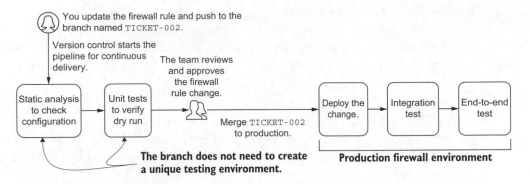

Figure 7.16   You can omit your branches' integration and end-to-end tests to mitigate the cost of multiple environments and pipeline concurrency.

You'll also encounter the challenge of long-lived branches. Imagine your teammate has been working on updating the license for a month. They create a new branch named TICKET-005. Every few days, they need to check for updates in the main branch and add them to their fix.

One day, you need to make a change that depends on your teammate's license update. You start working on your changes on a branch named TICKET-002, as shown in figure 7.17 You finish but realize that your teammate still has work to do on TICKET-005! You wait two more months for your teammate to finish their firewall license update. Once they finish, you spend hours updating your TICKET-002 branch so you can finally deploy your changes to production.

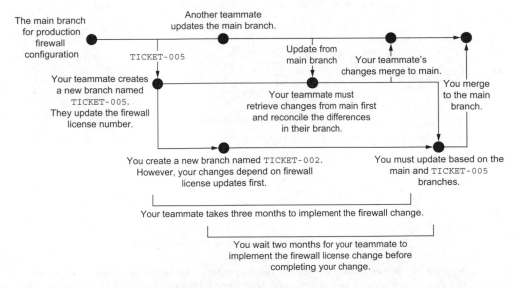

Figure 7.17   Branches with long lifetimes can prevent other changes from deploying to production and introduce complexity during the branching process.

Feature-based development encourages you to keep branches for a long time. You have to vigilantly update long-lived branches to keep up with the main one. Otherwise, you'll encounter conflicts you cannot easily resolve. On occasion, your only solution involves deleting your abandoned branch and restarting your changes on a new, updated branch.

CHALLENGES OF TRUNK-BASED DEVELOPMENT

Trunk-based development works well with infrastructure changes and the need to mitigate configuration drift between environments and states. You omit the complexities of merging and managing feature branches, especially if you need to build confidence in Git skills.

Trunk-based development favors small changes instead of large, significant ones. You implement changes progressively instead of testing them in one batch. In chapter 10, I cover the use of feature toggling to gradually implement a set of changes and mitigate risk to infrastructure.

Trunk-based development has a few disadvantages. It requires a dedicated testing environment before pushing changes to production. Figure 7.18 outlines the ideal workflow for trunk-based development. After you run unit tests, you deploy the change to a long-lived testing environment for integration and end-to-end tests. If the change passes tests in the testing environment, it can undergo review from your teammates. Once they approve the change, it goes to the production environment for integration and end-to-end testing.

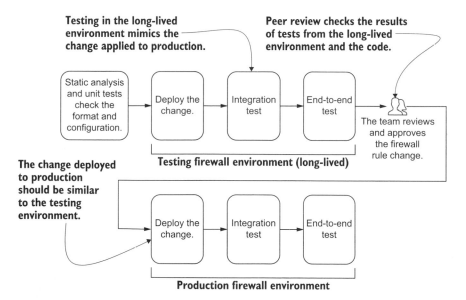

Figure 7.18   Trunk-based development requires a dedicated testing environment to mimic the changes to production and help build confidence for peer review.

You need thorough unit tests to format and lint for your team's standards, and integration tests to verify functionality. A persistent testing environment increases the overall cost of trunk-based development. Smaller, more modular infrastructure configurations can reduce the conflicts within a resource or module and lower the overall cost of required infrastructure for tests.

You may find that trunk-based development conflicts with manual change approval. Manual change approval can happen only after someone pushes the changes to the main branch. Your reviewer needs to know if your change worked before they can verify its formatting and configuration. If you push a broken configuration to the testing environment, you identify and revert quickly before someone else reviews it.

Table 7.3 summarizes the benefits and limitations of feature-based and trunk-based development. The choice depends on the type of infrastructure your team configures and its familiarity with version control.

Table 7.3 Comparison of feature-based and trunk-based development

Development model	Benefits	Limitations
Feature-based development	Isolates changes using branches Isolates tests using branches Organizes manual review of code Scales across multiple teams and collaborators	Requires diligence and familiarity with updating branches Encourages long-lived branches Increases cost in money and time
Trunk-based development	Provides better representation of change behavior Uses one version control workflow for all changes Encourages incremental infrastructure changes to reduce blast radius	Requires long-lived testing environment Does not include a stage for manual review Requires discipline and organization to scale across multiple teams and collaborators

You must establish and agree on a development model within your team. Agreement on a development model helps promote reproducibility of changes and the overall availability of the system. Beware of the limitations with each approach, and always keep your changes as small as possible. No matter which model your team adopts, apply changes to production as frequently as possible to reduce the blast radius of changes.

7.3 Peer review

Throughout this chapter and chapter 5, I emphasized the importance of including a review step in delivery pipelines and module changes. Why should you take the time to review your teammate's IaC? What should you look for as you review it?

Peer review allows your teammates to examine your infrastructure configuration for recommendations, standards, and formatting.

DEFINITION   *Peer review* is a practice that allows your teammates or other teams to examine your infrastructure configuration for recommendations, standards, and formatting.

As a reviewer, I focus on whether a configuration will scale across teams, remain secure, or affect higher-level infrastructure dependencies. This perspective on review sometimes blocks the merging of the change to production. However, the peer review process serves as a team education opportunity for standardized practices and new patterns. You and your team may need to spend time debating the merits or drawbacks of a design or implementation.

To understand the importance and drawbacks of peer review, imagine a new inventory team needs read access to a GCP project. In listing 7.1, you update the code for access management rules to read a list of users from a JSON object. The new code passes all the tests, and you wait for a few days for your teammate to review the change.

Listing 7.1   First implementation to add a new team to a GCP project

```
import json

GCP_PROJECT_USERS = [        ⟵── Defines a list of users and groups
    (                             to add to the GCP project
        'operations',
        'group:team-operations@example.com',
        'roles/editor'
    ),
    (
        'inventory',
        'group:inventory@example.com',        Adds the inventory team as a
        'roles/viewer'                        read-only group to the project
    )
]
                                         Creates a module for the GCP project
                                         users, which uses the factory pattern
class GCPProjectUsers:        ⟵──        to attach users to roles
    def __init__(self, project, users):
        self._project = project
        self._users = users
        self.resources = self._build()
                                         Uses the module to create the JSON configuration
                                         for the list of users to append to GCP roles
    def _build(self):
        resources = []
        for user, member, role in self._users:
            resources.append({
                'google_project_iam_member': [{      For each group in the list,
                    user: [{                         creates a Google project IAM
                        'role': role,                member with the user
                        'member': member,            attached to their assigned
                        'project': self._project     role. This resource appends
                    }]                               the user to the roles in GCP.
                }]
            })
        return {
```

```
            'resource': resources
    }


if __name__ == "__main__":
    with open('main.tf.json', 'w') as outfile:
        json.dump(GCPProjectUsers(
            'infrastructure-as-code-book',
            GCP_PROJECT_USERS).resources, outfile,
            sort_keys=True, indent=2)
```

When you write out the JSON file to be executed by Terraform, use an indentation of two spaces.

Writes the Python dictionary out to a JSON file to be executed by Terraform later

AWS and Azure equivalents

To convert the code listing to AWS, you would map references to the GCP project to an AWS account. GCP project users align with an AWS IAM user. Similarly, you would create an Azure subscription and add a user account to Azure Active Directory.

You wait three days before your teammate returns with the following feedback:

- You must indent your JSON infrastructure configuration with four spaces.
- You must rename the group to `team-inventory@example.com`.
- You must add the inventory team to the list of users for the `viewer` role instead of defining the role for the group.

Your teammate explains that the first two conform to team standards. The last requirement conforms to a security standard for authoritative bindings for access control (it defines a list of users for the role instead of adding a role to the user). You already delayed your change by three days waiting for peer review! Now, you need to fix it and wait another few days to get approval.

Remember from chapter 6 that you want to capture the unknown knowns of siloed knowledge into tests. Your teammate had some knowledge that you did not know. You decide to add some unit tests to help you remember the team standards.

The new code in listing 7.2 includes new unit tests (linting rules) to validate your team's configuration and security standards. One test checks for the correct indentation of four spaces in the JSON. Another checks that all groups conform to a naming standard. The last test checks that you use the correct resource to bind users to roles.

Listing 7.2 Adding unit tests to lint for team development standards

```
import pytest
from main import GCP_PROJECT_USERS, GCPProjectUsers

GROUP_CONFIGURATION_FILE = 'main.tf.json'


@pytest.fixture
def json():
    with open(GROUP_CONFIGURATION_FILE, 'r') as f:
        return f.readlines()
```

Imports the list of GCP users and roles

Uses Python to read in the Terraform JSON configuration file. The test uses this fixture to verify that the JSON has an indentation of four spaces.

```
@pytest.fixture
def users():
    return GCP_PROJECT_USERS
```

Imports the list of GCP users and roles, including the inventory team, as a fixture to the test. The test checks that each user has a prefix of "team-" to identify it as a group.

```
@pytest.fixture
def binding():
    return GCPProjectUsers(
        'testing',
        [('test', 'test', 'roles/test')]).resources['resource'][0]
```

Uses Python to read in the Terraform JSON configuration file. The test uses this fixture to verify that the JSON has an indentation of four spaces.

Uses a fixture to create a sample GCP project user using the factory module

```
def test_json_configuration_for_indentation(json):
    assert len(json[1]) - len(json[1].lstrip()) == 4, \
        "output JSON with indent of 4"


def test_user_configuration_for_standard_team_name(users):
    for _, member, _ in GCP_PROJECT_USERS:
        assert member.startswith('team-'), \
            "group should always start with `team-`"


def test_authoritative_project_iam_binding(binding):
    assert 'google_project_iam_binding' in binding.keys(), \
        "use `google_project_iam_binding` to add team members to roles"
```

Checks that the factory module uses the correct Terraform resource of Google project IAM binding and not members. This uses an authoritative binding to add team members to a specific role.

AWS and Azure equivalents

A GCP project IAM binding is similar to an `aws_iam_policy_attachment` Terraform resource (http://mng.bz/5QW7). The binding or attachment authoritatively revokes any users not defined as part of the Terraform resource. At the time of publication, Azure's access control model uses an additive policy approach and does not have an explicit way to define authoritative role attachments or binding definitions.

You correct your mistakes before peer review and shorten the feedback loop, thanks to automated linting and unit tests. Your teammate doesn't have to nitpick for formatting and standards. However, you and your teammate still debate whether you should add the user to the role or the role to the user. You decide to raise this architectural decision to the broader team for consideration.

Figure 7.19 demonstrates that effective peer review follows the example's workflow of combining automated testing with broader architectural discussions. Between automated tests, peer review, and collaborating together, you maintain secure, resilient, and scalable IaC.

**Effective peer review for IaC requires a combination
of automated and manual processes.**

Write automated tests for linting and formatting configuration.   Review the configuration to identify dependent infrastructure and changes to architecture.*   Use pair programming to communicate changes and identify problems early.

* Be aware of how long manual review may take. The larger the change, the more complex the review, and the longer it will take.

Figure 7.19   Automating some of the checks and maintaining awareness of any manual review processes will help expedite peer review.

However, test automation and reviewers do not catch everything. Peer review later in your development process can get frustrating as well. To address any gaps and raise architectural concerns earlier in the IaC writing process, you can program with a teammate. This technique, called *pair programming*, uses two engineers to mitigate the friction of peer review.

> **DEFINITION**   *Pair programming* is the practice of two programmers working together at one workstation.

One engineer may catch something the other does not realize, and vice versa. Pair programming has many challenges, including resource constraints and personality conflicts. Most companies don't adopt it because it initially slows the delivery pace and affects team capacity. Some individuals dislike it because their pairing partner may work at a different pace. Pair programming takes self-awareness and discipline.

Try to pair program IaC when you can. Infrastructure often includes particular terminology and institutional knowledge. For instance, current and future team members must understand *why* someone used an authoritative binding for project access control. Pair programming facilitates knowledge sharing and bakes in change review during development. Over time, your team becomes more proficient at delivering infrastructure changes quickly without the friction of manual change review.

> **NOTE**   Peer (or code) review and pair programming should promote a safe space for everyone on the team to learn how to code with best practices in mind. Specific details about these processes are beyond the scope of this book. For more information on code review, I recommend examining Google's Engineering practices at http://mng.bz/6XNR. For more on pair programming, see http://mng.bz/o2GD. You can use various techniques to balance the pairing relationship, such as switching the keyboard every 30 minutes or assigning a driver and navigator.

A change to infrastructure can affect the availability of business-critical systems. Batching many changes can exacerbate the failure by making it challenging to troubleshoot to one root cause. If you can shorten the peer-review process with a combination of pair programming and test automation, you can focus on reviewing the architecture and impact of infrastructure changes.

7.4   GitOps

What happens when you combine continuous deployment, declarative configuration, drift detection, and version control? All of these patterns seem fairly disparate, but using them together offers an opinionated approach to managing infrastructure. You declare the configuration you want for your infrastructure, add it to version control, and deploy it to production.

Imagine you want to update a payment service from version 3.0 to 3.2. The payment service runs on a workload orchestrator (e.g., Kubernetes). The orchestrator offers a declarative configuration interface using a DSL. You can pass YAML files to configure resources in the orchestrator.

Figure 7.20 implements a workflow that responds to changes by combining continuous deployment, the declarative configuration, and version control. You update the declarative configuration with version 3.2. A controller detects drift between the current configuration and the one in version control. It starts a delivery pipeline to deploy the new version and run tests to check its functionality.

Why do you have a controller detect and apply changes continuously? The controller reduces the drift between the expected configuration and actual state. This ensures that your system stays updated.

You might get a sense of déjà vu from this workflow. After all, it combines all the practices on writing IaC, testing, and delivery. This book takes a very opinionated stance on IaC, aligning with a concept called GitOps. *GitOps* defines an approach that allows teams to manage infrastructure changes in version control, make declarative changes via IaC, and continuously deploy updates to infrastructure.

> **DEFINITION**   *GitOps* is an approach that uses declarative IaC to manage infrastructure changes through version control and continuously deploy them to production.

You'll associate GitOps most frequently with the Kubernetes ecosystem. However, GitOps offers an opinionated paradigm for scaling IaC practices across an organization. You no longer implement changes by filling tickets with the relevant details.

Instead, anyone in the organization can branch IaC and commit changes. Continuous deployment reduces drift, keeps infrastructure updated, and always runs the tests. You can track who requested and made the change through the pull request and commit history.

> **NOTE**   To learn more about GitOps and Kubernetes, check out *GitOps and Kubernetes* by Billy Yuen et al. (Manning, 2021). You can find general practices about GitOps on https://opengitops.dev.

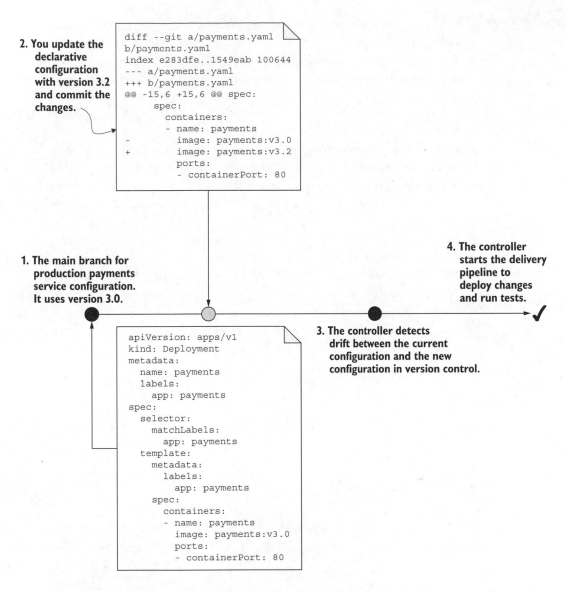

2. You update the declarative configuration with version 3.2 and commit the changes.

```
diff --git a/payments.yaml
b/payments.yaml
index e283dfe..1549eab 100644
--- a/payments.yaml
+++ b/payments.yaml
@@ -15,6 +15,6 @@ spec:
    spec:
      containers:
      - name: payments
-       image: payments:v3.0
+       image: payments:v3.2
        ports:
        - containerPort: 80
```

1. The main branch for production payments service configuration. It uses version 3.0.

4. The controller starts the delivery pipeline to deploy changes and run tests.

```
apiVersion: apps/v1
kind: Deployment
metadata:
  name: payments
  labels:
    app: payments
spec:
  selector:
    matchLabels:
      app: payments
  template:
    metadata:
      labels:
        app: payments
    spec:
      containers:
      - name: payments
        image: payments:v3.0
        ports:
        - containerPort: 80
```

3. The controller detects drift between the current configuration and the new configuration in version control.

Figure 7.20 An implementation of GitOps can use feature-based development to open a pull request, test changes on a branch, add reviewers, and merge the changes.

Summary

- Delivering infrastructure changes to production usually involves a change review process, which manually verifies the architecture and impact of the change.
- Continuous integration involves frequently merging changes to the main branch of infrastructure configuration.
- Continuous delivery deploys changes to a testing environment for automated testing and waits for manual approval before pushing them to production.

- Continuous deployment directly deploys changes to production without a manual approval stage.
- You can use continuous integration, delivery, or deployment to push IaC changes with automated tests, depending on the type of change and its frequency.
- Your team can collaborate on IaC by using feature-based development or trunk-based development.
- Feature-based development creates a branch for each change, enabling isolated testing but requiring familiarity with version control practices.
- Trunk-based development applies all changes to the main branch, which identifies conflicts between changes but requires a testing environment before production.
- You can automate checks for formatting and standards and manually review the configuration for architecture and dependencies.
- Pair programming can help identify conflicts and problems with a change earlier in the development process.
- GitOps incorporates version control, declarative infrastructure configuration, and continuous deployment to empower anyone to automate infrastructure changes through code commits.

Security and compliance

In previous chapters, I alluded to the importance of securing infrastructure as code and checking its conformance with your organization's security and compliance requirements. Oftentimes, you don't address these requirements until later in your engineering process. By that point, you may have already deployed an insecure configuration or violated a compliance requirement about data privacy!

For example, imagine you work for a retail company called uDress. Your team has six months to build a new frontend application on GCP. The company needs it available by the holiday season. Your team works very hard and develops enough functionality to go live. However, a month before you deploy and test the new application, the compliance and security team performs an audit—and you fail.

Now, you have new items in your backlog to fix the security and compliance issues and adhere to company policy. Unfortunately, these fixes delay your delivery timeline or, at worst, break functionality. You might wish that you knew about these from the very beginning, at least so you could plan for them!

Your company's *policy* ensures that systems comply with security, audit, and organizational requirements. In addition, your security or compliance teams often define policies based on industry, country, and more.

> **DEFINITION**   A *policy* is a set of rules and standards in your organization to ensure compliance to security, industry, or regulatory requirements.

This chapter will teach you to protect credentials and secrets and write tests to enforce policies for security and compliance. If you think about these practices before you write IaC, you can build secure, compliant infrastructure and avoid delays in your delivery timeline. Inspired by a manager I used to work with, "We're baking security into the infrastructure instead of icing it later."

8.1   *Managing access and secrets*

I already introduced the idea of "baking" security into IaC in chapter 2. IaC uses two sets of secrets. You use API credentials to automate infrastructure and sensitive variables such as passwords to pass to resources. You can store both secrets in secrets managers to handle their protection and rotation.

In this section, I focus on securing IaC delivery pipelines. IaC expresses the expected state of the infrastructure, which often includes root passwords, usernames, private keys, and other sensitive information. Infrastructure delivery pipelines control the deployment and release of infrastructure that needs this information.

Let's imagine you build delivery pipelines for the new uDress system to deploy infrastructure. The pipelines use a set of infrastructure provider credentials to create and update resources. Each pipeline also reads a database password from a secrets manager and passes it as an attribute to create the database.

Your security team points out two problems with your approach. First, the infrastructure delivery pipeline uses full administrative credentials to configure GCP. Second, your team's delivery pipeline accidentally prints out the root database password in its logs!

Your delivery pipeline just increased the *attack surface* (sum of the different points of attack) of your system.

> **DEFINITION**   The *attack surface* describes the sum of different points of attack where an unauthorized user can compromise a system.

Anyone can use the administrative credentials or root database password to gain information and compromise your system. You need a solution to better secure the credentials and the database password. The solution should hopefully minimize the attack surface.

8.1.1 *Principle of least privilege*

IaC delivery pipelines have points of attack that allow unauthorized users to use credentials with elevated access. For example, you used chapter 7 to build a pipeline that continuously delivers infrastructure changes to production. The pipeline needs some permissions to change infrastructure in GCP.

Initially, your team gives the pipeline full administrative credentials so it can create all of the resources in GCP. If someone accesses those credentials, they could create and update anything in the uDress system. Someone could exploit your team's pipeline to run machine learning models or access other customer data!

The pipeline does not *need* access to every resource. You decide to update the credentials so it uses only the minimal set of permissions it needs to update specific resources. You determine that the IaC creates only network, Google App Engine, and Cloud SQL resources. You remove administrative access from the credentials and replace them with write access to the three resources.

When the pipeline runs, as shown in figure 8.1, the new credentials have just enough access to update the three sets of resources. It also retrieves the database password from the secrets manager before deploying updates to the network, application, and database. After deploying the changes to a testing environment, you add a unit test to verify that the credentials no longer have administrative access.

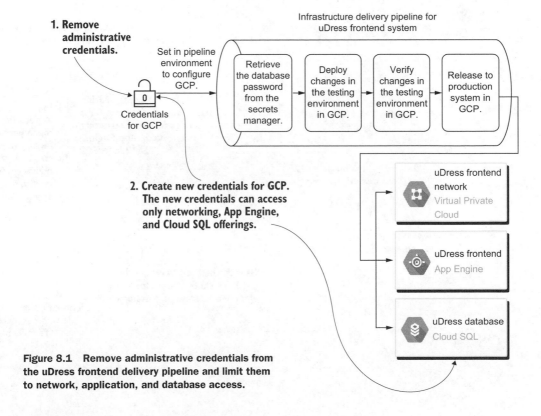

Figure 8.1 Remove administrative credentials from the uDress frontend delivery pipeline and limit them to network, application, and database access.

You remediated the security concern of pipeline credentials by using the *principle of least privilege*. This principle ensures that a user or service account gets only the minimum access they require to complete their task.

> **DEFINITION**   The *principle of least privilege* indicates that users or service accounts should have minimum access requirements to a system. They should have only enough to complete their tasks.

Maintaining the principle of least privilege takes time and effort. You usually change access as you add new resources to IaC. In general, attach roles to delivery pipeline credentials. Grouping access permissions into roles helps promote composability so you can add and remove access as needed.

Apply the module practices from chapter 3 to offer modules of permission sets. For example, you may offer a factory module for uDress's web applications to customize network, application, and database write access. Any web application can use the module and properly reproduce the minimum set of privileges it needs.

Let's use the access management module to implement least privilege access management for uDress's frontend delivery pipeline in listing 8.1. You limit the pipeline to network, application, and Cloud SQL administrative credentials. These credentials allow the pipeline to create, delete, and update the network, application, and database, but not update any other resource types.

Listing 8.1   Least privilege access management policy for the frontend

```python
import json
import iam                                        ◁─── Imports the application access management
                                                       factory module to create access management
                                                       roles for the frontend application

def build_frontend_configuration():
    name = 'frontend'
    roles = [                                     ◁─── Creates the role configuration based on a list
        'roles/compute.networkAdmin',                  of roles for a service account, including
        'roles/appengine.appAdmin',                    networking, App Engine, and Cloud SQL
        'roles/cloudsql.admin'
    ]

    frontend = iam.ApplicationFactoryModule(name, roles)
    resources = {
        'resource': frontend._build()             ◁─── Uses the method to create the JSON
    }                                                  configuration for the pipeline's access permissions
    return resources

if __name__ == "__main__":
    resources = build_frontend_configuration()    ◁─── Writes the Python dictionary out to a JSON
                                                       file to be executed by Terraform later

    with open('main.tf.json', 'w') as outfile:
        json.dump(resources, outfile, sort_keys=True, indent=4)
```

AWS and Azure equivalents

Google App Engine is similar to AWS Elastic Beanstalk or Azure App Service, which deploy web applications and services to provider-managed infrastructure.

Google Cloud SQL is similar to Amazon Relational Database Service (RDS), which deploys different managed databases. Azure has different services for specific databases, such as Azure Database for PostgreSQL or Azure SQL Database offerings.

As you adhere to the principle of least privilege, take care when you remove permissions. Sometimes a pipeline needs more specific permissions to read or update dependencies. You can break infrastructure or applications if they do not have sufficient permissions.

Some infrastructure providers, including GCP, analyze the permissions used for a service account or user and output a set of excess permissions. You can also run other third-party tools to analyze access and identify unused permissions. I recommend using these tools to check and update your access control each time you add a new infrastructure resource.

8.1.2 Protecting secrets in configuration

Besides using administrative credentials from a pipeline to access an infrastructure provider, someone could alter the pipeline to print out sensitive information about infrastructure. For example, the frontend delivery pipeline outputs the root database password in the logs. Anyone accessing the logs from the pipeline can use the root password to log into the database!

To address this security concern, you decide to mark the password as a *sensitive variable* by using your IaC tool. The tool redacts the password in the logs. You also *install a plugin* in your pipeline tool to identify and redact any sensitive information, such as the password. You add these two configurations to your pipeline in figure 8.2 to avoid compromising the database password in the pipeline logs. As a safety precaution, you rotate the database password in the secrets manager and directly change the password in the database, rather than using IaC.

You can use tools to *mask* the password in the delivery pipeline by either suppressing or redacting the plaintext information.

> **DEFINITION** *Masking* your sensitive information means suppressing or redacting its plaintext format to prevent someone from reading the information.

Using one or both mechanisms will prevent the sensitive information from appearing in the pipeline logs. Sensitive information can include passwords, encryption keys, or infrastructure identifiers like IP addresses. If you think someone can use the information to gain access to your system, consider masking the value in your pipeline.

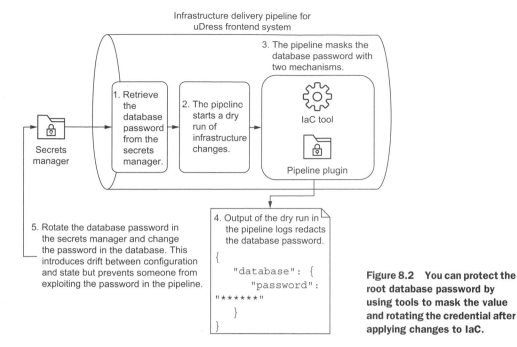

Figure 8.2   You can protect the root database password by using tools to mask the value and rotating the credential after applying changes to IaC.

However, masking sensitive information doesn't guarantee protection from unauthorized access. You still need a workflow to *remediate* the exposed credentials as quickly as possible. As a solution, store and rotate the credentials with a secrets manager after you use them to configure your IaC.

Separately managing secrets introduces mutability, or in-place changes, to your IaC. While it introduces drift between the actual root database password and the one expressed in IaC, managing the password mutably prevents someone from exploiting the IaC pipeline and using the credentials.

As you build IaC, think about this checklist of security requirements in your delivery pipeline to minimize its attack surface:

1 Check for *least privilege access* for infrastructure provider credentials from the beginning. You should provide enough permissions to apply and secure your IaC.

2 Generate a secret by *using a function* to generate a random string or read the secret from a secrets manager. Avoid passing secrets as static variables to your configuration.

3 Check that your pipeline *masks sensitive configuration data* in its dry-run capability or command outputs.

4 Provide a mechanism to *revoke and rotate compromised credentials* or data quickly.

You can solve many of the requirements in the checklist with a secrets manager. The secrets manager can omit the need for statically defining secrets in configuration.

While some requirements serve as general security practices for delivery pipelines, they also apply to secure IaC. You can review chapter 2 for the pattern of securing secrets with a secrets manager.

8.2 Tagging infrastructure

After securing your infrastructure, you have the challenge of running and supporting it. Operating infrastructure requires a set of troubleshooting and auditing patterns and practices. As you continue to add infrastructure to your system, you need a way to identify the purpose and life cycle of resources.

Imagine the uDress frontend application goes live. However, your team gets a message from the finance team. Your infrastructure provider billing has exceeded the expected budget for the past two or three months. You search in the provider's interface to determine which resources have contributed most to the cost. How do you know the owner and environment of each resource?

GCP offers the use of labels, which allows you to add metadata to your resources for identification and audit purposes. You update these labels to include owner and environment. In figure 8.3, uDress includes identification of owner and environment, standards for tag format, and automation metadata. You decide to dash-delimit tag names and values so the tags work with GCP.

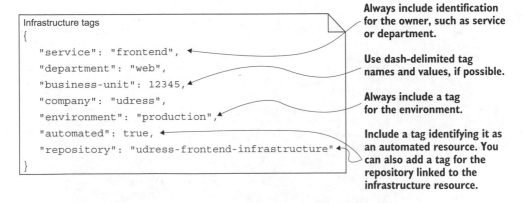

Figure 8.3 Tags should include identification of owner, environment, and automation for easy troubleshooting.

Outside of GCP, other infrastructure providers allow you to add metadata to identify resources. In your organization, you'll develop a *tagging strategy* to define a standard set of metadata used for auditing your infrastructure system.

> **DEFINITION** A *tagging strategy* defines a set of metadata (also known as *tags*) used for auditing, managing, and securing infrastructure resources in your organization.

Why use metadata in the form of tags? Tags help you search and audit resources, actions necessary for billing and compliance. You can also use tags to do bulk automation of infrastructure resources. Bulk automation includes cleanup or break-glass (manual changes to stabilize or fix system failures) updates to a subset of resources.

Let's implement standard tags for uDress in the following listing. From chapter 3, you apply the prototype pattern to define a list of standard tags for your uDress. You reference the uDress tag module to create a list of labels for a GCP server in your code.

Listing 8.2   Using the tags module to set standard tags for the server

```
class TagsPrototypeModule():
    def __init__(                          ◁————  The tag module uses the
            self, service, department,            prototype pattern to define
            business_unit, company, team_email,   a standard set of tags.
            environment):
        self.resource = {
            'service': service,
            'department': department,
            'business-unit': business_unit,            Sets tags to
            'company': company,                        identify owner,
            'email': team_email,                       department,
            'environment': environment,                business unit
            'automated': True,                         for billing, and
            'repository': f"${company}-${service}-infrastructure"   repository for
        }                                              the resource


class ServerFactory:
    def __init__(self, name, network, zone='us-central1-a', tags={}):
        self.name = name
        self.network = network
        self.zone = zone
        self.tags = TagsPrototypeModule(          Passes the required
            'frontend', 'web', 12345, 'udress',   parameters to set tags for
            'frontend@udress.net', 'production')   the frontend application
        self.resource = self._build()

    def _build(self):
        return {                        ◁——┐  Uses the module to create the
            'resource': [                   │  JSON configuration for the server
                {
                    'google_compute_instance': [
                        {
                            self.name: [
                                {
                                    'allow_stopping_for_update': True,
                                    'boot_disk': [
                                        {
                                            'initialize_params': [
                                                {
                                                    'image': 'ubuntu-1804-lts'
                                                }
                                            ]
```

Creates the Google compute instance (server) by using a Terraform resource

```
                                                                }
                                                              ],
                                                              'machine_type': 'f1-micro',
                                                              'name': self.name,
                                                              'network_interface': [
                                                                  {
                                                                      'network': self.network
                                                                  }
Add the tags from the tag                                     ],
module as labels to the                                       'zone': self.zone,
Google compute instance  ⟶                                    'labels': self.tags
                                          }
                                      ]
                                  }
                              ]
                          }
                      ]
                  }
```

AWS and Azure equivalents

To convert listing 8.2 to another cloud provider, change the resource to an Amazon EC2 instance or Azure Linux virtual machine. Then, pass `self.tags` to the `tags` attribute for the AWS or Azure resource.

How do you know which tags to add? Recall from chapter 2 that you must standardize the naming *and* tagging of your infrastructure resources. Discuss these considerations with compliance, security, and finance teams. That will help determine which tags you need and how to use them. At a minimum, I *always* have a tag for the following:

- Service or team
- Team email or communication channel
- Environment (development or production)

For example, let's say the uDress security team audits the frontend resources and discovers some misconfigured infrastructure. The team members can check the tags, identify the service and environment with the problem, and reach out to the team that created the resource.

You may also include tags for the following:

- Automation, which helps you identify manually created resources from automated ones
- Repository, which allows you to correlate the resource with its original configuration in version control
- The business unit, which identifies the billing or charge-back identifier for accounting
- Compliance, which identifies whether the resource has compliance or policy requirements for handling personal information

As you decide on your tagging, make sure it conforms to a general set of constraints so you can apply the same tags across any infrastructure provider. Most infrastructure providers have character restrictions on tags. I usually prefer *dash-case*, which uses lowercase tag names and values split with hyphens. While you can use camel case (stylistically, camelCase), not all providers have case-sensitive tagging.

Tag character limits also vary depending on the infrastructure provider. Most providers support a *maximum length* of 128 characters for the tag key and 256 characters for the tag value. You will have to balance the verbosity of descriptive names (described in chapter 2) with the provider's tag limits!

Another part of your tagging strategy involves deciding whether you *delete untagged resources*. Consider enforcing tags for all resources in the production environment. The testing environment can support untagged resources for manual testing. In general, I do not recommend immediately deleting untagged resources without careful examination. You don't want to delete an essential resource by accident.

8.3   *Policy as code*

Securing access and secrets in infrastructure delivery pipelines and managing tags in infrastructure providers can improve security and compliance practices. However, you might wish to identify insecure or noncompliant infrastructure configuration *before* it goes to production. You'd like to catch a problem before someone finds it in your production system.

Imagine connecting the uDress frontend application to another database. You open a firewall rule to allow all traffic inbound to a managed database for testing. After testing, you expect to remove the database, so you do not tag it.

You forget about the firewall and tag configuration and send it off for review. Unfortunately, your teammate misses them in code review and pushes the changes to production. Two weeks later, you discover that an unknown entity has accessed some data! However, you have no tags to identify the compromised database.

What could you have done differently? Recall the importance of unit tests or static analysis of infrastructure configuration in chapter 6. You can apply the *same* techniques to write tests specifically for security and policy.

Rather than depend on a teammate to catch the problem, you can express policy as code to statically analyze the configuration for the permissive firewall rule or lack of tags. *Policy as code* tests infrastructure metadata and verifies that it complies with security or compliance requirements.

> **DEFINITION**   *Policy as code* (also known as *shift-left security testing*, or *static analysis of IaC*) tests infrastructure metadata and verifies that values comply with security or compliance requirements before pushing changes to production. Policy as code includes the rules you write for dynamic analysis tools or vulnerability scanning.

I discussed the long-term benefit of automating and testing IaC in chapters 1 and 6. You similarly have an initial short-term time investment for writing policy as code. The policy checks continuously verify the compliance of each change you want to make to production. You minimize the surprises after the compliance and security teams audit your system. Over time, you decrease the long-term time investment with a shorter time to production.

8.3.1 Policy engines and standards

Tools can help run policy as code by evaluating metadata based on a set of rules. Most testing tools in this space use a policy engine. A *policy engine* takes policies as input and evaluates infrastructure resources for compliance.

> **DEFINITION** A *policy engine* takes policies as the input and evaluates resource metadata for compliance to policies.

Many policy engines parse and check fields in infrastructure configuration or state. In figure 8.4, a policy engine extracts JSON or other metadata from the IaC or system state. Then it passes the metadata to a security or policy test. The engine runs the test to parse fields, check their values, and fail if the actual values do not match the expected values.

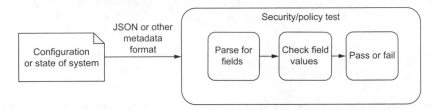

Figure 8.4   Tests for security and policy parse the configuration or state of the system for the correct field values and fail if they do not match an expected value.

This workflow applies to policy as code tools *and* any tests you write yourself. Policy as code tools make testing for values more straightforward because the tools abstract the complexity of parsing for fields and checking the values. However, tools don't cover every value or use case you want to test.

As a result, you usually write your own policy engine to suit your purposes. In the examples for this chapter, I use pytest, a Python testing framework, as a primitive "policy engine" to check for a secure and compliant configuration.

POLICY ENGINES

The policy as a code ecosystem has different tools for different purposes. Most tools fall into one of three use cases, all of which address very different functions and vary widely in behavior:

1 Security tests for specific platforms
2 Policy tests for industry or regulatory standards
3 Custom policies

Table 8.1 includes a non-exhaustive list of policy engines for *provisioning* tools, both vendor and open source. I've outlined a few of the technology integrations and the use case category for each tool.

Table 8.1   Examples of policy engines for provisioning tools

Tool	Use case(s)	Technology integration(s)
AWS CloudFormation Guard	Security tests for specific platforms Custom policies	AWS CloudFormation
HashiCorp Sentinel	Security tests for specific platforms Custom policies	HashiCorp Terraform
Pulumi CrossGuard	Security tests for specific platforms Custom policies	Pulumi SDK
Open Policy Agent (Underlying technology for Fugue, Conftest, Kubernetes Gatekeeper, and more)	Security tests for specific platforms (tool-dependent) Policy tests for industry or regulatory standards (tool-dependent) Custom policies	Various (for a complete list, see www.openpolicyagent.org/docs/latest/ecosystem/)
Chef InSpec	Security tests for specific platforms Custom policies	Various (for a complete list, search the Chef marketplace at https://supermarket.chef.io)
Kyverno	Security tests for specific platforms Custom policies	Kubernetes

You often need to *mix and match* tools to cover all use cases. No single tool covers all use cases. Some tools offer customization, which you can use to build policies of your own. In general, consider extending an existing tool with custom policies so you can establish opinionated patterns and defaults with your security, compliance, and engineering teams. In reality, you'll probably adopt five or six policy engines to cover the tools, platforms, and policies you need.

Note that I do not include any security or policy tooling specific to data center appliances, which often depend on your organization's procurement requirements. You may also find some community projects outside of the examples listed in table 8.1. I often find these tools and their integrations replaced by newer ones since the ecosystem changes rapidly.

Image building and configuration management

Image building tools do not have too many security or policy tools, as you tend to write your tests for them. Configuration management tools follow a similar approach to provisioning tools. You will need to find community or built-in tools that verify security and policy configuration.

INDUSTRY OR REGULATORY STANDARDS

You might examine table 8.1 and discover that few tools include policy tests for industry or regulatory standards. Most of these policies exist in documentation form, and you often have to write them yourself. On occasion, you can find policy test suites created by the community that you'll need to augment with your own.

For example, the National Institute of Standards and Technology (NIST) in the United States publishes a list of security benchmarks as part of the National Checklist Program (https://ncp.nist.gov/repository). A reviewer for this book also recommended Security Technical Implementation Guides (STIGs) from the US Department of Defense, including technical testing and configuration standards.

> **NOTE** Yes, I am missing many tools or standards in this section. The standards I included apply to the United States and not necessarily worldwide. By the time you read this, policy engines will have changed features, integrations, or open source status, and the industry or regulatory standards will have updated drafts. If you'd like to recommend one, please let me know at https://github.com/joatmon08/tdd-infrastructure.

8.3.2 Security tests

What should you test to secure your infrastructure? Some policy as code tools offer opinionated defaults that capture best practices for a secure system. However, you might need to write your own for your company's specific platforms and infrastructure.

Let's start fixing your database security breach. Fortunately, the testing data did not have anything important. However, in the future, you don't want your teammate copying and deploying the configuration to production. To prevent the testing environment's IaC from deploying to production, you write a test to secure a network for a database.

The database needs a very restrictive, least-privilege (minimum access) firewall rule. Figure 8.5 shows how you implement a test to retrieve the firewall configuration from IaC. The configuration goes to a test, which parses the source range from the firewall rule. If the range contains a permissive rule, `0.0.0.0/0`, the test fails.

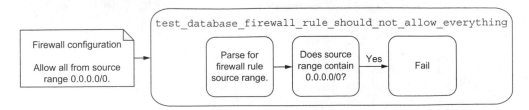

Figure 8.5 Retrieve the source range value from the firewall rule configuration and determine if it contains an overly permissive range.

GCP uses `0.0.0.0/0` to denote that any IP address can access the database. If someone gains access to your network, they can access your database if they have the username and password. Your new test fails before an overly permissive rule like `0.0.0.0/0` goes to production.

Listing 8.3 implements the test for the firewall rule in Python. In your test, you implement code to open the JSON configuration file, retrieve the `source_ranges` list, and check if the list contains `0.0.0.0/0`.

Listing 8.3   Using a test to parse the firewall rule for `0.0.0.0`

```
import json
import pytest
from main import APP_NAME, CONFIGURATION_FILE


@pytest.fixture(scope="module")
def resources():
    with open(CONFIGURATION_FILE, 'r') as f:        Loads the infrastructure
        config = json.load(f)                        configuration from a JSON file
    return config['resource']              ◁──── Parses the resource
                                                  block out of the JSON

@pytest.fixture
def database_firewall_rule(resources):              Parses the Google compute firewall
    return resources[0][                            resource defined by Terraform from
        'google_compute_firewall'][0][APP_NAME][0]  the JSON configuration

                                                             Uses a descriptive
                                                             test name
def test_database_firewall_rule_should_not_allow_everything(  ◁── explaining the policy
        database_firewall_rule):                             for the firewall rule,
    assert '0.0.0.0/0' not in \                               which should not
        database_firewall_rule['source_ranges'], \           allow all traffic
        'database firewall rule must not ' + \
        'allow traffic from 0.0.0.0/0, specify source_ranges ' + \
        'with exact IP address ranges'
```

Checks that `0.0.0.0/0`, or allow all, is not defined in the rule's source ranges

Uses a descriptive error message describing how to correct the firewall rule, such as removing 0.0.0.0/0 from source ranges

---

AWS and Azure equivalents

A firewall rule in GCP is equivalent to an AWS security group (http://mng.bz/Qvvm) or Azure network security group (http://mng.bz/XZZY). To update the code, create a security group resource in the cloud provider of your choice. Then, edit the test to switch GCP's `source_ranges` with the `security_rule.source_port_range` attribute for Azure or `ingress.cidr_blocks` attribute for AWS.

Imagine your new teammate wants to run some tests on the database from their laptop. They make a change to open the firewall rule to `0.0.0.0/0` in IaC. The pipeline runs the Python code to generate JSON:

```
$ python main.py
```

The pipeline runs unit tests checking the JSON file with the configuration. It recognizes the firewall rule contains 0.0.0.0/0 in the list of allowed source ranges and throws an error:

```
$ pytest test_security.py
====== short test summary info ======
FAILED
      test_security.py::test_database_firewall_rule_should_not_allow_everything -
      ➥AssertionError: database firewall rule must not allow traffic
      ➥from 0.0.0.0/0, specify source_ranges with exact IP address ranges
===== 1 failed in 0.04s ======
```

Your teammate reads the error description and realizes that the firewall rule should not allow all traffic. They can correct their configuration to add their laptop IP address to source ranges.

Just like functional tests in chapter 6, security tests *educate* the rest of your team on ideal secure practices for infrastructure. While the tests do not necessarily catch all security violations, they communicate important information about security expectations. Moving the *unknown knowns* of security best practices to *known knowns* eliminates a repeated mistake.

These tests also help scale security practices in your organization. Your teammate feels empowered to correct the configuration. Furthermore, your security team has fewer investigations and follow-ups for security violations. Making security part of everyone's responsibility reduces the time and effort for future remediation.

Positive versus negative testing

In the example of the database IP address range, you checked that an IP address range does *not* match every IP address (0.0.0.0/0). Called *negative testing*, this process asserts that the value does not match. You can also use *positive testing* to assert that attributes do match an expected value.

Some references suggest that you express all security or policy tests with one type. However, I usually write tests with both positive and negative testing assertions. The combination better expresses the intent of the security and policy requirement. For example, you can use the negative test to check for any IP address range against *any* infrastructure configuration written by any team. On the other hand, if you have an IP address range that every firewall rule *must include*, such as a VPN connection, you can use a positive test.

You can write tests to check other secure configurations, including these:

- Ports, IP ranges, or protocols on other network policies
- Access control for no administrative or root access of infrastructure resources, servers, or containers
- Metadata configuration to mitigate exploitation of instance metadata
- Access and audit logging configuration for security information and event management (SIEM), such as for load balancers, IAM, or storage buckets

- Package or configuration versions for fixed vulnerabilities

This non-exhaustive list covers some general configurations. However, you should consult with your security team or other industry benchmarks for additional information and tests.

8.3.3   *Policy tests*

Security tests verify that you minimize the attack surface of misconfiguration in your IaC. However, you need other tests for auditing, reporting, billing, and troubleshooting. For example, your testing database should have a tag on it so someone can identify its owner and report the security breach.

The uDress compliance team reminds you to add tags to your GCP database so they can identify the database owner. They also notify you that the security breach caused the database resources to scale, which increased your cloud computing bill. Without tags, the compliance team had a difficult time identifying who to contact about the security problem and the increased bill.

You add tags to the database configuration. To remind yourself of tagging in the future, you use the workflow shown in figure 8.6 to implement a unit test to check for tags. As with the security test for the firewall rule configuration, you parse a JSON file with the database configuration to check that you correctly filled the labels with tags. If the test has empty labels, the test fails.

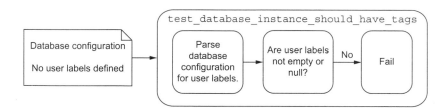

Figure 8.6   You implement a test that parses the database configuration and checks for a list of tags in the database's user labels.

The policy test behaves similarly to the security test. However, it tests the tags instead of the IP source ranges. While the policy does not better secure the infrastructure, it improves your ability to troubleshoot and identify resources.

Let's implement the test workflow. In the following listing, you write a test to check that you have more than zero tags under the GCP `user_labels` parameter.

Listing 8.4   Using a test to parse the database configuration for tags

```
import json
import pytest
from main import APP_NAME, CONFIGURATION_FILE
```

```
@pytest.fixture(scope="module")
def resources():
    with open(CONFIGURATION_FILE, 'r') as f:          Loads the infrastructure
        config = json.load(f)                          configuration from a JSON file
    return config['resource']    ◁─────
                                        Parses the resource block out
                                        of the JSON configuration file        Parses user labels in
                                                                              the Google SQL
                                                                              database instance
@pytest.fixture                                                               defined by Terraform
def database_instance(resources):                                             from the JSON
    return resources[2][                                                      configurations
        'google_sql_database_instance'][0][APP_NAME][0]

                                                                              Checks that the user
                                                                              labels on the database
                                                                              do not have an empty
  ▷ def test_database_instance_should_have_tags(database_instance):          list or null value
        assert database_instance['settings'][0]['user_labels'] \
            is not None
        assert len(
            database_instance['settings'][0]['user_labels']) > 0, \
            'database instance must have `user_labels`' + \
            'configuration with tags'

 Uses a descriptive test name explaining     Uses a descriptive error message describing
 the policy for tagging the database            the addition of tags to GCP user labels
```

> ### AWS and Azure equivalents
>
> To convert listing 8.4 to AWS or Azure, change the Google SQL database instance to a PostgreSQL offering from either cloud. You can use AWS RDS (http://mng.bz/yvvJ) or Azure Database for PostgreSQL (http://mng.bz/M552). Then, parse the database instance resource for the `tags` attribute. Both Azure and AWS use tags.

You add the test to your security tests. The next time your teammate makes a change and forgets tags, the test fails. Your teammate reads the error message and corrects their IaC to include the tags. You can implement tests for other organizational policies, including these:

- Required tags for all resources
- Number of approvers for a change
- The geographic location of an infrastructure resource
- Log outputs and target servers for auditing
- Separate development data from production data

This non-exhaustive list covers some general configurations. However, you should consult with your compliance team or other industry benchmarks for additional information and tests. As you write your tests, ensure that you include clear error messages outlining which policies the test checks.

8.3.4 Practices and patterns

As you write more security and policy tests, you gain confidence that your configuration remains secure and compliant. How can you teach this across your team and company?

You can apply some of the practices and patterns for testing to checking infrastructure security and compliance. Next, I'll cover the practices and patterns for writing security and policy tests in greater detail.

USE DETAILED TEST NAMES AND ERROR MESSAGES

You'll notice *detailed test names and error messages* for the uDress policy and security tests. These names and messages seem verbose but communicate to teammates precisely what the policy looks for and how they should correct it! I introduced a technique in chapter 2 to verify the quality of your naming and code. Try asking someone else to read the test. If they can understand its purpose, they can update their configuration to conform to the policy as code.

MODULARIZE TESTS

You can apply some of the *module patterns* from chapter 3 to policy as code. For example, the uDress payments team asks to borrow your security and policy tests for their infrastructure. You divide your database policies into `database-tests`, and firewall policies into `firewall-tests`.

The security team also asks you to add a Center for Internet Security (CIS) benchmark. This industry benchmark includes tests to verify the best practices for secure configuration on GCP. After adding the security benchmark, you realize that you have too many tests to track in multiple repositories.

Figure 8.7 moves all of these tests into a repository named `gcp-security-test`. The repository organizes all tests for uDress's GCP infrastructure. The uDress frontend and payments teams can reference a shared repository, import the tests, and run them against their configuration. Meanwhile, the security team can update the security benchmarks in one place in the `gcp-security-tests` repository.

As with your infrastructure approach to code repository structures, you can choose to put your organization's policy as code in a single repository or divide it across multiple repositories based on the environment. In either structure, make sure all

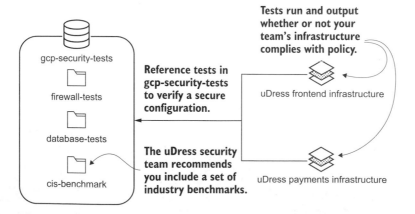

Figure 8.7   Add policy as code to a shared repository for distribution across all teams creating infrastructure.

teams have visibility into security and policy tests for the organization to learn how to deploy compliant infrastructure.

Furthermore, divide the tests based on business unit, function, environment, infrastructure provider, infrastructure resource, stack, or benchmark. You want to evolve the types of tests individually as your business changes. Some business units may need one type of test, while another may not. Dividing the tests and running them selectively helps.

ADD POLICY AS CODE TO DELIVERY PIPELINES

Your team wants to make sure to run the security and policy tests before pushing to production, so they add them as a *stage of their delivery pipeline*. Policy as code runs *after* deploying the changes to a testing environment but *before* releasing to production. You get fast feedback on infrastructure changes, prioritizing functionality but checking policy before production.

The security team also adds policy as code to scan the *running* production environment. This dynamic analysis continuously verifies the security and compliance of any emergency or break-glass changes to infrastructure.

Figure 8.8 shows the workflow of static analysis in a delivery pipeline and dynamic analysis of running infrastructure to check configuration changes and address issues in resources proactively. After deploying the changes to a testing environment, you

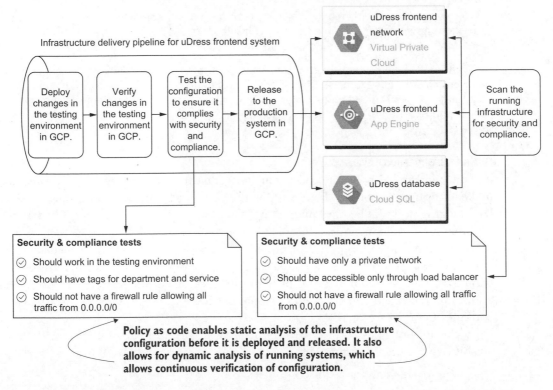

Figure 8.8   Tests for security and policy check for improper infrastructure configuration and prevent the changes from going to production.

run the security and policy tests. They should pass before releasing the changes to production. When the resources get the changes, you scan the running infrastructure with similar tests for runtime security and policy checks.

You may have different tests for static and dynamic analysis. Some tests, such as live verification of endpoint access, can work on only running infrastructure. As a result, you want to run some tests *before* and *after* you push to production.

If your static analysis tests take too long, you could run a subset of tests after you push the change to production. However, you will have to quickly remediate any security or compliance violations. As a result, I recommend running the most critical security and policy tests as part of your pipeline.

> ## Image building
>
> You might encounter the practice of building immutable server or container images. By baking the packages you want into a server or container image, you can create new servers with updates without the problems of in-place updates.
>
> Use the same workflow of the infrastructure pipeline with policy as code to build the immutable images. The workflow includes unit tests to check the scripts for specific installation requirements, such as a company package registry, and integration tests against a test server to verify that the package versions comply with policy and security.
>
> You can always use dynamic analysis in the form of an agent to scan a server and make sure its configuration complies with rules. For example, Sysdig offers Falco, a runtime security tool that runs on a server and checks for rule compliance.
>
> Most teams *do not* want their security or policy tests to block all changes from going to production. For example, what if customers need to access public endpoints for infrastructure? The test to check for a private network only may not apply. Sometimes you find exceptions in your security policy.

DEFINE ENFORCEMENT LEVELS

As you build more policy as code, you must identify the most important ones and make exceptions for others. For example, the uDress security team identifies the database tagging policy to be hard mandatory. The delivery pipeline *must fail* if it does not find tags, and someone must add the tags.

You define three categories of policy, as shown in figure 8.9. The security team mandates that you fix the database tags before pushing to production. However, the team makes an exception for your firewall rule because customers need access to your endpoint. The team also includes some advice on more secure infrastructure configurations.

I classify policy as code into three categories of enforcement (borrowed from HashiCorp Sentinel's terminology):

- *Hard mandatory* for required policies
- *Soft mandatory* for policies that may require manual analysis for an exception
- *Advisory* for knowledge-sharing of best practices

Hard mandatory

Soft mandatory

Advisory

You must fix the database tags before pushing the change to production.

The security team must review your firewall rule and manually approve the change to production.

Your infrastructure configuration may not be compliant with industry standards; try to correct what you can.

Figure 8.9   You can divide policy as code into three enforcement categories that gate changes before production.

The security team classifies the firewall rule as a soft mandatory. Some public load balancers must allow access from 0.0.0.0/0. If the firewall rule test fails, someone from the security team must review the rule and manually approve the change to production in the pipeline.

The security team sets the CIS benchmarks as `advisory` for knowledge sharing and best practices. They ask you to correct the configuration, if possible, but they do not require enforcement before production.

Do you have to run security tests before changes go to production? They take a while to run, after all! If you worry that security and policy tests will gate the changes too long, run the *hard mandatory* tests before deploying to production.

You can run the soft mandatory or advisory tests asynchronously, so only the necessary tests block your pipeline. I *do not* recommend running *all* security and policy tests asynchronously because you may temporarily introduce a noncompliant configuration to production, even if you fix it quickly after running asynchronous tests!

Figure 8.10 summarizes testing patterns and practices, such as writing detailed test names and error messages. Similar to infrastructure, you can modularize tests based on function and add tests to delivery pipelines for production.

No matter the tool, security benchmark, or policy rules, you should express and communicate the practices in the form of tests. Following these patterns and practices will help you and your teammates improve your security and compliance knowledge.

Write detailed names and error messages to communicate the security and policy requirement.

Divide security and policy tests by business unit, function, environment, infrastructure provider, or stack.

Add security and policy tests to delivery pipelines as a gate for production.

Define enforcement levels to indicate mandatory vs. advisory policies.

Figure 8.10   Tests for security and policy check for improper infrastructure configuration and prevent the changes from going to production.

As your organization grows and sets more policies, you expand your security and policy tests with it. Early adoption of policy as code sets a foundation for baking security and compliance practices into your IaC. If you cannot find a tool to run the tests you need, consider writing your own tests to parse IaC.

Summary

- A company policy ensures that systems comply with security, audit, and organizational requirements. Your company defines policies based on industry, country, and other factors.
- The principle of least privilege gives a user or service account only the minimum access they require.
- Ensure that your IaC uses credentials with least privilege access to the infrastructure provider. Least privilege prevents someone from exploiting the credentials and creating unauthorized resources in your environment.
- Use a tool to suppress or redact plaintext, sensitive information in a delivery pipeline.
- Rotate any usernames or passwords generated by IaC after applying it in the pipeline.
- Tagging infrastructure with service, owner, email, accounting information, environment, and automation details makes it easier to identify and audit security and billing.
- Policy as code tests some infrastructure metadata and verifies that it complies with a secure or compliant configuration.
- Use policy as code to test the security and compliance of your infrastructure before pushing to production but after functional testing of your system.
- Apply clean IaC and module patterns to managing and scaling policy as code.
- Classify each security and policy test into one of three enforcement categories, such as hard mandatory (must fix), soft mandatory (manual review), and advisory (best practice, but not blocking production).

Part 3

Managing production complexity

Once multiple teams use infrastructure as code and build a common practice, you must learn to make changes and manage the complexity of production infrastructure. This final part describes techniques for updating infrastructure through IaC and changing IaC itself. You will, after all, change your infrastructure and evolve your tools and configuration!

In chapter 9, you'll learn how to make changes to infrastructure and minimize the potential for change failure. Chapter 10 describes the process of refactoring IaC, which you may need after growing your practice or system. If your refactor causes infrastructure failure, you can use the general techniques in chapter 11 to roll forward, troubleshoot, and fix your changes.

However, as you continue to grow your system, you will encounter cost concerns. Chapter 12 offers guidance for IaC techniques to manage the cost of infrastructure. Finally, chapter 13 concludes with techniques for using open source tools and modules and replacing or upgrading existing tools.

Making changes 9

This chapter covers

- Determining when to use patterns like blue-green deployments to update infrastructure
- Establishing immutability to create environments across multiple regions with IaC
- Determining change strategies for updating stateful infrastructure

In previous chapters, we started with helpful practices and patterns for modularizing, decoupling, testing, and deploying infrastructure changes. However, you also need to manage changes to infrastructure with infrastructure as code techniques. In this chapter, you'll learn how to change IaC with strategies that apply immutability to minimize the impact of potential failure.

Let's return to Datacenter for Veggies and its struggles to modularize IaC from chapter 5. The company acquires Datacenter for Carnivorous Plants as a subsidiary. Its carnivorous plants, like Venus flytraps, require particular growing conditions.

As a result, Datacenter for Carnivorous Plants needs global networking and network-optimized servers and components. Most teams configure their IaC but realize that their code can't handle such a widespread change. They ask you, a Datacenter for Veggies engineer with some experience in IaC, to help them.

The engineering team directs you to the Cape sundew team to update its infrastructure first. As a hardy carnivorous plant, the Cape sundew can best handle any system downtime that causes fluctuations in temperature and watering. All of the infrastructure resources for the Cape sundew infrastructure exist in a single repository with a few configuration files.

You investigate and diagram the architecture of the sundew system. Figure 9.1 shows a regional forwarding rule (load balancer) that sends traffic to a regional network with a container cluster and three servers. All traffic circulates in the same region and not globally.

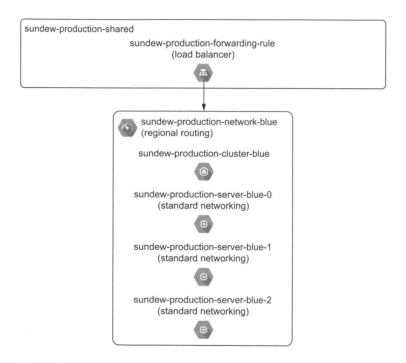

Figure 9.1   The Cape sundew applications use an infrastructure system with shared load balancing resources, three servers, and one container cluster.

You want to change all resources to send traffic globally instead of routing in a single region. However, the sundew team defined all of these resources in the same IaC, also known as the singleton pattern (refer to chapter 3). The resources also share infrastructure state.

How do you roll out the network changes to the system and minimize their impact? You worry about disrupting the watering application if you treat the infrastructure mutably by making the change in place. For example, changing your network to use global routing may affect the servers supporting the watering application.

You remember from chapter 2 that you can use the idea of immutability to build new infrastructure with new changes. If you can apply these techniques to the system, you can isolate and test the changes in a new environment without affecting the old one. In this chapter, you'll learn how to isolate and make changes to IaC.

NOTE Demonstrating change strategies requires a sufficiently large (and complex) example. If you run the complete example, you will incur a cost that exceeds the GCP free tier. This book includes only the relevant lines of code and omits the rest for readability. For the listing in its entirety, refer to the book's code repository at https://github.com/joatmon08/manning-book/tree/main/ch09. If you convert these examples for AWS and Azure, you will also incur a cost. When possible, I offer notations on converting the examples to the cloud provider of your choice.

9.1 Pre-change practices

You jump right into changing the sundew system. Unfortunately, you accidentally delete a configuration attribute that tags a server with `blue`, which allows traffic between all blue instances in the network. You push your change to your delivery pipeline to test the configuration and apply it to production.

Testing misses the deleted tag. Fortunately, your monitoring system sends you an alert that the watering application cannot communicate with your new server! You divert all requests to a duplicate server instance to ensure that the sundews still get watered while you debug.

You realize that you should *not* start changing the system. The sundew system has existing architecture and tools you need to understand before you start. You also need to know if the system has backups or alternative environments ready for use if you break something. What should you do *before* you make a change?

9.1.1 Following a checklist

You always run the risk of introducing bugs and other problems when changing IaC. You need testing, monitoring, and observability (the ability to infer a system's internal state from its outputs) to ensure that you haven't affected the system during your change. If you do not have some visibility into your system, you cannot quickly troubleshoot problems from broken changes.

Before you change the sundew system, you decide to review a few things about your system. Figure 9.2 shows what you review. You first add a test to check for your deleted tag. Next, you examine your monitoring system for both system and application health checks and metrics. Finally, you create duplicate servers as backup, just in case you break the existing servers. You can send traffic to the backup server if you accidentally affect the updated server.

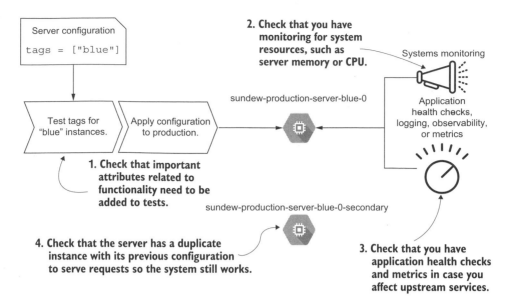

Figure 9.2   Before updating the network, you need to verify test coverage, systems and application monitoring, and redundancy.

Why did you create the duplicate servers as backup? It helps to have extra resources that duplicate the previous configuration that you use only if the primary resources fail. This *redundancy* keeps your system running.

> **DEFINITION**   *Redundancy* is the duplication of resources to improve the system's performance. If updated components fail, the system can use working resources with a previous configuration.

In general, review the following checklist before you make a change:

- Can you preview each change and *test* the changes in an isolated environment?
- Does the system have *monitoring and alerts* configured to identify any anomalies?
- Does the application track error responses with *health checks, logging, observability, or metrics?*
- Do the applications and their systems have any *redundancy?*

The items on the list focus on visibility and awareness. Without monitoring systems or tests to help identify problems, you may have trouble identifying or resolving broken changes. I once pushed a change that broke an application and did not find out until *two weeks* after release. It took so long to realize the problem because we did not have alerts on the application!

A pre-change checklist sets the foundation for debugging any problems and establishing any backup plans should the change fail. You can even use the practices from chapters 6 and 8 to build this checklist into delivery pipelines as quality gates.

9.1.2 Adding reliability

After reviewing the pre-change checklist, you realize that you need a better backup environment in your system. To ensure that you don't bring down the entire sundew system in your continued refactoring efforts, you need additional redundancy. When you finally deploy a change to the sundew team's modules, you do not need to worry about disrupting the system.

Unfortunately, the sundew system exists only in `us-central1`. The sundews don't get watered if the region fails! You decide to build an idle production sundew system in another region (`us-west1`) so you can restart the watering application. You use IaC to *reproduce* the active region in `us-central1` to the passive (idle) region in `us-west1`.

You can now use the environment in the passive region as a backup. In figure 9.3, you update the sundew team's configuration to use a server module and push the change to the active environment. If it does not work, you temporarily send all traffic to the passive environment while you debug the problem. Otherwise, you run tests and update the passive environment with the module changes.

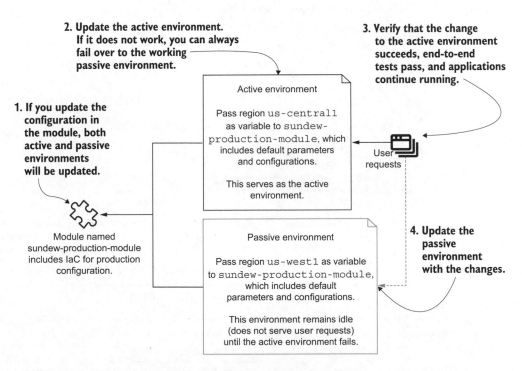

Figure 9.3   You use IaC to implement an active-passive configuration for the sundew system to improve its reliability during changes.

The sundew system now uses an *active-passive configuration*, in which one environment sits idle and serves as a backup.

> **DEFINITION**   In an *active-passive configuration*, one system is the active environment for completing user requests, and the other is the backup environment.

If the environment in `us-central1` stops working, you can always send traffic to the other passive environment in `us-west1`. Switching from a failed active environment to the working passive one follows the process of *failover*.

> **DEFINITION**   *Failover* is the practice of using passive (or standby) resources to take over when the primary resources fail.

Why would you want an active-passive configuration? Building a passive environment in a second region improves the overall reliability of the system. *Reliability* measures how long a system performs correctly within a time period.

> **DEFINITION**   *Reliability* measures how long a system performs correctly within a time period.

You want to keep your system reliable as you make IaC changes. Improving reliability minimizes disruption to business-critical applications and, ultimately, end users. You reduce your blast radius to the active environment with the option to cut over traffic to a working passive environment.

Let's create the active-passive configuration in code. In your terminal, you copy the file named blue.py containing the sundew's infrastructure resources to a new file named passive.py:

```
$ cp blue.py passive.py
```

For passive.py in listing 9.1, you update a few variables to create the passive sundew environment, including region and name.

Listing 9.1   Updating the passive sundew environment for `us-west1`

```
TEAM = 'sundew'
ENVIRONMENT = 'production'
VERSION = 'passive'                  Sets the version to identify    Changes the region from
REGION = 'us-west1'                  the passive environment          us-central1 to us-west1 for
IP_RANGE = '10.0.1.0/24'                                              the passive environment

                                     Updates a different IP address
                                     range for the passive environment
                                     to avoid sending requests
zone = f'{REGION}-a'
network_name = f'{TEAM}-{ENVIRONMENT}-network-{VERSION}'
server_name = f'{TEAM}-{ENVIRONMENT}-server-{VERSION}'               Remaining variables
                                                                     and functions
cluster_name = f'{TEAM}-{ENVIRONMENT}-cluster-{VERSION}'             reference the
cluster_nodes = f'{TEAM}-{ENVIRONMENT}-cluster-nodes-{VERSION}'      constants for the
cluster_service_account = f'{TEAM}-{ENVIRONMENT}-sa-{VERSION}'       passive environment,
                                                                     including region.
```

```
labels = {
    'team': TEAM,
    'environment': ENVIRONMENT,
    'automated': True
}
```

Defines labels for resources so you can identify the production environment

> ## AWS and Azure equivalents
>
> GCP labels are similar to AWS and Azure tags. You can take the object defined in the `labels` variable and pass it to AWS and Azure resource tags.

You now have a backup environment in case your module change goes wrong. Imagine you push the change and break the active environment in `us-central1`. You can update and push the configuration for a production global load balancer to failover and send everything to the passive environment. In the following listing, you change the weight on your global load balancer to send 100% of traffic to the passive environment.

Listing 9.2 Failover to passive sundew environment in `us-west1`

```
import blue
import passive
```

Imports IaC for both blue (active environment) and passive environment

```
services_list = [
    {
        'version': 'blue',
        'zone': blue.zone,
        'name': f'{shared_name}-blue',
        'weight': 0
    }, {
        'version': 'passive',
        'zone': passive.zone,
        'name': f'{shared_name}-passive',
        'weight': 100
    }
]
```

Defines a list of versions for each environment to attach to the load balancer, blue and passive

Configures the load balancer with a weight to send 0% of traffic to the blue version

Configures the load balancer with a weight to send 100% of traffic to the passive version

```
def _generate_backend_services(services):
    backend_services_list = []
    for service in services:
        version = service['version']
        weight = service['weight']
        backend_services_list.append({
            'backend_service': (
                '${google_compute_backend_service.'
                f'{version}.id}}'
            ),
            'weight': weight,
        })
    return backend_services_list
```

Adds the two versions to the load balancer with their weights as routes to the load-balancing rule

Defines backend services for the blue and passive environments with a weight to direct traffic to each one

```
def load_balancer(name, default_version, services):
    return [{
        'google_compute_url_map': {
            TEAM: [{
                'name': name,
                'path_matcher': [{
                    'name': 'allpaths',
                    'path_rule': [{
                        'paths': [
                            '/*'
                        ],
                        'route_action': {
                            'weighted_backend_services':
                                _generate_backend_services(
                                    services)
                        }
                    }]
                }]
            }]
        }
    }]
```

Creates the Google compute URL map (load-balancing rule) using a Terraform resource based on the path, blue (active) and passive servers, and weight

Sets up a path rule that directs all paths to the active or passive servers

Adds the two versions to the load balancer with their weights as routes to the load-balancing rule

---

AWS and Azure equivalents

The Google Cloud URL map is similar to AWS Application Load Balancer (ALB) or Azure Traffic Manager and Application Gateway. To convert listing 9.2 to AWS, you will need to update the resource to create an AWS ALB and listener rule. Then, add path routing and weight attributes to the ALB listener rule.

For Azure, you will need to link an Azure Traffic Manager profile and endpoint to an Azure Application Gateway. Update the Azure Traffic Manager with weights and route them to the correct backend address pool attached to an Azure Application Gateway.

After you fail over the system to the passive environment, the sundew team reports the return of the watering application. You have a chance to debug problems with your module in the blue (active) environment. The active-passive configuration will protect from failures in individual regions in the future.

The sundew team members tell you that, eventually, they want to send traffic to both regions. Both environments in each region process requests. Figure 9.4 shows their dream configuration. The next time, they want to update the module and push it out to one region. If a region breaks, *most* requests will still get processed by the system. You water the sundews less frequently but have an opportunity to fix the broken region.

Why aspire to run two active environments? Many distributed systems run in *an active-active configuration*, which means both systems process and accept requests and replicate data between them. Public cloud architectures recommend using a multiregion, active-active configuration to improve the system's reliability.

DEFINITION In an *active-active configuration*, multiple systems are the active environments for completing user requests and replicating data between them.

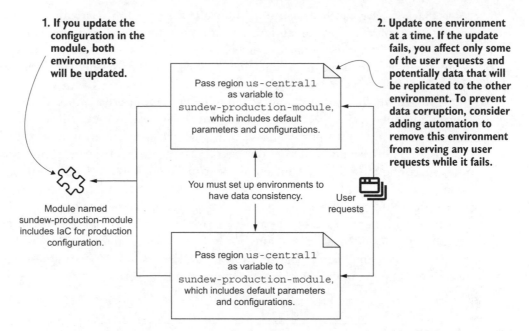

Figure 9.4 In the future, the sundew team will further refactor the system configuration to support an active-active configuration and send requests to both regions.

Your changes to IaC will differ depending on active-passive or active-active configuration. The sundew team's active-active configuration must refactor the IaC into more modular components and support data replication between environments. Assuming the sundew team refactors its applications to support an active-active configuration, you will need to implement some form of global load balancing in your IaC and connect it to each region.

IaC conforms to *reproducibility*, which we covered in chapter 1. Thanks to this principle, we can create a new environment in a new region with a few updates to attributes. You do not have to painstakingly rebuild an environment resource by resource as we did in chapter 2.

However, you may find yourself copying and pasting a lot of the same configuration. Try to pass regions as inputs and modularize your IaC to reduce copying and pasting. Separate shared resources configuration, like global load balancer definitions, away from the environment configurations.

Multiregion environments always incur a cost in terms of money and time but can help improve system reliability. IaC expedites creating copies of new environments in other regions and enforces consistent configurations across regions. Inconsistencies between regions can introduce significant system failures and increase maintenance effort! Chapter 12 discusses cost management and its considerations.

9.2   *Blue-green deployment*

Now that you have another environment to fall back on if you accidentally corrupt the active one, you can start updating the sundew system to use global networking and premium tier network access for servers. The sundew system uses an active-passive configuration, which means duplicating a whole new environment in a new region just to make changes.

You realize that some changes don't require duplicating entire environments across multiple regions. Why have an entire passive environment just to update a server? Can't you just update one server? After all, we want to minimize the blast radius of failures and optimize our resource efficiency. Instead of using active-passive configuration, you can apply the pattern to fewer resources on a much smaller scale.

In figure 9.5, you reproduce a new *network* with global networking instead of the entire environment. You label the new network green and deploy a set of three servers and one cluster on it. After testing the new resources, you use your global load balancer to send a small percentage of traffic to the new resources. The requests succeed, indicating that the update to global routing worked.

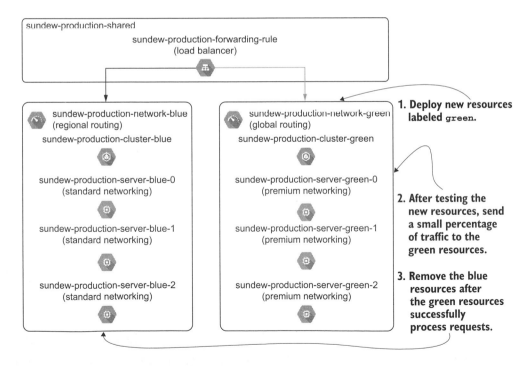

Figure 9.5   Use blue-green deployment to create a green environment for the global network, send some traffic to the new resources, and remove the old resources.

The pattern of creating a new set of resources and gradually cutting over to them applies the principles of composability and evolvability of your system. You add a new `green` set of resources to your environment and allow them to evolve independently of the old resources. If you want to make changes to infrastructure, repeat this workflow to reduce your blast radius of changes and test new resources before sending traffic to them.

   This pattern, called a *blue-green deployment*, creates a new subset of infrastructure resources that stages the changes you want to make, labeled `green`. You then direct a few requests to the green staging infrastructure resources and ensure that everything works. Over time, you send all requests to the green infrastructure resources and remove the old production resources, labeled `blue`.

> **DEFINITION**   *Blue-green deployment* is a pattern that creates a new subset of infrastructure resources with the changes you want to make. You gradually shift traffic from the old set of resources (blue) to the new set of resources (green) and eventually remove the old ones.

Blue-green deployment allows you to isolate and test changes in a (temporarily) new staging environment before sending requests to it. After validating the green environment, you can switch the new environment to the production one and delete the old one. You temporarily pay for two environments for a few weeks but minimize the overall cost of maintaining persistent environments.

> **NOTE**   Blue-green deployment has a few different labels, occasionally with subtle nuances depending on the context. It doesn't matter what color or names you label the environments, as long as you can identify which environment serves as the existing production one or the new staging one. I have also used production/staging and version numbering (v1/v2) to identify old and new resources during blue-green deployment.

You should use a blue-green deployment pattern to refactor or update your IaC beyond a few minimal configurations. Blue-green deployment depends on the principle of immutability to create new resources, cut over traffic or functionality to them, and remove old resources. Most of the patterns for refactoring (chapter 10) and changing IaC often involve the principle of reproducibility.

Image building and configuration management

You can similarly mitigate the risk of a failed machine image or configuration by applying a blue-green deployment pattern. Isolate machine image or configuration management updates to a new server (green), send traffic to it, and test its functionality before removing the old server (blue).

You already have a global load balancer for the existing blue network that you can use later to connect the new green network. In the following sections, let's implement each step of a blue-green deployment for the sundew system.

9.2.1   *Deploying the green infrastructure*

To start a blue-green deployment for the sundew system's global networking and premium tier servers, you copy the configuration for the existing blue network. You create the file named green.py and paste the blue network configuration. In the following listing, you make changes to the network definition so it uses a global routing mode.

Listing 9.3   Creating the green network

```
TEAM = 'sundew'
ENVIRONMENT = 'production'          Sets the name of the new
VERSION = 'green'         ◄         network version to "green"
REGION = 'us-central1'
IP_RANGE = '10.0.0.0/24'     ◄

zone = f'{REGION}-a'
network_name = f'{TEAM}-{ENVIRONMENT}-network-{VERSION}'    ◄

labels = {
    'team': TEAM,
    'environment': ENVIRONMENT,
    'automated': True
}


def build():
    return network()


def network(name=network_name,
            region=REGION,
            ip_range=IP_RANGE):
    return [
        {
            'google_compute_network': {     ◄
                VERSION: [{
                    'name': name,
                    'auto_create_subnetworks': False,
                    'routing_mode': 'GLOBAL'     ◄
                }]
            }
        },
        {
            'google_compute_subnetwork': {     ◄
                VERSION: [{
                    'name': f'{name}-subnet',
                    'region': region,
```

Keeps the IP address range for green the same as the blue network. GCP allows the two networks to have the same CIDR block if you have not set up peering.

Uses the module to create the JSON configuration for the network and subnetwork for the green network

Creates the Google network by using a Terraform resource based on the name and a global routing mode

Updates the green network's routing mode to global to expose routes globally

Creates the Google subnetwork by using a Terraform resource based on the name, region, network, and IP address range

```
                         'network': f'${{google_compute_network.{VERSION}.name}}',
                         'ip_cidr_range': ip_range
                }]
        }
    }
]
```

> **AWS and Azure equivalents**
>
> If you convert listing 9.3 to AWS or Azure, the global routing mode *does not apply*. You can still update the code listing to AWS or Azure by changing Google's network and subnetwork to a VPC or virtual network, and changing the subnets and routing tables.

You want to keep the same configuration for blue and green resources when possible. They should differ only in the changes you want to make to the green sources. However, you might have some differences!

For example, if I had some specific peering configuration for my networks, I *could not* use the blue network's IP address range for the green network. Instead, I would need a different IP address range, like 10.0.1.0/24, and update any dependencies to communicate to another IP address range.

Blue-green deployment favors immutability, creating new, updated resources and isolating the changes away from the old resources. However, deploying a new version of a low-level resource like networking does not mean you can immediately send live traffic to it. You always start by changing and testing the infrastructure resource you want to update. Then, you must change and test *other* resources that depend on it.

9.2.2 Deploying high-level dependencies to the green infrastructure

When you use the blue-green deployment pattern, you always need to deploy a new infrastructure resource with the changes *and* a new set of high-level resources that depend on it. You finished updating the network but cannot use it unless you have servers and applications on it. The new network needs high-level infrastructure that depends on it.

You communicate to the sundew teams to deploy new clusters and servers onto the green network, as shown in figure 9.6. The servers must use premium networking on the global network. The sundew team also deploys its applications onto the cluster and servers.

In this example, changing a low-level infrastructure resource like the network affects the high-level resources. The servers must run with premium networking. Updating the original `blue` network in-place from regional to global routing would likely have affected the servers and cluster. With a blue-green deployment, you *evolve* the network attributes for the servers without affecting the live environment.

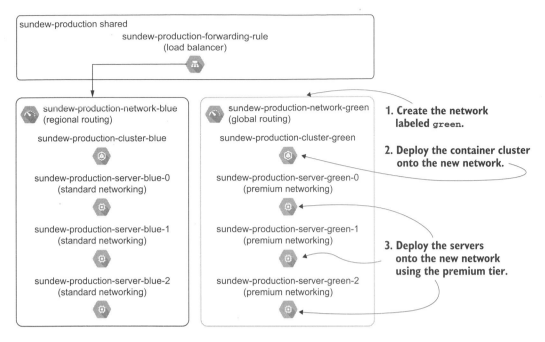

Figure 9.6   After creating the network, a low-level infrastructure resource, you also need to create new high-level resources like the server and container cluster that depend on it.

Let's review a sample of the IaC that the sundew team members added to deploy the cluster onto the green network in the following listing. They copied the cluster configuration from the blue resource and updated its attributes to run on the green network.

Listing 9.4   Adding a new cluster to the green network

```
VERSION = 'green'

cluster_name = f'{TEAM}-{ENVIRONMENT}-cluster-{VERSION}'
cluster_nodes = f'{TEAM}-{ENVIRONMENT}-cluster-nodes-{VERSION}'
cluster_service_account = f'{TEAM}-{ENVIRONMENT}-sa-{VERSION}'

def build():
    return network() + \
        cluster()

def cluster(name=cluster_name,
        node_name=cluster_nodes,
        service_account=cluster_service_account,
        region=REGION):
    return [
        {
```

Labels the new version of the cluster "green"

Uses the module to create the JSON configuration for the network, subnetwork, and cluster for the green network

Builds the cluster on the green network and subnetwork

Passes required attributes to the cluster, including name, node names, service accounts for automation, and region

```
                  'google_container_cluster': {          ◄─┐
                      VERSION: [                            │  Creates the Google container cluster
                          {                                 │  by using a Terraform resource with
                              'initial_node_count': 1,      │  one node and on the green network
                              'location': region,        ◄─┘
                              'name': name,
                              'remove_default_node_pool': True,
                              'network':
                 f'${{google_compute_network.{VERSION}.name}}',
                              'subnetwork': \
                                  f'${{google_compute_subnetwork.{VERSION}.name}}'
                          }
                      ]
                  }
              }
          ]
```

Builds the cluster on the green network and subnetwork

AWS and Azure equivalents

You can update the code by changing the Google container cluster to an Amazon EKS cluster or Azure Kubernetes Service (AKS) cluster. You will need an Amazon VPC and Azure virtual network for the Kubernetes node pools (also called *groups*).

The cluster does not require any changes to adapt to the global networking configuration. However, the servers need premium networking. You copy the server configuration from blue and change it to use premium networking attributes in green.py.

Listing 9.5 Adding premium networking to servers on the green network

```
VERSION = 'green'   ◄─┐ Labels the new version
                      └─ of the network "green"
```
Creates a template for the server name, which includes the team, environment, and version (blue or green)
```
server_name = f'{TEAM}-{ENVIRONMENT}-server-{VERSION}'   ◄──┘
```

```
def build():     ◄──┐ Uses the module to create the JSON configuration for the network,
    return network() + \  subnetwork, cluster, and server for the green network
        cluster() + \
        server0() + \
        server1() + \        Builds the three servers on the
        server2()            green network with the cluster
```
Copies and pastes each server configuration. This code snippet features the first server, server0. Other server configurations are omitted for clarity.

```
def server0(name=f'{server_name}-0',
            zone=zone):
    return [
        {
            'google_compute_instance': {   ◄──
                f'{VERSION}_0': [{
                    'allow_stopping_for_update': True,
                    'boot_disk': [{
```
Creates a small Google compute instance (server) by using a Terraform resource on the green network

```
            'initialize_params': [{
                'image': 'ubuntu-1804-lts'
            }]
        }],
        'machine_type': 'f1-micro',
        'name': name,
        'zone': zone,
        'network_interface': [{
            'subnetwork': \
                f'${{google_compute_subnetwork.{VERSION}.name}}',
            'access_config': {
                'network_tier': 'PREMIUM'                        <───┐
            }                                                        │
        }]                              Sets the network tier to use │
    }]                                  premium networking. This enables
}                                       compatibility with the underlying
}                                       subnet, which uses global routing.
]
```

> **AWS and Azure equivalents**
>
> If you convert listing 9.5 to AWS or Azure, the network tier *does not apply*. You can still update the code by changing the Google compute instance to an Amazon EC2 instance or Azure Linux virtual machine with an Ubuntu 18.04 image. You will need an Amazon VPC and Azure virtual network first.

Updating the network tier to premium *should* not affect the functionality of the applications, although you don't quite know! The green environment allows you to identify and mitigate any problems before affecting sundew growth. After the sundew team makes the updates, it pushes the changes and checks the test results in the delivery pipeline.

The tests include unit, integration, and end-to-end testing to ensure that you can run the applications on the new container cluster and send requests to the new green servers. Fortunately, the tests pass, and you feel ready to send live traffic to the green resources.

9.2.3 *Using a canary deployment to the green infrastructure*

You could immediately send all traffic to the green network, servers, and cluster. However, you don't want to bring down the sundew system! Ideally, you want to switch all traffic back to blue when you find a problem with your system. In figure 9.7, you adjust the global load balancer to send 90% of traffic to the blue network and 10% of traffic to the services on the green network.

If this small amount of traffic sent to your system, known as a *canary deployment*, results in errors in requests, you need to debug and fix your changes.

> **DEFINITION**   *Canary deployment* is a pattern that sends a small percentage of traffic to the updated resources in the system. If the requests complete successfully, you increase the percentage of traffic over time.

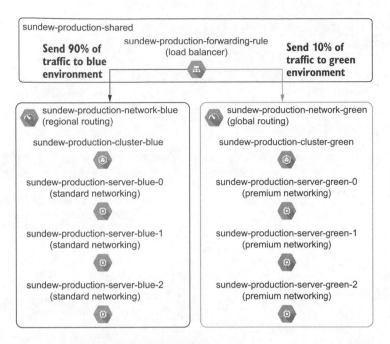

Figure 9.7 **Configure the global load balancer to run a canary test and send a small percentage of traffic to green resources.**

Why send a small amount of traffic first? You do not want all of your requests failing. Sending a few requests to the updated resources helps identify critical problems before you affect your entire system.

Canary in a coal mine

A *canary* in software or infrastructure serves as a first indicator of whether your new system, feature, or application will work. The term comes from the expression "canary in a coal mine." Miners would bring caged birds with them into mines. If the mine had dangerous gas, the birds would serve as the first indicator.

You'll often find references to canary *testing* in software development, which measures user experience for a new version of an application or feature. I highly recommend canary *deployment*, the technique of sending a small percentage of traffic to new resources, anytime you make significant infrastructure changes.

Note that you *do not* have to use load balancers to achieve a canary deployment. You can use any method to send a few requests to updated infrastructure resources. For example, you could add one updated application instance to an existing pool of three application instances. A round-robin load-balancing scheme sends about 25% of your requests to the new, updated instance and 75% to old, existing application instances.

For the sundew team, you separate the global load balancer configuration away from the green and blue environments in your configuration. This improves the load balancer's evolvability. You add the green servers as a separate backend service to the load balancer and control requests between green and blue environments.

You define the load balancer in a file named shared.py in the following listing. Let's add the green version of the network (servers and cluster, too!) to the list of versioned environments with a weight of 10.

Listing 9.6   Adding a green version to the list of load-balancing services

```python
import blue                              Imports IaC for both blue
import green                             and green environments

                                                            Creates the name for the shared
                                                            global load balancer based on
shared_name = f'{TEAM}-{ENVIRONMENT}-shared'       ◁───     the team and environment

                              Defines a list of versions for
                              each environment to attach
services_list = [        ◁─── to the load balancer, blue          Adds the blue network, servers, and
    {                         and green environments              cluster to the load balancer list.
        'version': 'blue',                                        Retrieves the availability zone of the
        'zone': blue.zone,                                        blue environment from its IaC.
        'name': f'{shared_name}-blue',
        'weight': 90      ◁───   Sets the weight of traffic to the blue server
    },                           instances to 90, representing 90% of requests
    {
        'version': 'green',
        'zone': green.zone,                                   Adds the green network,
        'name': f'{shared_name}-green',                       servers, and cluster to
        'weight': 10      ◁───                                the load balancer list.
    }                                                         Retrieves the availability
]                  Sets the weight of traffic to the          zone of the green
                   green server instances to 10,             environment from its IaC.
                   representing 10% of requests
def _generate_backend_services(services):    ◁───
    backend_services_list = []                            Creates a function to
    for service in services:                              generate a list of backend
        version = service['version']                      services for a load balancer
        weight = service['weight']
        backend_services_list.append({
            'backend_service': (                   For each environment,
                '${google_compute_backend_service.' defines a Google load-
                f'{version}.id}}'                   balancing backend service
            ),                                      with a version and weight
            'weight': weight,           ◁───
        })
    return backend_services_list
```

> ## AWS and Azure equivalents
>
> The backend services in listing 9.6 are similar to an AWS target group for an AWS ALB. However, Azure requires additional resources. You will need to create an Azure Traffic Manager profile and endpoint to the backend address pool attached to the Azure Application Gateway.

The load balancer in shared.py already accepts a list of backend services with differing weights. Once you deploy the list of weights and services in the following listing, the load balancer configuration starts sending 10% of traffic to the green network.

> **Listing 9.7   Updating the load balancer to send traffic to green**

```
default_version = 'blue'

def load_balancer(name, default_version, services):
    return [{
        'google_compute_url_map': {
            TEAM: [{
                'default_service': (
                    '${google_compute_backend_service.'
                    f'{default_version}.id}}'
                ),
                'description': f'URL Map for {TEAM}',
                'host_rule': [{
                    'hosts': [
                        f'{TEAM}.{COMPANY}.com'
                    ],
                    'path_matcher': 'allpaths'
                }],
                'name': name,
                'path_matcher': [{
                    'default_service': (
                        '${google_compute_backend_service.'
                        f'{default_version}.id}}'
                    ),
                    'name': 'allpaths',
                    'path_rule': [{
                        'paths': [
                            '/*'
                        ],
                        'route_action': {
                            'weighted_backend_services':
                                _generate_backend_services(
                                    services)
                        }
                    }]
                }]
            }]
        }
    }]
```

Annotations:
- Uses the module to create the JSON configuration for the load balancer to send 10% of traffic to green and 90% of traffic to blue
- Creates the Google compute URL map (load-balancing rule) by using a Terraform resource based on the path, blue and green environments, and weight
- Sends all traffic from the load balancer to the blue environment by default
- Sets routing rules on the load balancer to send 10% of traffic to green and 90% of traffic to blue

AWS and Azure equivalents

The Google Cloud URL map is similar to an AWS ALB or Azure Traffic Manager and Application Gateway. To convert listing 9.7 to AWS, you will need to update the resource to create an AWS ALB and listener rule. Then, add path routing and weight attributes to the ALB listener rule.

> **(continued)**
>
> For Azure, you will need to link an Azure Traffic Manager profile and endpoint to an Azure Application Gateway. Update the Azure Traffic Manager with weights and route them to the correct backend address pool attached to an Azure Application Gateway.

You run Python in listing 9.8 to build the Terraform JSON configuration for review. The JSON configuration for the load balancer includes the instance groups that organize the blue servers and green servers, backend services to target the blue and green instances' groups, and the weighted routing actions.

Listing 9.8   JSON configuration for the load balancer

```
{
    "resource": [
        {
            "google_compute_url_map": {            ◁——  Defines the Google compute URL map
                "sundew": [                               (load-balancing rule) using a Terraform
                    {                                      resource based on the path, blue and
                        "default_service": \               green environments, and weight
                            "${google_compute_backend_service.blue.id}",
                        "description": "URL Map for sundew",
                        "host_rule": [
                            {
                                "hosts": [
                                    "sundew.dc4plants.com"
                                ],
                                "path_matcher": "allpaths"
                            }
                        ],
                        "name": "sundew-production-shared",
                        "path_matcher": [
                            {
                                "default_service":
                                    "${google_compute_backend_service.blue.id}",
                                "name": "allpaths",
                                "path_rule": [
                                    {
                                        "paths": [
                                            "/*"
                                        ],
                                        "route_action": {
                                            "weighted_backend_services": [
                                                {
                                                    "backend_service":
                                                    "${google_compute_backend_
                                                    service.blue.id}",
                                                    "weight": 90,
                                                },
                                                {
                                                    "backend_service":
```

Annotations:
- **Defines the default service for the Google compute URL map (load-balancing rule) to the blue environment** (points to `"default_service": "${google_compute_backend_service.blue.id}"`)
- **Sends all requests to the blue or green environments based on weight** (points to `"paths": [ "/*" ]`)
- **Sends 90% of traffic to blue backend services, which use the blue network** (points to `"backend_service": "${google_compute_backend_service.blue.id}", "weight": 90`)

Sends 10% of traffic to green backend services, which use the green network

```
                              "${google_compute_backend_
                          service.green.id}",
                                          "weight": 10,
                                  }
                              ]
                          }
                      }
                  ]
              }
          ]
      }
  ]
}
```

Why send all traffic by default to the blue environment? You know the blue environment processes requests successfully. If your green environment breaks, you can quickly switch the load balancer to send traffic to the default blue environment.

In general, copy, paste, and update the green resources. If you express the blue resources in a module, you need to change only the attributes passed to the module. I separate the green and blue environment definitions in separate folders or files, when possible. This makes it easier to identify the environments later.

You may notice some Python code in shared.py that makes it easier to evolve the list of environments and the default environment attached to the load balancer. I usually define a list of environments and a variable for the default environment. Then, I iterate over the list of environments and attach the attributes to a load balancer. This ensures that the high-level load balancer can evolve to accommodate the different resources and environments.

As you add new resources, you can adjust your load balancer to send traffic to additional environments. You may find yourself updating your load balancer's IaC each time you want to run a blue-green deployment. Taking the time and effort to configure the load balancer helps mitigate any problems from changes and controls the rollout of potentially disruptive updates.

9.2.4 *Performing regression testing*

If you immediately send all traffic to the green network and it fails, you could disrupt the watering system for the Cape sundews. As a result, you start with a canary deployment and increase the ratio of traffic to the green network by 10% each day. The process takes about two weeks, but you feel confident that you updated the network correctly! If you find a problem, you reduce traffic to the green network and debug.

Figure 9.8 shows your gradual process of increasing traffic and testing the green environment over time. You gradually decrease traffic to the blue environment until it reaches 0%. You inversely increase traffic to the green environment until it reaches 100%. You run the green environment for a week or two before disabling the blue network just in case the change broke the system in the green environment.

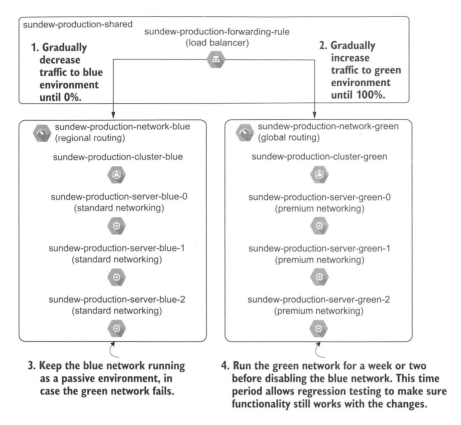

Figure 9.8   Allow a week for a regression test before cutting all traffic to the new network and removing the old one, which allows for time to verify functionality.

The process of gradually increasing traffic and waiting a week before proceeding seems so painful! However, you need to allow the system to run enough traffic through the green environment to determine if you can proceed. Some failures appear with only enough traffic through the system, while others take time to detect.

The window of time you spend testing, observing, and monitoring the system for errors becomes part of a regression test for the system. *Regression testing* checks whether changes to the system affect existing or new functionality. Gradually increasing the traffic over time allows you to assess the system's functionality while mitigating the potential failure impact.

> **DEFINITION**   *Regression testing* checks whether changes to the system affect existing or new functionality.

How much should you increase traffic to the green environment? Increasing traffic by 1% each day does not provide much information unless your system serves millions of requests. *Gradual* doesn't offer clear criteria on which increments you should use. I recommend assessing the number of requests your system serves daily and the cost of failure (such as errors on user requests).

I usually start with increments of 10% and check how many requests that means for the system. If I do not get a sufficient sample size of requests to identify failures, I increase the increment. You want to insert a regression-testing window between each percentage increase to identify system failures.

Even after increasing the load balancer to send all the traffic to the green network, you still want to keep running tests and monitor system functionality for a week or two. Why run regression tests for a few weeks? Sometimes you might encounter edge cases from application requests that break functionality. By allowing a period for regression tests, you can observe whether the system can handle unexpected or uncommon payloads or requests.

9.2.5 Deleting the blue infrastructure

You observe the sundew system for two weeks and resolve any errors. You know that the blue network has not processed any requests or data for about two weeks, which means you can remove it without additional migration steps. You confirm the inactivity with a peer or change advisory board review. Figure 9.9 updates the default service to the green environment before deleting the blue environment from IaC.

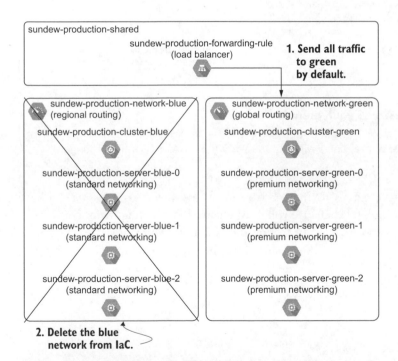

Figure 9.9 Decommission the old network by deleting it from IaC and removing all references.

I consider deleting the blue environment with the network a major change that requires additional peer review. You may not know who uses the network. Other resources that you do not share with other teams, like servers, may not need additional peer review or change approval. Assess the potential impact of deleting an environment and categorize the change based on patterns in chapter 7. Let's adjust the load balancer in shared.py by setting the default service to the green network and removing the blue network from its backend services, as shown in the following listing.

Listing 9.9   Removing the blue environment load balancer

```
import blue                    Imports IaC for both blue
import green                   and green environments

TEAM = 'sundew'
ENVIRONMENT = 'production'
PORT = 8080

shared_name = f'{TEAM}-{ENVIRONMENT}-shared'
                                           Changes the default
                                           version of the network for
default_version = 'green'                  the load balancer to green

services_list = [                  Removes the blue network and
    {                              instances from the list of
        'version': 'green',        backend services to generate
        'zone': green.zone,
        'name': f'{shared_name}-green',
        'weight': 100                Sends all traffic to
    }                                the green network
]
```

> **AWS and Azure equivalents**
>
> Listing 9.9 stays the same for AWS and Azure. You will want to map the version, availability zone, name, and weight to the AWS ALB or Azure Traffic Manager.

You apply the changes to the load balancer. However, you do *not* delete the blue resources immediately because you must ensure that the load balancer does not reference any blue resources. After testing the changes, you remove the code to build the blue environment from main.py and leave the green environment, as follows.

Listing 9.10   Removing the blue environment from main.py

```
import green
import json

if __name__ == "__main__":
    resources = {                  Uses the shared module to
        'resource':                create the JSON configuration
            shared.build() +       for the global load balancer
```

```
        green.build()
}
```

Uses the green module to create the JSON
configuration for the network with global routing,
servers with premium networking, and the cluster

```
with open('main.tf.json', 'w') as outfile:
    json.dump(resources, outfile,
                sort_keys=True, indent=4)
```

Writes the Python dictionary
out to a JSON file to be
executed by Terraform later

You apply the changes, and your IaC tool deletes all blue resources. You decide to delete the blue.py file to prevent anyone from creating new blue resources. I recommend removing any files you do not use to reduce confusion for your teammates in the future. Otherwise, you may have a system with more resources than you need.

Exercise 9.1

Consider the following code:

```
if __name__ == "__main__":
  network.build()
  queue.build(network)
  server.build(network, queue)
  load_balancer.build(server)
  dns.build(load_balancer)
```

The queue depends on the network. The server depends on the network and queue. How would you run a blue-green deployment to upgrade the queue with SSL?

See appendix B for answers to exercises.

9.2.6 *Additional considerations*

Imagine the sundew team needs to change the network again. Instead of creating a new green network, the team can create a new blue network and repeat the deployment, regression test, and deletion process! Since the old blue network no longer exists, this update does not conflict with an existing environment.

What you name your versions or iterations of changes does not matter, as long as you differentiate between old and new resources. For networking specifically, you consider allocating two sets of IP address ranges. You should permanently reserve one for the blue network and the other for the green network. The allocation will allow you the flexibility to make changes by using blue-green deployment without the need to search for open network space.

In general, I decide to use a blue-green deployment strategy when I encounter the following:

- Reverting changes to the resource takes a long time.
- I am not confident that I can revert changes to the resource after deployment.
- The resource has many high-level dependencies that I cannot easily identify.
- The resource change affects critical applications that cannot have downtime.

Not all infrastructure resources should use blue-green deployment. For example, you can update IAM policies in place and quickly revert them if you identify a problem. You'll learn more about reverting changes in chapter 11.

A blue-green deployment strategy costs less in time and money than maintaining multiple environments. However, this strategy will cost *more* when you have to deploy low-level infrastructure resources like networks, projects, or accounts! I usually consider the pattern worth the cost. It isolates the change to specific resources and provides a lower-risk methodology for deploying changes and minimizing disruption to systems.

9.3 *Stateful infrastructure*

Throughout this chapter, the example omitted an essential class of infrastructure resources. However, the sundew system includes numerous resources that process, manage, and store data. For example, the sundew system includes a Google SQL database running on a network with regional routing.

9.3.1 *Blue-green deployment*

The sundew application team members remind you that they need to update their database to use the new network with global routing. You update the private network ID in IaC and push the changes to your repository. Your deployment pipeline fails on a compliance test (something you learned about in chapter 8).

You notice that the test checks the dry run (plan) for whether the database deletions have failed:

```
$ pytest . -q

F                                                          [100%]
====== FAILURES ======
_____ test_if_plan_deletes_database _____

database = {'address': 'google_sql_database_instance.blue', 'change':
➡{'actions': ['delete'], 'after': None, 'after_sensitive': False,
➡'after_unknown': {}, ...}, 'mode': 'managed', 'name': 'blue', ...}

    def test_if_plan_deletes_database(database):
>       assert database['change']['actions'][0] != 'delete'
E       AssertionError: assert 'delete' != 'delete'

test/test_database_plan.py:35: AssertionError
======= short test summary info =======
FAILED test/test_database_plan.py::test_if_plan_deletes_database -
➡AssertionError: assert 'delete' != 'delete'
1 failed in 0.04s
```

The compliance test prevents you from deleting a critical database! If you applied the change without the test, you would delete *all* of the sundew data! The sundew team raises concerns about updating the database's network in place, so you need to do a blue-green deployment.

In figure 9.10, you manually verify that you can migrate the database to the green network. However, you discover you cannot migrate the database. The sundew system can accommodate for missing data, so you copy the IaC for the blue database and create a new green database instance in the premium network. After migrating the data from the blue to the green database, you switch applications to use the new database and remove the old one.

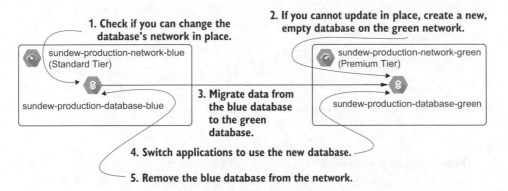

Figure 9.10 If you can't update the database in place, you must deploy a new green database, migrate and reconcile the data, and change the database endpoint from blue to green.

The blue-green deployment strategy applies to the database, a class of infrastructure resource that focuses on state. *Stateful* infrastructure resources like the database store and manage data. In reality, all applications process and store some amount of data. However, stateful infrastructure requires additional care because changes can directly affect data. This type of infrastructure includes databases, queues, caches, or stream-processing tools.

> **DEFINITION** *Stateful* infrastructure describes infrastructure resources that store and manage data.

Why use a blue-green deployment for infrastructure resources with data? Sometimes you cannot update the resource in place with IaC. Replacing the resource may corrupt or lose data, which affects your applications. A blue-green deployment helps you test the functionality of your new database before your applications use it.

9.3.2 *Update delivery pipeline*

Let's return to the sundew team. You must fix the delivery pipeline to automate the update for the database. In figure 9.11, you update your delivery pipeline with a step that automatically migrates data from the blue to the green database. When you add the green database and deploy it, your pipeline deploys the new database, runs integration tests, automatically migrates data from the blue to the green database, and completes the pipeline with end-to-end tests.

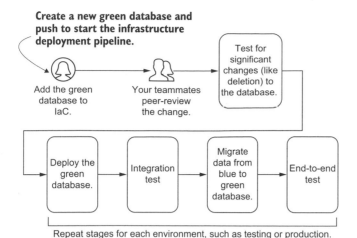

Figure 9.11   The infrastructure deployment pipeline should add the green database and copy data from blue to green.

Preserve *idempotency* with the automation for your migration step. Your script or automation for migration should result in the same database state each time. It should avoid duplicating data each time you run the automation. The data migration process differs depending on the kind of stateful infrastructure you have (database, queue, cache, or stream-processing tools).

> **NOTE** You can dedicate entire books to migrating and managing stateful infrastructure with minimal (or zero) downtime. I recommend *Database Reliability Engineering* by Laine Campbell and Charity Majors (O'Reilly, 2017) for other patterns and practices on managing databases. You can refer to specific documentation on migration, upgrading, and availability for other stateful infrastructure resources.

Depending on how often you update your stateful infrastructure, you should capture the automated data migration to your deployment pipelines and *not* within your IaC. Separating data migration allows you to change any steps and debug problems with the migration independent of creating and removing the stateful resources.

9.3.3   *Canary deployment*

To complete the database update for the sundew team, you make changes to application configuration to use the green database. As high-level resources, the applications depend on the database like a load balancer sends traffic to servers. You can use a modified form of canary deployment to cut over to the new database.

Figure 9.12 shows the pattern of regression testing and configuring the application to use the database. After a period of regression testing (to ensure that functionality still works), you update the application to *write* data exclusively to the green database. After another period of regression testing, you update the application to *read* data from the green database.

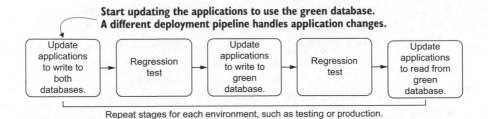

**Start updating the applications to use the green database.
A different deployment pipeline handles application changes.**

Repeat stages for each environment, such as testing or production.

Figure 9.12 You incrementally update the application deployment pipeline to write to both databases, write to the green database, and then read from the green database.

You incrementally roll out the changes to the application to revert to the blue database if you encounter an issue. Since the application writes to two databases, you may have to write additional automation to reconcile data. However, writing to new stateful infrastructure ensures that you test any critical functionality related to storing and updating data. Only then can applications properly read and process data.

Now that the sundew applications use the green database, figure 9.13 removes the blue database by deleting it from the IaC. Note that the compliance tests will fail when you remove the database because you deleted a database! You update the test to fail if you plan on deleting a green database and not a blue one. The manual override allows you to remove the blue database since applications no longer use it.

Techniques like canary deployment provide rapid feedback to mitigate the impact of failure, especially in a situation involving data processing. It can mean the difference between fixing a few wrong entries in a database versus restoring it entirely from backup! I get a sense of comfort knowing that I am making changes to stateful infrastructure in an isolated green environment instead of the live production system.

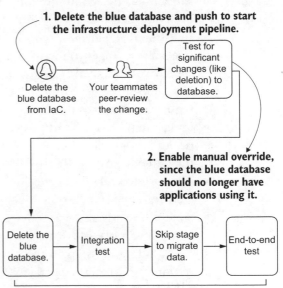

1. Delete the blue database and push to start the infrastructure deployment pipeline.

Delete the blue database from IaC.

Your teammates peer-review the change.

Test for significant changes (like deletion) to database.

2. Enable manual override, since the blue database should no longer have applications using it.

Delete the blue database.

Integration test

Skip stage to migrate data.

End-to-end test

Repeat stages for each environment, such as testing or production.

Figure 9.13 Delete the blue database by removing it from IaC and pushing the changes into your deployment pipeline.

Strategies using immutability like blue-green deployment offer a structured process to make changes and minimize the blast radius of potential failures. Thanks to the principle of reproducibility, you can typically use an immutable approach for changing IaC by duplicating and editing configuration. The principle also allows you to improve the redundancy of your infrastructure system with a similar process of duplication.

Summary

- Ensure that your system has testing, monitoring, and observability for infrastructure and applications before starting any infrastructure updates.
- Redundancy in IaC means adding extra, idle resources to the configuration so you can fail over in case of component failure.
- Adding redundant configuration to IaC can improve system reliability, measuring how long a system performs correctly over a certain period of time.
- An active-passive configuration includes an active environment serving requests and a duplicate idle environment for when the active environment fails.
- Failover switches traffic from a failing active environment to an idle passive environment.
- An active-active configuration sets two active environments serving requests, both of which you can duplicate and manage with IaC.
- Blue-green deployment creates a new subset of infrastructure resources that stages the changes you want to make and gradually switches requests to the new subset. You can then remove the old set of resources.
- In a blue-green deployment, deploy the resource you want to change and the high-level resources that depend on it.
- Canary deployment sends a small percentage of traffic to the new infrastructure resources to verify whether the system works correctly. Over time, you increase the percentage of traffic.
- Allow a few weeks for regression testing to check whether changes to the system affect existing or new functionality.
- Stateful infrastructure resources—like databases, caches, queues, and stream-processing tools—store and manage data.
- Add a migration step to the blue-green deployment of stateful infrastructure resources. You must copy data between blue and green stateful infrastructure.

Refactoring

This chapter covers

- Determining when to refactor IaC to avoid impacting systems
- Applying feature flagging to change infrastructure attributes mutably
- Explaining rolling updates to complete in-place updates

Over time, you might outgrow the patterns and practices you use to collaborate on infrastructure as code. Even change techniques like blue-green deployment cannot solve conflicts in configuration or changes as your team works on some IaC. You must deliver a series of major changes to your IaC and address problems with scaling the practice.

For example, the sundew team for Datacenter for Carnivorous Plants expresses that it can no longer comfortably and confidently roll out new changes to its system. The team puts all infrastructure resources in one repository (as per the singleton pattern) to quickly deliver the system and just kept adding new updates on top of it.

The sundew team outlines a few problems with its system. First, the team finds its updates to infrastructure configuration constantly overlapping. One teammate works on updating servers, only to find another teammate has updated the network and will affect their changes.

Second, it takes more than 30 minutes to run a single change. One change makes hundreds of calls to your infrastructure API to retrieve the state of resources, which slows the feedback cycle.

Finally, the security team expresses concern that the sundew infrastructure may have an insecure configuration. The current configuration does not use standardized, hardened company infrastructure modules.

You realize you need to change the sundew team's configuration. The configuration should use an existing server module approved by the security team. You also need to break the configuration into separate resources to minimize the blast radius of changes.

This chapter discusses some IaC patterns and techniques to break down large singleton repositories with hundreds of resources. As the IaC helper on the sundew team, you'll refactor the system's singleton configuration into separate repositories and structure the server configurations to use modules to avoid conflicts and comply with security standards.

NOTE Demonstrating refactoring requires a sufficiently large (and complex) example. If you run the complete example, you will incur a cost that exceeds the GCP free tier. This book includes only the relevant lines of code and omits the rest for readability. For complete listings, refer to the book's code repository at https://github.com/joatmon08/manning-book/tree/main/ch10. If you convert these examples for AWS and Azure, you will also incur a cost. When possible, I offer notations on converting the examples to the cloud provider of your choice.

10.1 *Minimizing the refactoring impact*

The sundew team needs help breaking down its infrastructure configuration. You decide to refactor the IaC to isolate conflicts better, reduce the amount of time to apply changes to production, and secure them according to company standards. *Refactoring* IaC involves restructuring configuration or code without impacting existing infrastructure resources.

DEFINITION *Refactoring* IaC is the practice of restructuring configuration or code without impacting existing infrastructure resources.

You communicate to the sundew team that its configuration needs to undergo a refactor to fix the problems. While the team members support your effort, they challenge you to minimize the impact of your refactor. Challenge accepted: you apply a few techniques to reduce the potential blast radius as you refactor IaC.

Technical debt

Refactoring often resolves technical debt. *Technical debt* began as a metaphor to describe the cost of any code or approach that makes the overall system challenging to change or extend.

To understand technical debt applied to IaC, recall that the sundew team put all its infrastructure resources into one repository. The sundew team accumulates debt in time and effort. A change to a server that *should* take a day takes four days because the team needs to resolve conflicts with another change and wait for hundreds of requests to the infrastructure API. Note that you'll always have some technical debt in complex systems, but you need continuous efforts to minimize it.

A management team dreads hearing that you need to address technical debt because you don't work on features. I argue that the technical debt you accumulate in infrastructure will always come back to haunt you. The gremlin of technical debt comes in the form of someone changing infrastructure and causing application downtime, or worse, a security breach that exposes personal information and incurs a monetary cost. Assessing the impact of *not* fixing technical debt helps justify the effort.

10.1.1 Reduce blast radius with rolling updates

The Datacenter for Carnivorous Plants platform and security team offer a server module with secure configurations, which you can use for the sundew system. The sundew team's infrastructure configuration has three server configurations but no usage of the secure module. How do you change the sundew IaC to use the module?

Imagine you create three new servers together and immediately send traffic to them. If the applications do not run correctly on the server, you could disrupt the sundew system entirely, and the poor plants do not get watered! Instead, you might reduce the blast radius of your server module refactor by gradually changing the servers one by one.

In figure 10.1, you create one server configuration using the module, deploy the application to the new server, validate that the application works, and delete the old

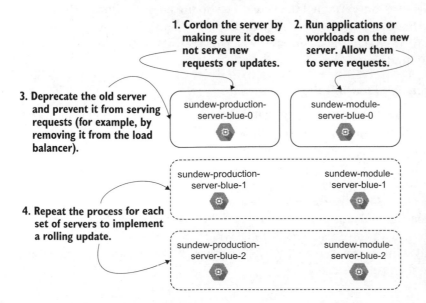

Figure 10.1 Use rolling updates to create each new server, deploy the application, and test its functionality while minimizing disruption to other resources.

server. You repeat the process two more times for each server. You gradually roll out the change to one server before updating the next one.

A *rolling update* gradually changes similar resources one by one and tests *each* one before continuing the update.

> **DEFINITION**   A *rolling update* is a practice of changing a group of similar resources one by one and testing them before implementing the change to the next one.

Applying a rolling update to the sundew team's configuration isolates failures to individual servers each time you make the update and allows you to test the server's functionality before proceeding to the next one.

The practice of rolling updates can save you the pain of detangling a large set of failed changes or incorrectly configured IaC. For example, if the Datacenter for Carnivorous Plants module doesn't work on one server, you have not yet rolled it out and affected the remaining servers. A rolling update lets you check that you have the proper IaC for each server before continuing to the next one. A gradual approach also mitigates any downtime in the applications or failures in updating the servers.

> **NOTE**   I borrowed *rolling updates* for refactoring from workload orchestrators, like Kubernetes. When you need to update new nodes (virtual machines) for a workload orchestrator, you may find it uses an automated rolling update mechanism. The orchestrator cordons the old node, prevents new workloads from running on it, starts all of the running processes on a new node, drains all of the processes on the old node, and sends workloads and requests to the new node. You should mimic the workflow when you refactor!

Thanks to the rolling update and incremental testing, you know that the servers can run with the secure module. You tell the team that you finished refactoring the servers and confirmed that they work with internal services. The sundew team can now send all customer traffic to the newly secured servers. However, the team members tell you that they need to update the customer-facing load balancer first!

10.1.2 Stage refactoring with feature flags

You need a way to hide the new servers from the customer-facing load balancer for a few days and attach them when the team approves. However, you have all the configurations ready! You want to hide the server attachments with a single variable to simplify for the sundew team. When the team members complete their load balancer update, they need to update only one variable to add the new servers to the load balancer.

Figure 10.2 outlines how you set up the variable to add new servers created by the module. You create a Boolean to enable or disable the new server module, using `True` or `False`. Then, you add an `if` statement to IaC that references the Boolean value. A `True` variable adds the new servers to the load balancer. A `False` variable removes the servers from the load balancer.

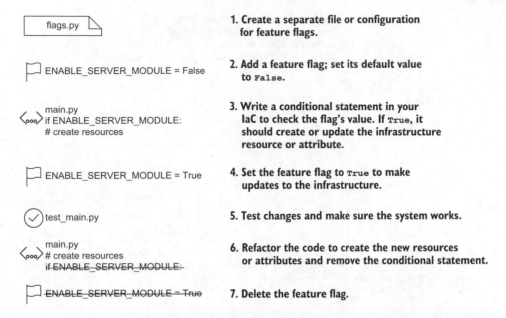

Figure 10.2 Feature flags in IaC involve a process of creation, management, and removal.

The Boolean variable helps with the composability or evolvability of IaC. A single change to the variable adds, removes, or updates a configuration. The variable, called a *feature flag* (or *feature toggle*), is used to enable or disable infrastructure resources, dependencies, and attributes. You often find feature flags in software development with a trunk-based development model (these work only on the main branch).

DEFINITION *Feature flags* (also known as *feature toggles*) enable or disable infrastructure resources, dependences, or attributes by using a Boolean.

Flags hide certain features or code and prevent them from impacting the rest of the team on the main branch. For the sundew team, you hide the new servers from the load balancer until the team completes the load balancer change. Similarly, you can use feature flags in IaC to stage configuration and push the update with a single variable.

SET UP THE FLAG

To start implementing a feature flag and stage changes for the new servers, you add a flag and set it to False. You default a feature flag to False to preserve the original infrastructure state, as shown in figure 10.3. The sundew configuration disables the server module by default so that nothing happens to the original servers.

Let's implement the feature flag in Python. You set the server module flag's default to False in a separate file called flags.py. The file defines the flag, ENABLE_ SERVER_MODULE, and sets it to False:

```
ENABLE_SERVER_MODULE = False
```

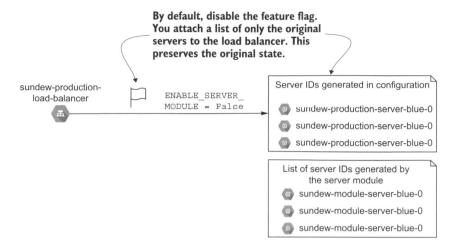

By default, disable the feature flag. You attach a list of only the original servers to the load balancer. This preserves the original state.

Figure 10.3   Set the feature flag to `False` by default to preserve the infrastructure resources' original state and dependencies.

You could also embed feature flags as variables in other files, but you might lose track of them! You decide to put them in a separate Python file.

NOTE   I always define feature flags in a file to identify and change them in one place.

The following listing imports the feature flag in main.py and adds the logic to generate a list of servers to add to the load balancer.

Listing 10.1   Including the feature flag to add servers to the load balancer

```
import flags

def _generate_servers(version):
    instances = [
        f'${{google_compute_instance.{version}_0.id}}',
        f'${{google_compute_instance.{version}_1.id}}',
        f'${{google_compute_instance.{version}_2.id}}'
    ]
    if flags.ENABLE_SERVER_MODULE:
        instances = [
            f'${{google_compute_instance.module_{version}_0.id}}',
            f'${{google_compute_instance.module_{version}_1.id}}',
            f'${{google_compute_instance.module_{version}_2.id}}',
        ]
    return instances
```

Imports the file that defines all of the feature flags

Defines a list of existing Google compute instances (servers) by using a Terraform resource in the system

Uses a conditional statement to evaluate the feature flag and adds the server module's resources to the load balancer

A feature flag set to True will attach the servers created by the module to the load balancer. Otherwise, it will keep the original servers.

> ### AWS and Azure equivalents
>
> To convert listing 10.1 to AWS or Azure, use the AWS EC2 Terraform resource (http://mng.bz/VMMr) or the Azure Linux virtual machine Terraform resource (http://mng.bz/xnnq). You will need to update only the references within the list of instances.

Run Python with the feature flag toggled off to generate a JSON configuration. The resulting JSON configuration adds only the original servers to the load balancer, which preserves the existing state of infrastructure resources.

Listing 10.2   JSON configuration with feature flag disabled

```
{
    "resource": [
        {
            "google_compute_instance_group": {          ← Creates a Google compute instance
                "blue": [                                   group using a Terraform resource
                    {                                       to attach to the load balancer
                        "instances": [
                            "${google_compute_instance.blue_0.id}",
                            "${google_compute_instance.blue_1.id}",
                            "${google_compute_instance.blue_2.id}"
                        ]
                    }                                    Configuration includes a list of
                ]                                        the original Google compute
            }                                            instances, preserving the current
        }                                                state of infrastructure resources
    ]
}
```

> ### AWS and Azure equivalents
>
> A Google Compute instance group has no straightforward equivalent in AWS or Azure. Instead, you will need to replace the compute instance group with a resource definition for an AWS Target Group (http://mng.bz/AyyE) for a load balancer. For Azure, you will need a backend address pool and three addresses to the virtual machine instances (http://mng.bz/ZAAj).

The feature flag set to `False` by default uses the principle of idempotency. When you run the IaC, your infrastructure state should not change. Setting the flag ensures that you do not accidentally change existing infrastructure. Preserving the original state of the existing servers minimizes disruption to dependent applications.

ENABLE THE FLAG
The sundew team made its changes and provided approval to add the new servers created by the module to the load balancer. You set the feature flag to `True`, as shown in

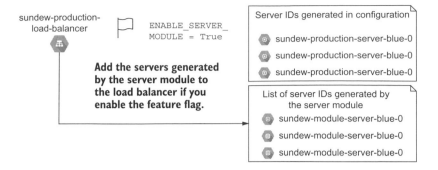

Figure 10.4   Set the feature flag to `True`, attach the three new servers created by the module to the load balancer, and detach the old servers.

figure 10.4. When you deploy the change, you attach servers from a module to the load balancer and remove the old servers.

Let's examine the updated feature flag in action. You start by setting the feature flag for the servers to `True`:

```
ENABLE_SERVER_MODULE = True
```

Run Python to generate a new JSON configuration. The configuration in the following listing now includes the servers created by the module that you will attach to the load balancer.

Listing 10.3   JSON configuration with feature flag enabled

```
{
    "resource": [
        {
            "google_compute_instance_group": {
                "blue": [
                    {
                        "instances": [
                            "${google_compute_instance.module_blue_0.id}",
                            "${google_compute_instance.module_blue_1.id}",
                            "${google_compute_instance.module_blue_2.id}"
                        ]
                    }
                ]
            }
        }
    ]
}
```

The new servers created by the module replace the old servers because you enabled the feature flag.

The feature flag allows you to stage the module's low-level server resources without affecting the load balancer's high-level dependency. You can rerun the code with the feature toggle off to reattach the old servers.

Why use the feature flag to switch to the server module? A feature flag hides functionality from production until you feel ready to deploy resources associated with it.

You offer one variable to add, remove, or update a set of resources. You can also use the same variable to revert changes.

REMOVE THE FLAG

After running the servers for some time, the sundew team reports that the new server module works. You can now remove the old servers in listing 10.4. You no longer need the feature flag, and you don't want to confuse another team member when they read the code. You refactor the Python code for the load balancer to remove the old servers and delete the feature flag.

Listing 10.4 Removing the feature flag after the change completes

```
import blue                                          You can remove the import for the
                                                     feature flags because you no
                                                     longer need it for your servers.
def _generate_servers(version):
    instances = [
        f'${{google_compute_instance.module_{version}_0.id}}',
        f'${{google_compute_instance.module_{version}_1.id}}',
        f'${{google_compute_instance.module_{version}_2.id}}',
    ]
    return instances
```

Permanently attaches the servers created by the module to the load balancer and removes the feature flag

---

Domain-specific languages

Listing 10.4 shows a feature flag in a programming language. You can also use feature flags in DSLs, although you must adapt them based on your tool's syntax. In Terraform, you can mimic a feature flag by using a variable and the count meta-argument (http://mng.bz/R44n):

```
variable "enable_server_module" {
  type        = bool
  default     = false
  description = "Choose true to build servers with a module."
}

module "server" {
  count   = var.enable_server_module ? 1 : 0
  ## omitted for clarity
}
```

In AWS CloudFormation, you can pass a parameter and set a condition (http://mng.bz/2nnN) to enable or disable resource creation:

```
AWSTemplateFormatVersion: 2010-09-09
Description: Truncated example for CloudFormation feature flag
Parameters:
  EnableServerModule:
    AllowedValues:
      - 'true'
      - 'false'
```

```
(continued)
    Default: 'false'
    Description: Choose true to build servers with a module.
    Type: String
Conditions:
 EnableServerModule: !Equals
   - !Ref EnableServerModule
   - true
Resources:
 ServerModule:
   Type: AWS::CloudFormation::Stack
   Condition: EnableServerModule
   ## omitted for clarity
```

Besides feature flags to enable and disable entire resources, you can use conditional statements to enable or disable specific attributes for a resource.

As a general rule, *remove* the feature flag after you finish the change. Too many feature flags can clutter your IaC with complicated logic, making it hard to troubleshoot infrastructure configuration.

USE CASES

The example uses feature flags to *refactor singleton configurations into infrastructure modules.* I often apply feature flags to this use case to simplify the creation and removal of infrastructure resources. Other use cases for feature flags include the following:

- Collaborating and avoiding change conflicts on the *same infrastructure* resources or dependencies
- Staging a *group of changes* and rapidly deploying them with a single update to the flag
- *Testing* a change and quickly disabling it on failure

A feature flag offers a technique to hide or isolate infrastructure resource, attribute, and dependency changes during the refactoring of infrastructure configuration. However, changing the toggle can still disrupt a system. In the example of the sundew team's servers, we cannot simply toggle the feature flag to `True` and expect the servers to run the application. Instead, we combine the feature flag with other techniques like rolling updates to minimize disruption to the system.

10.2 *Breaking down monoliths*

The sundew team members express that they still have a problem with their system. You identify the singleton configuration with hundreds of resources and attributes as the root cause. Whenever someone makes a change, the teammate must resolve conflicts with another person. They also have to wait 30 minutes to make a change.

A *monolithic architecture* for IaC means defining all infrastructure resources in one place. You need to break the monolith of IaC into smaller, modular components to minimize working conflicts between teammates and speed up the deployment of changes.

DEFINITION   A *monolithic architecture* for IaC defines all infrastructure resources in a single configuration and the same state.

In this section, we'll walk through a refactor of the sundew team's monolith. The most crucial step begins with identifying and grouping high-level infrastructure resources and dependencies. We complete the refactor with the low-level infrastructure resources.

Monolith vs. monorepository

Recall that you can put your infrastructure configuration into a single repository (chapter 5). Does a single repository mean you have a monolithic architecture? Not necessarily. You can subdivide a single repository into separate subdirectories. Each subdirectory contains separate IaC.

A monolithic architecture means you manage many resources together and tightly couple them, making it difficult to change a subset in isolation. The monolith usually results from an initial singleton pattern (all configurations in one place) that expands over time.

You might have noticed that I started immediately with patterns for modularizing infrastructure resources and dependencies in chapters 3 and 4. Why not present this chapter on refactoring earlier? If you can identify and apply some of the patterns early in IaC development, you can avoid the monolithic architecture. However, you sometimes inherit a monolith and often need to refactor it.

10.2.1 Refactor high-level resources

The sundew team manages hundreds of resources in one set of configuration files. Where should you start breaking down the IaC? You decide to look for *high-level infrastructure resources* that do not depend on other resources.

The sundew team has one set of high-level infrastructure in GCP project-level IAM service accounts and roles. The IAM service accounts and roles don't need to create a network or server before setting user and service account rules on the project. None of the other resources depend on the IAM roles and service accounts. You can group and extract them first.

You cannot use a blue-green deployment approach because GCP does not allow duplicate policies. However, you cannot simply delete roles and accounts from the monolithic configuration and copy them to a new repository. Deleting them prevents everyone from logging into the project! How can you extract them?

You can copy and paste the configuration into its separate repository or directory, initialize the state for the separated configuration, and import the resources into the infrastructure state associated with the new configuration. Then, you delete the IAM configuration in the monolithic configuration. As with the rolling update, you gradually change each set of infrastructure resources, test the changes, and proceed to the next one.

Figure 10.5 outlines the solution to refactoring a monolith for high-level resources. You copy the code from the monolith to a new folder and import the live

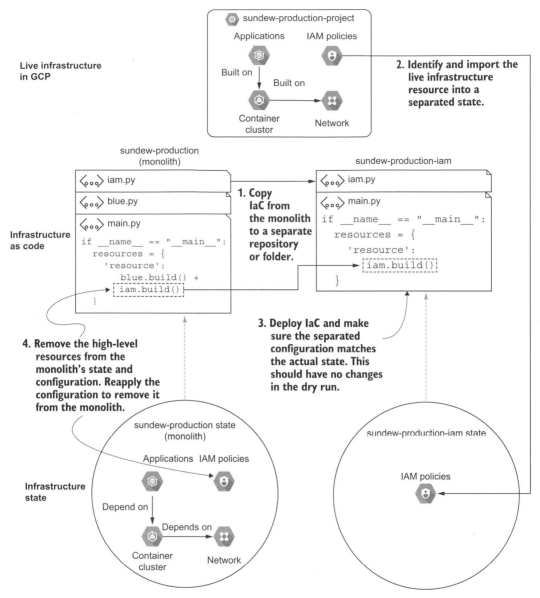

Figure 10.5   The sundew system's IAM policies for the GCP project have no dependencies, and you can easily refactor them without disrupting other infrastructure.

infrastructure resource into the state of the code in the new folder. You redeploy the code to make sure it does not change existing infrastructure. Finally, remove the high-level resources from the monolith.

As with feature flags, we use the principle of idempotency to run IaC and verify that we do not affect the active infrastructure state. Anytime you refactor, make sure you deploy the changes and check the dry run. You do not want to accidentally change an existing resource and affect its dependencies.

We will refactor the example in the following few sections. Stay with it! I know refactoring tends to feel tedious, but a gradual approach ensures that you do not introduce widespread failures into your system.

COPY FROM THE MONOLITH TO A SEPARATE STATE

Your initial refactor begins by copying the code to create the IAM roles and service accounts to a new directory. The sundew team wants to keep a single repository structure that stores all the IaC in one source control repository but separates the configurations into folders.

You identify the IAM roles and service accounts to copy the team's code to a new folder, as shown in figure 10.6. The active IAM policies and their infrastructure state in GCP do not change.

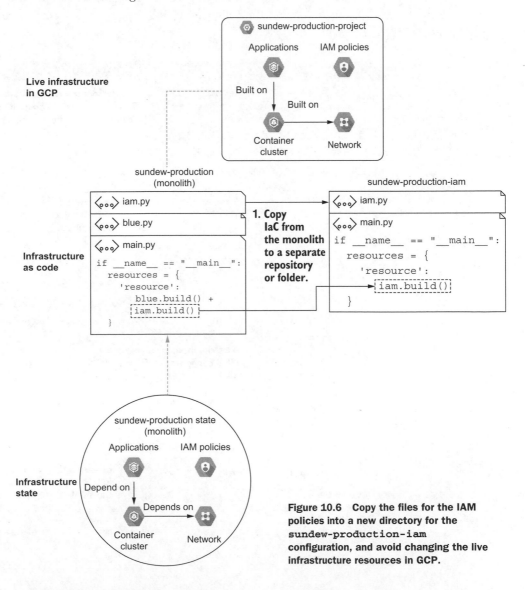

Figure 10.6 Copy the files for the IAM policies into a new directory for the `sundew-production-iam` configuration, and avoid changing the live infrastructure resources in GCP.

Why reproduce the IaC for the IAM policies in a separate folder? You want to split up your monolithic IaC without affecting any of the active resources. The most important practice when refactoring involves preserving idempotency. Your active state should never change when you move your IaC.

Let's start refactoring the IAM policies out of the monolith. Create a new directory that manages only the IAM policies for the GCP project:

```
$ mkdir -p sundew_production_iam
```

Copy the IAM configuration from the monolith into the new directory:

```
$ cp iam.py sundew_production_iam/
```

You don't need to change anything since the IAM policies do not depend on other infrastructure. The file iam.py in the following listing separates the creation and role assignment for a set of users.

Listing 10.5   IAM configuration separated from the monolith

```
import json

TEAM = 'sundew'
TERRAFORM_GCP_SERVICE_ACCOUNT_TYPE = 'google_service_account'
TERRAFORM_GCP_ROLE_ASSIGNMENT_TYPE = 'google_project_iam_member'


users = {
    'audit-team': 'roles/viewer',
    'automation-watering': 'roles/editor',
    'user-02': 'roles/owner'
}


def get_user_id(user):
    return user.replace('-', '_')


def build():
    return iam()


def iam(users=users):
    iam_members = []
    for user, role in users.items():
        user_id = get_user_id(user)
        iam_members.append({
            TERRAFORM_GCP_SERVICE_ACCOUNT_TYPE: [{
                user_id: [{
                    'account_id': user,
                    'display_name': user
                }]
            }]
        })
        iam_members.append({
```

> Sets the resource types that Terraform uses as constants so you can reference them later if needed

> Keeps all of the users you added to the project as part of the monolith

> Uses the module to create the JSON configuration for the IAM policies outside the monolith

> Creates a GCP service account for the project for each user in the sundew production project

```
            TERRAFORM_GCP_ROLE_ASSIGNMENT_TYPE: [{
                user_id: [{
                    'role': role,
                    'member': 'serviceAccount:${google_service_account.'
                    + f'{user_id}' + '.email}'
                }]
            }]
        })
    return iam_members
```

Assigns the specific role defined for each service account, such as viewer, editor, or owner

---

AWS and Azure equivalents

Listing 10.5 creates all users and groups as service accounts in GCP so you can run the example to completion. You typically use service accounts for automation.

A service account in GCP is similar to an AWS IAM user dedicated to service automation or Azure Active Directory application registered with a client secret. To rebuild the code in AWS or Azure, adjust the roles for viewer, editor, and owner to fit AWS or Azure roles.

Set constants and create methods that output resource types and identifiers when separating configuration. You can always use them for other automation and continued system maintenance, especially as you continue to refactor the monolith!

In the following listing, create a main.py file in the sundew_production_iam folder that references the IAM configuration and outputs the Terraform JSON for it.

Listing 10.6 Entry point to build the separate JSON configuration for IAM

```
import iam
import json

if __name__ == "__main__":
    resources = {
        'resource': iam.build()
    }

    with open('main.tf.json', 'w') as outfile:
        json.dump(resources, outfile,
                sort_keys=True, indent=4)
```

Imports the IAM configuration code and builds the IAM policies

Writes the Python dictionary out to a JSON file to be executed by Terraform later

Do not run Python yet to create the Terraform JSON or deploy the IAM policies! You already have IAM policies defined as part of GCP. If you run `python main.py` and apply the Terraform JSON with the separated IAM configuration, GCP throws an error that the user account and assignment already exists:

```
$ python main.py

$ terraform apply -auto-approve
## output omitted for clarity
| Error: Error creating service account: googleapi:
Error 409: Service account audit-team already exists within project
projects/infrastructure-as-code-book., alreadyExists
```

The sundew team members do not want you to remove and create new accounts and roles. If you delete and create new accounts, they cannot log into their GCP project. You need a way to migrate the existing resources defined in the monolith and link them to code defined in its own folder.

IMPORT THE RESOURCES TO THE NEW STATE

Sometimes creating new resources with your refactored IaC will disrupt development teams and business-critical systems. You cannot use the principle of immutability to

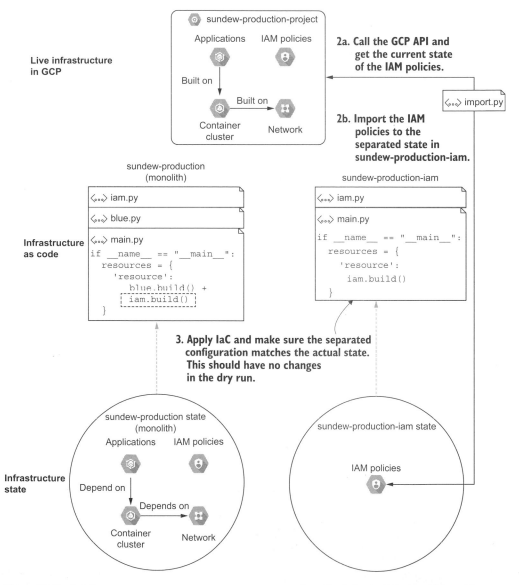

Figure 10.7   Get the current state of the separated resources from the infrastructure provider and import the identifiers before reapplying IaC.

delete the old resources and create new ones. Instead, you must migrate active resources from one IaC definition to another.

In the case of the sundew team, you extract the identifiers for each service account from the monolithic configuration and "move" them to the new state. Figure 10.7 demonstrates how to detach each service account and its role assignments from the monolith and attach them to the IaC in the sundew_production_iam directory. You call the GCP API for the current state of the IAM policies and *import* the live infrastructure resources into the separated configuration and state. Running the IaC should reveal no changes to its dry run.

Why import the IAM policy information with the GCP API? You want to import the updated, active state of the resource. A cloud provider's API offers the most up-to-date configuration for resources. You can call the GCP API to retrieve the user emails, roles, and identifiers for the sundew team.

Rather than write your own import capability and save the identifiers in a file, you decide to use Terraform's import capability to add existing resources to the state. You write some Python code in the following listing that wraps around Terraform to automate a batch import of IAM resources so that the sundew team can reuse it.

Listing 10.7 File import.py separately imports sundew IAM resources

```
import iam                              Retrieves the list of sundew users from
import os                               iam.py in sundew_production_iam
import googleapiclient.discovery
import subprocess

PROJECT = os.environ['CLOUDSDK_CORE_PROJECT']    Retrieves the GCP project
                                                 ID from the
                                                 CLOUDSDK_CORE_PROJECT
                                                 environment variable

def _get_members_from_gcp(project, roles):
    roles_and_members = {}
    service = googleapiclient.discovery.build(
        'cloudresourcemanager', 'v1')         Uses the Google Cloud Client
    result = service.projects().getIamPolicy( Libraries for Python to get a
        resource=project, body={}).execute()  list of members assigned to
    bindings = result['bindings']             a role in the GCP project
    for binding in bindings:
        if binding['role'] in roles:
            roles_and_members[binding['role']] = binding['members']
    return roles_and_members


def _set_emails_and_roles(users, all_members):
    members = []                                       Gets the email
    for username, role in users.items():               and user IDs for
        members += [(iam.get_user_id(username), m, role) the sundew IAM
                    for m in all_members[role] if username in m] members only
    return members
```

```
def check_import_status(ret, err):
    return ret != 0 and \
        'Resource already managed by Terraform'
        ➥not in str(err)
```

Imports the service account to the sundew_production_iam state based on project and user email, using the resource type constant you set in iam.py

```
def import_service_account(project_id, user_id, user_email):
    email = user_email.replace('serviceAccount:', '')
    command = ['terraform', 'import', '-no-color',
               f'{iam.TERRAFORM_GCP_SERVICE_ACCOUNT_TYPE}.{user_id}',
               f'projects/{project_id}/serviceAccounts/{email}']
    return _terraform(command)


def import_project_iam_member(project_id, role,
                              user_id, user_email):
    command = ['terraform', 'import', '-no-color',
               f'{iam.TERRAFORM_GCP_ROLE_ASSIGNMENT_TYPE}.{user_id}',
               f'{project_id} {role} {user_email}']
    return _terraform(command)


def _terraform(command):
    process = subprocess.Popen(
        command,
        stdout=subprocess.PIPE,
        stderr=subprocess.PIPE)
    stdout, stderr = process.communicate()
    return process.returncode, stdout, stderr
```

Both import methods wrap around the Terraform CLI command and return any errors and output.

Gets the email and user IDs for the sundew IAM members only

Retrieves the list of sundew users from iam.py in sundew_production_iam

```
if __name__ == "__main__":
    sundew_iam = iam.users
    all_members_for_roles = _get_members_from_gcp(
        PROJECT, set(sundew_iam.values()))
    import_members = _set_emails_and_roles(
        sundew_iam, all_members_for_roles)
    for user_id, email, role in import_members:
        ret, _, err = import_service_account(PROJECT, user_id, email)
        if check_import_status(ret, err):
            print(f'import service account failed: {err}')
        ret, _, err = import_project_iam_member(PROJECT, role,
                                                user_id, email)
        if check_import_status(ret, err):
            print(f'import iam member failed: {err}')
```

Uses the Google Cloud Client Libraries for Python to get a list of members assigned to a role in the GCP project

If the import fails and it did not already import the resource, outputs the error

Imports a role assignment to the sundew_production_iam state based on project, role, and user email, using the resource type constant you set in iam.py

Libcloud vs. Cloud Provider SDKs

The examples in this chapter need to use the Google Cloud Client Library for Python instead of Apache Libcloud, which I showed in chapter 4. While Apache Libcloud works for retrieving information about virtual machines, it does not work for other resources in GCP. For more information about the Google Cloud Client Library for Python, review http://mng.bz/1ooZ.

You can update listing 10.7 to use the Azure libraries for Python (http://mng.bz/ Pnn2) or AWS SDK for Python (https://aws.amazon.com/sdk-for-python/) to retrieve information about users. These would replace the GCP API client library.

As with defining dependencies, you want to *dynamically retrieve identifiers* from the infrastructure provider API for your resources to import. You never know when someone will change the resource, and the identifier you thought you needed no longer exists! Use your tags and naming conventions to search the API response for the resources you need.

When you run `python import.py` and perform a dry run of the Terraform JSON with the separated IAM configuration, you get a message that you do not have to make any changes. You successfully imported the existing IAM resources into their separate configuration and state:

```
$ python main.py

$ terraform plan
No changes. Your infrastructure matches the configuration.

Terraform has compared your real infrastructure against your configuration
↪and found no differences, so no changes are needed.

Apply complete! Resources: 0 added, 0 changed, 0 destroyed.
```

Sometimes your dry run indicates drift between the active resource state and the separated configuration. Your copied configuration does not match the active state of the resource. The differences often come from someone changing the active state of an infrastructure resource during a manual change or during updates to the default value for an attribute. Update your separated IaC to *match the attributes of the active infrastructure resource.*

Import with and without a provisioning tool

Many provisioning tools have a function for importing resources. For example, AWS CloudFormation uses the `resource import` command. The example uses Python wrapped around `terraform import` to move service accounts. Breaking down monolithic configuration will become tedious without it.

If you write IaC without a tool, you do not need a direct import capability. Instead, you need logic to check that the resources exist. The sundew service accounts and role assignments can work without Terraform or IaC import capability:

1 Call the GCP API to check whether the sundew team's service accounts and role attachments exist.
2 If they do, check whether the API response for the service account attributes matches your desired configuration. Update the service account as needed.
3 If they do not, create the service accounts and role attachments.

REMOVE THE REFACTORED RESOURCES FROM THE MONOLITH

You managed to extract and move the sundew team's service accounts and role assignments to separate IaC. However, you don't want the resources to stay in the monolith. You remove the resources from the monolith's *state and configuration* before reapplying and updating your tool, as shown in figure 10.8.

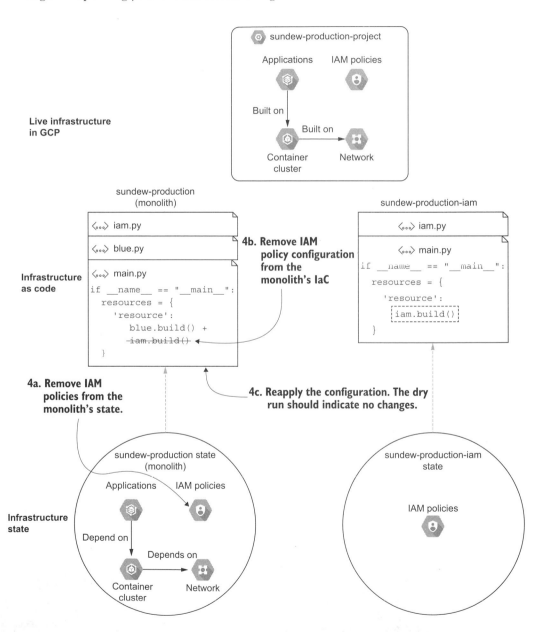

Figure 10.8 Remove the policies from the monolith's state and configuration before applying the updates and completing the refactor.

This step helps maintain IaC hygiene. Remember from chapter 2 that our IaC should serve as the *source of truth*. You do not want to manage one resource with two sets of IaC. If they conflict, the two IaC definitions for the resource may affect dependencies and the configuration of the system.

You want the IAM policy directory to serve as the source of truth. Going forward, the sundew team needs to declare changes to its IAM policy in the separate directory and not in the monolith. To avoid confusion, let's remove the IAM resources from the IaC monolith.

To start, you must remove the sundew IAM resources from Terraform state, represented in a JSON file. Terraform includes a state removal command that you can use to take out portions of the JSON based on the resource identifier. Listing 10.8 uses Python code to wrap around the Terraform command. The code allows you to pass any resource type and identifier you want to remove from the infrastructure state.

Listing 10.8 File remove.py removes resources from the monolith's state

```python
from sundew_production_iam import iam
import subprocess


def check_state_remove_status(ret, err):
    return ret != 0 \
        and 'No matching objects found' not in str(err)


def state_remove(resource_type, resource_identifier):
    command = ['terraform', 'state', 'rm', '-no-color',
            f'{resource_type}.{resource_identifier}']
    return _terraform(command)


def _terraform(command):
    process = subprocess.Popen(
        command,
        stdout=subprocess.PIPE,
        stderr=subprocess.PIPE)
    stdout, stderr = process.communicate()
    return process.returncode, stdout, stderr


if __name__ == "__main__":
    sundew_iam = iam.users
    for user in iam.users:
        ret, _, err = state_remove(
            iam.TERRAFORM_GCP_SERVICE_ACCOUNT_TYPE,
            iam.get_user_id(user))
```

If the removal failed and did not already remove the resource, outputs the error

Opens a subprocess that runs the Terraform command to remove the resource from the state

Retrieves the list of sundew users from iam.py in sundew_production_iam. Referencing the variable from the separated IaC allows you to run the removal automation for future refactoring efforts.

Removes the GCP service account from the monolith's Terraform state based on its user identifier

Creates a method that wraps around Terraform's state removal command. The command passes the resource type, such as service account and identifier to remove.

For each user in sundew_production_iam, removes their service account and role assignment from the monolith's state

```
        if check_state_remove_status(ret, err):
            print(f'remove service account from state failed: {err}')
        ret, _, err = state_remove(
            iam.TERRAFORM_GCP_ROLE_ASSIGNMENT_TYPE,
            iam.get_user_id(user))
        if check_state_remove_status(ret, err):
            print(f'remove role assignment from state failed: {err}')
```

Checks that the subprocess's Terraform command successfully removed the resource from the monolith's state

Removes the GCP role assignment from the monolith's Terraform state based on its user identifier

Do not run `python remove.py` yet! Your monolith still contains a definition of the IAM policies. Open your monolithic IaC's main.py. In the following listing, remove the code that builds the IAM service accounts and role assignments for the sundew team.

Listing 10.9   Removing the IAM policies from the monolith's code

```
import blue
import json
```
Removes the import for the IAM policies

```
if __name__ == "__main__":
    resources = {
        'resource': blue.build()
    }
```
Removes the code to build the IAM policies within the monolith and leaves the other resources

```
    with open('main.tf.json', 'w') as outfile:
        json.dump(resources, outfile,
                    sort_keys=True, indent=4)
```
Writes the configuration out to a JSON file to be executed by Terraform later. The configuration does not include the IAM policies.

You can now update your monolith. First, use `python remove.py` to delete the IAM resources from the monolith's state:

```
$ python remove.py
```

This step signals that your monolith no longer serves as the source of truth for the IAM policies and service accounts. You *do not* delete the IAM resources! You can imagine this as handing over ownership of the IAM resources to the new IaC in a separate folder.

In your terminal, you can finally update the monolith. Generate a new Terraform JSON without the IAM policies and apply the updates; you should not have any changes:

```
$ python main.py

$ terraform apply
```

```
google_service_account.blue: Refreshing state...
google_compute_network.blue: Refreshing state...
google_compute_subnetwork.blue: Refreshing state...
google_container_cluster.blue: Refreshing state...
google_container_node_pool.blue: Refreshing state…

No changes. Your infrastructure matches the configuration.

Terraform has compared your real infrastructure against your configuration
➥and found no differences, so no changes are needed.

Apply complete! Resources: 0 added, 0 changed, 0 destroyed.
```

If your dry run *includes* a resource you refactored, you know that you did not remove it from the monolith's state or configuration. You need to examine the resources and identify whether to remove them manually.

10.2.2 *Refactor resources with dependencies*

You can now work on the lower-level infrastructure resources with dependencies, such as the sundew team's container orchestrator. The sundew team members ask you to avoid creating a new orchestrator and destroying the old one since they do not want to disrupt applications. You need to refactor and extract the low-level container orchestrator in place.

Start copying the container configuration out of the monolith, repeating the same process you used for refactoring the IAM service accounts and roles. You create a separate folder labeled sundew_production_orchestrator:

```
$ mkdir -p sundew_production_orchestrator
```

You select and copy the method to create the cluster into sundew_production_orchestrator/cluster.py. However, you have a problem. The container orchestrator *needs the network and subnet names.* How do you get the name of the network and subnet when the container orchestrator cannot reference the monolith?

Figure 10.9 implements dependency injection with an existing monolith using the infrastructure provider's API as the abstraction layer. The IaC to create the cluster calls the GCP API to get network information. You pass the network ID to the cluster to use.

A monolith passes the dependency explicitly between resources. When you create a new folder, your separated resources need information about its low-level dependencies. Recall that you can decouple infrastructure modules with the *dependency injection* (previously in chapter 4). A high-level module calls an abstraction layer to get identifiers for low-level dependencies.

When you start refactoring resources with dependencies, you must implement an interface for dependency injection. In the sundew team's code for listing 10.10, update sundew_production_orchestrator/cluster.py to use the Google Cloud Client Library and retrieve the subnet and network names for the cluster configuration.

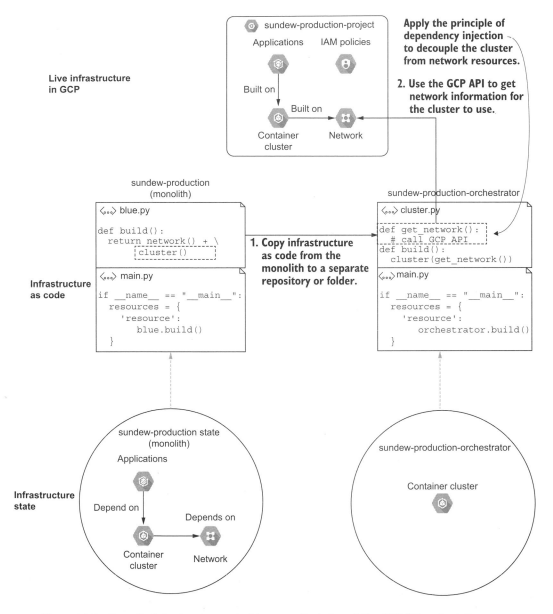

Figure 10.9   Copy the infrastructure and add new methods to call the GCP API and get the network ID for the cluster.

NOTE Several dependencies, variables, and imports have been removed from listing 10.10 for additional clarity. Refer to the book's code repository at https://github.com/joatmon08/manning-book/tree/main/ch10/s03/s02 for the full example.

Listing 10.10 Using dependency inversion for the network name in the cluster

```python
import googleapiclient.discovery

def _get_network_from_gcp():
    service = googleapiclient.discovery.build(
        'compute', 'v1')
    result = service.subnetworks().list(
        project=PROJECT,
        region=REGION,
        filter=f'name:"{TEAM}-{ENVIRONMENT}-*"').execute()
    subnetworks = result['items'] if 'items' in result else None
    if len(subnetworks) != 1:
        print("Network not found")
        exit(1)
    return subnetworks[0]['network'].split('/')[-1], \
        subnetworks[0]['name']

def cluster(name=cluster_name,
            node_name=cluster_nodes,
            service_account=cluster_service_account,
            region=REGION):
    network, subnet = _get_network_from_gcp()
    return [
        {
            'google_container_cluster': {
                VERSION: [
                    {
                        'name': name,
                        'network': network,
                        'subnetwork': subnet
                    }
                ]
            },
            'google_container_node_pool': {
                VERSION: [
                    {
                        'cluster':
                        '${google_container_cluster.' +
                            f'{VERSION}' + '.name}'
                    }
                ]
            },
            'google_service_account': {
                VERSION: [
```

Sets up access to the GCP API using the Google Cloud Client Library for Python

Creates a method that retrieves the network information from GCP and implements dependency injection

Queries the GCP API for a list of subnetworks with names that start with sundew-production

Throws an error if the GCP API did not find the subnetwork

Returns the network name and subnetwork name

Applies the dependency inversion principle and calls the GCP API to retrieve the network and subnet names

Uses the network and subnet names to update the container cluster

Creates the Google container cluster, node pool, and service account by using a Terraform resource

Several dependencies, variables, and imports have been removed from the code listing for additional clarity. Refer to the book's code repository for the full example.

```
                              {
                                  'account_id': service_account,
                                  'display_name': service_account
                              }
                          ]
                      }
                  }
              }
          ]
```

When refactoring an infrastructure resource with dependencies, you must implement dependency injection to retrieve the low-level resource attributes. Listing 10.10 uses an infrastructure provider's API, but you can use any abstraction layer you choose. An infrastructure provider's API often provides the most straightforward abstraction. You can use it to avoid implementing your own.

After copying and updating the container cluster to reference network and subnet names from the GCP API, you repeat the refactoring workflow shown in figure 10.10. You import the live infrastructure resource into sundew_production_orchestrator, apply the separate configuration, check for any drift between the active state and the IaC, and remove the resource's configuration and reference in the monolith's state.

The main difference between refactoring a high-level resource versus a lower-level resource out of a monolith involves the implementation of dependency injection. You can choose the type of dependency injection you want to use, such as the infrastructure provider's API, module outputs, or infrastructure state. Note that you might need to change the monolithic IaC to output the attributes if you do not use the infrastructure provider's API.

Otherwise, ensure that you apply idempotency by rerunning your IaC after refactoring. You want to avoid affecting the active resources and isolate all changes to the IaC. If your dry run reflects changes, you must fix the drift between your refactored code and infrastructure state before moving forward with other resources.

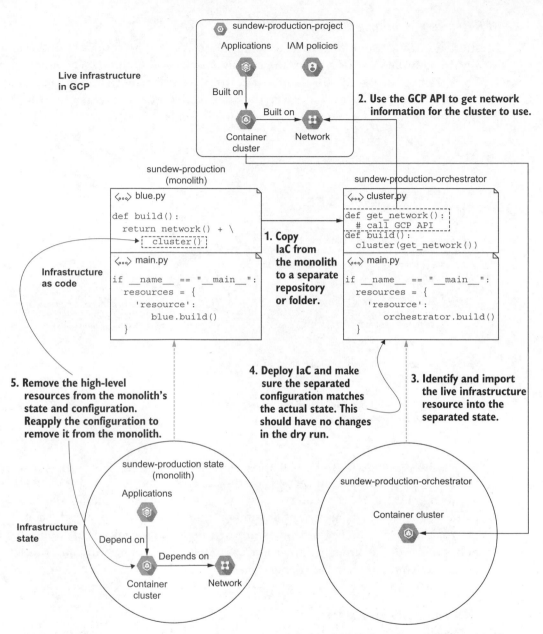

Figure 10.10   Refactor higher-level resources to get low-level identifiers with the GCP API before continuing to refactor low-level resources.

10.2.3 *Repeat refactoring workflow*

After you extract the IAM service accounts and roles and the container orchestrator, you can continue to break down the sundew system's monolithic IaC configuration. The workflow in figure 10.11 summarizes the general pattern for breaking down monolithic IaC. You identify which resources depend on each other, extract their configuration, and update their dependencies to use dependency injection.

How to refactor an IaC monolith

1. Extract high-level infrastructure resources with no dependencies and nothing depending on them (e.g., IAM roles & service accounts).

2. Extract higher-level resources that depend on another infrastructure resource (e.g., applications running on a container orchestrator).

    → ☁ Refactor to use dependency injection for low-level resource attributes (e.g., container orchestrator name).

    ⋮ Depends on

3. Extract lower-level resources that depend on another infrastructure resource (e.g., container orchestrator running on a network).

    → ☁ Refactor to use dependency injection for low-level resource attributes (e.g., network and subnet names).

    ⋮ Depends on

4. Extract low-level resources with no dependencies (e.g., network).

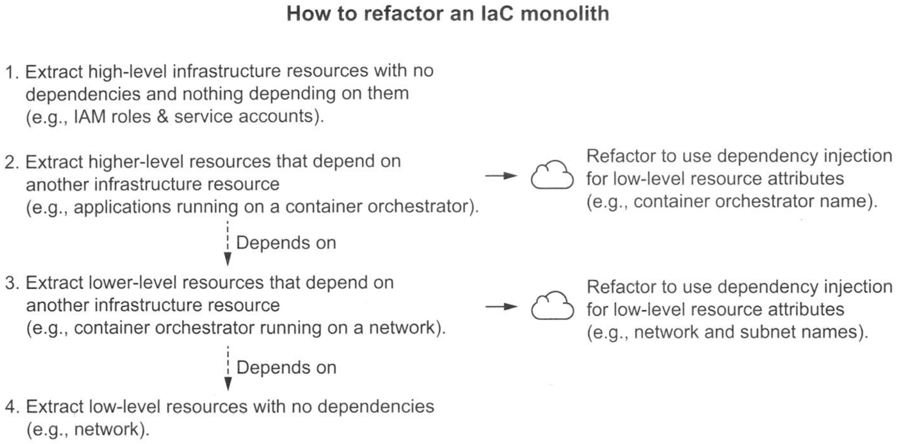

Figure 10.11   The workflow for refactoring an IaC monolith starts by identifying high-level resources with no dependencies.

Identify the high-level infrastructure resources that do not depend on anything or have anything depending on them. I use the high-level resources to test the workflow of copying, separating, importing, and deleting them from the monolith. Next, I identify the higher-level resources that depend on other resources. During the copying, I refactor them to reference attributes through dependency injection. I identify and repeat the process through the system, eventually concluding with the lowest-level resources that do not have any dependencies.

Configuration management

While this chapter focused primarily on IaC provisioning tools, configuration management can also turn into a monolith of automation and result in the same challenges, including taking a long time to run or having conflicting changes to parts of the configuration. You can apply a similar refactoring workflow to monolithic configuration management:

1 Extract the most independent parts of the automation with no dependencies and separate them into a module.

> 2 Run the configuration manager and make sure you did not change your resource state.
>
> 3 Identify configuration that depends on the outputs or existence of lower-level automation. Extract them and apply dependency injection to retrieve any required values for the configuration.
>
> 4 Run the configuration manager and make sure you did not change your resource state.
>
> 5 Repeat the process until you effectively reach your configuration manager's first step.

As you refactor IaC monoliths, identify ways to decouple the resources from one another. I find refactoring a challenge and rarely without some failures and mistakes. Isolating individual components and carefully testing them will help identify problems and minimize disruption to the system. If I do encounter failures, I use the techniques in chapter 11 to fix them.

Exercise 10.1

Given the following code, what order and grouping of resources would you use to refactor and break down the monolith?

```
if __name__ == "__main__":
  zones = ['us-west1-a', 'us-west1-b', 'us-west1-c']
  project.build()
  network.build(project)
  for zone in zones:
    subnet.build(project, network, zone)
  database.build(project, network)
  for zone in zones:
    server.build(project, network, zone)
  load_balancer.build(project, network)
  dns.build()
```

  A DNS, load balancer, servers, database, network + subnets, project
  B Load balancer + DNS, database, servers, network + subnets, project
  C Project, network + subnets, servers, database, load balancer + DNS
  D Database, load balancer + DNS, servers, network + subnets, project

See appendix B for answers to exercises.

Summary

- Refactoring IaC involves restructuring configuration or code without impacting existing infrastructure resources.
- Refactoring resolves technical debt, a metaphor to describe the cost of changing code.

- A rolling update changes similar infrastructure resources one by one and tests each resource before moving to the next one.
- Rolling updates allow you to implement and troubleshoot changes incrementally.
- Feature flags (also known as *feature toggles*) enable or disable infrastructure resources, dependencies, or attributes.
- Apply feature flags to test, stage, and hide changes before applying them to production.
- Define feature flags in one place (such as a file or configuration manager) to identify their values at a glance.
- Remove feature flags when you do not need them anymore.
- Monolithic IaC happens when you define all of your infrastructure resources in one place, and removing one resource causes the entire configuration to fail.
- Refactoring a resource out of a monolith involves separating and copying the configuration into a new directory or repository, importing it into a new separate state, and removing the resources from the monolithic configuration and state.
- If your resource depends on another resource, update your separated resource configuration to use dependency injection and retrieve identifiers from an infrastructure provider API.
- Breaking down a monolith starts by refactoring high-level resources or configurations with no dependencies, then resources or configurations with dependencies, and concluding with low-level resources or configurations with no dependencies.

Fixing failures

This chapter covers

- Determining how to roll forward failed changes to restore functionality
- Organizing an approach for IaC troubleshooting
- Categorizing repairs for failed changes

We took many chapters to discuss writing and collaborating on infrastructure as code. All of the practices and principles you learned for IaC accumulate to the crucial moment when you push a change, it causes your system to fail, and you need to roll it back! However, IaC doesn't support rollback. You do not fully revert IaC changes. What does it mean to fix failures if you don't roll them back?

This chapter focuses on fixing failed changes from IaC. First, we'll discuss what it means to "revert" IaC changes by rolling *forward*. Then, you'll learn workflows for troubleshooting and fixing the failed change. While the techniques in this chapter might not apply to every scenario you'll encounter in your system, they establish a broad set of practices you can use to start repairing IaC failures.

> ### Troubleshooting and site reliability engineering
>
> I do not dive too deeply into the process and principles of troubleshooting failed systems in this book. Most of the discussion around troubleshooting centers around how to manage it in the context of IaC. For more information on troubleshooting and building reliable systems, I recommend *Site Reliability Engineering* by Betsy Beyer et al. (O'Reilly, 2016).
>
> As a general rule, *prioritize stabilization and restoration of functionality* for services and customers before you debug further for a root cause (the issue that led to the problem). A temporary bandage provides you the opportunity to troubleshoot and implement a longer-term fix for the system.

11.1 *Restoring functionality*

Imagine you work for a company called Cool Caps for Keys. It creates custom keyboard caps and connects customers with artists to design the caps. As the security engineer, you need to narrow down the access control for applications and users across GCP projects.

You copy the Google Cloud SQL database configuration and update the access control to implement least-privilege access for team members and applications. You choose the policies required for different applications to use infrastructure and verify that the applications still work.

Next, you talk to the promotions team. Its application accesses the database directly by using a database username and password. Direct access to the database means that you can remove the policy for `roles/cloudsql.admin` from the promotions application's service account. You remove the policy, test the changes, confirm with the promotions team that the change did not affect its application in its testing environment, and push it to production; see figure 11.1.

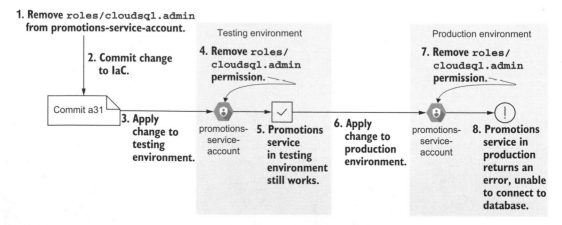

Figure 11.1   After removing the administrative database access for the promotions service, you discover that the change broke the service's ability to access the database.

An hour later, the promotions team tells you that its application keeps throwing an error that it can't access the database! You suspect that your change might have introduced a problem. While you could start digging around for the problem, you prioritize fixing the promotions service so it can access the database before investigating further.

11.1.1   Rolling forward to revert changes

You need to fix the service so users can make requests to the system. However, you cannot simply return the system to a previously working state. IaC prioritizes immutability, which means any changes to the system, including *reverted* changes, must create new resources!

For example, let's fix the promotions service for Cool Caps for Keys by reverting the change and adding the role to the service account. In figure 11.2, you revert the commit and add `roles/cloudsql.admin` back to the service account. Then, you push the changes to your testing and production environments.

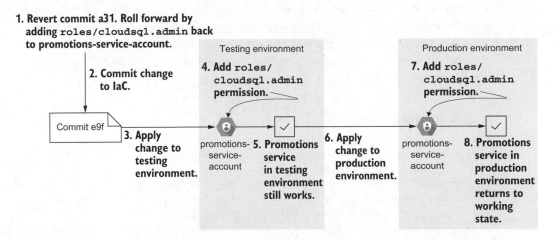

Figure 11.2   You add the administrative database role for the promotions service to roll forward the system to a working state.

You revert the commit and push *forward* the changes to the testing and production environments. You *roll forward* IaC because it uses immutability to return the system to a working state.

> **DEFINITION**   The practice of *rolling forward* IaC reverts changes to a system and uses immutability to return the system to a working state.

Rollback implies that you return infrastructure to a previous state. In reality, the immutability of IaC means that you create a *new* state anytime you make changes. You cannot fully restore the state of infrastructure back to its previous state. Sometimes you can't actually restore the infrastructure to a previous state because your change has a large blast radius.

Let's revert your changes to the service account and roll forward changes to add back the permission. First, check your commit history because version control keeps track of all the changes you make. The commit prefixed with a31 includes your removal of roles/cloudsql.admin:

```
$ git log --oneline -2
a3119fc (HEAD -> main) Remove database admin access from promotions
6f84f5d Add database admin to promotions service
```

Applying the GitOps practices from chapter 7, you want to avoid making manual, break-glass changes. Instead, you favor operational changes through IaC! You revert the commit to push updates to restore the promotions service to a working state:

```
$ git revert a3119fc
```

You push the commit, and the pipeline adds the role back to the service account. After you roll forward, the application works again. You've successfully returned the infrastructure state to a working state. However, you never achieve a full restore of state. Instead, you rolled out a new state that matched the previous working state.

Rolling back IaC often means rolling forward changes to the infrastructure state. You use git revert as a forward-moving undo to preserve immutability and roll forward undo updates to infrastructure.

> **Configuration management**
>
> Configuration management does not prioritize immutability but still rolls forward reverted changes to a server or resource. For example, imagine you install a package with version 3.0.0 and need to revert to 2.0.0. Your configuration management tool may choose to uninstall the new version and reinstall the old version. You do not restore the package and its configuration to its previous state. You just restore the server to a new working state with an older package.

11.1.2 Rolling forward for new changes

The benefit of taking a roll-forward mentality means that you expand your trouble-shooting approach. In the example, you reverted a broken commit and restored functionality to the promotions service by matching the new state to a prior working one. However, sometimes reverting a commit doesn't fix your system and makes everything worse! Instead, you can roll forward *new changes* and restore functionality.

Let's imagine the promotions service still doesn't work after you roll forward changes. Rather than try to fix the application, you create a new environment with the change and a new promotions service. You start a canary deployment technique from chapter 9 to gradually increase the traffic to fully restore the application, as shown in figure 11.3. You disable the failed environment after all requests go to the new service instance for debugging.

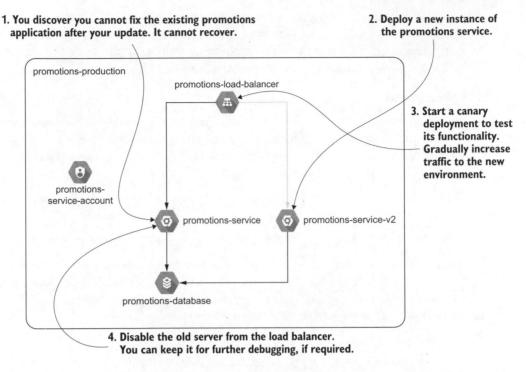

1. You discover you cannot fix the existing promotions application after your update. It cannot recover.

2. Deploy a new instance of the promotions service.

promotions-production

promotions-load-balancer

3. Start a canary deployment to test its functionality. Gradually increase traffic to the new environment.

promotions-service-account

promotions-service

promotions-service-v2

promotions-database

4. Disable the old server from the load balancer. You can keep it for further debugging, if required.

Figure 11.3   When you cannot recover the promotions application, you can use a canary deployment to cut over traffic to a new instance and restore the system.

IaC allows you to reproduce environments with less effort. Furthermore, conforming to immutability means that you already have a pattern of creating new environments for changes. The combination of the two principles helps mitigate higher-risk changes with a larger blast radius.

Use cases that involve data or completely irrecoverable resources cannot roll forward to a prior state. You could corrupt application data or affect other infrastructure while detangling a cascading failure. Rather than roll forward to revert, you can roll forward and implement new changes by applying the change techniques from chapter 9.

You may also restore functionality with a combination of reverts and completely new changes. Expanding your roll-forward mentality to include new changes outside of undoing old ones offers a helpful alternative to restore functionality quickly and minimize disruption to other parts of your system.

11.2 Troubleshooting

You put a bandage on your system so the promotions team can still send out promotional offers for Cool Caps for Keys. However, you still need to secure the IAM of the application! Where do you start to find out why the promotions service failed when you removed administrative permission that the promotions team shouldn't need?

Troubleshooting your IaC also follows specific patterns. Even in the most complex infrastructure systems, many failed changes from IaC usually come from three causes: drift, dependencies, or differences. Examining your configuration for any of these causes helps you identify the problem and a potential fix.

11.2.1 Check for drift

Many broken infrastructure changes stem from configuration drift between configuration and resource state. In figure 11.4, you start by checking for drift. Make sure the IaC for the service account matches the state of the service account in GCP.

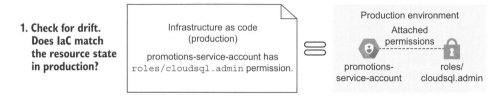

Figure 11.4   Start by checking for drift between IaC and state.

Checking for drift between code and state ensures that you eliminate any failures due to differences between the two. Differences between code and state can introduce unexpected problems. Removing those differences ensures that your change behavior works as expected.

In the case of Cool Caps for Keys, you review the permissions for the promotions service account that you define in IaC. The following listing outlines the IaC that defines the service and roles.

Listing 11.1   Promotions service account with database admin permission

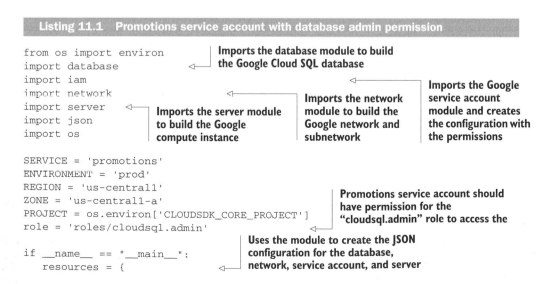

Imports the network module to build the Google network and subnetwork

Imports the Google service account module and creates the configuration with the permissions

```
        'resource':
        network.Module(SERVICE, ENVIRONMENT, REGION).build() +
        iam.Module(SERVICE, ENVIRONMENT, REGION, PROJECT,
                  role).build() +
        database.Module(SERVICE, ENVIRONMENT, REGION).build() +
        server.Module(SERVICE, ENVIRONMENT, ZONE).build()
    }

    with open('main.tf.json', 'w') as outfile:
        json.dump(resources, outfile,
                  sort_keys=True, indent=4)
```

Imports the database module to build the Google Cloud SQL database

Imports the server module to build the Google compute instance

Writes out the Python dictionary to a JSON file to be executed by Terraform later

> **AWS and Azure equivalents**
>
> The AWS equivalent of the GCP Cloud SQL administrator permission is similar to `AmazonRDSFullAccess`. Azure does not have an exact equivalent. Instead, you will need to add an Azure Active Directory account to the database directly and grant administrative consent for Azure SQL Database API permissions.

Then, compare the code to the promotions application's service account permissions in GCP. The service account has only `roles/cloudsql.admin` permissions consistent with your IaC:

```
$ gcloud projects get-iam-policy $CLOUDSDK_CORE_PROJECT
bindings:
- members:
  - serviceAccount:promotions-prod@infrastructure-as-code-book
  ➥ .iam.gserviceaccount.com
  role: roles/cloudsql.admin
version: 1
```

If you find configuration drift between IaC and the active resource state, you can further investigate whether it affects system functionality. You may choose to eliminate some of the drift to ensure that it doesn't contribute to the root cause. However, just because you detect some drift does not mean that it breaks your system! Some drift may have nothing to do with the failure.

11.2.2 Check for dependencies

If you determine drift does not contribute to the failure, you can check for resources that depend on your updated one. In figure 11.5, you start graphing which resources depend on the service account. In both the IaC and production environment, the server depends on the service account.

2. Check for infrastructure resources that depend on your updated one. Is there an unexpected dependency?

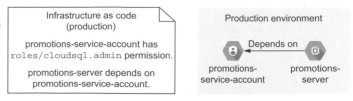

Infrastructure as code (production)

promotions-service-account has `roles/cloudsql.admin` permission.

promotions-server depends on promotions-service-account.

Production environment

Depends on

promotions-service-account ← promotions-server

Figure 11.5   Troubleshoot any resources that depend on the one you want to update.

You want to check that the expected dependencies match the actual. Unexpected dependencies disrupt change behavior. When you review the code in the following listing, you verify that the service account's email gets passed to the server.

Listing 11.2   Promotions server depends on the promotions service account

```
class Module():
    def __init__(self, service, environment,
                 zone, machine_type='e2-micro'):
        self._name = f'{service}-{environment}'
        self._environment = environment
        self._zone = zone
        self._machine_type = machine_type

    def build(self):
        return [
            {
                'google_compute_instance': {
                    self._environment: {
                        'allow_stopping_for_update': True,
                        'boot_disk': [{
                            'initialize_params': [{
                                'image': 'ubuntu-1804-lts'
                            }]
                        }],
                        'machine_type': self._machine_type,
                        'name': self._name,
                        'zone': self._zone,
                        'network_interface': [{
                            'subnetwork':
                            '${google_compute_subnetwork.' +
                            f'{self._environment}' + '.name}',
                            'access_config': {
                                'network_tier': 'STANDARD'
                            }
                        }],
                        'service_account': [{
                            'email': '${google_service_account.' +
                            f'{self._environment}' + '.email}',
                            'scopes': ['cloud-platform']
                        }]
                    }
                }
            }
        ]
```

Uses the module to create the JSON configuration for the server

Creates the Google compute instance by using a Terraform resource based on the name, address, region, and network

The factory for the promotions application's server uses a service account to access GCP services.

However, the promotions team mentions that its application *directly* accesses the database by using its IP address, username, and password. Why would the server need the service account if the application reads the database connection string from a file?

You realize this highlights a discrepancy. You ask the promotions team to show you the application code. The application configuration does not use the database IP address, username, or password!

After additional debugging with the promotions team, you discover that the promotions application connects to the database on `localhost`. The configuration uses the Cloud SQL Auth proxy (https://cloud.google.com/sql/docs/mysql/sql-proxy), which handles the connection and logs into the database! Therefore, the service account connected to the server needs database access.

Figure 11.6 shows that the promotions application accesses the database through a proxy. The proxy uses the service account to authenticate and access the database. The service account needs access to the database with a policy.

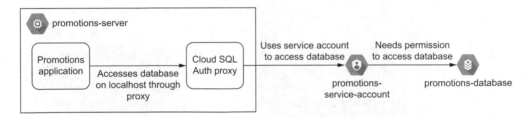

Figure 11.6   The promotions application accesses the database through a proxy, which needs a service account with database permissions.

Congratulations, you discovered why the promotions application broke when you removed the service account! However, you get a little suspicious. Shouldn't you have found the same problem in the testing environment? After all, you tested the change in a testing environment, and the application did not break.

11.2.3 *Check for differences in environments*

Why did the change work in testing but not in production? You examine the promotions application in testing. The application *does not* connect to the database on `localhost`. Instead, it uses the database IP address, username, and password.

You explain to the application team that the production IaC uses the Cloud SQL Auth proxy, while the testing IaC directly calls the database; see figure 11.7. Both configurations use the `roles/cloudsql.admin` permission.

3. Check for differences between testing and production environments. Do they match?

Infrastructure as code (production)

promotions-service-account has `roles/cloudsql.admin` permission.

promotions-server depends on promotions-service-account.

promotions-service uses Cloud SQL Auth proxy.

Infrastructure as code (testing)

promotions-service-account has `roles/cloudsql.admin` permission.

promotions-service directly calls Cloud SQL database.

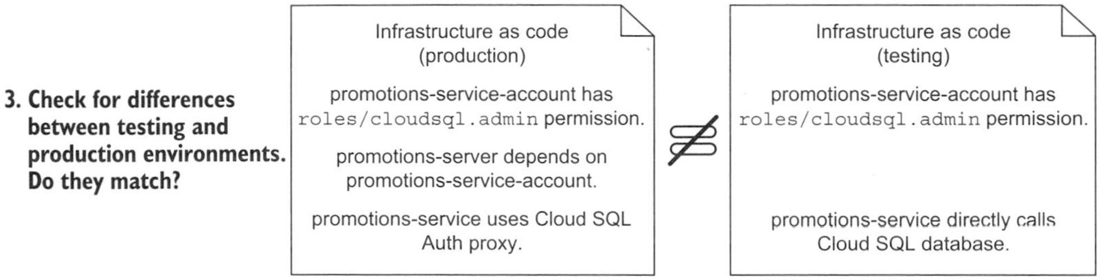

Figure 11.7   Check for differences between testing and production to reconcile any tested changes that fail.

After further discussion with the promotions team, you discover that the team implemented an emergency change to secure production with the Cloud SQL Auth proxy. However, the team did not have a chance to update the testing environment to match! The mismatch allowed your updates to succeed in the testing environment but fail in the production environment.

You want to keep the testing and production environments as similar as possible. However, you cannot always reproduce production in testing environments. As a result, you will encounter failed changes due to discrepancies in both. Systematically identifying differences between testing and production environments helps highlight gaps in testing and change delivery.

While IaC should document all changes and configuration to your system, you might still discover a few surprises between IaC and environments. Figure 11.8 summarizes your structured approach to debugging failed changes in the promotions application's IaC. You check for drift, dependencies, and finally, differences between environments.

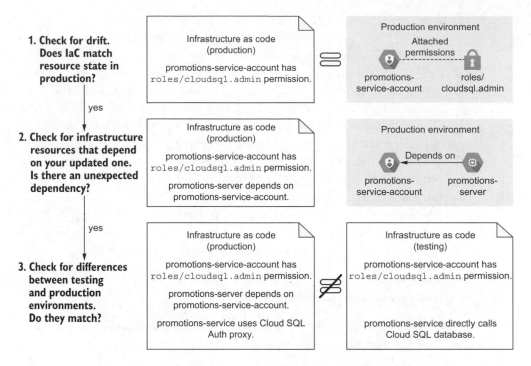

**1. Check for drift.
Does IaC match
resource state in
production?**

yes

**2. Check for infrastructure
resources that depend
on your updated one.
Is there an unexpected
dependency?**

yes

**3. Check for differences
between testing
and production
environments.
Do they match?**

Figure 11.8   You use IaC to troubleshoot your broken change by checking for drift, unexpected dependencies, and differences between testing and production.

After determining a root cause, you can finally implement a long-term fix. You must now reconcile the difference between the testing and production environment and revisit least-privilege access to secure the promotions application's service account.

Exercise 11.1

A team reports that that its application can no longer connect to another application. The application worked last week, but requests have failed since Monday. The team has made no changes to its application and suspects the problem may be a firewall rule. Which steps can you take to troubleshoot the problem? (Choose all that apply.)

A Log into the cloud provider and check the firewall rules for the application.

B Deploy new infrastructure and applications to a green environment for testing.

C Examine the changes in IaC for the application.

D Compare the firewall rules in the cloud provider with IaC.

E Edit the firewall rules and allow all traffic between the applications.

See appendix B for answers to exercises.

11.3   *Fixing*

Your original task for Cool Caps for Keys involved updating the service account permissions for each application to ensure least-privilege access to services. You tried to remove database administrative access from the promotions application's service account but failed. After troubleshooting the issue, you can now fix the problem.

You might find yourself a bit impatient at this point! After all, you have not finished updating the access for other applications in Cool Caps for Keys. However, don't just go in and change everything at once. Pushing a batch of changes can make it difficult to debug the source of failure (previously referenced in chapter 7). Your testing environment still doesn't match production, and you can still affect the promotions application if you make too many changes at once.

Throughout the book, I mention the process of making minor changes to minimize the blast radius of potential failure. Similarly, *incremental fixes* break down the changes you need to make to a system to prevent future failure.

> **DEFINITION**   *Incremental fixes* break changes into smaller parts to gradually improve a system and prevent future failure.

Making minor configuration changes and gradually deploying them helps you recognize the first sign of trouble and stage your IaC for future success.

11.3.1   *Reconcile drift*

As I mentioned in chapter 2, you need to reconcile any manual changes to the infrastructure state with IaC. If you find some drift, you need to address it first! Your system should not have too many break-glass changes if you prioritize the use of IaC.

Recall that the promotions application for Cool Caps for Keys implemented a break-glass change that resulted in a difference between testing and production environments. The production application uses the Cloud SQL Auth proxy to connect to the database, while the testing application directly connects to the database through the IP address and password. You need to build a Cloud SQL Auth proxy in the testing environment.

To start fixing drift, you need to reconstruct the current state of infrastructure in configuration. Figure 11.9 reconstructs the installation commands for the Cloud SQL Auth proxy based on the production server. Then, you add the commands to IaC and apply them to the testing environment.

In this example, the team did not add IaC for the manual change. As a result, you spend additional time rebuilding the installation of the Cloud SQL Auth proxy. An out-of-band change such as the proxy caused a failed change, which takes even more time and effort to fix.

To help minimize some of these problems, use the process of migrating to IaC described in chapter 2. Capturing the manual change as IaC helps minimize differences between environments and drift between IaC and actual state. If you need to

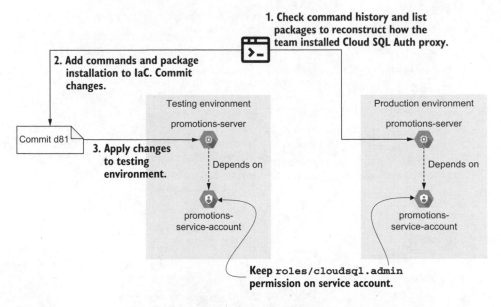

Figure 11.9 In testing, you need to install the Cloud SQL Auth proxy package onto the promotions application's server to reconcile drift from the break-glass change.

reconstruct the state of infrastructure, remember that chapter 2 includes a high-level example of migrating existing infrastructure into IaC. However, you typically have to find or write a tool to transform the state to IaC.

Let's write the IaC to install the proxy. You checked the command history on the promotions application's server in production and reconstructed the installation of the Cloud SQL Auth proxy. The following listing automates the commands and installation process in a startup script for the promotions application's server.

Listing 11.3   Installing the Cloud SQL Auth proxy in the server startup script

Creates a startup script that reconstructs
the manual installation commands for
the Cloud SQL Auth proxy

```
class Module():
    def _startup_script(self):
        proxy_download = 'https://dl.google.com/cloudsql/' + \
            'cloud_sql_proxy.linux.amd64'
        exec_start = '/usr/local/bin/cloud_sql_proxy ' + \
            '-instances=${google_sql_database_instance.' + \
            f'{self._environment}.connection_name}}=tcp:3306'

        return f"""
#!/bin/bash
wget {proxy_download} -O /usr/local/bin/cloud_sql_proxy
chmod +x /usr/local/bin/cloud_sql_proxy
```

Sets a variable
as the proxy
download URL

Sets a variable that
runs the Cloud SQL
Auth proxy binary
on port 3306

Returns a shell
script that
installs the proxy
and starts it up
with the server

```
cat << EOF > /usr/lib/systemd/system/cloudsqlproxy.service
[Install]
WantedBy=multi-user.target

[Unit]
Description=Google Cloud Compute Engine SQL Proxy
Requires=networking.service
After=networking.service

[Service]
Type=simple
WorkingDirectory=/usr/local/bin
ExecStart={exec_start}
Restart=always
StandardOutput=journal
User=root
EOF

systemctl daemon-reload
systemctl start cloudsqlproxy
"""
```

Configures the systemd daemon to start and stop the Cloud SQL Auth proxy

Uses the module to create the JSON configuration for the Google compute instance and includes a startup script to install the proxy

```
def build(self):
    return [
        {
            'google_compute_instance': {
                self._environment: {
                    'metadata_startup_script': self._startup_script()
                }
            }
        }
    ]
```

Adds the startup script to the server. I omit other attributes for clarity.

AWS and Azure equivalents

For AWS and Azure, you do not have to install software for the proxy on the instance. If you would like to reproduce listing 11.3 in AWS and Azure for practice, you can pass the startup script to the resource as `user_data` to the AWS instance or `custom_data` to the Azure Linux virtual machine.

You *do not* update the service account with new permissions! In the spirit of incremental fixes, you want to avoid adding more changes to track as you push to production. You add the startup script to the promotions application's server and change the testing environment without more updates.

Startup script, configuration manager, or image builder?

I use the startup script field in this example to avoid introducing more syntax. Instead, you should implement the configuration of any new packages or processes with a *configuration manager* or *image builder*.

For example, the configuration manager would push the Cloud SQL Auth proxy instal-lation process to any server with the promotions application. Similarly, the image builder configures the proxy for each image you bake! Whenever you reference the image for the promotions application, you always have the proxy built into the server.

11.3.2 Reconcile differences in environments

While you updated your IaC to account for drift, you also need to make sure testing and production environments use your new IaC. For Cool Caps for Keys, you make sure the database connection works in the testing environment. Then, you ask the promotions team to update its application configuration to connect to the database through the proxy on `localhost`.

The promotions team pushes its application configuration to use the Cloud SQL Auth proxy into the testing environment, run tests, and update production, as shown in figure 11.10. You keep the `roles/cloudsql.admin` permission on the service account because the proxy needs it.

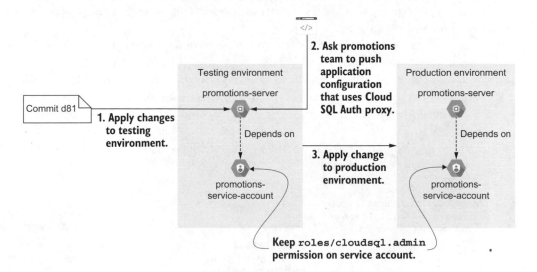

Figure 11.10   You need to push your IaC changes onto the promotions application's server in testing and production environments.

The push re-creates the production server with the new startup script. After additional end-to-end testing for the promotions application, you confirm that you successfully updated both testing and production environments.

Why start with reconciling drift before differences between production and testing environments? In this example, you opt to reconcile drift first because you will spend more time manually installing the packages in the testing environment. If you update your IaC and automate the package installation, you can ensure that the change works in the testing environment before pushing it to the production environment.

You might choose to reconcile testing and production environments first because you have a large amount of drift. In that case, match testing and production environments before fixing drift. You want an accurate testing environment before you implement your reconciliation changes.

Reconcile drift and differences in environments to help the next person make updates to the system. They do not have to worry about knowing the difference in configuration or manually configuring the proxy. The extra time you spend updating your IaC helps you avoid additional time debugging!

11.3.3 *Implement the original change*

Now that you've minimized the blast radius of potential failure by reconciling drift and updating your environments, you can finally push forward the original change. Your debugging and incremental fixes change your infrastructure. When you return to implementing the original change, you may need to adjust your code.

Let's finish the original change for the Cool Caps for Keys promotions application. Recall that the security team asked you to remove administrative permissions from the service account. This process ensures least-privilege access and accounts for using the Cloud SQL Auth proxy.

You know that the service account must have database access because the application uses the Cloud SQL Auth proxy. Now, you try to figure out what kind of minimal access the application *should* use. The roles/cloudsql.client permission offers enough access for a service account to get a list of instances and connect to them.

In figure 11.11, you change the service account's permissions from administrative access to roles/cloudsql.client. You push this change to the testing environment, verify that promotions still work, and deploy the roles/cloudsql.client permission to production.

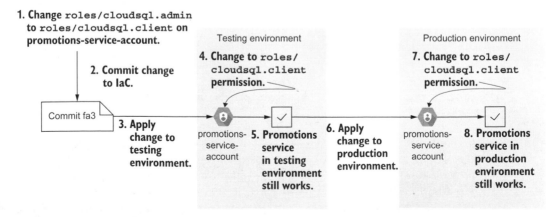

Figure 11.11   You need to push your IaC changes onto the promotions application's server in testing and production environments.

You reconciled the difference between testing and production environments for the proxy. In theory, the testing environment should now catch any issues with your change. Any failed changes should now appear in the testing environment. Let's change the permission for the service account in the following listing from `roles/cloudsql.admin` to `roles/cloudsql.client`.

Listing 11.4 Changing the service account role to the database client

```
from os import environ
import database
import iam
import network
import server
import json
import os


SERVICE = 'promotions'
ENVIRONMENT = 'prod'
REGION = 'us-central1'
ZONE = 'us-central1-a'
PROJECT = os.environ['CLOUDSDK_CORE_PROJECT']
role = 'roles/cloudsql.client'

if __name__ == "__main__":
    resources = {
        'resource':
        network.Module(SERVICE, ENVIRONMENT, REGION).build() +
        iam.Module(SERVICE, ENVIRONMENT, REGION, PROJECT,
                role).build() +
        database.Module(SERVICE, ENVIRONMENT, REGION).build() +
        server.Module(SERVICE, ENVIRONMENT, ZONE).build()
    }

    with open('main.tf.json', 'w') as outfile:
        json.dump(resources, outfile,
                sort_keys=True, indent=4)
```

Changes the promotions service account role to client access, which allows connecting to the database instance (annotation pointing to `role = 'roles/cloudsql.client'`)

Imports the network, database, and server modules without changing the resources (annotation pointing to the network, database, and server module lines)

Imports the service account and attaches the "roles/cloudsql.client" role to its permissions (annotation pointing to the iam.Module line)

AWS and Azure equivalents

The AWS equivalent of the GCP Cloud SQL administrator permission is similar to `AmazonRDSFullAccess`. Azure does not have an exact equivalent. Instead, you will need to add an Azure Active Directory account to the database directly and grant administrative consent for Azure SQL Database API permissions.

In AWS, you can add the `rds-db:connect` action to the IAM role attached to the EC2 instance. In Azure, you will need to revoke administrative access and grant `SELECT` access to the Azure AD user linked to the database user (http://mng.bz/woo7).

You commit and apply the change. The testing environment applies the change and validates that the application still works! You confirm with the promotions team, which approves the production change.

The team promotes the new permissions change to production, runs end-to-end tests, and confirms that the promotions application can access the database! After a few weeks of debugging and making changes, you can *finally* fix the other applications in Cool Caps for Keys.

Why dedicate an entire chapter with a single example of fixing failed changes? It represents the reality of fixing IaC. You want to resolve the failure as quickly as possible without making it worse.

Rolling *forward* helps restore the system's working state and minimize disruption to infrastructure resources. Then, you can work on troubleshooting the root cause. Many infrastructure failures come from drift, dependencies, or differences between testing and production environments. After you address these discrepancies, you implement your original change.

Learning the art of rolling forward IaC takes time and experience. While you could just log into the cloud provider console and make manual changes to get the system working, remember that the bandage will fall off very quickly and won't promote long-term system healing. Using IaC to track and fix the system incrementally minimizes the impact of the repairs and provides context for anyone else updating the system.

Summary

- Repairing failures for IaC involves rolling forward fixes instead of rolling them back.
- Rolling forward IaC uses immutability to return the system to a working state.
- Before debugging and implementing long-term fixes, prioritize stabilizing and restoring the system to a working state.
- When troubleshooting IaC, check for drift, unexpected dependencies, and differences between environments as part of the root cause.
- Work on incremental fixes to quickly recognize and reduce the blast radius of potential failure.
- Before you re-implement the original change that failed, make sure you reconcile drift and differences between environments for accurate testing and future system updates.
- Reconstructing state in IaC to reconcile drift involves aggregating manual commands for server configuration or transforming infrastructure metadata into IaC.

Cost of cloud computing

When you use a cloud provider, you get very excited at the ease of provisioning. After all, you can create a resource at the click of a mouse or a single command. However, the cost of cloud computing becomes a concern as your organization scales and grows. Your updates to infrastructure as code can affect the overall cost of the cloud!

We must build cost considerations into our infrastructure just as we build security into it. If you make your system and find out you overran your cost, you could break the system while trying to remove resources and reduce your cloud computing bill. In chapter 8, I recommended baking security into IaC like a cake. The cost of ingredients affects how many cakes we could bake, essential to know *before* you start.

This chapter covers the practices you can combine with IaC to manage the cost of cloud computing and reduce unused resources. You will find some high-level, general cost-control practices and patterns that I describe in the context of IaC. However, regularly apply these practices to re-optimize costs as your system evolves based on customer demand, organizational scale, and cloud provider billing.

What about the cost of my data center or managed services?

I focus primarily on cloud computing because of its flexibility and on-demand billing. You often account for the cost of data center computing with your organization's chargeback system. Each business unit establishes a budget for its data center resources, and the technology department issues *chargeback* based on resource usage, taking into account the operating cost of the data center.

You can always apply the practices for managing your cost drivers with cost control and estimation. However, the techniques I outline for cost reduction and optimization may or may not work for every situation (no matter whether you're using the cloud, data center, or managed service). Depending on your scale, geographic architecture, business domain, or data center usage, your use cases and systems may require specialized assessment or re-platforming.

12.1   *Manage cost drivers*

Say you work as a consultant for a company that needs to migrate its platform that supports conferences and events to the public cloud. The company asks you to "lift and shift" its configuration in its data center to the public cloud. You help the company's teams build out infrastructure in GCP, applying all of the principles and practices you learned from this book. Eventually, your team rolls out the platform on GCP and successfully supports its first customer: a small three-hour community conference.

A few weeks after the event, your client schedules a cryptic meeting. When the meeting starts, the client shows you their cloud bill. It totals over $10,000 for the development and support of a single three-hour conference! The finance team does not seem happy with the cost, especially since the company lost money running the conference. You get your next task: *reduce the cost per conference as much as possible.*

Are you using an actual cloud bill?

The preceding example uses a fictitious, *very* simplified cloud bill that approximates the cost of a conference platform service based on GCP's pricing calculator (https://cloud.google.com/products/calculator) as of 2021. The estimates may not include all of the offerings you need, updated pricing for the platform, differences between environments, or the sizes you might use in a comparable system. I rounded the subtotals to streamline the example.

If you run the example, you may reach a GCP quota for the N2D machine type instances. The servers will exceed the platform's free tier! You can change the machine type to free-tier instances to run the examples without a charge.

Thanks to the tagging practices you borrowed from chapter 8, the bill uses the tag to identify which resources belong to the community conference and their environment. You manage to break down your cloud computing bill, as shown in table 12.1, and identify the costs by the type and size of the infrastructure resource.

Table 12.1 Your cloud bill by offering and the environment

Offering	Subtotal, testing environment	Subtotal, production environment	Subtotal
Compute (servers)	$400	$3,600	$4,000
Database (Cloud SQL)	$250	$2,250	$2,500
Messaging (Pub/Sub)	$100	$900	$1,000
Object storage (Cloud Storage)	$100	$900	$1,000
Data transfer (networking egress)	$100	$900	$1,000
Other (Cloud CDN, Support)	$50	$450	$500
Total	$1,000	$9,000	$10,000

> **AWS and Azure equivalents**
>
> The cloud bill mostly abstracts the specific names for equivalent Azure and AWS services. For clarity, I list some of the GCP offerings with approximations to AWS or Azure ones:
>
> - *Database (Cloud SQL)*—Amazon RDS, Azure SQL Database
> - *Messaging (Pub/Sub)*—Amazon Simple Queue Service (SQS) and Simple Notification Service (SNS), Azure Service Bus
> - *Object storage (Cloud Storage)*—Amazon S3, Azure Blob Storage
> - *Other (Cloud CDN, Support)*—Amazon CloudFront, Azure Content Delivery Network (CDN)

Separating cost by offerings and environments helps you identify which factors contribute to the cost and where you should investigate further. To start reducing the bill, you must determine the *cost drivers*, the factors or activities that affect the total cost.

DEFINITION　*Cost drivers* are the factors or activities that affect your total cloud computing cost.

When you assess cost drivers, calculate the percentage cost of cloud offerings. Some offerings will always cost more than others. You can still use the breakdown to help you identify services to optimize. Breaking down cost by environment helps you identify the footprint of testing versus production environments. Comparing the two will give you a better picture of which environment has inefficiencies you can reduce.

Based on your breakdown, you calculate the percentage for each offering and environment. In figure 12.1, you chart out that compute resources take 40% of the bill. You also discover that the team spent 10% of the total on the testing environment and 90% on the production environment.

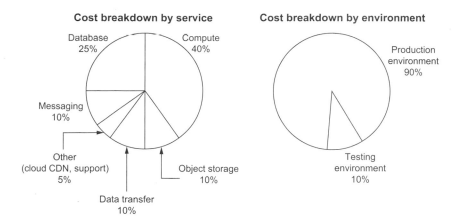

Figure 12.1   The resource tags break down the cost by service and environment.

A large part of the bill goes to compute resources—specifically, servers. If your team members need to support an even larger conference, they need to control the type of resources they create and to optimize the resource size based on usage. You decide to investigate methods of controlling the size and types of servers the team can use.

12.1.1 Implement tests to control cost

You examine the metrics for the conference and the resource usage for each server. None of the servers exceeded their virtual CPU (vCPU) or memory usage. For the most part, you determine that you need at most 32 vCPUs for your production environment. Your client's infrastructure team confirms that the maximum usage does not exceed 32 vCPUs.

> **NOTE** GCP uses the term *machine type* to refer to a predefined virtual machine shape with specific vCPU and memory ratios to fit your workload requirements. Similarly, AWS uses the term *instance type*, and Azure uses the term *size*.

However, the public cloud makes it easy for anyone to adjust a server to use 48 vCPU. Your bill increases by 50% because of the additional CPU, and you don't even use all of it. To more proactively control the cost using IaC, you combine unit testing from chapter 6 and policy enforcement from chapter 8.

Figure 12.2 adds a new policy test to the server's delivery pipeline. The test checks every server defined in IaC for its number of vCPUs and compares it to the value

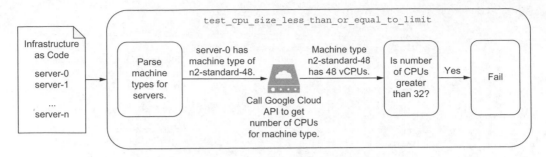

Figure 12.2   Your test should parse machine types from server configurations, check the GCP API for the number of CPUs, and verify they do not exceed the limit.

returned by the GCP API. If the API's information exceeds your maximum vCPU limit of 32, your test fails.

Why call the infrastructure provider's API for vCPU information? Many infrastructure providers offer an API or client library to retrieve information about a given machine type from their catalogs. You can use this to dynamically get information about the number of CPUs and memory.

Infrastructure providers change offerings frequently. Furthermore, you cannot account for every possible server type. Writing your test to call the infrastructure provider API for the most updated information helps improve the overall evolvability of the test.

In listing 12.1, let's implement the policy test to check for the maximum vCPU limit. First, you build a method to call the GCP API for the number of vCPUs for a given machine type.

Listing 12.1   Retrieving vCPU count for machine type from the GCP API

```
import googleapiclient.discovery


class MachineType():
    def __init__(self, gcp_json):
        self.name = gcp_json['name']
        self.cpus = gcp_json['guestCpus']
        self.ram = self._convert_mb_to_gb(
            gcp_json['memoryMb'])
        self.maxPersistentDisks = gcp_json[
            'maximumPersistentDisks']
        self.maxPersistentDiskSizeGb = gcp_json[
            'maximumPersistentDisksSizeGb']
        self.isSharedCpu = gcp_json['isSharedCpu']

    def _convert_mb_to_gb(self, mb):
        GIGABYTE = 1.0/1024
        return GIGABYTE * mb
```

> **Defines a machine type object to store any attributes you might need to check, including number of vCPUs**

> **Converts megabytes of memory to gigabytes for consistent unit measure**

```
def get_machine_type(project, zone, type):
    service = googleapiclient.discovery.build(
        'compute', 'v1')
    result = service.machineTypes().list(
        project=project,
        zone=zone,
        filter=f'name:"{type}"').execute()
    types = result['items'] if 'items' in result else None
    if len(types) != 1:
        return None
    return MachineType(types[0])
```

Calls the GCP API to retrieve
the number of vCPUs for a
given machine type

Returns a machine type object
with vCPU and disk attributes

AWS and Azure equivalents

You can use AWS's Python SDK to retrieve the EC2 instances and parse the instance type. Then, describe the instance types to get the vCPU and memory information (http://mng.bz/qYYK).

To get the machine type and stock-keeping units (SKUs) from Azure, use the Azure library for Python. After retrieving the size from a list of instances, you can call the Resource Skus API for information on the number of CPUs and memory (http://mng.bz/YG1N).

Anytime you use a new machine type, you can use the same function to retrieve vCPUs and memory. Next, you write a test to parse every server defined in your configuration for its machine type. In the following listing, you retrieve the number of vCPUs for the machine type for a list of servers and verify that the vCPUs do not exceed the limit of 32.

Listing 12.2   Writing a policy test to check that servers do not exceed 32 vCPUs

```
import pytest
import os
import compute
import json

ENVIRONMENTS = ['testing', 'prod']
CONFIGURATION_FILE = 'main.tf.json'

PROJECT = os.environ['CLOUDSDK_CORE_PROJECT']

                                            Parses and extracts any
                                            server JSON configurations
                                            across testing and
                                            production environments

@pytest.fixture(scope="module")
def configuration():
    merged = []
    for environment in ENVIRONMENTS:
        with open(f'{environment}/{CONFIGURATION_FILE}', 'r') as f:
            environment_configuration = json.load(f)
            merged += environment_configuration['resource']
    return merged
```

```
def resources(configuration, resource_type):
    resource_list = []
    for resource in configuration:
        if resource_type in resource.keys():
            resource_name = list(
                resource[resource_type].keys())[0]
            resource_list.append(
                resource[resource_type]
                [resource_name])
    return resource_list


@pytest.fixture
def servers(configuration):
    return resources(configuration,
                     'google_compute_instance')

def test_cpu_size_less_than_or_equal_to_limit(servers):
    CPU_LIMIT = 32
    non_compliant_servers = []
    for server in servers:
        type = compute.get_machine_type(
            PROJECT, server['zone'],
            server['machine_type'])
        if type.cpus > CPU_LIMIT:
            non_compliant_servers.append(server['name'])
    assert len(non_compliant_servers) == 0, \
        f'Servers found using over {CPU_LIMIT}' + \
        f' vCPUs: {non_compliant_servers}'
```

Parses and extracts any server JSON configurations across testing and production environments

Initializes a list of noncompliant servers that exceed the 32 vCPU limit

Sets the CPU limit to 32, the maximum required for the application

For each server configuration, retrieves the machine type attribute and calls the GCP API for more information

If the server configuration includes a machine type that exceeds 32 vCPUs, add it to a list of noncompliant servers.

Checks that all servers comply with the CPU limit. If not, fail the test and throw an error for the servers that exceed 32 CPUs.

You configure the test with a soft mandatory enforcement policy. *Soft mandatory enforcement* means your team reviews and approves the more expensive resource type before you create it. You can override the machine type to a larger size if you have a business justification.

Outside of checking machine types for vCPU and memory limits, you may also need to add overrides for unique architectures or machine types that apply to certain use cases, like machine learning. However, they cost more than a general-purpose resource type.

You can test that IaC uses general-purpose resources by default. General-purpose machine or resource types offer lower-cost options. If someone needs a specialized, more expensive resource, you can enable it with soft mandatory enforcement.

Other tests might include checks for specific configurations like scheduled reboots, automatic scaling, or private networking. Each of these configurations contributes to optimizing the cost of your resources. Expressing them in IaC lets you verify that configuration conforms to best practices to reduce cost early in the development process.

12.1.2 *Automate cost estimation*

You react to too large or expensive resource changes with policy tests to control costs. What if you want a proactive way to check how you change your budget by changing cost drivers? Imagine you want to know how adjusting your production server size to the machine type of n2d-standard-16 (16 vCPUs) might affect the future cost of a different three-hour conference.

Figure 12.3 outlines the workflow to *estimate* the cost of five servers with the machine type n2d-standard-16. Once you calculate the price, you can add a policy test to verify that the total does not exceed your monthly budget.

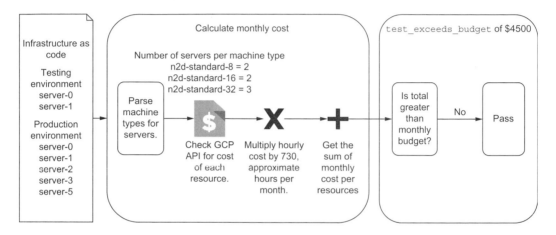

Figure 12.3   Cost estimation parses IaC for machine types, calculates the monthly cost of the resource, and generates a value to compare with your expected budget.

Cost estimation parses your IaC for resource attributes and generates an estimate of their cost. You can use cost estimation to check that your changes stay within your budget or assess adjustments to cost drivers.

> **DEFINITION**   *Cost estimation* extracts infrastructure resource attributes and generates an estimate of their total cost.

How does cost estimation help you evolve your infrastructure? Cost estimation offers additional transparency into cost drivers that may affect your architecture. As you change your system, you can use these tests to help budget and communicate charge-back across teams.

Cost estimation example and tools

I wrote minimal code to demonstrate the general workflow of cost estimation. For clarity, I omitted some of the code from the text. You can find all of the code organized at https://github.com/joatmon08/manning-book/tree/main/ch12.

The example uses the Google Cloud Billing Catalog API, which offers a service catalog with pricing. I also use a specialized Python client library for the Cloud Catalog to access the billing API (http://mng.bz/mOOn). The example does not account for specialized pricing, such as sustained use discounts or preemptible (equivalent to spot instances in AWS).

You will find a few tools that offer cost estimation. Each cloud provider offers its own cost estimator user interface for entering your resources. Other tools implement a more scalable workflow than my example code to parse configuration, call a cloud provider's API, and calculate a cost estimate. I will not list them in this chapter, as they change frequently and depend on the cloud provider and your IaC tooling.

GET THE PRICE PER UNIT

I recommend dynamically requesting information from a cloud provider's service catalog API. Price per unit can change, and hardcoding the prices often results in the wrong cost estimation. To start implementing cost estimation in the example, you need some logic to call the cloud provider's catalog and retrieve the price per unit based on your machine type.

The Google Cloud Billing Catalog API offers a list of services and SKUs based on price per unit of CPU or memory (RAM). In listing 12.3, you get the service identifier for the Google Compute Engine service. The Google Cloud Billing Catalog API categorizes prices based on service identifiers, which you must retrieve dynamically.

Listing 12.3   Getting the Google Compute Engine service from the catalog

```
from google.cloud import billing_v1

class ComputeService:
    def __init__(self):
        self.billing = \
            billing_v1.services.cloud_catalog.CloudCatalogClient()
        for result in self.billing.list_services():
            if result.display_name == 'Compute Engine':
                self.name = result.name
```

Creates a client with the Python library for Google Cloud Billing Catalog API

Gets the service identifier for Google Compute Engine in the catalog

AWS and Azure equivalents

Update the GCP client library to call the AWS Cost Explorer API (http://mng.bz/5Qm4) for AWS. On the other hand, Azure offers an open REST API endpoint for retail prices (http://mng.bz/6X9G). You can write some additional code to request catalog information.

You can call the Google Cloud Billing Catalog API a second time for the price of a machine type in listing 12.4. Using the service identifier from the preceding step, you get a list of SKUs for the Google Compute Engine service. You write some code to parse its response list of SKUs to match the machine type and purpose, and retrieve the unit price per CPU or gigabyte of memory.

Listing 12.4   Getting the CPU and RAM price for Compute Engine SKUs

```
from google.cloud import billing_v1


class ComputeSKU:
    def __init__(self, machine_type, service_name):
        self.billing = \
            billing_v1.services.cloud_catalog.CloudCatalogClient()
        self.service_name = service_name
        type_name = machine_type.split('-')
        self.family = type_name[0]
        self.exclude = [
            'custom',
            'preemptible',
            'sole tenancy',
            'commitment'
        ] if type_name[1] == 'standard' else []

    def _filter(self, description):
        return not any(
            type in description for type in self.exclude
        )

    def _get_unit_price(self, result):
        expression = result.pricing_info[0]
        unit_price = expression. \
            pricing_expression.tiered_rates[0].unit_price.nanos \
            if expression else 0
        category = result.category.resource_group
        if category == 'CPU':
            self.cpu_pricing = unit_price
        if category == 'RAM':
            self.ram_pricing = unit_price

    def get_pricing(self, region):
        for result in self.billing.list_skus(parent=self.service_name):
            description = result.description.lower()
            if region in result.service_regions and \
                    self.family in description and \
                    self._filter(description):
                self._get_unit_price(result)
        return self.cpu_pricing, self.ram_pricing
```

Creates a client with the Python library for the Google Cloud Billing Catalog API

For a machine type like n2d-standard-16, extracts the machine family (N2D) and purpose (standard) to identify the SKU

If you use a standard machine type, do not search for any specialized Compute Service SKUs in the catalog.

Retrieves the unit price per CPU or RAM in nano-dollars (10^{-9})

Calls the Google Cloud Billing Catalog and retrieves a list of SKUs for the Compute Service

Finds SKUs that match the region, machine family, and purpose of the machine type based on its description

The Google Cloud Billing Catalog sets a unit price based on the number of CPUs and gigabytes of memory. As a result, you cannot search based on the name of the machine type. Instead, you need to correlate the general-purpose machine type with the catalog's description.

CALCULATE THE MONTHLY COST FOR A SINGLE RESOURCE

Once you retrieve the CPU and RAM unit price for a given machine type, you can use it to calculate a monthly cost for a single instance of the machine. Some cloud catalogs set up a unit price by a factor. For example, GCP uses nano units, which means you need to also multiply by the factor. Listing 12.5 implements the code to calculate the monthly cost for a single server. You multiply the unit price by the average number of hours per month, 730, and the nano units.

Listing 12.5 Calculating the monthly cost for a single server

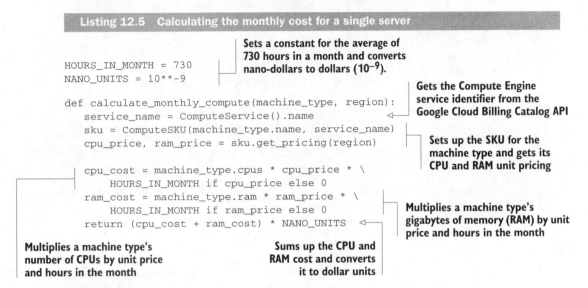

```
HOURS_IN_MONTH = 730
NANO_UNITS = 10**-9

def calculate_monthly_compute(machine_type, region):
    service_name = ComputeService().name
    sku = ComputeSKU(machine_type.name, service_name)
    cpu_price, ram_price = sku.get_pricing(region)

    cpu_cost = machine_type.cpus * cpu_price * \
        HOURS_IN_MONTH if cpu_price else 0
    ram_cost = machine_type.ram * ram_price * \
        HOURS_IN_MONTH if ram_price else 0
    return (cpu_cost + ram_cost) * NANO_UNITS
```

Sets a constant for the average of 730 hours in a month and converts nano-dollars to dollars (10^{-9}).

Gets the Compute Engine service identifier from the Google Cloud Billing Catalog API

Sets up the SKU for the machine type and gets its CPU and RAM unit pricing

Multiplies a machine type's gigabytes of memory (RAM) by unit price and hours in the month

Multiplies a machine type's number of CPUs by unit price and hours in the month

Sums up the CPU and RAM cost and converts it to dollar units

You now have a minimal form of cost estimation that calculates the cost of a single server. With the initial cost calculation for a single server, you can parse your IaC for all servers, retrieve their machine types and regions, and calculate a total cost. In the future, you can add more logic to retrieve SKUs for other services, like databases or messaging.

CHECK THAT YOUR COST DOES NOT EXCEED THE BUDGET

You decide that you can do more with your cost estimation. You write a test with a soft mandatory enforcement approach to check whether your estimated cost exceeds your monthly budget. For example, your client tells you that a conference should not exceed a monthly budget of $4,500. You can compare your cost estimation to the budget and proactively identify any cost drivers.

Let's write a test to estimate the new cost of servers and compare it to the budget. In the following listing, you parse your IaC for all servers and count the number of servers with specific machine types and regions.

Listing 12.6 Parsing IaC for all servers

```
from compute import get_machine_type
import pytest
import os
import json
```

```
ENVIRONMENTS = ['testing', 'prod']
CONFIGURATION_FILE = 'main.tf.json'

@pytest.fixture(scope="module")          Reads every configuration file
def configuration():            ◁────    that defines each environment,
    merged = []                          such as testing and production
    for environment in ENVIRONMENTS:
        with open(f'{environment}/{CONFIGURATION_FILE}', 'r') as f:
            environment_configuration = json.load(f)
            merged += environment_configuration['resource']
    return merged
                                         For each server in the
@pytest.fixture                          configuration file, creates a list of
def servers(configuration):     ◁────    their regions and machine types
    servers = dict()
    server_configs = resources(configuration,
                               'google_compute_instance')
    for server in server_configs:
        region = server['zone'].rsplit('-', 1)[0]
        machine_type = server['machine_type']
        key = f'{region},{machine_type}'
        if key not in servers:           Calls the Google Compute API and gets
            type = get_machine_type(     details on the machine type, such as its
                PROJECT, server['zone'], number of CPUs and memory
                machine_type)
            servers[key] = {
                'type': type,            Tracks the number of servers
                'num_servers': 1         with the specific machine type
            }                            and region to streamline the
        else:                            SKUs you need to retrieve
            servers[key]['num_servers'] += 1
    return servers
```

You can call these methods in your test to retrieve cost information for each machine type in a specific region and sum the total cost. The test in the following listing checks whether the total cost exceeds the monthly budget of $4,500.

Listing 12.7   Getting CPU and RAM price for Compute Engine SKUs

```
from estimation import calculate_monthly_compute
                                         Sets a constant to
PROJECT = os.environ['CLOUDSDK_CORE_PROJECT']   communicate the expected
MONTHTLY_COMPUTE_BUDGET = 4500          ◁──── monthly compute budget


def test_monthly_compute_budget_not_exceeded(servers):   ◁──  Tests that the cost of
    total = 0                                            your servers does not
    for key, value in servers.items():                   exceed the monthly
        region, _ = key.split(',')                       compute budget
```

```
total += calculate_monthly_compute(value['type'], region) * \
    value['num_servers']
assert total < MONTHTLY_COMPUTE_BUDGET
```

Confirms that the estimated total cost does not exceed the monthly compute budget

Calculates the monthly total per server based on machine type and region, multiplied by servers for that machine type, and sums up the total

You now have a test to estimate the total monthly cost of computing resources and compare it to your budget! Each time someone changes the infrastructure, the test recalculates the new cost of the system.

A cost estimation gives you a general view of your infrastructure cost but may not accurately reflect your actual bill. You'll have to account for a certain margin of error. If your estimation exceeds the monthly budget, it may indicate that you need to reassess size and resource usage. You'll also refine your monthly budget over time depending on the growth of your systems.

CONTINUOUS DELIVERY WITH COST ESTIMATION

How do you check that infrastructure changes do not exceed your budget? Each time you change your IaC and push it to a repository, your cost estimation and test for budget runs. Budget tests in your pipeline help you identify costly infrastructure changes and refine the resource in a testing environment. The process prevents chargeback in the production environment.

For example, let's say you want to add another server to the testing environment for a different conference. In figure 12.4, you create a configuration to add another server with the machine type of n2d-standard-8. The pipeline runs a test to calculate the monthly cost with the new server and check it against the monthly budget.

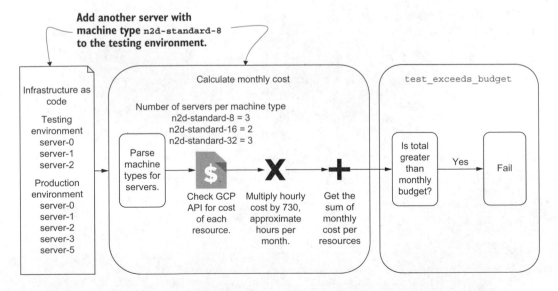

Figure 12.4   Adding another server exceeds your budget of $4,500, causing the test to fail.

You push the configuration to the repository, and your delivery pipeline runs the tests to check for budget compliance. The pipeline fails! You check the logs and discover that your cost estimation exceeds the expected monthly budget:

```
$ pytest test_budget.py
FAILED test_budget.py::test_monthly_compute_budget_not_exceeded -
  assert 4687.6161600000005 < 4500
```

You speak with your finance team. The finance analyst confirms that the budget can increase to accommodate the new testing instance. You update the monthly budget within the test to $4,700 for future changes!

Whether you write a cost estimation mechanism or use a tool, you should consider adding it to your delivery pipelines as another test for policy. Estimation helps guide instance sizing and usage. It should *never* stop a change before production. Instead, it should provide an *opportunity* for you to reassess the need for the resource.

Do not account for every cost driver as part of your cost estimation. Instead, choose the resources that make up the bulk of your bill. The example focuses on computing resources like servers, which often contribute significantly to the cost. You might implement cost estimation for other resources, like databases or messaging frameworks.

Always question the accuracy of your cost estimation! You cannot predict the resources you will create or how you use them. For example, you might find it hard to estimate the cost to transfer data between regions or services until it happens. Reconcile your cost estimate with your monthly bill and assess which cost drivers contribute to the difference.

A monthly comparison can help you identify any changes and budget for the actual cost based on a multiplier of the estimate. In the remainder of the chapter, we'll discuss ways to reduce cloud waste and optimize cost outside of proactive measures like testing or estimation.

Exercise 12.1

Given the following code, which of the following statements are true? (Choose all that apply.)

```
HOURS_IN_MONTH = 730
MONTHLY_BUDGET = 5000
DATABASE_COST_PER_HOUR = 5
NUM_DATABASES = 2
BUFFER = 0.1


def test_monthly_budget_not_exceeded():
    total = HOURS_IN_MONTH * NUM_DATABASES * DATABASE_COST_PER_HOUR
    assert total < MONTHLY_BUDGET + MONTHLY_BUDGET * BUFFER
```

A The test will pass because the cost of the database is within the budget.
B The test estimates the monthly cost of databases.
C The test does not account for different database types.

12.2   *Reduce cloud waste*

You can use IaC to implement proactive measures to manage cost drivers for cloud computing. However, you need to combine them with other practices to continue to reduce and optimize costs. After all, your client in the example still doesn't appreciate a $10,000 cloud bill for a three-hour conference!

If you provision a large server but do not use all the CPU or memory, you have wasted unused CPU or memory. You have an opportunity to reduce your cloud computing cost! One approach you can take to improve your bill's state involves eliminating *cloud waste*, unused or underutilized infrastructure resources.

> **DEFINITION**   *Cloud waste* is unused or underutilized infrastructure resources.

You can reduce cloud waste by deleting, expiring, or stopping unused resources; scheduling or scaling instances based on usage; and assessing the right resource size or type for your system; see figure 12.5.

Reducing Cloud Waste

| Stop untagged or unused resources. | Start and stop resources on a schedule. | Choose the right resource type, size, and reservation. | Enable autoscaling for resources. | Set a tag for resource expiration. |

Figure 12.5   You can reduce cloud waste by removing unused resources, or scheduling and sizing resources to accommodate usage patterns.

Identifying cloud waste often starts as the first response to a surprising cost on your public cloud bill. However, you can use these techniques in your data center, especially for a private cloud. While they do not provide an immediate short-term benefit, they help optimize data center resource usage and long-term cost reduction.

12.2.1   *Stop untagged or unused resources*

Sometimes you and your team will create infrastructure resources for testing or other configuration. You end up forgetting about them until they show up on your cloud bill. As a first iteration of reducing cloud waste, you can identify unused resources and remove them.

Recall that you have a mission of reducing the cost of running a conference for your client. Could you reduce costs by identifying unused resources? Yes! Sometimes our teams create resources for testing and forget to remove them.

For example, you retrieve a list of servers in your Google Cloud projects and examine them in table 12.2. While many of them in testing and production have tags, you notice two instances with no tags. The n2d-standard-16 machines cost about $700 (7% of the total monthly bill).

Table 12.2 Cost of servers by type and environment

Machine type	Environment	Number of servers	Subtotal
n2d-standard-8	Testing	2	$400
n2d-standard-16	Production	2	$700
n2d-standard-32	Production	3	$2,900
Total			$4,000

You ask the team about the untagged instances in production. They created the servers for a sandbox to verify the application but never used them. Just to make sure, you check the server usage metrics over the month, and they all stayed at zero. You identified some cloud waste!

The team did create the servers with IaC. You delete the configuration and push the changes to remove the unused instances. Deleting the configuration removes the disks and resources attached to the instances. Fortunately, the cloud bill for your next conference reflects the reduction.

Why would you confirm usage of the server by metrics and team members? You do not want to remove the resource by accident. Sometimes you have unexpected dependencies on what seems like an unused resource.

Make sure that any resources you intend to delete do not have additional dependencies. If you have concerns about deleting an untagged or unused resource, you can always stop the resource for a week or two, wait to determine if it breaks the system, and then delete it.

12.2.2 *Start and stop resources on a schedule*

Your next cloud bill comes back 7% less, thanks to the removal of unused servers. However, the finance team wants you to reduce it even more. You puzzle over this until you talk to one of the client's team members. They mention that they never run testing or use any of their infrastructure resources over the weekends. The client needs the platform available the weekend before the conference.

Could you find a way to turn off the servers on a Friday night and turn them on each Monday? You do not get charged for the 48 hours you shut down the servers. Scheduling a regular shutdown means cost reduction.

You discover that GCP defines an instance shutdown schedule with a compute resource policy (http://mng.bz/o25N). You start the servers each Monday and shut them down each Saturday, as outlined in figure 12.6.

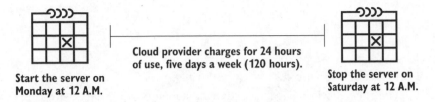

Start the server on Monday at 12 A.M.

Cloud provider charges for 24 hours of use, five days a week (120 hours).

Stop the server on Saturday at 12 A.M.

Figure 12.6   You can reduce cost by scheduling a resource to start and stop when not in use.

Shutting down instances on a schedule alleviates the cost of running servers. However, this technique works *only* if you understand the behavior of your system. Starting and stopping resources on a schedule can disrupt development work.

Some applications do not have fault tolerance and would continue to fail even if a resource restarts successfully. In general, most reboot schedules run only in testing environments. The schedule provides an opportunity for you to verify your system's resilience because you have a planned outage each weekend.

Listing 12.8 implements the resource policy for instance scheduling in GCP. The schedule expires the week before the conference, so it does not shut down the servers over the weekend. The development team might need to work on the platform in the few days before the conference.

Listing 12.8   Creating a resource policy for instance scheduling

```
def build(name, region, week_before_conference):
    expiration_time = datetime.strptime(
        week_before_conference,
        '%Y-%m-%d').replace(
            tzinfo=timezone.utc).isoformat().replace(
                '+00:00', 'Z')
    return {
        'google_compute_resource_policy': {
            'weekend': {
                'name': name,
                'region': region,
                'description':
                'start and stop instances over the weekend',
                'instance_schedule_policy': {
                    'vm_start_schedule': {
                        'schedule': '0 0 * * MON'
                    },
```

Expires the schedule the week before the conference, using the RFC 3339 date format

Creates a compute resource policy with an instance schedule

Starts the virtual machines every Monday at midnight

Stops the virtual
machines every
Saturday at midnight

```
'vm_stop_schedule': {
    'schedule': '0 0 * * SAT'
},
'time_zone': 'US/Central',
'expiration_time': expiration_time
        }
      }
    }
  }
```

Runs the schedule in the US
central time zone since
development teams work in
the central United States

AWS and Azure equivalents

Other public cloud providers usually offer a similar automation capability to start and stop the virtual machines on a schedule. For example, AWS uses Instance Scheduler to start and stop servers and databases (http://mng.bz/nNev). Similarly, Azure uses a start/stop virtual machine workflow based on Azure functions (http://mng.bz/v6Xx).

If your public or private cloud platform does not offer scheduled shutdown capabilities, you will need to write your automation to run on a regular schedule. I implemented this before using various tools, including serverless functions, cron jobs on container orchestrators, or scheduled runs on continuous integration frameworks.

Instead of running seven servers 730 hours per month, you run it about 144 hours less (assuming three weekends in a month and a 48-hour shutdown). Using your cost estimation code, you update your calculation for 586 hours per month. It outputs that you reduced the overall cost by $700 (7% of the total monthly bill)!

The example adds the schedule to the testing environment. However, you could add a reboot schedule to a production environment if it has cyclical usage patterns. For example, the conference platform runs on demand for three hours and serves user traffic only during the week. Shutting down servers and databases for 48 hours does not disrupt user traffic. However, you may not want to implement a reboot schedule in a production environment that serves requests continuously.

12.2.3 *Choose the correct resource type and size*

If your production environment needs to serve customers 24 hours a day, seven days a week, you can still reduce cloud waste without a resource schedule by assessing your resource types and sizes. Many resources do not utilize their CPU or memory fully.

Many times, we provision larger resources because we don't know how much we need. After running a system for some time, you can adjust the size of the resource for its actual usage. You can reduce cost by changing a resource type, size, reservation, replicas, or even cloud provider, as shown in figure 12.7.

If the following does not affect your application and its ability to fulfill requests:

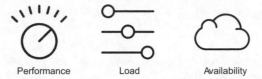

Performance   Load   Availability

You can reduce the cost of infrastructure by changing a resource's...

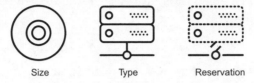

Size   Type   Reservation

Figure 12.7   You can change a resource's attributes to utilize it better and reduce its cost.

You decide to investigate your client's conference platform to find cloud waste in resource type and size. You realize you cannot reduce the cost of computing resources, so you check the database (Cloud SQL). The team provisioned the production database for 4 TB of solid-state drive (SSD) storage, detailed in table 12.3.

Table 12.3   Your cloud bill by offering and resource

Offering	Type	Environment	Number	Subtotal
Cloud SQL				$2,500
	db-standard-1, 400 GB SSD, 600 GB backup	Testing	1	$250
	db-standard-4, 4 TB SSD, 6 TB backup	Production	1	$2,250

After checking metrics and database usage, you realize that it needs only a 1 TB SSD. You update the disk size of the database in your IaC. Fixing the size reduces the cost of the database by $1,350 (22.5% of the total monthly bill)!

You might not use a resource to its full potential in many other ways. You might consider changing the type of resource if it uses a more expensive machine type. You need to ask yourself and your team, "Do we need this high-performance database in my testing environment if we do not run performance tests?"

Probably not! Choosing the right size and type for a given environment may take a few iterations. You want to choose a resource type, size, and replicas that simulate production without making it an exact duplicate in cost.

For the conference example, you might have three `n2d-standard-32` instances in production and three `n2d-standard-8` instances in your testing environment. The configuration still tests the three application instances without incurring a cost of 72 CPUs.

Other times, you can change the resource's reservation type. GCP and many other cloud providers offer an *ephemeral* (also known as *spot* or *preemptible*) resource type. The resource costs less, but the cloud provider reserves the right to stop the resource and give CPU or memory to another customer. While an ephemeral resource reservation can reduce cost, you need to carefully consider whether your application and system can handle the disruption.

12.2.4 *Enable autoscaling*

You tried to identify as much cloud waste as possible in your environment but still want to reduce costs further. Many systems have customer usage patterns that do not require their CPU, memory, or bandwidth in the system every hour of every day.

For example, the conference platform needed 100% of its capacity during only the three hours of the conference! Could you have automatically increased or decreased the number of servers based on demand?

Figure 12.8 sets the target utilization to 75% of CPU usage so that the GCP managed instance group starts and stops servers to match the target metric. It increases and decreases the size of the group based on demand.

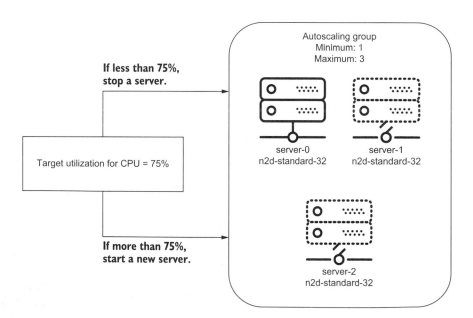

Figure 12.8   An autoscaling group includes a target utilization rate, which allows it to start and stop resources to adjust for usage automatically.

You added autoscaling for each group of servers. *Autoscaling* increases or decreases the number of resources in a group based on a metric, such as CPU or memory. Many public cloud providers offer an autoscaling group resource that you can create with IaC.

> **DEFINITION** *Autoscaling* is the practice of automatically increasing or decreasing the number of resources in a group based on a metric.

GCP autoscaling requires that you set a target metric to scale up or scale down resources to achieve. For most of the month with low traffic, you expect to use only one server. However, when peak traffic runs through your conference platform, you need a maximum of three. You decide to use a metric for CPU utilization and set the target to 75%.

You update the IaC for the servers. In listing 12.9, you replace the original servers and instance scheduling resource policy with a managed instance group and autoscaling policy. The autoscaling schedule starts each morning, increases or decreases instances to achieve 75% CPU utilization, and scales the instances to zero each evening.

Listing 12.9 Creating an autoscaling group based on CPU utilization

```
def build(name, machine_type, zone,
          min, max, cpu_utilization,
          cooldown=60,
          network='default'):
    region = zone.rsplit('-', 1)[0]
    return [{
        'google_compute_autoscaler': {
            name: {
                'name': name,
                'zone': zone,
                'target': '${google_compute_instance_group_manager.' +
                f'{name}.id}}',
                'autoscaling_policy': {
                    'max_replicas': max,
                    'min_replicas': 0,
                    'cooldown_period': cooldown,
                    'cpu_utilization': {
                        'target': cpu_utilization
                    },
                    'scaling_schedules': {
                        'name': 'weekday-scaleup',
                        'min_required_replicas': min,
                        'schedule': '0 6 * * MON-FRI',
                        'duration_sec': '57600',
                        'time_zone': 'US/Central'
                    }
                }
            }
        }
    }]
```

Annotations:
- Attaches an instance group to the autoscaling resource. We omitted the instance group for clarity.
- Sets the maximum number of replicas to scale up if CPU utilization increases above 75%
- Sets the minimum number of replicas to zero by default, which means it stops the virtual machines
- Uses CPU utilization as the target metric for the autoscaling group
- Sets a scaling schedule that increases the minimum number of replicas each Monday through Friday morning for the development team's usage patterns

AWS and Azure equivalents

GCP attaches managed instance groups to autoscaling policies. GCP does not allow you to attach a resource policy. You must implement the schedule in the autoscaling group.

Other public cloud providers also offer autoscaling capabilities for servers and sometimes databases. AWS uses autoscaling groups. Azure uses autoscale rules for scale sets.

You can set a scaling schedule in the example to mimic a weekend shutdown that you previously implemented. In general, use the patterns for modules to create an autoscaling module. The module should set an opinionated, default target metric depending on your workload.

If you have a unique workload that does not fit the module's preset target metrics, you can set its default to target CPU utilization or memory and assess its behavior over time. When you roll out the instance group, apply the blue-green deployment pattern from chapter 9 to replace active workloads or instances. Rolling out a schedule and autoscaling group should not disrupt applications.

To encourage teams to use autoscaling groups and scheduling, you can create several policy tests to make sure your autoscaling group reduces cloud waste. For example, one test could verify that your IaC has no individual servers and contains only autoscaling groups. The test encourages the team to take advantage of elasticity.

Another test you can add involves checking the maximum replica limit. Suppose your application suddenly consumes a lot of CPU or memory, or a bad actor injects a cryptocurrency mining binary on your machine. In that case, you don't want the autoscaling group to automatically increase its capacity to 100 machines.

12.2.5 *Set a resource expiration tag*

You may reduce cloud waste by dynamically scaling up and down resources based on utilization, but you also need to accommodate on-demand, manually created resources. For example, the client team members complain that they often need to create sandbox servers for further testing. However, they often forget about the servers. Can you "expire" the servers after some time if no one updates them?

You decide to update your tag module to attach a new tag for the *expiration date* in the testing environment. Recall that you can use the prototype pattern (chapter 3) to establish standard tags. After applying the policy tests to check for tag compliance in chapter 8, you know that each resource in the testing environment will have an expiration date.

For example, the team members might create a server with an initial expiration date of February 2, as shown in figure 12.9. However, they decide to update the server. As part of the change, the tag module retrieves the current date (February 5), adds seven days, and updates the tag on the server to a new date (February 12).

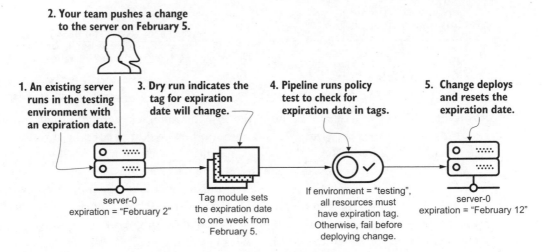

Figure 12.9   Create an expiration date in the tag module that resets the expiration date of the module to one week from the change.

Why use set expiration as part of the tag module? Your tag module should get applied across all your IaC. This allows you to establish a *default duration* of seven days and apply it to all infrastructure resources.

You can also control when to apply the expiration tag as part of a module. The module applies the expiration tag only if you don't create a resource in the production environment or continuously run it in the testing environment. The following listing updates the prototype module for default tags with an expiration date.

Listing 12.10   Tag module with an expiration date

```
import datetime

EXPIRATION_DATE_FORMAT = '%Y-%m-%d'          Formats the date to a string
                                             of year, month, and day
EXPIRATION_NUMBER_OF_DAYS = 7
                                             Calculates the expiration
                                             date for seven days from
                                             the current date
class DefaultTags():
    def __init__(self, environment, long_term=False):
        self.tags = {
            'customer': 'community',
            'automated': True,
            'cost_center': 123456,
            'environment': environment     Sets the expiration tag if you
        }                                  do not create the resource in
        if environment != 'prod' and not long_term:   production or mark it as a
            self._set_expiration()         long-term resource

    def get(self):
        return self.tags
```

```
def _set_expiration(self):
    expiration_date = (
        datetime.datetime.now() +
        datetime.timedelta(
            days=EXPIRATION_NUMBER_OF_DAYS)
    ).strftime(EXPIRATION_DATE_FORMAT)
    self.tags['expiration'] = expiration_date
```

Calculates the expiration date for seven days from the current date

Formats the date to a string of year, month, and day

You set one week as a default because it gives team members enough time to develop and test a resource. They can always renew another week if needed by running their delivery pipeline to update the tag automatically. However, you do need to enable an override to allow long-term resources in testing environments.

How do you enforce expiration date tagging by default but exempt resources from an expiration date? You can create a policy test with soft mandatory enforcement. A soft mandatory policy makes exceptions and audits long-term resources in testing environments.

Let's write a test that enforces the expiration tag for each server resource in listing 12.11. If the server does not exist in the list of exempt resources, it fails the test and stops the delivery pipeline from deploying all changes to production.

Listing 12.11   Test checks that testing resources have an expiration date

```
import pytest
```

Retrieves a list of servers in configuration and those exempt from the policy

```
def test_all_nonprod_resources_should_have_expiration_tag(
        servers, server_exemptions):
    noncompliant = []
    for name, values in servers.items():
        if 'expiration' not in values['labels'].keys() and \
                name not in server_exemptions:
            noncompliant.append(name)
    assert len(noncompliant) == 0, \
        'all nonprod resources should have ' + \
        f'expiration tag, {noncompliant}'
```

Checks if the tag for expiration exists in server tags

If you did not exempt the server, you must flag the server as noncompliant with the policy.

Adding the resource to an exemption list means that your teammates will carefully examine which resources persist in the testing environment. During peer review (chapter 7), you can identify any new, persistent resource based on changes to the exemption list. A single source of persistent resources in a testing environment ensures that you can audit and discuss cost control early in the development process.

After implementing the expiration tag in IaC, you need to write a script that runs daily. Figure 12.10 shows the script's workflow. It checks whether the expiration date matches the current date. If so, the automation deletes the resource.

Why set an expiration date by using IaC? The workflow of setting an expiration date using a tag module *builds in* the ability to renew the resource expiration date! Rather than introduce development friction by adding separate automation, you build renewals into the development process.

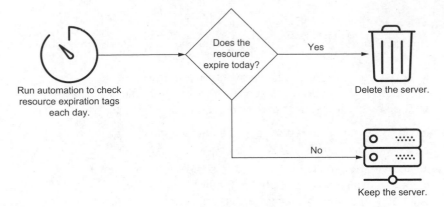

Figure 12.10 Setting an expiration tag allows daily automation to determine whether to delete a temporary resource and thus reduce cost.

For example, if a team still needs the resource, it can always rerun its IaC delivery pipeline to reset the expiration date for another seven days. Active changes to the resource also reset the expiration date. If you change your infrastructure, you probably still need the resource.

What happens when a resource expires and you still need it? You can always rerun your IaC and create a new one. Using IaC to add and renew the expiration date provides cost compliance and functional visibility across teams.

> **NOTE** Sometimes you'll find separate automation for automatic tagging. The automation adds the expiration date to infrastructure resources after their creation. While the automatic tagging means greater control for cost compliance, it also introduces drift between the actual and intended configurations. Furthermore, automatic expiration often confuses team members. Unless they paid attention to your communications, they might find their resource deleted after a few days!

You can always set the expiration time interval to something other than several days. If you want to offer more flexibility to teams, you can offer a range of days through the tag module. I recommend calculating the absolute expiration date and adding it to the tag instead of the time interval for easier cleanup automation.

With all of the changes in the example, what happened to your client's cloud computing bill? Your bill went from a little over $10,000 to about $6,500 (a 35% reduction)! Your client appreciates the efficient use of their cloud resources.

In reality, you might not achieve the same dramatic cost reduction as the example. However, you can always apply the practices and techniques to your IaC to introduce minor changes that reduce cost when possible. Capturing cost reduction practices in IaC with tests ensures that everyone writes it with the constraint of cost in mind.

Exercise 12.2

Imagine you have three servers. You examine their utilization and notice the following:

- You need one server to serve the minimum traffic.
- You need three servers to serve the maximum traffic.
- The server handles traffic 24 hours a day, seven days a week.

What can you do to optimize the cost of the servers for the next month?

A Schedule the resources to stop on the weekends.
B Add an `autoscaling_policy` to scale based on memory.
C Set an expiration of three hours for all servers.
D Change the servers to smaller CPU and memory machine types.
E Migrate the application to containers and pack applications more densely on servers.

See appendix B for answers to exercises.

12.3   *Optimize cost*

You can apply other IaC principles and practices to reduce cloud waste and manage cost drivers. Techniques like building environments on demand, updating routes between regions, or testing in production can use IaC to further optimize cost, as shown in figure 12.11.

Cost optimization techniques

Build environments on demand.   **Use multiple clouds and choose based on workload, offering, or time of day.**   **Assess routes between regions and clouds.**   **Allow testing in production.**

Figure 12.11   Cost optimization requires IaC practices for scaling and deploying infrastructure resources.

In particular, the principles of reproducibility, composability, and evolvability can help with creative techniques to further optimize cost. These techniques include reproducing environments on demand to reduce persistent testing environments, composing infrastructure across cloud providers, and evolving production infrastructure across regions and cloud providers.

Recall that you reduced your client's cloud computing cost for a conference by 35%. A year later, the finance team asks for your help to optimize the cost of their platform. They've grown their business and want to optimize costs across hundreds of customers and a managed service.

12.3.1   *Build environments on demand*

From a broader perspective, you need to examine which environments exist in testing and production. You might start by reducing cloud waste across all environments. However, as your company grows, it adds more environments to support and test more products.

Imagine you examine your client's infrastructure. The client has many testing environments. You determine that three or four of them run continuously and support specialized testing. For example, the quality assurance (QA) team uses one of the environments for performance testing twice a year. For the rest of the year, these environments remain dormant.

You decide to *remove the continuously running environments.* If the QA team wants an environment for performance testing, it can do that on demand. The team copies the production environment with its factory and builder modules that allow inputs. The modules provide flexibility to specify variables and parameters for different environments.

Figure 12.12 shows the rest of the workflow for creating an on-demand environment. The QA team copies the IaC to a new repository specific to the testing environment in the organization's multirepository structure. The team updates the parameters and variables, runs its tests, and removes the environment.

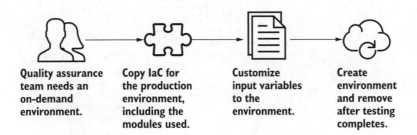

Quality assurance team needs an on-demand environment. **Copy IaC for the production environment, including the modules used.** **Customize input variables to the environment.** **Create environment and remove after testing completes.**

Figure 12.12   You can copy the configuration for production to create and customize on-demand environments for testing.

Why use reproducibility to create new environments on demand and delete them? A new, updated environment ensures that the latest configuration matches production. If you use the environment only once a year, you do not want to keep it constantly running for 11 months.

While it takes time to create a new environment, you probably take the same amount of time trying to fix drift between your testing and production environment.

Identifying unnecessary long-running environments and switching them to an on-demand model can help mitigate costs, especially if you can easily re-create them.

12.3.2 Use multiple clouds

With a few cloud provider options, you may also consider deploying to other clouds and optimizing cost based on resource, workload, and time of day. IaC can help standardize and organize your configuration for multiple clouds. Deploying to multiple clouds can accommodate specialized workloads or teams that want specific infrastructure resources.

For example, imagine your client uses Google Cloud Dataflow for stream data processing. However, the cost varies depending on the type of pipeline. You convince some reporting teams to convert a few of the batch-processing pipelines to Amazon EMR to reduce the overall cost.

> **Azure equivalent**
>
> The Azure equivalent of Amazon EMR or Google Cloud Dataflow is Azure HDInsight.

In figure 12.13, the report service team switches its IaC to use the Amazon EMR module. To minimize the disruption of jobs, the team members use the blue-green deployment pattern from chapter 9 to gradually increase the number of jobs they run in Amazon EMR.

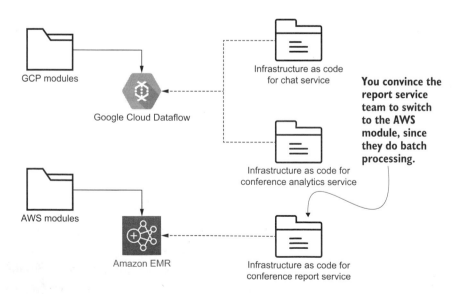

Figure 12.13   The report service switches its batch-processing job to use Amazon EMR instead of Google Cloud Dataflow by referencing a different module.

The principle of composability becomes an important part of a multicloud configuration. IaC makes it easier to manage and identify infrastructure resources across different cloud providers. Using modules to express dependencies between clouds also helps you evolve your resources over time.

In chapter 5, we separated IaC configuration into different folders based on tools and providers. Many IaC tools do not offer a unified data model for cloud provider resources. Build a different module for each cloud you plan to support. Separating modules by provider reduces the complexity and supports isolated testing of modules. Maintaining separate modules for each cloud provider also enables easy identification of infrastructure resources and providers.

12.3.3 *Assess data transfer between regions and clouds*

With the adoption of multiple clouds, you might discover that you didn't reduce your overall cloud computing bill. You need to consider multiple clouds carefully because providers will charge for data transfer between regions and outside their cloud network. Data transfer costs add up in surprising ways!

You check your client's cloud computing bill and notice that a lot of the cost comes from data transfers across regions and out of the network. After some investigation, you discover that many of the services and testing environments communicate across regions, availability zones, and over the public internet.

For example, integration tests for the chat service in us-central1-a use the public IP address of the user profile service in us-central1-b! You realize that all of the services in the integration testing environment do not need to test across regions, availability zones, or out of the network.

Integration testing tests the functionality of the service only relative to other services and not the system itself. Figure 12.14 uses the refactoring techniques from chapter 10 to consolidate the infrastructure resources in the integration testing environment into one availability zone.

What happens if the availability zone fails? You can always switch the IaC to a different zone or region. The applications still communicate over a private network and do not charge for data transfer out of Google Cloud's network or between regions and zones.

Favor private over public networking, not just for security but also for cost and efficiency. If you use multiple clouds, know which resources need to communicate across clouds. Sometimes you might find it more cost-efficient to shift an entire set of services to another cloud than pay for data transfer between clouds. Applying the change and refactoring techniques in chapters 9 and 10 can help consolidate services and communications.

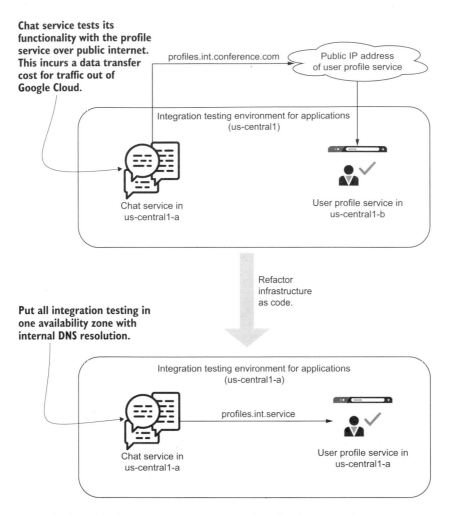

Chat service tests its functionality with the profile service over public internet. This incurs a data transfer cost for traffic out of Google Cloud.

profiles.int.conference.com

Public IP address of user profile service

Integration testing environment for applications (us-central1)

Chat service in us-central1-a

User profile service in us-central1-b

Refactor infrastructure as code.

Put all integration testing in one availability zone with internal DNS resolution.

Integration testing environment for applications (us-central1-a)

Chat service in us-central1-a

profiles.int.service

User profile service in us-central1-a

Figure 12.14   Refactor your IaC to support an integration testing environment in a single availability zone and resolve to a private IP address.

12.3.4 *Test in production*

Even after shifting to multiple clouds and optimizing data transfer, you might find that your testing environment cannot fully mimic production and costs too much to run. At some point, you cannot get away with testing in an isolated environment. Rather than simulate the production environment in its entirety, you can continue to optimize costs by testing directly in the production environment.

In the case of the conference platform, you help the video service team implement changes to test in production. In figure 12.15, the team members stage a new set of infrastructure resources with the expected changes hidden behind a feature flag. Then, they toggle the flag to direct all applications and user traffic and verify its func-

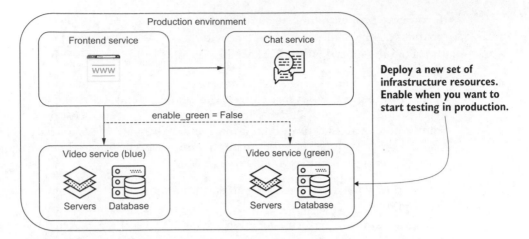

Figure 12.15 Testing in production for IaC applies blue-green deployments and feature flagging for a set of resources.

tionality in production. The two sets of resources run simultaneously for a few weeks. After a few weeks, they delete the old infrastructure resources.

The team tested its service in production by using blue-green services without using a testing environment. *Testing in production* involves a set of practices that enable you to run tests against production data and systems.

> **DEFINITION** *Testing in production* is a set of practices that allow you to run tests against production data and systems.

In software development, you use techniques like feature flagging to hide certain functionality in production for testing. Similarly, you use canary deployments to test functionality with a small group of users before offering it to everyone on the platform.

For IaC, testing in production does not fit entirely with the software development practices. You don't want to test that the code works with a small group of users. You just want to know if you create broken infrastructure systems that might *affect* the users! You can apply a few techniques, like feature flagging and canary deployment. We did this in chapters 9 and 10.

You could test IaC directly in production without a blue-green deployment pattern or feature flagging. However, you will need an established roll-forward plan in case of failure. I worked in one organization that depended entirely on local testing before pushing changes to production. If our change failed, we would attempt to update the system to a previous state. If all else failed, we would create a whole new infrastructure environment and direct all application and user traffic to the new environment.

You might go through all cost optimization, cloud waste reduction, and cost driver control techniques and *still* never fully optimize your cloud bill! Over time, your organization's usage and product demands change.

If you have proper monitoring and instrumentation in your systems, you might discover that you have periods of greater or lower demand. For example, your client's platform has the most demand in May, June, October, and November, for peak conference season.

> **NOTE**   You might need to re-architect your systems to take advantage of public cloud *elasticity*, the ability to scale up or down, and reduce cost over time. Some software architectures do not make it easy for you to dynamically scale resources up or down. The solution often requires a refactor or re-platform of the application to improve system cost efficiency.

Understanding your system's resource usage and requirements over time can help you further optimize costs beyond the techniques I described in this chapter. You could reduce costs even further by negotiating a contract with the infrastructure provider. Choosing a new pricing model lets you save on a certain number of reserved instances or volume-based discounts.

The longer you run the system, the more metrics you aggregate. The information can help you iterate on cost driver control, cloud waste reduction, and overall cost optimization in IaC. You can also use the information to negotiate with your cloud provider and reduce the surprises on your cloud computing bill!

Summary

- Before changing IaC to optimize cost, identify the cost drivers (resources or activities) that may affect the total cost.
- Manage cost drivers in infrastructure, such as compute resources, by adding policy tests to check for resource type, size, and reservation.
- Cost estimation parses your IaC for resource attributes and generates an estimate of their cost based on a cloud provider's API.
- You can add a policy test to check the output of cost estimation to approximate whether you exceeded your budget.
- Cloud waste describes unused or underutilized infrastructure resources.
- Eliminating cloud waste can help decrease your cloud computing cost.
- Reduce cloud waste by removing or stopping untagged or unused resources, starting and stopping resources on a schedule, right-sizing infrastructure resources for better utilization, enabling autoscaling, and tagging a resource expiration date.
- Autoscaling increases or decreases the number or amount of resources in a given group based on a metric, such as CPU or memory.
- Techniques for optimizing cloud computing cost involve building environments on demand, using multiple clouds, assessing data transfer, and testing in production.
- Testing in production uses practices like blue-green deployments and feature flagging to test infrastructure changes without a testing environment.

Managing tools

This chapter covers

- Assessing the use of open source infrastructure modules and tools
- Applying techniques to update or migrate IaC tools
- Implementing module patterns for event-driven IaC

You've learned how to write infrastructure as code, update it with your team by using delivery pipelines and testing, and manage its security and cost within your organization. As you evolve your infrastructure system, you adapt these patterns and practices and adjust them to fit new workflows and use cases. Similarly, tools change but should not disrupt the patterns and practices to scale, collaborate, and operate your infrastructure.

Updating your tool can require several actions. You could upgrade to a new version, replace it with a new tool, or handle more dynamic use cases for IaC. This chapter discusses common patterns and practices to handle updates to IaC tools.

The patterns apply to any tools that cover *provisioning, configuration management, and image building* use cases. You'll find they also apply to software development, although I adapted them in an opinionated way to infrastructure. Use these patterns and practices to mitigate the blast radius of an update, scale the new tool across teams, and continue evolving your system to support business requirements.

> **NOTE** This chapter does not include any code listings. Adding an example means introducing yet another tool. I describe the patterns and approaches at a higher level. You can apply the techniques to any tool that supports DSLs or programming languages.

You've read the many chapters in this book and practiced IaC in different industries and companies. You've built a reputation for setting up and scaling IaC practices. One day, a social media company offers you a role in its platform team.

The company has already established its IaC practice for a few years now. The staff needs your help to maintain and keep the tools they use for IaC updated. You accept and get a backlog of projects to start on the very first day.

13.1 *Using open source tools and modules*

The accessibility of version control and public repositories makes it simpler to search for an existing tool or infrastructure module instead of writing your own. You can go onto GitHub or any other service to find the automation and tooling to serve your needs. However, you need to make sure you do your due diligence before introducing new tooling to any organization.

For example, let's imagine the team members who maintain the social media's feed functionality approach you. They searched online and found an infrastructure module to create a database. They want to use it. They hope to speed up their development process and avoid waiting for another team to review their database configuration. Why reinvent the wheel, after all?

You offer to help review the module for security and best practices. Before you introduce the module to the other teams at the social media company, you use figure 13.1 to assess the database module for its functionality, security, and life cycle before officially adopting it.

Each time the open source maintainers release a new database module, you reassess the module. You can apply this decision workflow to safely and securely adopt external IaC modules and tools. You want to make sure you can use the tool or module and avoid insecure configuration in your infrastructure system that would allow a bad actor to exploit your system.

13.1.1 *Functionality*

You may find a module or tool promising to start. It allows you to configure the attributes you need very flexibly. However, recall from chapters 2 and 3 that modules should include some opinionated defaults. Without them, a module or tool with too much flexibility may lead to one-off configurations that eventually break your system.

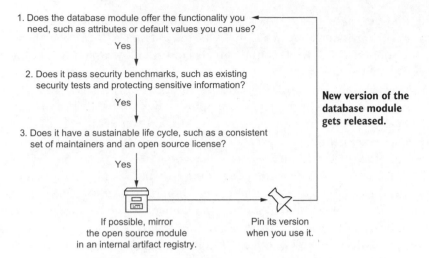

Figure 13.1 **You assess the functionality, security, and life cycle of a tool or module before you use it.**

You encourage the feed team to verify the default values in the database module. The team assesses the module, as shown in figure 13.2. The module uses very opinionated defaults, pins the version of the database, and tests compatibility thoroughly.

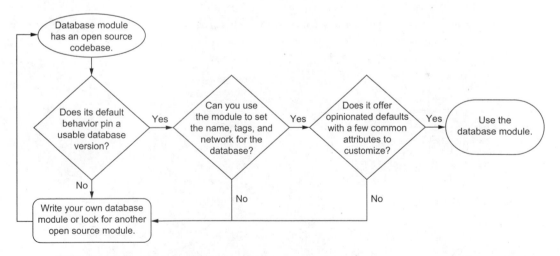

Figure 13.2 **Decision flow for assessing usage of a module or tool based on functionality**

The documentation notes that the module pins the database version to thoroughly test the configuration and its compatibility with specific versions. The feed team members confirm they use the database version and approve the module's default value for it.

Next, they assess the input variables for the module. The database module allows them to set the attributes they need, such as database name. It also lets them set the tagging and network. The feed team members confirm they do not need to set more than those variables.

Since the module does not offer every attribute as an input variable and offers opinionated defaults that fit the team, you approve the module based on functionality. In general, review the module's documentation and commit history. If the module tests for version compatibility and a set of opinionated defaults that suit your functionality, you can move forward with a security assessment.

If you find the module does not offer some specific default values or input variables you need to change, you can find another module, write your own, or proceed to use the module with its limitations in mind. Similarly, you can apply the decision flow to a tool and find it lacking. A single tool cannot do everything! You must balance its flexibility in functionality with its predictability in making infrastructure changes.

13.1.2 *Security*

While you might first assess the functionality of a module or tool, you should next evaluate its security. Security tends to serve as the make-or-break criteria for whether you should use an open source tool or module. Without carefully assessing an open source module or tool for secure configuration or code, you may inadvertently open a door for a bad actor to compromise the system.

Before the feed team members can use their database module, they need you to check the module for any security concerns. You check whether the database module exposes or outputs sensitive information, sends information to third-party endpoints, and passes existing security and compliance tests, as shown in figure 13.3.

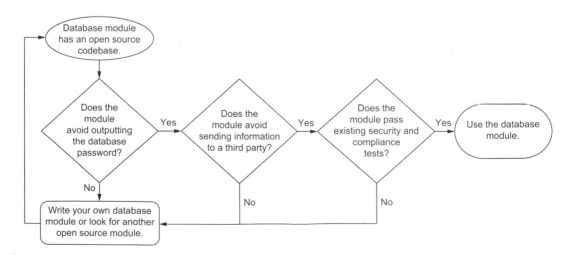

Figure 13.3 Decision flow for assessing usage of module or tool based on security

In the example, the database module does not output the password or any sensitive configuration or send information to a third-party endpoint. The module also passes your security and compliance tests for databases you wrote in chapter 8. Why should you verify all three checks before adopting a module?

A module may accidentally expose or output sensitive information. For example, a configuration could accidentally output a password during a dry run. If it does, make sure you have a way to mitigate or mask the password and rotate it.

Similarly, a module should not write or send information to an unauthorized third party. A bad actor might add a minor configuration that sends your network information to an HTTP endpoint. Review each resource and check that they do not send anything to a third party.

> **Security and open source**
>
> Software supply-chain attacks occur when an actor includes malicious code in a vendor's software, which gets shipped out to customers and compromises their data and systems. The benefit of open source means that you can examine *what* goes into code before you, as a customer, decide to use it.
>
> In this section, I recognize that I greatly oversimplified the risk assessments and guardrails for defending against supply-chain attacks. For more information, a NIST whitepaper (http://mng.bz/449B) better organizes some of the practices.

Finally, run existing security and compliance tests you wrote for the infrastructure resources. You want *secure* and *compliant* resources. Otherwise, you need to go back and update the module to suit your requirements.

Deploy the module in your IaC in an isolated testing environment. Then run the security and compliance tests against the module. Isolating the module in its own environment ensures that you do not introduce noncompliant configurations to running environments.

Keep in mind that not all security and compliance tests will pass. Those that fail need minor refactoring to work with the module. After all the tests pass, you can approve the module as secure for use.

Tools follow a similar decision workflow as you assess their security. However, security and compliance testing for IaC tools may include static code analysis and additional reviews from your organization. For tools that output configuration or other information during dry runs, you will want to apply the remediation steps from chapter 8.

13.1.3 *Life cycle*

You examined the functionality and security of the module, but the compliance team members raise a very good question. They ask about *who* maintains the public module. Your organization will need to take private (or maybe public) ownership of the module or tool if its maintainers no longer update it.

You examine the documentation to understand the life cycle of the module and who maintains it, as shown in figure 13.4. If the database module has company sponsorship and an appropriate license, you can likely use it.

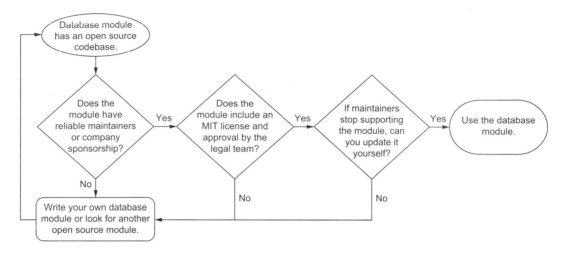

Figure 13.4   Decision flow for assessing usage of a module or tool based on tool or module life cycle

You examine the maintainers of the database module. The maintainers come from a well-known technology company and have many contributors, which means the project fosters an active community. They update and release a new version of the module every few months. Each contribution must pass a testing suite to verify that changes do not break the module.

Next, you retrieve information about the database module's open source license. You do not know how the open source license affects your company, so you contact your legal team. The legal team reviews the license before the feed team can use it.

The module includes an MIT license. As a *permissive open source license*, the MIT license means if you fork (maintain a copy) or modify the database module, you must include a copy of the license and the original copyright notice. If the maintainers deprecate the module or tool, the permissive license type allows you to modify and update the module yourself.

> **DEFINITION**   A *permissive open source license* allows you to fork or modify code as long as you include a copy of the license and original copyright notice.

Your legal team approves the license because the module poses minimal risk to the overall infrastructure configuration. The company can edit the module if needed but does not have to release it publicly. Perhaps you can even contribute to the open source module yourself, pending legal approval.

A module or tool can also include an open source license in the copyleft category. The *copyleft* category of licenses contains a clause that you must release the codebase with your modifications.

DEFINITION A *copyleft open source license* allows you to fork or modify code as long as you release the codebase with your modifications.

The copyleft category of licenses often includes more restrictions on modifying and distributing the tool or module. Your company's legal team will assess whether the company can use open source IaC with more restrictive licenses.

NOTE For more information on open source licenses, review the licenses and standards outlined by the Open Source Initiative (https://opensource.org/licenses).

The feed team (overjoyed) can use the database module. You recommend that the team pins the module version by mirroring it to an internal artifact repository. Mirroring the module ensures that teams can use the approved module only in the internal repository. If the public endpoint for the module goes down, the team always has a copy in the internal repository. Each time the maintainers release a new module version, you must check the changes and approve the latest version.

Consider contributing back to open source if your organization allows it. Forking an open source module or tool and maintaining it yourself while keeping it updated with the public release has an operational overhead. You can dedicate many hours reconciling changes between the open source version and your version. Creating a process to contribute changes directly to the public release helps reduce the overhead of maintaining unique changes that may break your infrastructure.

13.2 Upgrading tools

When you run your IaC practice for a few years, you inevitably reach a point where you need to upgrade your tool or the plugins it uses. A wider gap in your tool version to the latest version can make it much harder for you to update your infrastructure with minimal disruption!

We learned about this challenge for module versioning in chapter 5. In this section, I'll cover some of the considerations and patterns you can use when you need to upgrade your tool.

NOTE You will not find magic tools to migrate everything perfectly for you. Upgrading a tool will always have challenging obstacles. Unique patterns in your IaC (such as inline scripting) may break the system during the upgrade! As a result, try to limit the complexity of your IaC logic when possible.

Imagine you audit the company's IaC tools (provisioning, configuration management, and image building). Most of the company IaC uses tool version 1.7. However, the latest tool version is at 4.0. Your first major project involves updating the IaC to use the tool version 4.0.

13.2.1 *Pre-upgrade checklist*

Before you start upgrading a tool or plugin, you need to check a few essential practices that will help minimize potential disruption to your infrastructure. Your checklist should include a few steps to decouple, stabilize, and reconcile IaC.

Figure 13.5 shows this checklist. You decouple all dependencies, check versioning, pin all versions, and deploy your IaC to reduce drift.

Decouple infrastructure dependencies with dependency injection.   **Check that all modules have versioning.**   **Pin module versions across repositories.**   **Pin tool and its plugin versions.**   **Run IaC tool and make sure to apply any changes from versioning.**

Figure 13.5   Before you upgrade a tool, your checklist should include pinning and checking all versions for modules, plugins, and tools.

If the tool upgrade adds or removes fields, you need to pass the correct information expected by each resource subset. Dependency injection offers a layer of abstraction for configuration attributes between infrastructure resources (refer to chapter 4). It protects each subset from changes to the other.

You check that you added module versioning to all IaC modules (chapter 5). Similarly, you make sure any IaC or repositories using the module pin to a specific version.

For example, one of the teams at the social media company always uses the latest version of the module. You add module version 2.3.1 to the team's repository. When you release module version 3.0.0 with the tool upgrade, the team's IaC will not upgrade with breaking changes. You could update a module and push a breaking change to everyone using it without pinning the module version!

You also verify that each team pins the current version of the tool and its plugin versions. While the plugins may not have forward compatibility, you want to preserve the current version and avoid adding a new configuration in a different version. Finally, you push all your pinned module, tool, and plugin versions to each IaC module and configuration. You ensure that the version pinning does not introduce new changes.

After you complete your pre-upgrade checklist, you must plan your tool upgrade path. Figure 13.6 shows that upgrading from 1.0 to 4.0 of the tool introduces some breaking changes! You decide you can upgrade to 3.0, which provides backward compatibility with 1.7. Then you can upgrade from 3.0 to 4.0, which should reduce any other breaking changes.

Figure 13.6 You plan your tool upgrade path and account for backward-compatible versions and versions with breaking changes.

Do not upgrade to the latest version immediately. Instead, examine a list of breaking changes in your tool and assess whether you can accommodate those changes. I avoid upgrading more than two versions (or subversions in case of beta releases) at one time. Most tools have breaking changes in either behavior or syntax.

Consider testing the upgrade in a testing environment before rolling it out to production. Based on your system and its testing environment, you can identify if a tool upgrade may disrupt infrastructure. Upgrading will never go as smoothly as you expect, and a testing environment helps identify significant issues before you upgrade production.

13.2.2 *Backward compatibility*

Many IaC tools offer some kind of backward compatibility for changes. They typically support old and new features for a version or two before deprecating the old feature. Even if a tool supports backward compatibility, make sure to port and refactor to new features as soon as you can.

Your example upgrades the tool from version 1.7 to 3.0. Fortunately, version 3.0 does support backward compatibility with 1.7. It offers new features but no breaking changes that would affect your IaC. Just in case, you take a careful approach to the upgrade.

You start with the feed team members since they agree to your help during the upgrade. The feed team deploys all changes and makes sure not to add new changes to the IaC. Then, you examine the configuration for the best way to upgrade the tool without disrupting the social media feed.

In figure 13.7, you apply the refactoring techniques from chapter 10 to upgrading the tool. You start with high-level resources because other resources do not depend on them, deploy changes, test the system, and upgrade the lower-level resources.

You notify the feed team that you will upgrade DNS and load balancer infrastructure resources first. Other resources do not depend on them. Updating them first allows you to test whether your upgrade patterns work. You can upgrade the tool version for the resource by changing the version and running the IaC. You check the dry run and tests in your delivery pipeline to ensure that you did not disrupt anything.

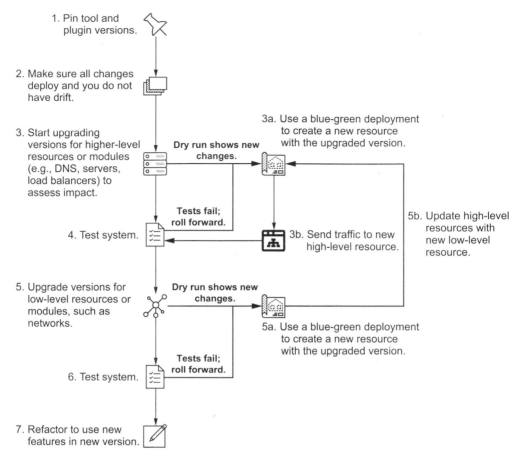

Figure 13.7   Apply refactoring techniques to upgrade a backward-compatible tool version from high-level to low-level resources.

The high-level resources like DNS and load balancer update without any disruption. Next, you move to lower-level resources. You start to update the servers with the rolling update pattern from chapter 10. Rather than upgrade all servers simultaneously, you start the upgrade on one and quickly run into a problem.

The production server configuration has an override script that breaks when you upgrade the tool. Fortunately, you affected only one server, since you used a rolling update. After all, you want to keep the social media feed running and available.

In figure 13.8, you apply the roll-forward techniques from chapter 11 to fix the server that no longer works. You implement a manual fix and debug the old server for the problem. Once you fix the problem in the testing environment, you push out a change to the override script and proceed with your rolling update of servers.

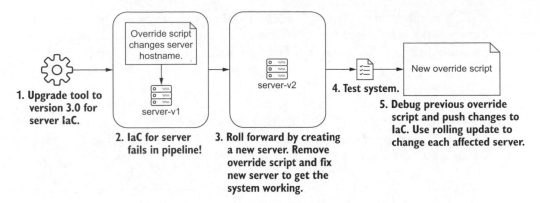

Figure 13.8 You can use a rolling update pattern to minimize the blast radius of a failed tool upgrade and roll forward if the change fails.

The servers pass the test. You move to the lowest-level resource, the network. Just in case, you deploy a second version of the network using a blue-green deployment pattern from chapter 9. After deploying everything onto the new network, you run all the end-to-end tests and check that the system still works. You completed the tool upgrade!

Why revisit patterns like refactoring, blue-green deployment, and rolling upgrades? You want to minimize the blast radius of a potential failure. Many of these patterns seem repetitive, but they offer a structured, less risky approach to upgrading your system. Changing your tool *does* change your infrastructure, so you can apply very similar techniques with the same result.

In general, use rolling upgrades for IaC upgrades to servers or other compute resources. Blue-green deployment helps tool upgrades for high-risk, low-level infrastructure resources. You can usually update high-level resources in place.

However, you can't prevent every failure. In that case, use the roll-forward practices and patterns from chapter 11 if the system breaks. High-level resources can revert the configuration in place, while lower-level resources benefit from creating new resources with previous changes.

13.2.3 Breaking changes in upgrades

Every once in a while, you'll find your infrastructure tool or plugin releases a new version that includes breaking changes. New versions with breaking changes often happen with early versions of a tool, such as when the tool handles new or edge use cases. If you need to do a tool upgrade with breaking changes or features, use the techniques for making changes in chapter 9.

For the social media company, you upgraded the feed team's tool from version 1.7 to 3.0. However, upgrading from version 3.0 to 4.0 involves some breaking changes! Version 4.0 contains backend schema changes that may affect your resources. How can you update your infrastructure to version 4.0 without impacting the system?

Remember, in chapter 4, I mentioned the existence of the *tool state*. Tools keep a copy of the infrastructure state to detect drift between actual resource state and configuration and to track which resources it manages. Tool state differs from the actual infrastructure state. When you update a tool, you want to break out the old tool state from the new one.

In our example, you want to isolate the old tool state with version 3.0 from a new tool state with version 4.0. Separating the tool state minimizes the blast radius of a potential failure by isolating the infrastructure resources a tool needs to change. Fewer resources means faster recovery and potentially less impact to other parts of the system.

In figure 13.9, each team in the social media company separates its tool state into a different location. Separate tool states ensure that changes to the feed team's blue infrastructure does not affect the green infrastructure.

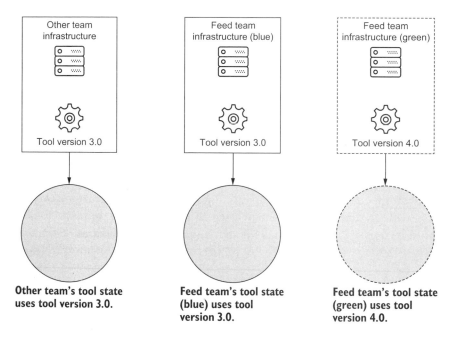

Figure 13.9 **A tool state captures the infrastructure state for the tool to make comparisons and can exist in separate locations for the tool to use.**

First, you pin tool and module versions across the feed team's IaC. Next, you update infrastructure modules to tool version 4.0. You release a new version of the module, making a note of breaking changes.

Next, you copy the existing configuration into a new folder. Each new folder creates a new tool state. Find the network folder and create a new network using tool version 4.0. You should now have the original "blue" resources from tool version 3.0 and the new "green" resources from tool version 4.0.

You applied a *blue-green deployment strategy to the tool state* to create new resources with the new tool! Creating a new set of resources with a new version ensures that any breaking changes will not affect the existing infrastructure.

> **DEFINITION** *Blue-green deployment for tool state* is a pattern that creates a new subset of infrastructure resources with a new tool version. You gradually shift traffic from the old set of resources (blue) to the new set of resources (green). The pattern isolates breaking changes to the new set of resources for testing.

After creating the low-level resources, copy the high-level resources to a new folder. Update its dependencies to use the low-level resources from tool version 4.0. After all, you want all resources using the new tool version.

Figure 13.10 summarizes the strategy. Create the high-level resources, run your tests, and send traffic to the new resources.

This approach differs from the blue-green deployment in chapter 9. You create a new set of resources *and* an entirely new tool state. If you loosely coupled your dependencies, subsets of resources can have different tool versions without affecting the system's functionality.

Recall that you can work on IaC with different repository structures (chapter 5) and branching models (chapter 7). Depending on your repository structure and branching model, you can isolate your tool state differently. You can always merge a new branch and alter its pipeline to deploy infrastructure or copy the separate folder into your main configuration for a repository.

Suppose your organization has an opinionated approach to delivery pipelines and allows production deployment only on the main branch. In that case, you can create a new repository for the tool upgrade and archive the old one.

You can apply an in-place upgrade if you dry-run and test the

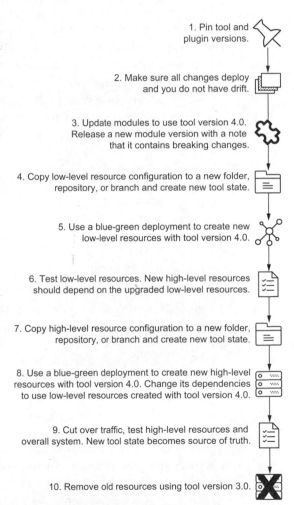

1. Pin tool and plugin versions.

2. Make sure all changes deploy and you do not have drift.

3. Update modules to use tool version 4.0. Release a new module version with a note that it contains breaking changes.

4. Copy low-level resource configuration to a new folder, repository, or branch and create new tool state.

5. Use a blue-green deployment to create new low-level resources with tool version 4.0.

6. Test low-level resources. New high-level resources should depend on the upgraded low-level resources.

7. Copy high-level resource configuration to a new folder, repository, or branch and create new tool state.

8. Use a blue-green deployment to create new high-level resources with tool version 4.0. Change its dependencies to use low-level resources created with tool version 4.0.

9. Cut over traffic, test high-level resources and overall system. New tool state becomes source of truth.

10. Remove old resources using tool version 3.0.

Figure 13.10 With breaking changes, consider creating a new resource in a different state and cutting over traffic to the resource with the latest version of the tool.

changes thoroughly. If it fails, you create an entirely new resource in a new tool state with the upgraded tool. When in doubt, refer to a tool's upgrade documentation. As a general practice, I will try an in-place upgrade if the tool offers some kind of migration tool or script to ease the update.

13.3   *Replacing tools*

I attempted to keep this book as tool-agnostic as possible while offering concrete examples to demonstrate the patterns and practices. I recognize I will probably have to update this book and replace all the tools with the latest and greatest technology! When running IaC for a while, you inevitably change tools for improved functionality or vendor support. What patterns should we use when migrating to a new tool?

Many of the patterns and practices in this book should help protect your system from these changes. Scoping and modularizing your infrastructure with patterns from chapter 3 and decoupling your dependencies with patterns from chapter 4 allows your teams to use tools that fit their use case and replace them as needed. If you do not have these patterns in place, you will encounter some difficulties migrating to a new tool.

Imagine completing your tool upgrades across the IaC for the social media company. You think about taking a break when the network team members ask for your help. They want to move from a vendor's DSL to an open source DSL. Their configuration will need an additional review from the social media feed team, which does not know anything about the vendor.

Your research cannot find a vendor or open source script to facilitate a straightforward migration. You wished you had something that could translate the vendor's DSL to the open source one. Without it, you and the network team need to proceed with the migration carefully.

13.3.1   *New tool supports import*

You could not find automation to "translate" between tools. However, you can apply patterns in this book to migrate across tools. Some tools support an import capability to add new resources to a tool's state. You can use the practices in chapter 2 to migrate existing resources to the new tool.

In figure 13.11, you upgrade the modules to use the new open source DSL. You also update its tests, which pass. To start, identify some low-level resources you can change. You create a separate folder, branch, or repository to isolate the new DSL from the vendor DSL. After writing the configuration for the new DSL, you import existing resources into the state of the new DSL.

Once again, you rewrite the tests to test the new syntax of the open source DSL. They pass, and you proceed to write configuration and import high-level resources. Finally, you delete the IaC.

Throughout each cycle of writing new IaC with the open source DSL, you want to check your dry run and rewrite your tests. The dry run shows if the defaults for the new tool do not match your existing state. You need to update the new IaC if they do not match and fix the drift.

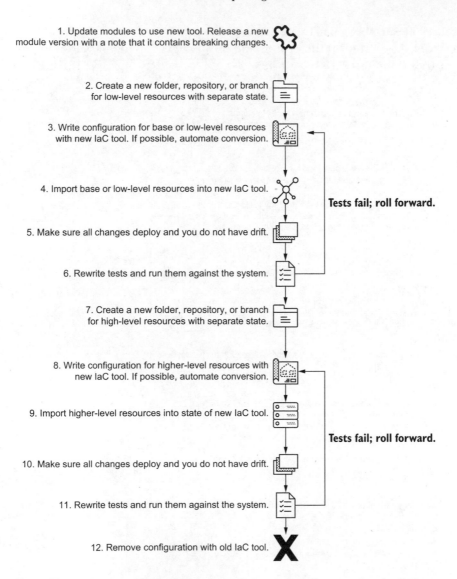

1. Update modules to use new tool. Release a new module version with a note that it contains breaking changes.

2. Create a new folder, repository, or branch for low-level resources with separate state.

3. Write configuration for base or low-level resources with new IaC tool. If possible, automate conversion.

4. Import base or low-level resources into new IaC tool.

Tests fail; roll forward.

5. Make sure all changes deploy and you do not have drift.

6. Rewrite tests and run them against the system.

7. Create a new folder, repository, or branch for high-level resources with separate state.

8. Write configuration for higher-level resources with new IaC tool. If possible, automate conversion.

9. Import higher-level resources into state of new IaC tool.

Tests fail; roll forward.

10. Make sure all changes deploy and you do not have drift.

11. Rewrite tests and run them against the system.

12. Remove configuration with old IaC tool.

Figure 13.11   A new tool that supports importing resources allows you to migrate to a new tool without changing existing resources.

13.3.2   *No import capability*

Some tools do not support import capabilities, and you need to create new resources for the new tool. Imagine if the network team asked you to help them convert from one vendor DSL to another. However, the new vendor DSL does not allow the import of existing resources into its state.

If your new tool does not support importing existing resources, you need to recreate resources with a blue-green deployment strategy for the tool state. In figure

13.12, you start by writing new IaC for the low-level resources and refactor tests for the new tool. As you repeat the process and finish migrating high-level resources, you cut over traffic and test the entire system.

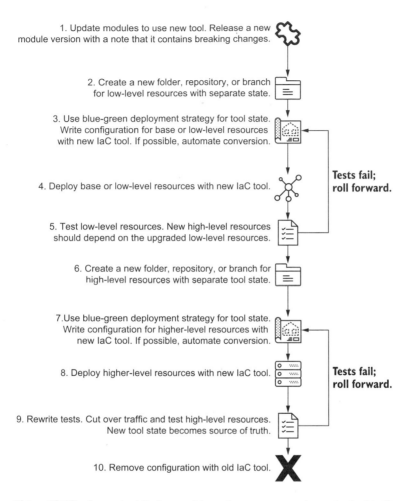

1. Update modules to use new tool. Release a new module version with a note that it contains breaking changes.

2. Create a new folder, repository, or branch for low-level resources with separate state.

3. Use blue-green deployment strategy for tool state. Write configuration for base or low-level resources with new IaC tool. If possible, automate conversion.

4. Deploy base or low-level resources with new IaC tool.

Tests fail; roll forward.

5. Test low-level resources. New high-level resources should depend on the upgraded low-level resources.

6. Create a new folder, repository, or branch for high-level resources with separate tool state.

7.Use blue-green deployment strategy for tool state. Write configuration for higher-level resources with new IaC tool. If possible, automate conversion.

8. Deploy higher-level resources with new IaC tool.

Tests fail; roll forward.

9. Rewrite tests. Cut over traffic and test high-level resources. New tool state becomes source of truth.

10. Remove configuration with old IaC tool.

Figure 13.12   A new tool that cannot import resources requires a tool migration using a blue-green deployment strategy.

The pattern of migrating tools remains consistent, import capability or none. However, migration without an import capability takes more effort because you re-create the system. Even if you had a magical script to migrate from one tool to another, you might consider applying some of these patterns and practices to avoid breaking critical infrastructure resources, like the network.

You will always replace or add tools to your infrastructure ecosystem. Your organization will choose the tools that fit its architectural objectives. Applying the techniques to modularize, isolate, and manage IaC will accommodate your IaC evolution. I always return to the practices and patterns to make infrastructure, IaC, module, tool, and organizational changes and mitigate their risk to critical systems.

Regardless of whether a tool has import capabilities, you need to rewrite the tests for each resource you refactor. Figure 13.13 shows that you must refactor the unit and contract tests for each module and subset of resources as you migrate. However, your end-to-end and integration tests may stay the same.

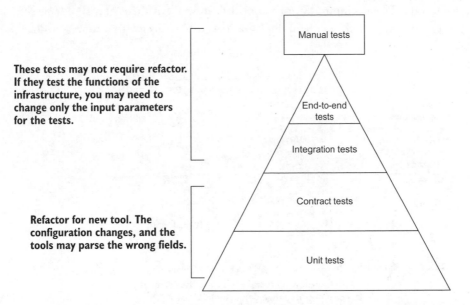

These tests may not require refactor. If they test the functions of the infrastructure, you may need to change only the input parameters for the tests.

Refactor for new tool. The configuration changes, and the tools may parse the wrong fields.

Figure 13.13   You will need to rewrite the unit and contract tests when you upgrade a tool, while the integration, end-to-end, and manual tests may stay mostly the same.

A new tool will affect unit and contract tests because the tool uses a different state and metadata format. Tests cannot parse the correct information from the new tool. Integration and end-to-end tests likely stay the same because they evaluate the functions of infrastructure and not the tool itself.

Refactoring the tests as you go along allows you to add more tests, remove redundant tests, or make updates to broader security or policy tests. You should update your manual, integration, and end-to-end tests with new input parameters because you have different resources. However, the tests themselves do not change too much because they test the system's functionality, not infrastructure attributes.

13.4   *Event-driven IaC*

Most of the book covers the practices of collaborating on and writing IaC to reduce the impact of a potential failure of critical systems. Once you get familiar with the principles and practices, you can extend them to more dynamic use cases.

For example, a development team wants some very dynamic automation with its IaC. Whenever the development team members deploy a new instance of an application, they need to update a firewall rule to allow access from the instance to the database. Rather than push a new instance and then remember to update the firewall rule later, they want some automation to run an infrastructure module to configure the firewall rule after an application instance starts.

Figure 13.14 demonstrates the automation you implement. You deploy a new application with a new IP address. An automated script captures the new IP address and runs some IaC. The configuration updates the firewall with the new IP address. This automation repeats each time you deploy a new application with a new IP address.

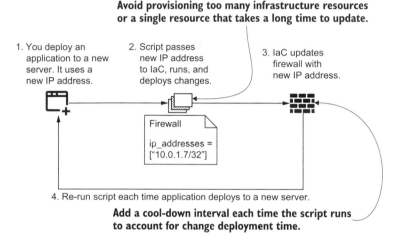

Figure 13.14   Whenever an application instance gets a new IP address, the infrastructure module updates the firewall rule with the new IP address.

You may consider running an infrastructure module automatically when the system changes. *Event-driven IaC* means running a minimally scoped infrastructure module to configure infrastructure in response to an event. You can use the automation to update another resource or fix the system based on the event.

> **DEFINITION**   *Event-driven IaC* runs a minimally scoped infrastructure module to configure infrastructure in response to an event.

Updating the application equals an event. Some script, application, or automation detects the event and responds by running an infrastructure module! You can write your own or find an open source tool to identify and respond to the event. Some real-world automation you can use to detect and react to an event includes an operator for Kubernetes, a serverless function, or an application that consumes from an event queue.

> ### Isn't this GitOps?
>
> In chapter 7, I mentioned that a number of practices and patterns in this book lean toward GitOps. GitOps combines declarative configuration, drift detection, version control, and continuous deployment. The approach achieves event-driven IaC. I think of GitOps as a subset of event-driven IaC because its automation responds to events in configuration drift.
>
> If the GitOps framework detects drift, it runs automation to reconcile the configuration. For example, the container orchestrator Kubernetes uses controllers to automatically reconcile the declarative configuration with resource state. However, event-driven IaC describes IaC automated by a broader set of events, not just drift.

The use case for event-driven IaC has become more prevalent with dynamic services and applications. If you do use event-driven IaC, keep a few practices in mind:

- Avoid infrastructure resources that take a long time to create or configure. You do not want to include an infrastructure resource that takes an hour to create.
- Do not add too many resources to an event-driven module. Otherwise, you will take a long time to create many instances.
- Balance the time it takes to run a change with the module versus the time interval between events.
- Combine the module practices from chapter 2 with the testing patterns from chapter 6 to verify that event-driven IaC runs quickly and correctly.

Some events happen with high frequency. You need infrastructure that deploys faster than the event's frequency or an automation script to batch changes at a specific interval. You should choose the most minimal subset of infrastructure resources to deploy with event-driven IaC.

From static IaC that you deploy based on code commits to dynamic IaC run for an event, you apply the same patterns, practices, and principles to managing and collaborating. Your objectives, your team's requirements, and your organization's business will evolve and change over time—hopefully, your IaC practice grows with it. Keep in mind your testing strategy, the cost of infrastructure, and maintaining its security and compliance.

Summary

- Review the functionality, security, and life cycle of an open source tool or module before adopting it in your organization.
- An open source tool or module should have default values or behaviors that offer predictability and stability in changes. Otherwise, you will have to write a layer of code to add opinionated default attributes within your organization.
- Protect your infrastructure from supply-chain attacks by scanning an infrastructure tool or module for security, checking for third-party data collection, and running your security and compliance tests.

- The type and number of maintainers and the license associated with the tool or module also affect your organization's use.
- Open source tools and modules can have two categories of licenses: permissive and copyleft.
- A permissive license lets you modify and update the module or tool as long as you include a copy of the license and its original copyright notice.
- A copyleft license allows you to modify and update the module or tool as long as you include a copy of the license, its original copyright notice, and release your copy open source.
- Before upgrading your IaC tool, decouple infrastructure dependencies and pin module, plugin, and tool versions.
- Start a tool update with backward compatibility by refactoring high-level resources mutably and proceeding to low-level resources.
- A blue-green deployment strategy for tool state means creating a new set of infrastructure resources with a state separate from the existing configuration.
- Tool state refers to a copy of the infrastructure state that an IaC tool uses to detect drift or resources under its management.
- Start a tool update with breaking changes by applying a blue-green deployment strategy to the tool state, starting from low-level to high-level resources.
- When replacing one tool with another, use the new tool's import capability to migrate existing resources to the new tool. Start with low-level resources and apply them to high-level resources. Then, remove the configuration for the old tool.
- If a new tool does not have an importing feature for existing infrastructure resources, you will need to apply a blue-green deployment strategy for the tool state.
- Event-driven IaC runs a minimal IaC module in response to a system event to automate infrastructure changes.
- Ensure that a module for event-driven IaC deploys quickly with as few resources as possible.

appendix A
Running examples

The examples in this book use Python to create a JSON configuration file for you to run with HashiCorp Terraform. This appendix provides guidance on running the examples. Why bother with this manual two-step process of generating the JSON file using Python and *then* creating the resources using Terraform?

First, I want to ensure that anyone who wants to run the examples but cannot use Google Cloud Platform (GCP) has an opportunity to examine them further. This allows for "local" development and testing and optionally creating live infrastructure resources.

Second, JSON files have a lot of content! They turned out quite verbose in code listings. A Python wrapper allows me to provide examples of the patterns without wading through lines of JSON configuration. Adding Python code around Terraform JSON syntax offers some future-proofing in case I need to rewrite the examples in another tool.

> **NOTE** Reference links, libraries, and tool syntax change. Review https:// github.com/joatmon08/manning-book for the most up-to-date code.

Figure A.1 reiterates the workflow you need to run the examples. If you run `python main.py`, you will get a JSON file with the file extension .tf.json. Run

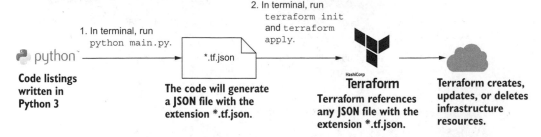

Figure A.1   Use the code listings written in Python to generate a JSON file and run it with Terraform.

`terraform init` in your CLI to initialize the tool state, and `terraform apply` to provision resources.

I will briefly discuss how to set up an account with various cloud providers. Then, I'll introduce Python and the libraries I referenced throughout the examples, such as infrastructure API access and testing. Finally, I will provide a short explanation of how to use Terraform with GCP.

A.1   *Cloud providers*

The examples in this book use Google Cloud Platform (GCP) as the cloud provider. If you prefer another cloud provider, many examples have sidebars on an equivalent implementation to achieve a similar architecture. Table A.1 maps the approximations for each resource type across GCP, Amazon Web Services (AWS), and Microsoft Azure.

Table A.1   Mapping resources across cloud providers

Resource	GCP	AWS	Azure
Grouping resources	Google project	AWS account	Azure subscription and resource groups
Identity and access management (IAM)	Google IAM	AWS IAM	Azure Active Directory
Linux servers (Ubuntu)	Google compute instance	Amazon EC2 instance	Azure Linux Virtual Machine
Networking	Google Virtual Private Cloud (VPC) Subnets Note: Has default network	Amazon Virtual Private Cloud (VPC) Subnets Route tables Gateways Note: Has default network	Azure Virtual Network Subnets Route table associations
Firewall rules	Firewall rules	Security groups Network access control lists	Network security groups
Load balancing	Google compute forwarding rule (L4) HTTP(S) load balancing (L7)	AWS Elastic Load Balancing (ELB) (L4) AWS Application Load Balancer (ALB) (L7)	Azure Load Balancer (L4) Azure Application Gateway (L7)
Relational database (PostgreSQL)	Google Cloud SQL	Amazon Relational Database Service (RDS)	Azure Database for PostgreSQL
Container orchestrator (Kubernetes)	Google Kubernetes Engine (GKE)	Amazon Elastic Kubernetes Service (EKS)	Azure Kubernetes Service (AKS)

In this section, I'll outline some initial setup you'll need to do for each cloud provider, if you choose.

A.1.1   Google Cloud Platform

When you start using GCP, create a new project (http://mng.bz/mOV2) and run all of the examples in that project. This allows you to delete the project and its resources when you finish the book.

Next, install the `gcloud` CLI (https://cloud.google.com/sdk/docs/install). The CLI will help you authenticate so Terraform can access the GCP API:

```
$ gcloud auth application-default login
```

This sets up credentials on your machine so Terraform can authenticate to GCP (http://mng.bz/5Qw1).

A.1.2   Amazon Web Services

When you start using AWS, create a new account (http://mng.bz/6XDD) and run all of the examples in that account. This allows you to delete the account and its resources when you finish the book.

Next, create a set of access keys in the AWS console (http://mng.bz/o21r). You will need to save these keys so Terraform can access the AWS API.

Copy the access key ID and secret access key and save it to environment variables:

```
$ export AWS_ACCESS_KEY_ID="<Access key ID>"
$ export AWS_SECRET_ACCESS_KEY="<Secret access key>"
```

Then, set the AWS region you want to use:

```
$ export AWS_REGION="us-east-1"
```

This sets up credentials on your machine so Terraform can authenticate to AWS (http://mng.bz/nNWg).

A.1.3   Microsoft Azure

When you start using Azure, create a new account (http://mng.bz/v6nJ). Creating a new account gives you a subscription by default. This allows you to create resources within the subscription and group them by resource groups. After you finish the book, you can delete the resource group.

Next, install the Azure CLI (http://mng.bz/44Da). The CLI will help you authenticate so Terraform can access the Azure API.

Log into the Azure CLI:

```
$ az login
```

List the subscriptions so you can get the ID for the default subscription:

```
$ az account list
```

Copy the subscription ID and save it to an environment variable:

```
$ export ARM_SUBSCRIPTION_ID="<subscription ID>"
```

This sets up credentials on your machine so Terraform can authenticate to Azure (http://mng.bz/QvPw). You should create an Azure resource group (http://mng.bz/XZNG) for each example. Delete the resource group to remove all infrastructure resources for the example.

A.2   *Python*

Before you start running the examples, you must download Python. I used Python 3 in the code listings. You can install Python in a few ways, such as using your package manager of choice or the Python downloads page (www.python.org/downloads/). However, I prefer to use pyenv (https://github.com/pyenv/pyenv) to download and manage my Python versions. pyenv allows you to choose the Python version you need and install it into a virtual environment using Python's venv library (https://docs.python.org/3/library/venv.html).

I use a virtual environment because I have many projects that require different Python versions. Installing different versions of each project in the same environment gets confusing and often breaks code. As a result, I want to separate each project into a development environment with its dependencies and Python version.

A.2.1   *Install Python libraries*

After you install Python 3 into your development or virtual environment, you need to install some external libraries. In listing A.1, I capture libraries and dependencies in requirements.txt, a plaintext file with a list of packages and versions.

> **Listing A.1   Python requirements.txt with libraries for this book**

```
apache-libcloud==3.3.1          ⟵── Installs Apache Libcloud library
google-api-python-client==2.17.0     Installs client libraries for
google-cloud-billing==1.3.3          GCP, including the Python client
netaddr==0.8.0                       and Cloud Billing client
pytest==6.2.4    ⟵── Installs pytest, a Python    Installs netaddr, a Python library
                    testing framework              for parsing network information
```

The example repository contains a requirements.txt file that freezes the library versions you need to install. In your Python development environment, use your CLI to install the libraries with pip, Python's package installer:

```
$ pip install -r requirements.txt
```

Some of the examples require more complex automation or testing. They reference libraries that you will need to import separately. Let's examine the libraries to download in more detail.

APACHE LIBCLOUD

Apache Libcloud (https://libcloud.apache.org/) offers a Python interface to create, update, read, and delete cloud resources. It includes a single interface agnostic of the cloud service or provider. I reference this library in the early sections of the book for examples on integration and end-to-end testing. To use Apache Libcloud in the following listing, you can import the `libcloud` package and set up a driver to connect to GCP.

Listing A.2 Import Apache Libcloud

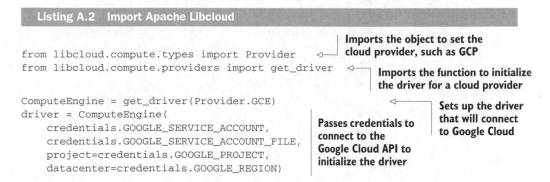

```
from libcloud.compute.types import Provider          Imports the object to set the
from libcloud.compute.providers import get_driver    cloud provider, such as GCP

                                                     Imports the function to initialize
                                                     the driver for a cloud provider

ComputeEngine = get_driver(Provider.GCE)             Sets up the driver
driver = ComputeEngine(                              that will connect
    credentials.GOOGLE_SERVICE_ACCOUNT,       Passes credentials to   to Google Cloud
    credentials.GOOGLE_SERVICE_ACCOUNT_FILE,  connect to the
    project=credentials.GOOGLE_PROJECT,       Google Cloud API to
    datacenter=credentials.GOOGLE_REGION)     initialize the driver
```

I use Apache Libcloud in the tests instead of Google Cloud's client libraries because it provides a unified API to access any cloud. If I want to switch my examples to AWS or Azure, I need to change only the driver for the cloud provider. The tests only read information from the cloud provider and do not run any complex operations with Apache Libcloud.

> ### AWS and Azure equivalents
> You will need to update the Apache Libcloud driver to use Amazon EC2 Driver (http://mng.bz/yvQG) or Azure ARM Compute Driver (http://mng.bz/M5B7).

PYTHON CLIENTS FOR GOOGLE CLOUD

The later part of the book includes more complicated IaC and tests, which I could not implement in Apache Libcloud. Apache Libcloud could not support my use case of retrieving specific information about Google Cloud resources, such as pricing information! The following listing shows how I used client libraries specific to Google Cloud in these use cases.

Listing A.3 Import Google Cloud Client Library

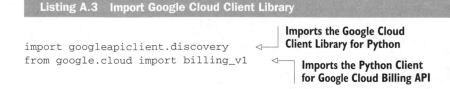

```
import googleapiclient.discovery        Imports the Google Cloud
from google.cloud import billing_v1     Client Library for Python

                                        Imports the Python Client
                                        for Google Cloud Billing API
```

> ### AWS and Azure equivalents
> You can import the AWS SDK for Python (https://aws.amazon.com/sdk-for-python/) or Azure library for Python (http://mng.bz/VMVO) to build the examples in AWS or Azure.

The examples use two libraries maintained by Google Cloud. The Google Cloud Client Library for Python (http://mng.bz/aJlz) allows you to access many of the APIs on Google Cloud and create, read, update, and delete resources. However, it *does not* include access to Google's Cloud Billing API.

As a result, for chapter 12 on cost, I had to import a different library maintained by Google Cloud to retrieve billing catalog information. The Python Client for Google Cloud Billing API (http://mng.bz/gwBl) allows me to read information from the Google Cloud service catalog.

When you have IaC that needs to reference specific resources or APIs not available in a unified API, like Apache Libcloud, you often need to find a separate library to retrieve the information you need. While we would like to minimize dependencies, we must recognize that not every library achieves every use case! Choose a different library if you feel that your existing one cannot accomplish the automation you need.

NETADDR

In chapter 5, I needed to modify an IP address block. While I entertained the possibility of mathematically calculating the correct address, I decided to use a library instead. Python does have a built-in ipaddress library, but it does not include the functionality I needed. I installed netaddr (https://netaddr.readthedocs.io/en/latest/) instead to reduce the additional code I needed to calculate the IP addresses.

PYTEST

Many of the tests in this book use pytest, a Python testing framework. You can use Python's unittest module to write and run tests as well. I prefer pytest since it offers a minimal interface to write and run tests without more complicated testing features. Rather than explain pytest in depth, I will outline some of the features I use in the tests and how to run them.

Pytest searches for Python files prefixed with test_. This filename signals that the file contains Python tests. Each test function also uses the prefix test_. Pytest selects and runs the tests based on the prefix.

Many of the tests in this book include test fixtures. A *test fixture* captures a known object, such as a name or constant, that you can use for comparison across multiple tests. In the following listing, I use fixtures to pass commonly processed objects, like network attributes, among multiple tests.

Listing A.4   An example using pytest

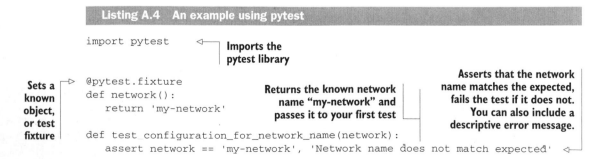

```
import pytest          ◁─┐  Imports the
                          │  pytest library

                                                        Asserts that the network
        @pytest.fixture                                 name matches the expected,
Sets a  def network():           Returns the known network   fails the test if it does not.
known       return 'my-network'    name "my-network" and      You can also include a
object,                            passes it to your first test  descriptive error message.
or test
fixture  def test_configuration_for_network_name(network):
            assert network == 'my-network', 'Network name does not match expected'  ◁─
```

The most important part of the test involves checking that the expected value matches the actual value, or *asserting*. Pytest suggests one `assert` statement for each test. I follow this convention because it helps me write more descriptive, helpful tests. Your tests should describe their intent and what they test as clearly as possible.

To run a set of tests with pytest, you can pass in the directory with the tests. However, make sure your testing directory has absolute paths to any files you read in via pytest! For example, the tests in chapter 4 read external JSON files. As a result, you need to change the working directory to the chapter and section:

```
$ cd ch05/s02
```

You can run all the tests in the directory by passing a dot (`.`) to pytest in the CLI:

```
$ pytest .
```

You can run one file by adding the filename to pytest in the CLI:

```
$ pytest test_network.py
```

Many of the tests in this book use similar patterns of fixtures and `assert` statements. For more information on other pytest features, review its documentation (https://docs.pytest.org). You will run either `pytest` or `python main.py` commands in your CLI for the examples.

A.2.2   Run Python

I separate each infrastructure resource into a Python file. Every directory contains a main.py file, as shown in listing A.5. The file always includes code that writes a Python dictionary to a JSON file. The object needs to use Terraform's JSON configuration syntax for an infrastructure resource.

Listing A.5   Example main.py file writes dictionary to JSON file

```
import json

if __name__ == "__main__":
    server = ServerFactoryModule(name='hello-world')     ⟵┐  Generates a Python
    with open('main.tf.json', 'w') as outfile:                dictionary for a GCP server
        json.dump(server.resources, outfile, sort_keys=True, indent=4)     ⟵
```

Creates a JSON file named "main.tf.json," which
contains Terraform-compatible JSON configuration

Writes out the server
dictionary to the JSON file

You can run the Python script in your terminal:

```
$ python main.py
```

When you list the files, you will find a new JSON file named main.tf.json:

```
$ ls
main.py      main.tf.json
```

Many examples require you to run Python for main.py and generate a JSON file named main.tf.json unless otherwise noted. However, some examples use other libraries or code for automation or testing.

A.3   *HashiCorp Terraform*

After you generate a main.tf.json file by using `python main.py`, you need to create the resources in GCP. The .tf.json files need HashiCorp Terraform to create, read, update, and delete the resources in GCP.

You can download and install Terraform with the package manager of your choice (www.terraform.io/downloads.html). You run it with a set of CLI commands, so you will need to download the binary and make sure you can run it in your terminal. Terraform searches for files with the .tf or .tf.json extension within a working directory and creates, reads, updates, and deletes the resources you define in those files.

A.3.1   *JSON configuration syntax*

Terraform offers various interfaces for you to create infrastructure resources. Most of its documentation uses HashiCorp Configuration Language (HCL), a DSL that defines infrastructure resources for each cloud provider. For more on Terraform, review its documentation (www.terraform.io/docs/index.html).

The examples in this book do not use HCL. Instead, they use a JSON configuration syntax (www.terraform.io/docs/language/syntax/json.html) specific to Terraform. This syntax uses the same DSL as the HCL, just formatted in JSON.

Each main.py file in Python writes a dictionary out to the JSON file. Listing A.6 shows how I create a dictionary that defines a Terraform resource in JSON configuration syntax. The JSON resource references the `google_compute_instance` resource defined by Terraform (http://mng.bz/e71z) and sets all of the required attributes.

Listing A.6   Python dictionary for a server in Terraform JSON

```
terraform_json = {
    'resource': [{                                          Signals to Terraform that you
                                                            will define a list of resources
        'google_compute_instance': [{
            'my_server': [{                                        Defines a
                'allow_stopping_for_update': True                  "google_compute_instance,"
                'boot_disk': [{                                    a Terraform resource that
                    'initialize_params': [{                        will create and configure a
                        'image': 'ubuntu-1804-lts'                 server in GCP
                    }]
                }],
                'machine_type': 'e2-micro',
                'name': 'my-server',
                'zone': 'us-central1-a',
            }]
        }]
    }]
}
```

Defines a unique identifier for the server so Terraform can track it

> ### AWS and Azure equivalents
>
> In AWS, you would use the `aws_instance` Terraform resource with a reference to the default VPC (http://mng.bz/pOPG).
>
> In Azure, you would need to create a virtual network and subnets. Then, create the `azurerm_linux_virtual_machine` Terraform resource (http://mng.bz/Ooxn) on the network.

The Python dictionary becomes Terraform JSON configuration syntax when you write it to a JSON file. Terraform will create the resources defined in its current working directory only with files that have the extension .tf or .tf.json. If you update the code to write the configuration to a JSON file that does not have the .tf.json extension, Terraform will not recognize the resources in the file.

A.3.2 Initialize state

After running Python and creating a JSON file, you need to initialize Terraform in the working directory. Figure A.2 outlines the commands you need to run in your terminal to initialize state and apply infrastructure changes.

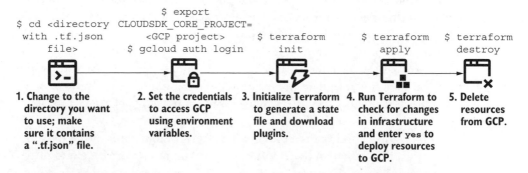

Figure A.2 Initialize and deploy resources using Terraform in a working directory; then destroy the resources when you complete the example.

In your terminal, change to a directory with a *.tf.json file. For example, I change to the directory that contains examples for section 2.3:

```
$ cd ch02/s03
```

Initialize Terraform in your terminal:

```
$ terraform init
Initializing the backend...

Initializing provider plugins...
- Reusing previous version of hashicorp/google from the dependency lock file
- Using previously-installed hashicorp/google v3.86.0
```

```
Terraform has been successfully initialized!

You may now begin working with Terraform. Try running "terraform plan"
➥to see any changes that are required for your infrastructure.
➥All Terraform commands should now work.

If you ever set or change modules or backend configuration
➥for Terraform, rerun this command to reinitialize
➥your working directory. If you forget, other
➥commands will detect it and remind you to do so if necessary.
```

Terraform runs an initialization step that creates a tool state called *backend* and installs plugins and modules. The initialization creates a series of files that you should not delete from your filesystem. After you initialize Terraform, you will find some hidden and new files when you list the contents of your directory:

```
$ ls -al
drwxr-xr-x  .terraform
-rw-r--r--  .terraform.lock.hcl
-rw-r--r--  main.py
-rw-r--r--  main.tf.json
-rw-r--r--  terraform.tfstate
-rw-r--r--  terraform.tfstate.backup
```

Terraform stores its tool state in a state file to quickly reconcile any changes that you make to infrastructure resources. Terraform can reference a state file stored locally or on a server, artifact registry, object store, or other. The examples store tool state in a local file named terraform.tfstate. If you accidentally delete this file, Terraform will no longer recognize resources under its management! Ensure that you do not remove the local state file or update the examples to use a remote backend. You may also find a terraform.tfstate.backup file, which Terraform uses to back up its tool state before it makes changes.

Initialization also installs a plugin for Terraform to communicate to Google. Terraform uses a plugin system to extend its engine and interface with cloud providers. The AWS examples use the same command of `terraform init` to download the AWS plugin for you automatically. Plugins or modules get downloaded to the .terraform folder.

Terraform also pins the versions of plugins for you, similar to the requirements.txt file for Python. You'll find a list of pinned versions for plugins in .terraform.lock.hcl. In the examples repository, I committed the .terraform.lock.hcl to version control so that Terraform installs only the plugins I've tested with at the time I generated the examples.

A.3.3   *Set credentials in your terminal*

Most Terraform plugins read credentials for infrastructure provider APIs by using environment variables. I usually set the GCP project environment variable, so Terraform connects to the correct GCP project:

```
$ export CLOUDSDK_CORE_PROJECT=<your GCP project ID>
```

I also authenticate to GCP by using the gcloud CLI tool. The command automatically sets credentials for Terraform to access GCP:

```
$ gcloud auth login
```

For other cloud providers, I recommend setting environment variables in your terminal to authenticate to your AWS or Azure account. Reference section A.1 for their configuration.

A.3.4 *Apply Terraform*

After setting your credentials, you can use Terraform to dry-run and deploy your infrastructure resources. In your terminal, you can run `terraform apply` to start the deployment of your changes:

```
$ terraform apply

Terraform used the selected providers to generate
➡the following execution plan. Resource actions
➡are indicated with the following symbols:
  + create

Terraform will perform the following actions:

  # google_compute_instance.hello-world will be created
  + resource "google_compute_instance" "hello-world" {

... OMITTED ...

Plan: 1 to add, 0 to change, 0 to destroy.

Do you want to perform these actions?
  Terraform will perform the actions described above.
  Only 'yes' will be accepted to approve.

  Enter a value:
```

The command will stop and wait for you to enter yes at `Enter a value`. It waits for you to review the changes and check that you want to add, change, or destroy resources. Always review changes before entering yes!

After you type yes, Terraform will start deploying the resources:

```
  Enter a value: yes

google_compute_instance.hello-world: Creating...
google_compute_instance.hello-world:
➡Still creating... [10s elapsed]
google_compute_instance.hello-world:
➡Creation complete after 15s [id=projects/infrastructure-as-code-book/zones
➡/us-central1-a/instances/hello-world]

Apply complete! Resources: 1 added, 0 changed, 0 destroyed.
```

You will find your resources in your GCP project after you use `terraform apply`.

A.3.5 *Clean up*

Many of the examples use overlapping names or network CIDR blocks. I recommend you clean up the resources between each chapter and section. Terraform uses the `terraform destroy` command to delete all the resources listed in terraform.tfstate from GCP. In your terminal, make sure you authenticate to GCP or your infrastructure provider.

When you run `terraform destroy`, it outputs the resources it will destroy. Review the list of resources and make sure you want to delete them!

```
$ terraform destroy


Terraform used the selected providers to generate
the following execution plan. Resource actions
are indicated with the following symbols:
  - destroy

Terraform will perform the following actions:

  # google_compute_instance.hello-world will be destroyed

 ... OMITTED ...

Plan: 0 to add, 0 to change, 1 to destroy.

Do you really want to destroy all resources?
  Terraform will destroy all your managed infrastructure,
  as shown above.
  There is no undo. Only 'yes' will be accepted to confirm.

  Enter a value:
```

After you review the resources you expect to delete, enter `yes` at the command prompt. Terraform will delete the resources from GCP. Deletion will take some time, so expect this to run for a few minutes. Some examples will take even longer to deploy and destroy because they have many resources involved:

```
  Enter a value: yes

google_compute_instance.hello-world: Destroying... elapsed]
google_compute_instance.hello-world: Still destroying…
  [id=projects/infrastructure-as-code-book/zones
  /us-central1-a/instances/hello-world, 2m10s elapsed]
google_compute_instance.hello-world: Destruction complete after 2m24s

Destroy complete! Resources: 1 destroyed.
```

After destroying the resources, you can remove the terraform.tfstate, terraform .tfstate.backup, and .terraform files if you would like. Remember to delete your resources from GCP (or delete the entire project) each time you finish an example so you can reduce your cloud bill!

appendix B
Solutions to exercises

EXERCISE 1.1

Choose an infrastructure script or configuration in your organization. Assess whether it adheres to the principles of IaC. Does it promote reproducibility, use idempotency, help with composability, and ease evolvability?

Answer:

You can use the following steps to identify whether your script of configuration follows IaC principles:

- *Reproducibility*—Copy and paste the script or configuration, share it with someone else, and ask them to create the resources without modifying or changing the configuration.
- *Idempotency*—Run the script a few times. It should not change your infrastructure.
- *Composability*—Copy a portion of the configuration and build it on top of other infrastructure resources.
- *Evolvability*—Add a new infrastructure resource to the configuration and verify that you can make changes without affecting other resources.

EXERCISE 2.1

Does the following use the imperative or declarative style of configuring infrastructure?

```
if __name__ == "__main__":
    update_packages()
    read_ssh_keys()
    update_users()
    if enable_secure_configuration:
        update_ip_tables()
```

Answer:

The code snippet uses the *imperative* style of configuring infrastructure. It defines how to configure a server *step-by-step* in a specific sequence rather than declaring a specific target configuration.

EXERCISE 2.2

Which of the following changes benefit from the principle of immutability? (Choose all that apply.)

- A Reducing a network to have fewer IP addresses
- B Adding a column to a relational database
- C Adding a new IP address to an existing DNS entry
- D Updating a server's packages to backward-incompatible versions
- E Migrating infrastructure resources to another region

Answer:

The correct answers are A, D, and E. Each change benefits from a new set of resources that implement the change. If you try to make the changes in place, you may accidentally bring down the existing system. For example, reducing a network to have fewer IP addresses may displace any resources using the network.

Updating packages to backward-incompatible versions means that a broken package update can affect the server's ability to handle user requests. Migrating infrastructure resources to another region takes time. Not all cloud provider regions support every type of resource. Creating new resources helps mitigate problems with migration. You can make changes for answers B and C mutably, likely without affecting the system.

EXERCISE 3.1

To which module pattern(s) does the following IaC apply? (Choose all that apply.)

```
if __name__ == "__main__":
  environment = 'development'
  name = f'{environment}-hello-world'
  cidr_block = '10.0.0.0/16'

  # NetworkModule returns a subnet and network
  network = NetworkModule(name, cidr_block)

  # Tags returns a default list of tags
  tags = TagsModule()

  # ServerModule returns a single server
  server = ServerModule(name, network, tags)
```

- A Factory
- B Singleton
- C Prototype
- D Builder
- E Composite

Answer:

The infrastructure as code applies A, C, and E. The network module uses the composite pattern to compose a subnet and a network. The tag module uses the prototype pattern to return status metadata. The server module uses the factory pattern to return a single server based on name, network, and tags.

The code does not use singleton or builder patterns. It does not create singular global resources or internal logic to build specific resources.

EXERCISE 4.1

How can we better decouple the database's dependency on the network via the following IaC?

```
class Database:
  def __init__(self, name):
    spec = {
      'name': name,
      'settings': {
        'ip_configuration': {
          'private_network': 'default'
        }
      }
    }
```

A   The approach adequately decouples the database from the network.

B   Pass the network ID as a variable instead of hardcoding it as `default`.

C   Implement and pass a `NetworkOutput` object to the database module for all network attributes.

D   Add a function to the network module to push its network ID to the database module.

E   Add a function to the database module to call the infrastructure API for the `default` network ID.

Answer:

You can implement the adapter pattern to output the network attributes (C). The database chooses which network attributes it uses, such as network ID or CIDR block. This approach best follows the principle of dependency injection. While D does implement dependency inversion, it does not implement inversion of control. Answer E does implement dependency injection but continues to hardcode the network ID.

EXERCISE 6.1

You notice that a new version of a load balancer module is breaking your DNS configuration. A teammate updated the module to output private IP addresses instead of public IP addresses. What can you do to help your team better remember the module needs public IP addresses?

A   Create a separate load balancer module for private IP addresses.

B   Add module contract tests to verify that the module outputs both private and public IP addresses.

c Update the module's documentation with a note that it needs public IP addresses.

d Run integration tests on the module and check the IP address is publicly accessible.

Answer:

Rather than creating a new module, you can add a contract test to help the team remember that high-level resources need both private and public IP addresses (B). You could create a separate load balancer module (A). However, it may not help your team remember that specific modules must output specific variables. Updating the module's documentation (C) means that your team must remember to read the documentation first. Integration tests have a time and financial cost for running (D) when contract tests adequately solve the problem.

EXERCISE 6.2

You add some firewall rules to allow an application to access a new queue. Which combination of tests would be most valuable to your team for the change?

A Unit and integration tests

B Contract and end-to-end tests

c Contract and integration tests

D Unit and end-to-end tests

Answer:

The two most valuable tests would be unit and end-to-end tests (D). Unit tests will help ensure that someone doesn't remove the new rules going forward. End-to-end tests check that the application can access the queue successfully. Contract tests would not provide any help because you do not need to test inputs and outputs for firewall rules.

EXERCISE 7.1

Choose a standard infrastructure change in your organization. What do you need in order to confidently continuously deliver the change to production? What about continuous deployment? Outline or diagram stages in your delivery pipelines for both.

Answer:

As you go through this exercise, consider the following:

- Do you have unit, integration, or end-to-end tests?
- What kind of branching model do you use?
- Does your company have compliance requirements? For example, two people must approve the change before production.
- What happens when someone needs to make a change?

EXERCISE 9.1

Consider the following code:

```
if __name__ == "__main__":
  network.build()
```

```
queue.build(network)
server.build(network, queue)
load_balancer.build(server)
dns.build(load_balancer)
```

The queue depends on the network. The server depends on the network and queue. How would you run a blue-green deployment to upgrade the queue with SSL?

Answer:

You create a green queue with SSL enabled. Then, you create a new green server that depends on the queue. Test that the application on the green server can access the queue with the SSL configuration. If it passes, you can add the green server to the load balancer. Gradually send traffic through the green server by using a canary deployment until you confirm that all requests succeed. Then, you remove the original server and queue.

Optionally, you can omit the step creating the green server and send traffic from the original server to SSL. However, this approach may not allow you to run a canary deployment. You update the server's configuration to directly communicate with the new queue.

EXERCISE 10.1

Given the following code, what order and grouping of resources would you use to refactor and break down the monolith?

```
if __name__ == "__main__":
  zones = ['us-west1-a', 'us-west1-b', 'us-west1-c']
  project.build()
  network.build(project)
  for zone in zones:
    subnet.build(project, network, zone)
  database.build(project, network)
  for zone in zones:
    server.build(project, network, zone)
  load_balancer.build(project, network)
  dns.build()
```

    A   DNS, load balancer, servers, database, network + subnets, project

    B   Load balancer + DNS, database, servers, network + subnets, project

    C   Project, network + subnets, servers, database, load balancer + DNS

    D   Database, load balancer + DNS, servers, network + subnets, project

Answer:

The order and grouping that mitigates the risk of refactor starts with DNS and proceeds with the load balancer, queue, database, servers, network and subnets, and project (A). You want to start with DNS as the highest-level dependency and evolve it separately from the load balancer, since the load balancer requires project and network attributes. Refactor the next resources as follows: the servers, database, network, and project.

You refactor the servers before the database because servers do not manage data directly but depend on the database. If you do not feel confident that you can refactor the database, at least you've moved the servers out of the monolith! You can always leave the database in the monolith with the network and project. Refactoring the bulk of resources out of the monolith sufficiently decouples the system to scale.

EXERCISE 11.1

A team reports that that its application can no longer connect to another application. The application worked last week, but requests have failed since Monday. The team has made no changes to its application and suspects the problem may be a firewall rule. Which steps can you take to troubleshoot the problem? (Choose all that apply.)

- A Log into the cloud provider and check the firewall rules for the application.
- B Deploy new infrastructure and applications to a green environment for testing.
- C Examine the changes in IaC for the application.
- D Compare the firewall rules in the cloud provider with IaC.
- E Edit the firewall rules and allow all traffic between the applications.

Answer:

The steps are A, C, and D. You can troubleshoot by checking for any drift in firewall rules. If you do not find drift, you can search the IaC running the application for other discrepancies. From a troubleshooting perspective, this problem may not need a new environment for testing or allowing all traffic between applications.

EXERCISE 12.1

Given the following code, which of the following statements are true? (Choose all that apply.)

```
HOURS_IN_MONTH = 730
MONTHLY_BUDGET = 5000
DATABASE_COST_PER_HOUR = 5
NUM_DATABASES = 2
BUFFER = 0.1


def test_monthly_budget_not_exceeded():
    total = HOURS_IN_MONTH * NUM_DATABASES * DATABASE_COST_PER_HOUR
    assert total < MONTHLY_BUDGET + MONTHLY_BUDGET * BUFFER
```

- A The test will pass because the cost of the database is within the budget.
- B The test estimates the monthly cost of databases.
- C The test does not account for different database types.
- D The test calculates the monthly cost per database instance.
- E The test includes a buffer of 10% for any cost overage as a soft mandatory policy.

Answer:

The answers are B, C, and E. The total estimated cost of the databases per month is $7,300, while the monthly budget with a 10% buffer is $5,500, which means the test fails. The test itself does not account for different database types or calculate monthly cost per database instance. It calculates based on the hourly rate and the number of databases. Adding a 10% buffer to the monthly budget creates a soft mandatory policy for the budget. Small changes that result in minor cost overage will reduce the friction of delivery to production but flag any major cost changes.

EXERCISE 12.2

Imagine you have three servers. You examine their utilization and notice the following:

- You need one server to serve the minimum traffic.
- You need three servers to serve the maximum traffic.
- The server handles traffic 24 hours a day, seven days a week.

What can you do to optimize the cost of the servers for the next month?

- **A** Schedule the resources to stop on the weekends.
- **B** Add an `autoscaling_policy` to scale based on memory.
- **C** Set an expiration of three hours for all servers.
- **D** Change the servers to smaller CPU and memory machine types.
- **E** Migrate the application to containers and pack applications more densely on servers.

Answer:

You can add an `autoscaling_policy` to scale based on memory (B). You cannot schedule a resource stop on weekends because you need at least one server on weekends. Setting an expiration or downsizing the servers does not help with cost in this situation. Migrating applications to containers involves a long-term solution that will not optimize cost for the next month.

index